TENRYU
THE DRAGON CYCLE

Volume 4

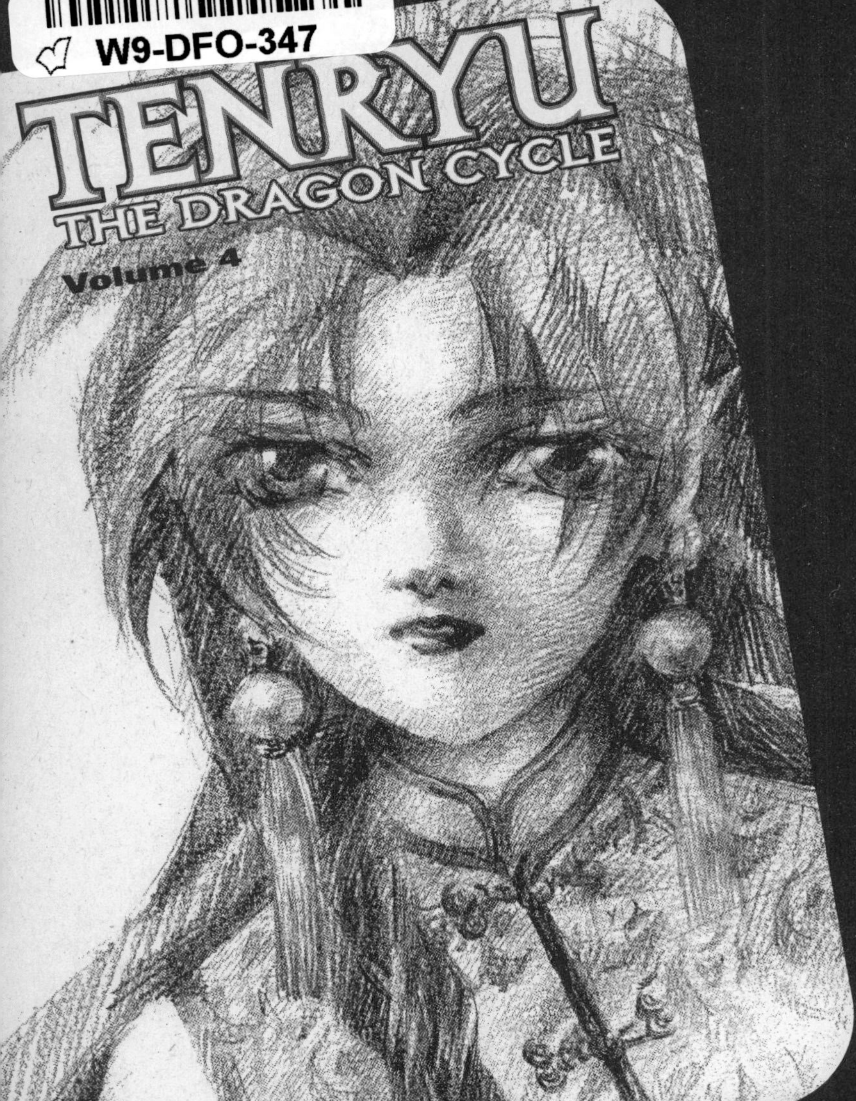

By Sanami Matoh

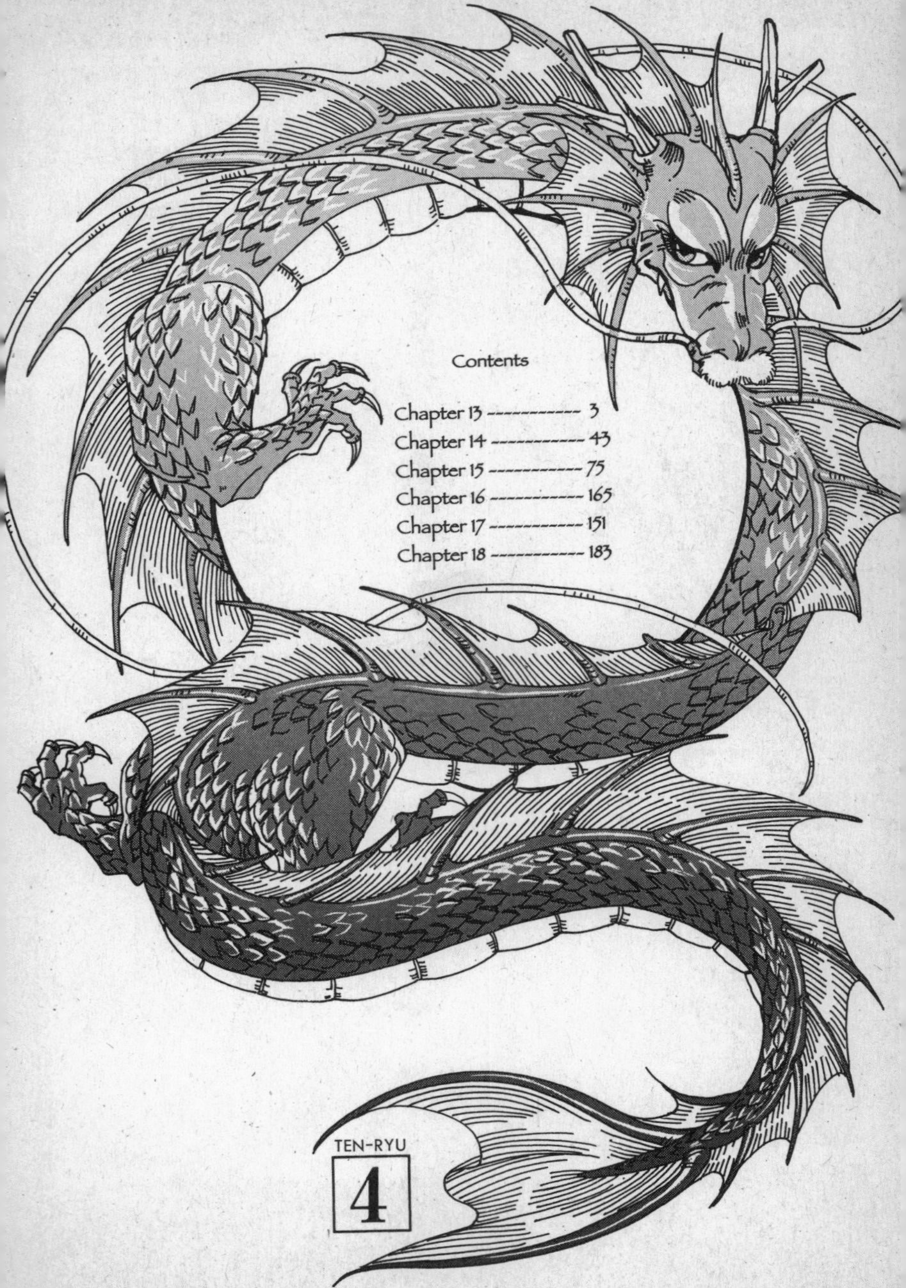

Contents

TEN-RYU

4

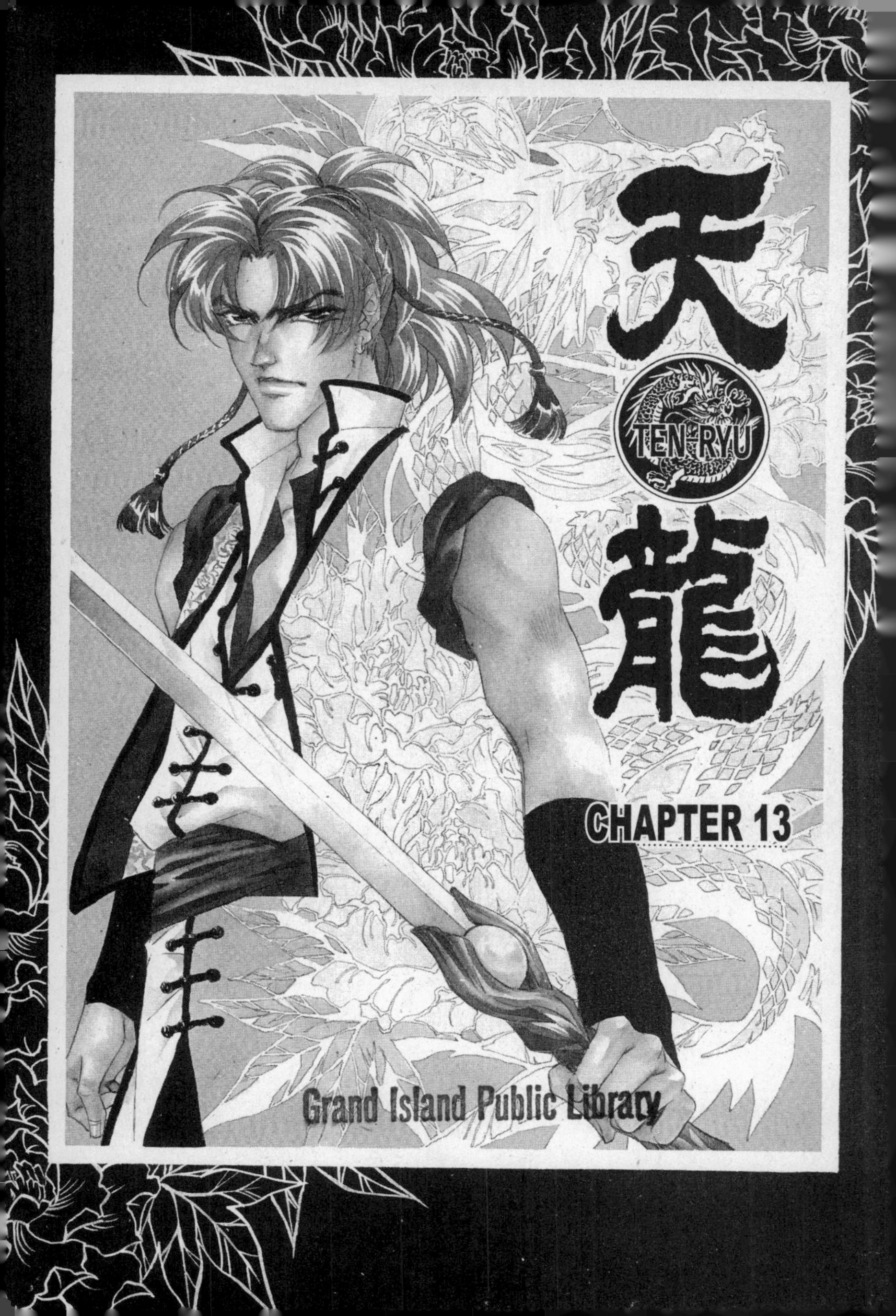
天龍
TEN-RYU
CHAPTER 13

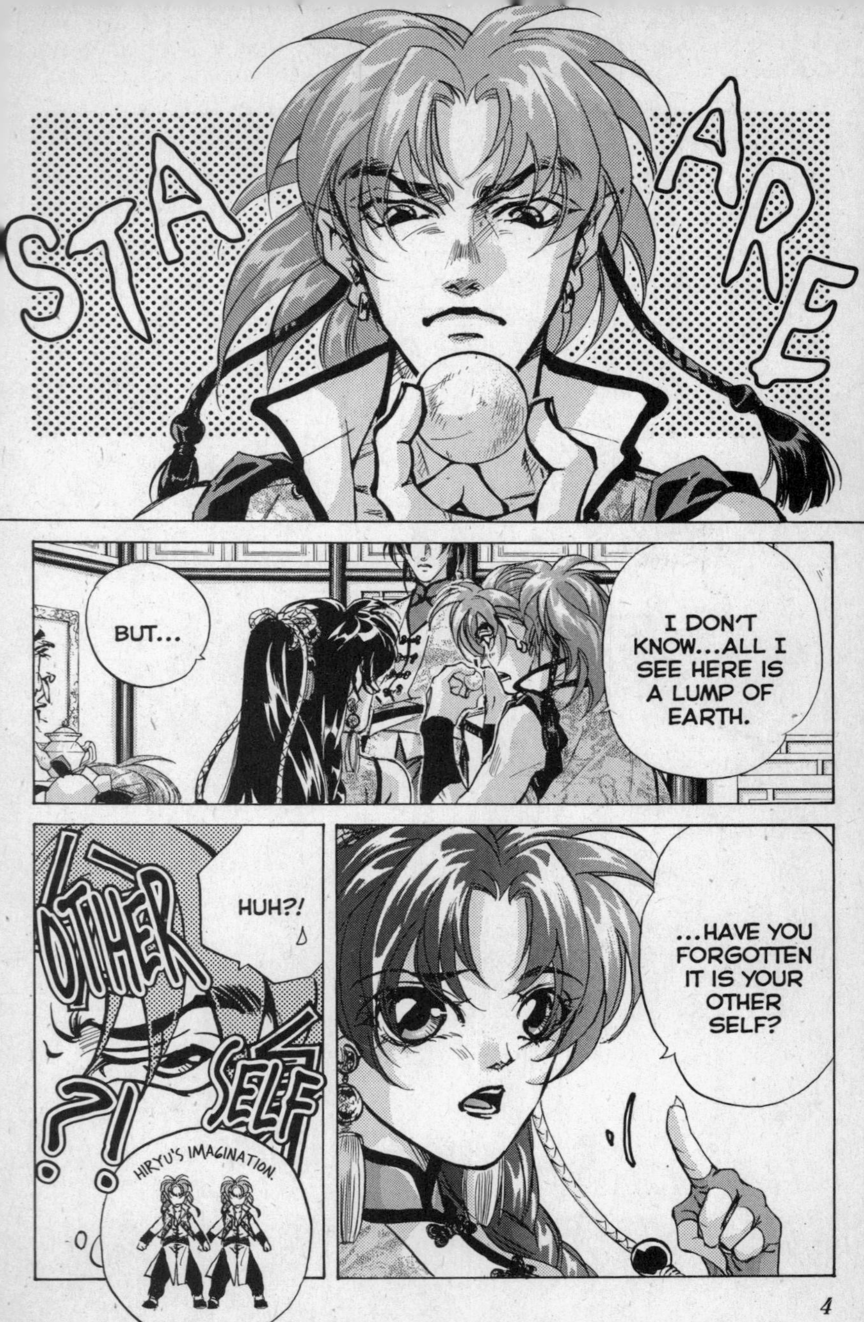
STAARE
I DON'T KNOW...ALL I SEE HERE IS A LUMP OF EARTH.
BUT...
...HAVE YOU FORGOTTEN IT IS YOUR OTHER SELF?
HUH?!
OTHER SELF
?!
HIRYU'S IMAGINATION.

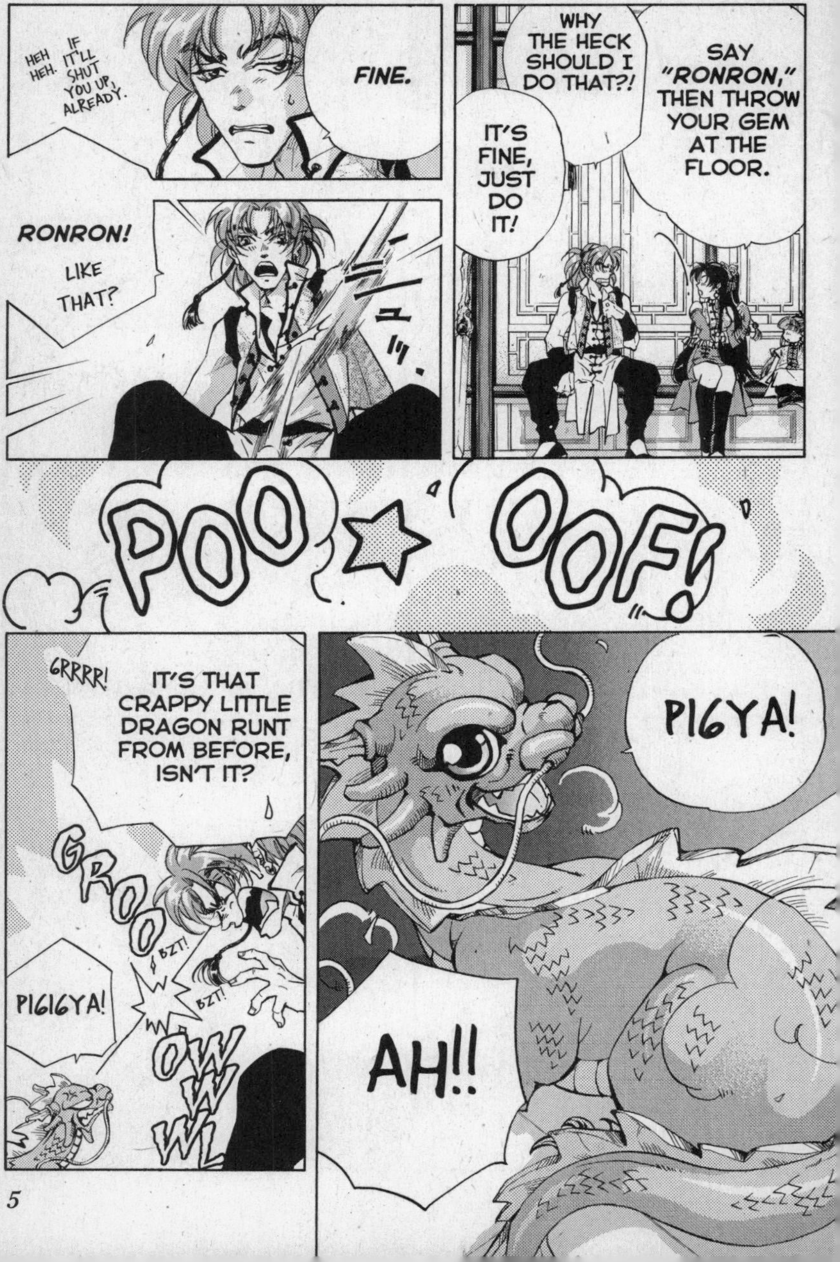
SAY "RONRON," THEN THROW YOUR GEM AT THE FLOOR.
WHY THE HECK SHOULD I DO THAT?!
IT'S FINE, JUST DO IT!
FINE.
HEH HEH.
IF IT'LL SHUT YOU UP, ALREADY.
RONRON!
LIKE THAT?
POO☆OOF!
PIGYA!
AH!!
GRRRR!
IT'S THAT CRAPPY LITTLE DRAGON RUNT FROM BEFORE, ISN'T IT?
GROOO
BZT!
BZT!
PIGIGYA!
OWWWL

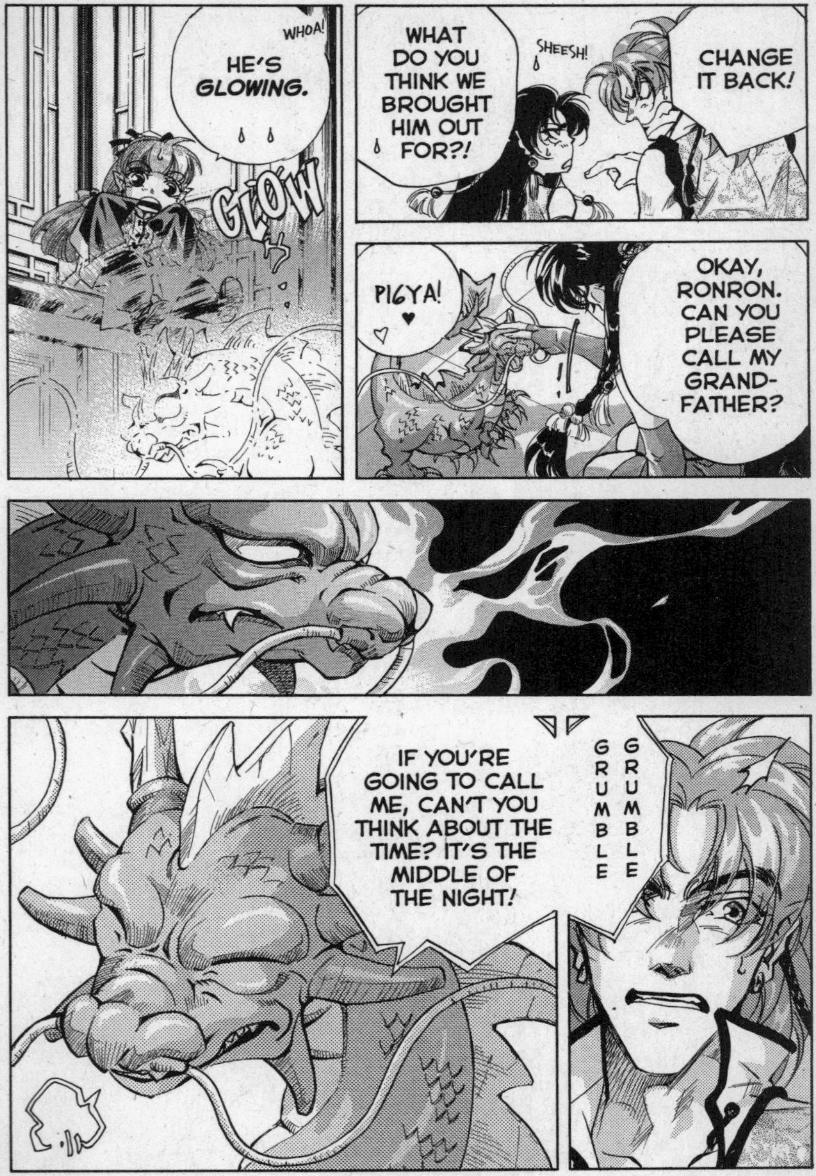
CHANGE IT BACK!
SHEESH!
WHAT DO YOU THINK WE BROUGHT HIM OUT FOR?!
OKAY, RONRON. CAN YOU PLEASE CALL MY GRAND-FATHER?
PIGYA!
WHOA!
HE'S GLOWING.
GLOW
GRUMBLE GRUMBLE
IF YOU'RE GOING TO CALL ME, CAN'T YOU THINK ABOUT THE TIME? IT'S THE MIDDLE OF THE NIGHT!

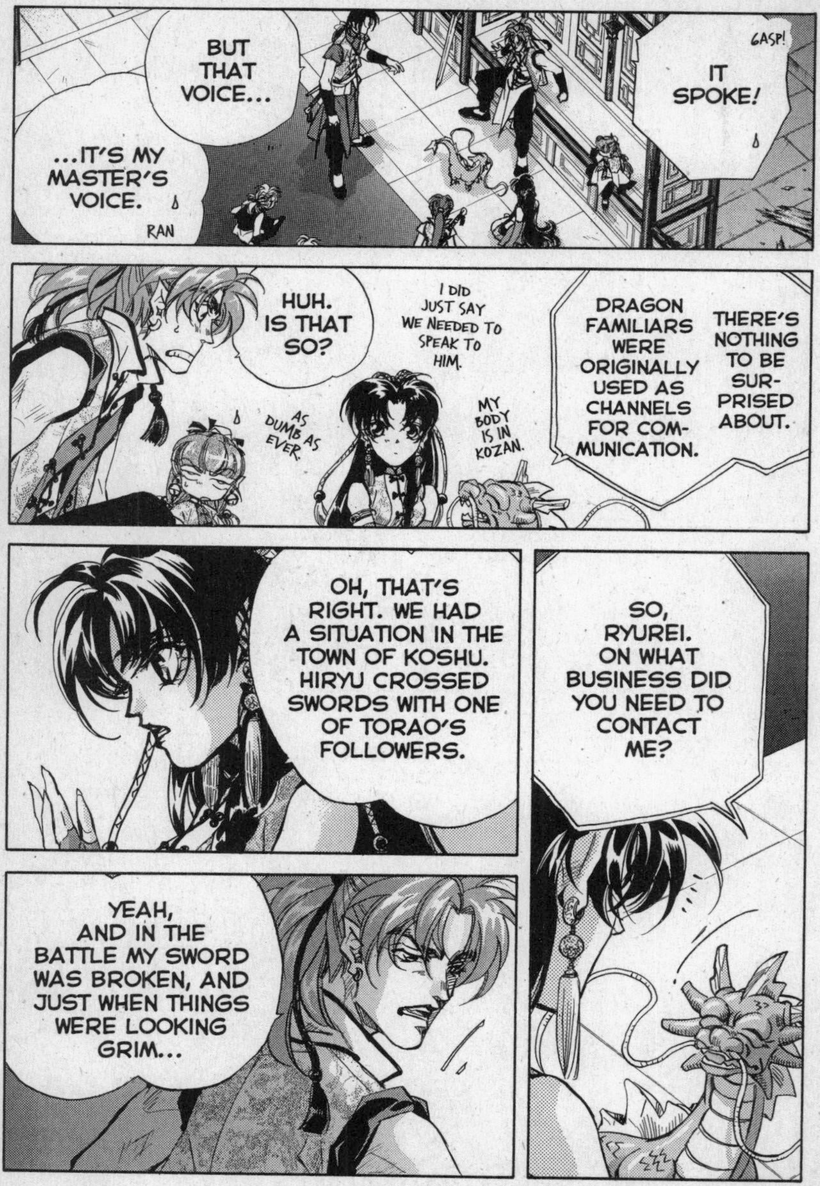
GASP!
IT SPOKE!
BUT THAT VOICE...
...IT'S MY MASTER'S VOICE.
RAN
THERE'S NOTHING TO BE SURPRISED ABOUT.
DRAGON FAMILIARS WERE ORIGINALLY USED AS CHANNELS FOR COMMUNICATION.
I DID JUST SAY WE NEEDED TO SPEAK TO HIM.
MY BODY IS IN KOZAN.
HUH. IS THAT SO?
AS DUMB AS EVER.
SO, RYUREI. ON WHAT BUSINESS DID YOU NEED TO CONTACT ME?
OH, THAT'S RIGHT. WE HAD A SITUATION IN THE TOWN OF KOSHU. HIRYU CROSSED SWORDS WITH ONE OF TORAO'S FOLLOWERS.
YEAH, AND IN THE BATTLE MY SWORD WAS BROKEN, AND JUST WHEN THINGS WERE LOOKING GRIM...

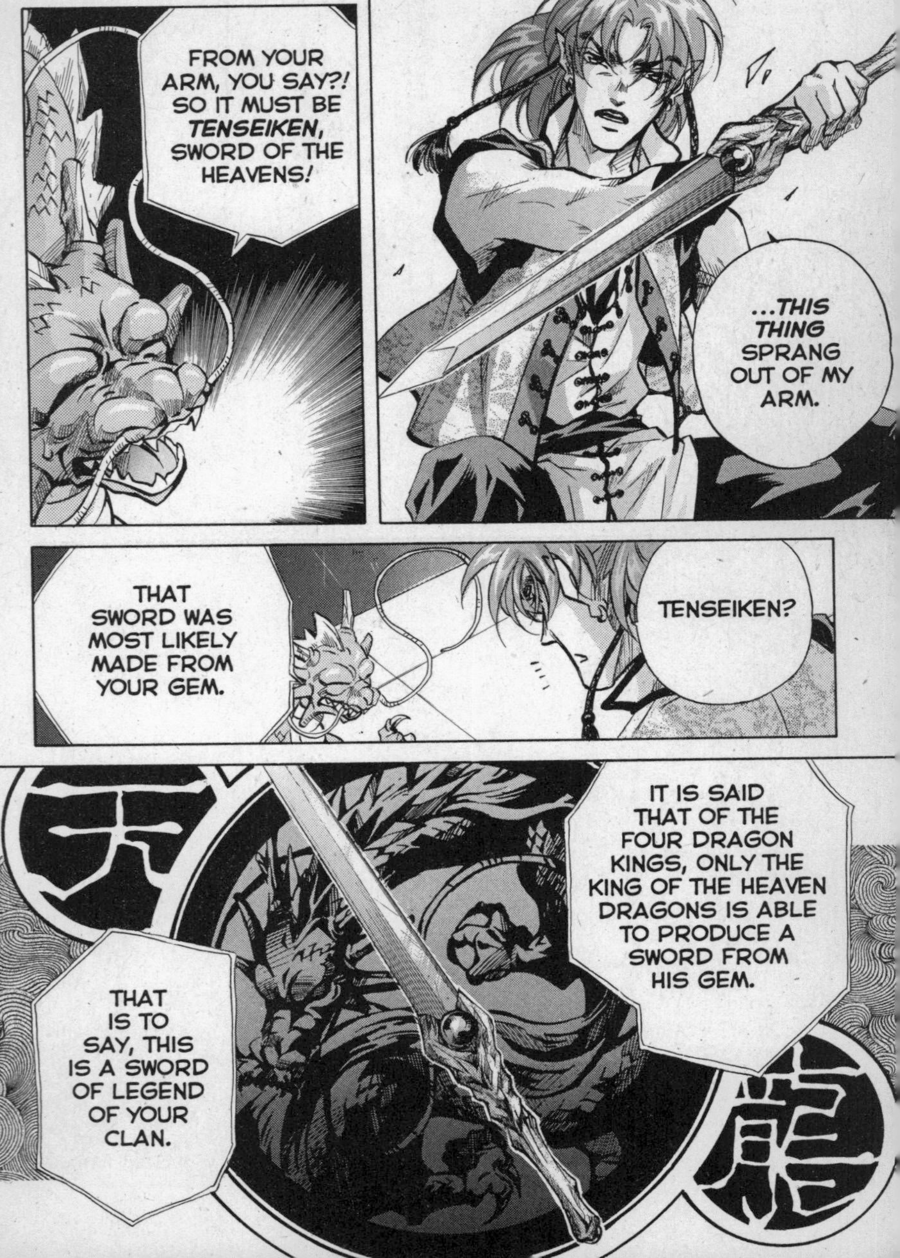
...THIS THING SPRANG OUT OF MY ARM.
FROM YOUR ARM, YOU SAY?! SO IT MUST BE TENSEIKEN, SWORD OF THE HEAVENS!
TENSEIKEN?
THAT SWORD WAS MOST LIKELY MADE FROM YOUR GEM.
IT IS SAID THAT OF THE FOUR DRAGON KINGS, ONLY THE KING OF THE HEAVEN DRAGONS IS ABLE TO PRODUCE A SWORD FROM HIS GEM.
THAT IS TO SAY, THIS IS A SWORD OF LEGEND OF YOUR CLAN.

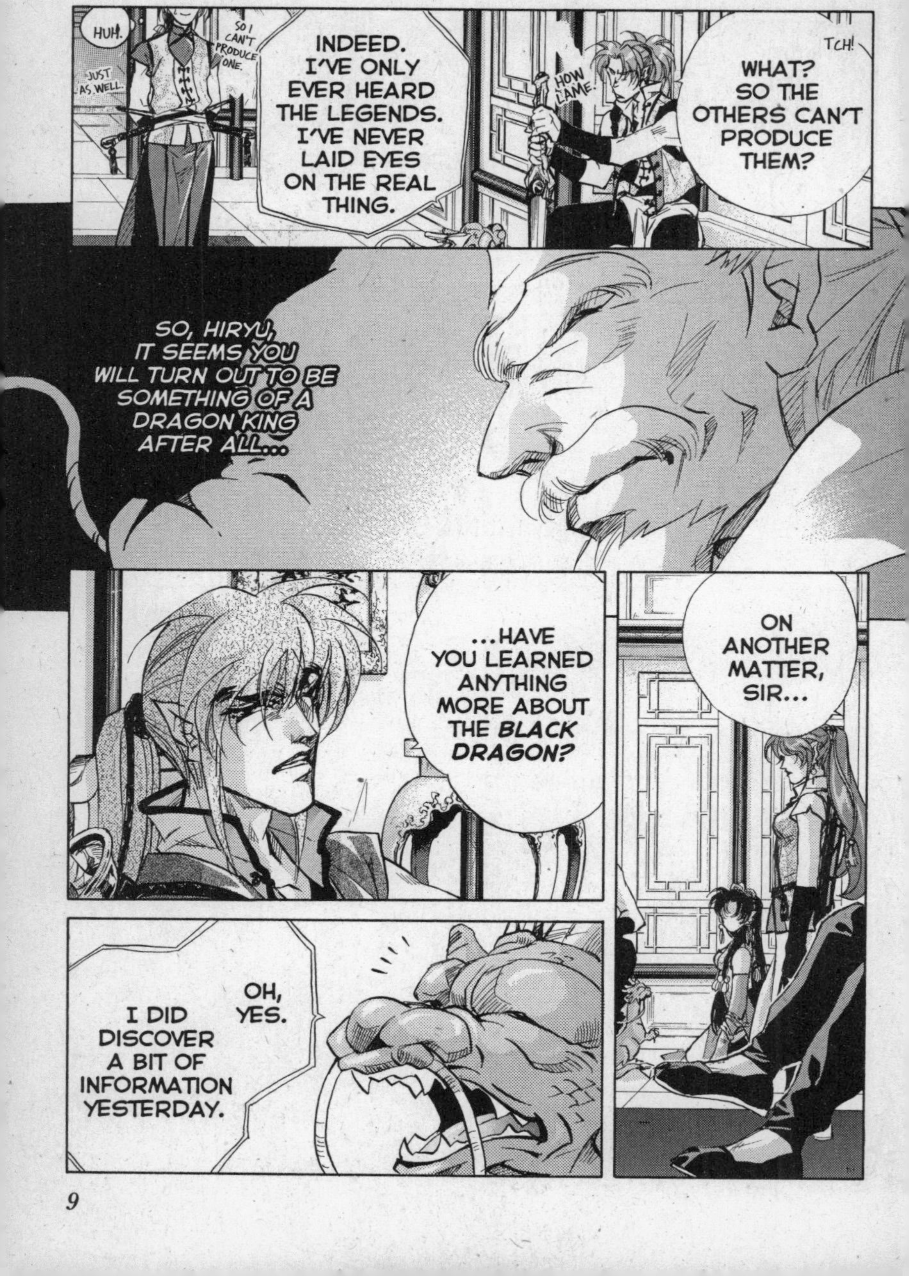
TCH!
WHAT? SO THE OTHERS CAN'T PRODUCE THEM?
HOW LAME.
INDEED. I'VE ONLY EVER HEARD THE LEGENDS. I'VE NEVER LAID EYES ON THE REAL THING.
SO I CAN'T PRODUCE ONE.
HUH.
JUST AS WELL.
SO, HIRYU, IT SEEMS YOU WILL TURN OUT TO BE SOMETHING OF A DRAGON KING AFTER ALL...
ON ANOTHER MATTER, SIR...
...HAVE YOU LEARNED ANYTHING MORE ABOUT THE *BLACK DRAGON?*
OH, YES.
I DID DISCOVER A BIT OF INFORMATION YESTERDAY.

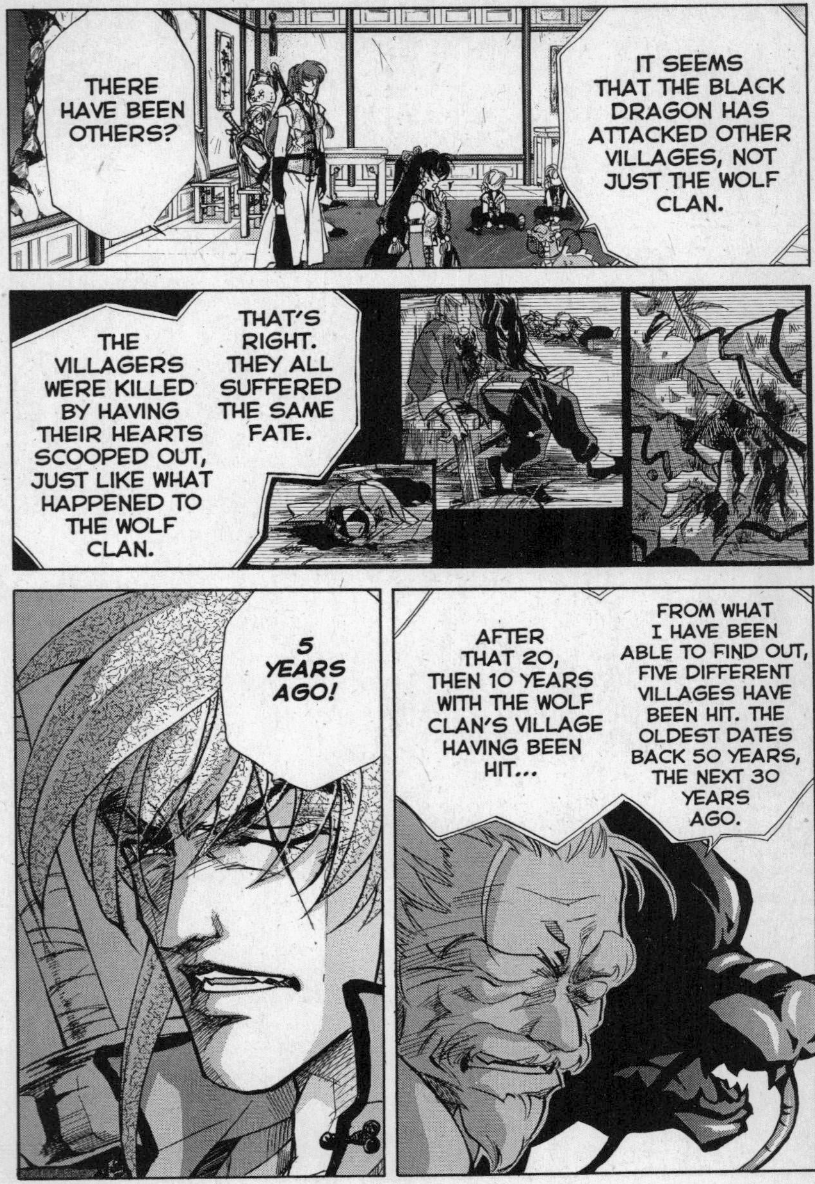
IT SEEMS THAT THE BLACK DRAGON HAS ATTACKED OTHER VILLAGES, NOT JUST THE WOLF CLAN.
THERE HAVE BEEN OTHERS?
THAT'S RIGHT. THEY ALL SUFFERED THE SAME FATE.
THE VILLAGERS WERE KILLED BY HAVING THEIR HEARTS SCOOPED OUT, JUST LIKE WHAT HAPPENED TO THE WOLF CLAN.
FROM WHAT I HAVE BEEN ABLE TO FIND OUT, FIVE DIFFERENT VILLAGES HAVE BEEN HIT. THE OLDEST DATES BACK 50 YEARS, THE NEXT 30 YEARS AGO.
AFTER THAT 20, THEN 10 YEARS WITH THE WOLF CLAN'S VILLAGE HAVING BEEN HIT...
5 YEARS AGO!

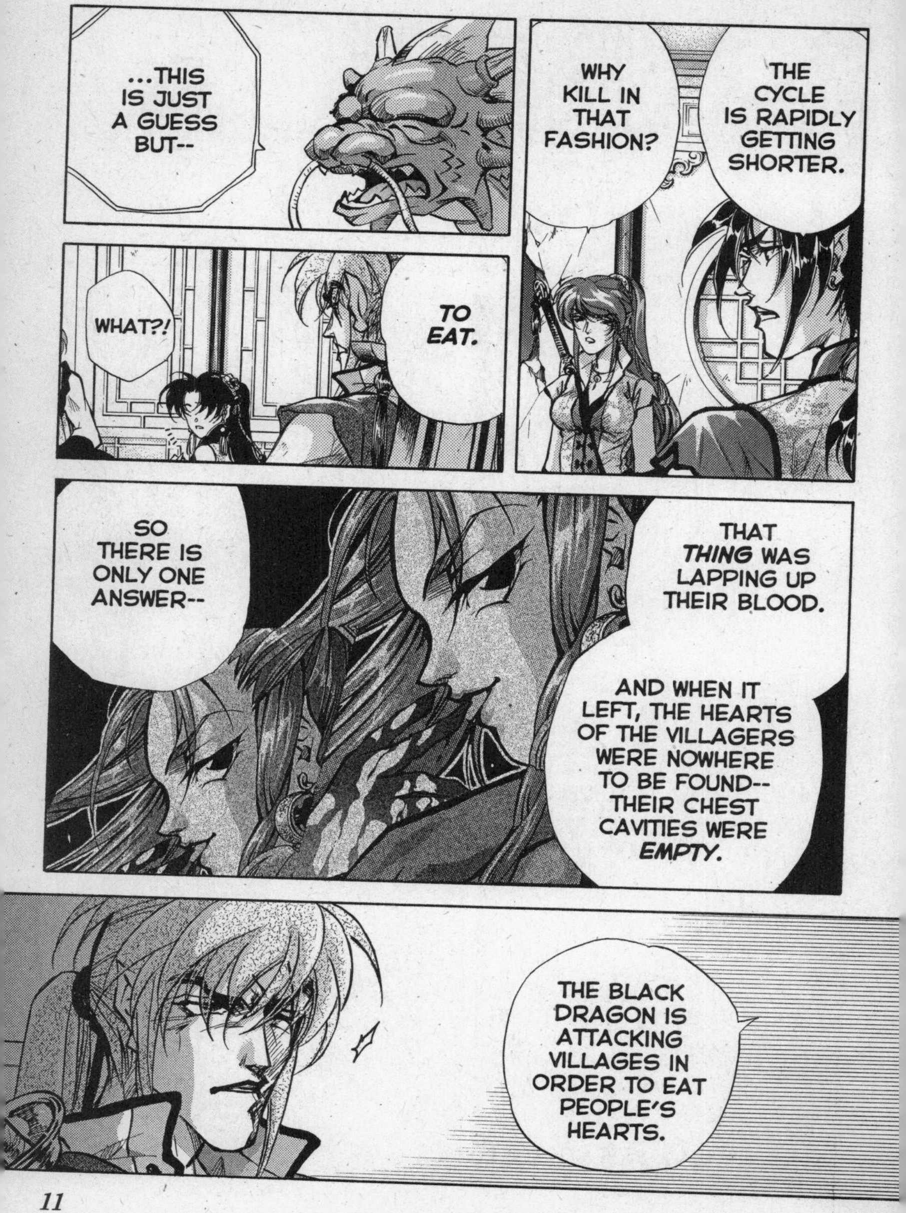
THE CYCLE IS RAPIDLY GETTING SHORTER.
WHY KILL IN THAT FASHION?
...THIS IS JUST A GUESS BUT--
TO *EAT*.
WHAT?!
THAT *THING* WAS LAPPING UP THEIR BLOOD.
AND WHEN IT LEFT, THE HEARTS OF THE VILLAGERS WERE NOWHERE TO BE FOUND-- THEIR CHEST CAVITIES WERE *EMPTY*.
SO THERE IS ONLY ONE ANSWER--
THE BLACK DRAGON IS ATTACKING VILLAGES IN ORDER TO EAT PEOPLE'S HEARTS.

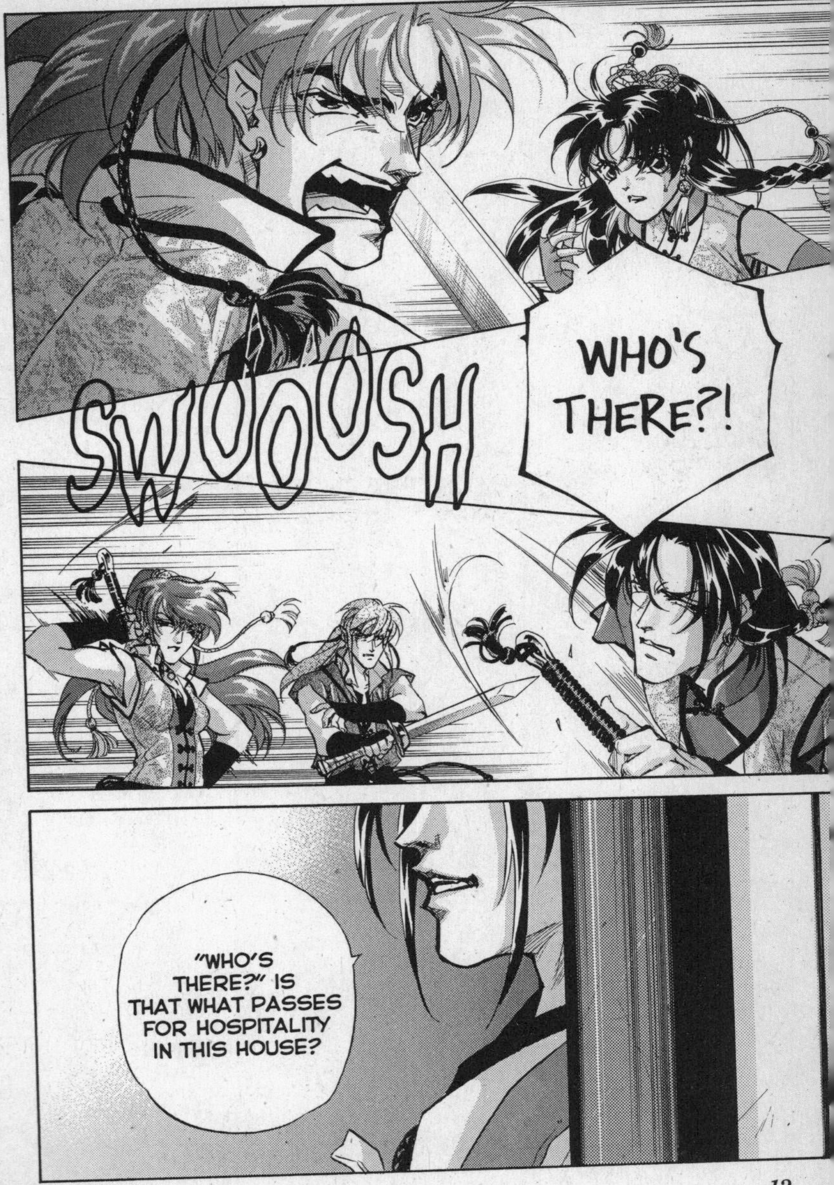
WHO'S THERE?!
SWOOOSH
"WHO'S THERE?" IS THAT WHAT PASSES FOR HOSPITALITY IN THIS HOUSE?

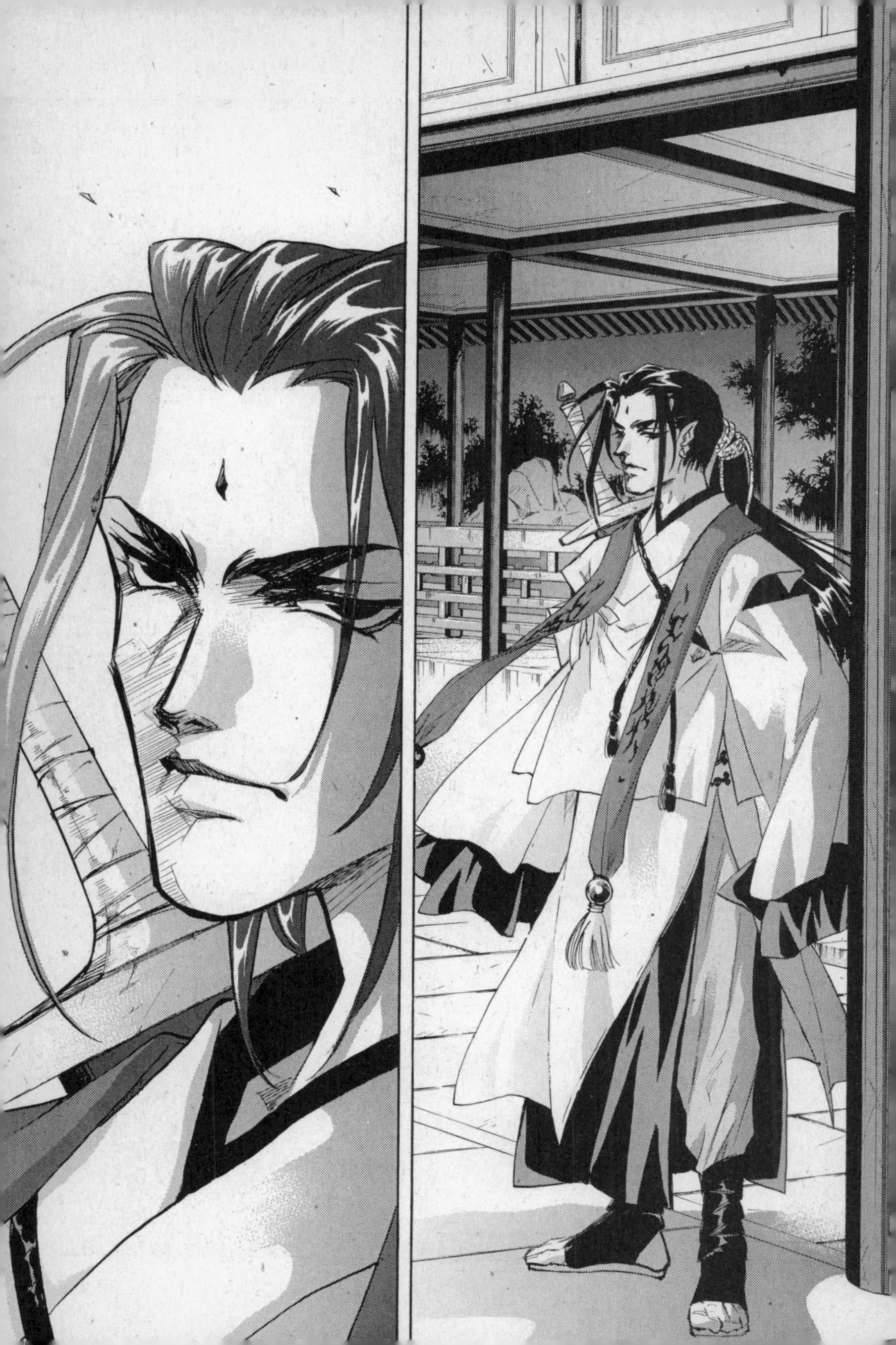

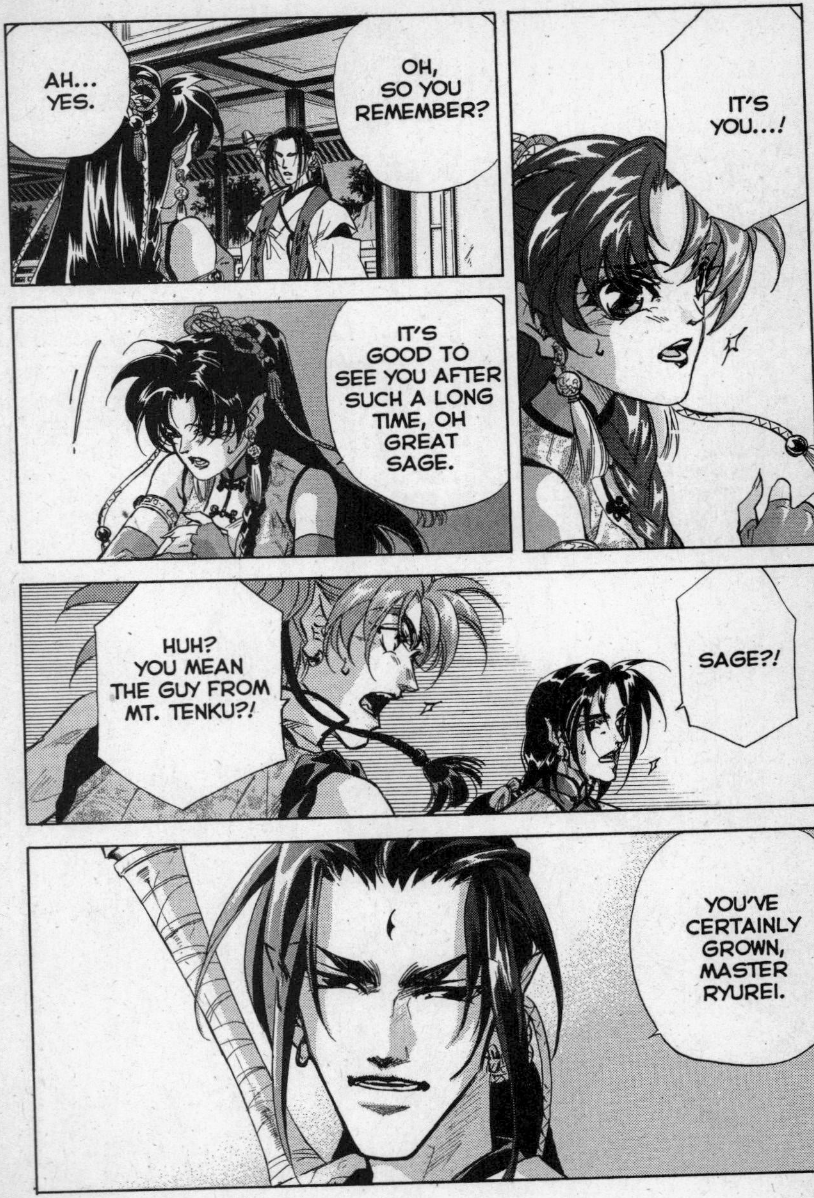
IT'S YOU...!
OH, SO YOU REMEMBER?
AH... YES.
IT'S GOOD TO SEE YOU AFTER SUCH A LONG TIME, OH GREAT SAGE.
SAGE?!
HUH? YOU MEAN THE GUY FROM MT. TENKU?!
YOU'VE CERTAINLY GROWN, MASTER RYUREI.

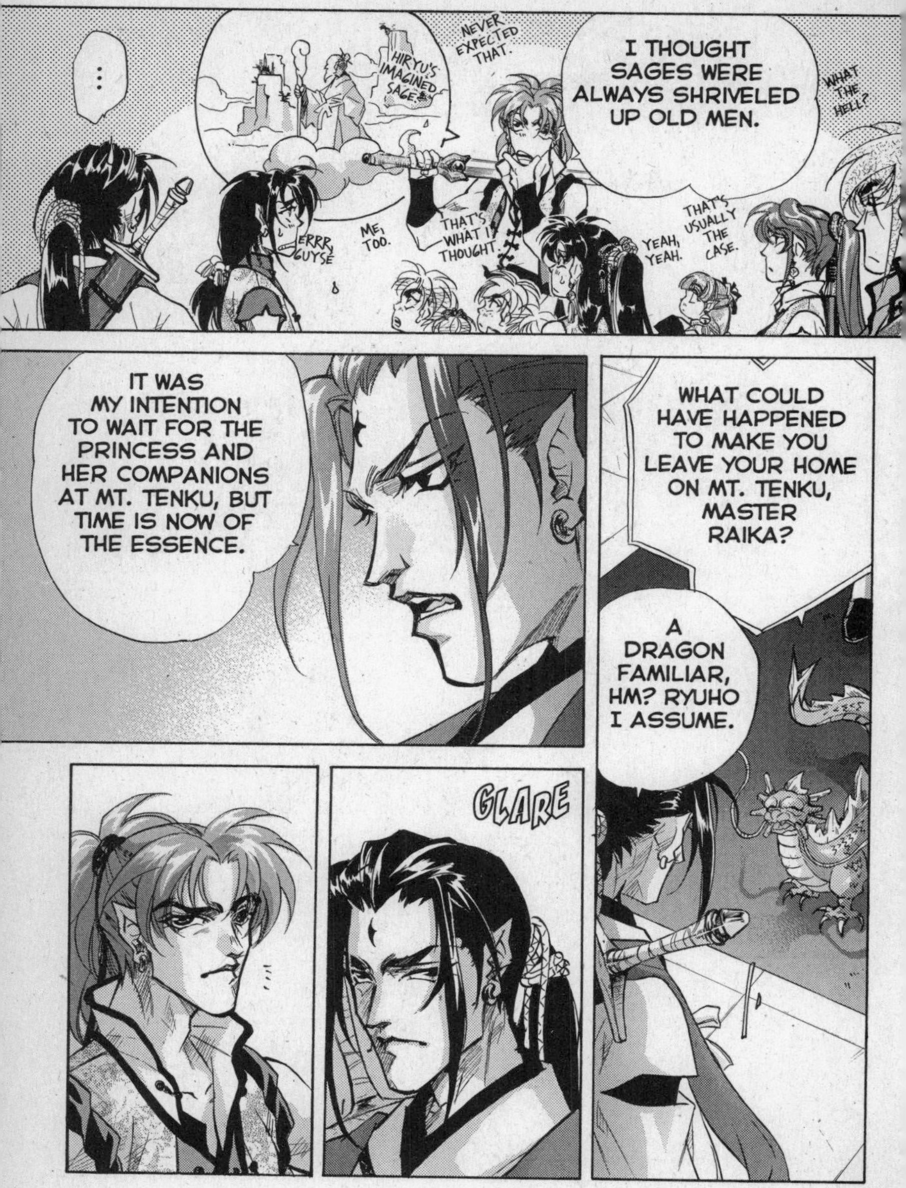
WHAT THE HELL?
I THOUGHT SAGES WERE ALWAYS SHRIVELED UP OLD MEN.
NEVER EXPECTED THAT.
HIRYU'S IMAGINED SAGE.
THAT'S USUALLY THE CASE.
YEAH, YEAH.
THAT'S WHAT I THOUGHT.
ME, TOO.
ERRR, GUYS?
...
WHAT COULD HAVE HAPPENED TO MAKE YOU LEAVE YOUR HOME ON MT. TENKU, MASTER RAIKA?
A DRAGON FAMILIAR, HM? RYUHO I ASSUME.
IT WAS MY INTENTION TO WAIT FOR THE PRINCESS AND HER COMPANIONS AT MT. TENKU, BUT TIME IS NOW OF THE ESSENCE.
GLARE

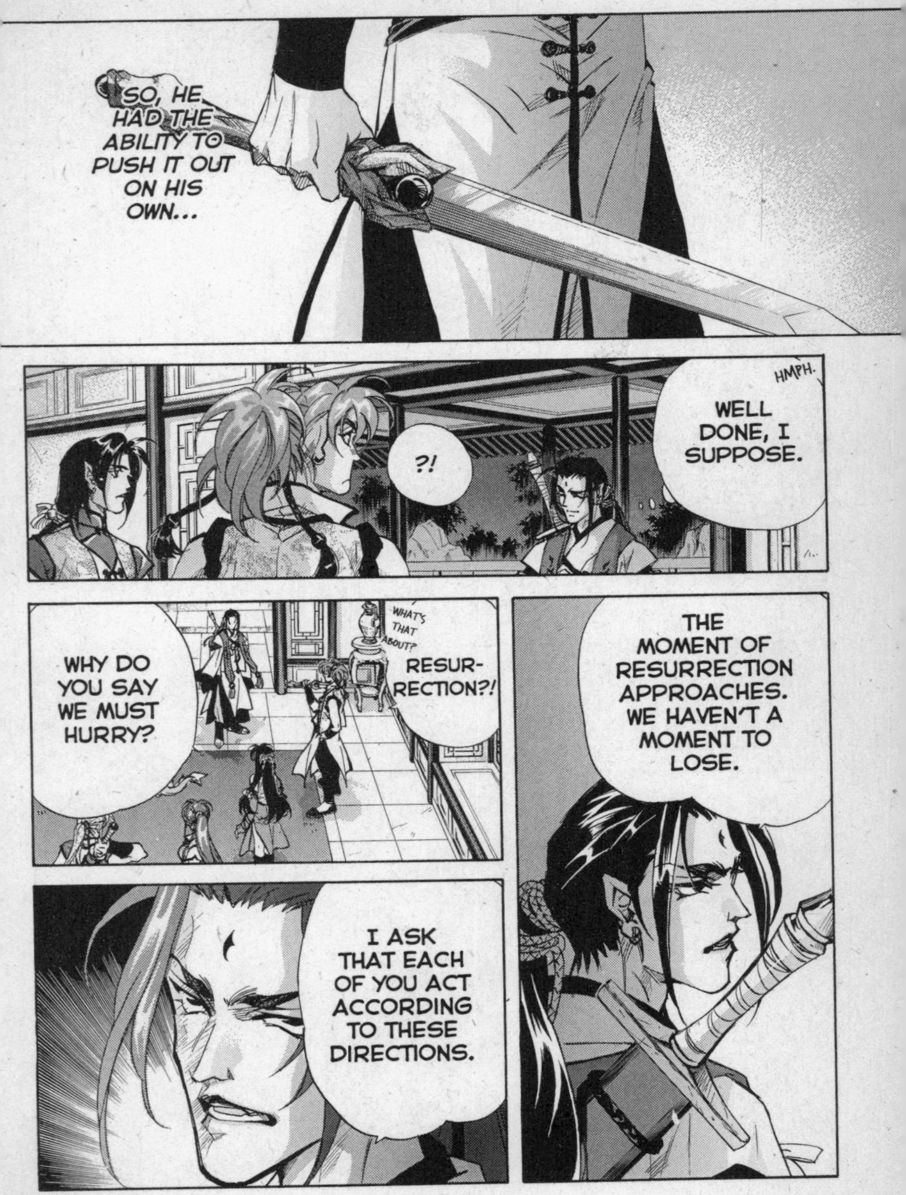
SO, HE HAD THE ABILITY TO PUSH IT OUT ON HIS OWN...
HMPH.
WELL DONE, I SUPPOSE.
?!
THE MOMENT OF RESURRECTION APPROACHES. WE HAVEN'T A MOMENT TO LOSE.
RESUR-RECTION?!
WHAT'S THAT ABOUT?
WHY DO YOU SAY WE MUST HURRY?
I ASK THAT EACH OF YOU ACT ACCORDING TO THESE DIRECTIONS.

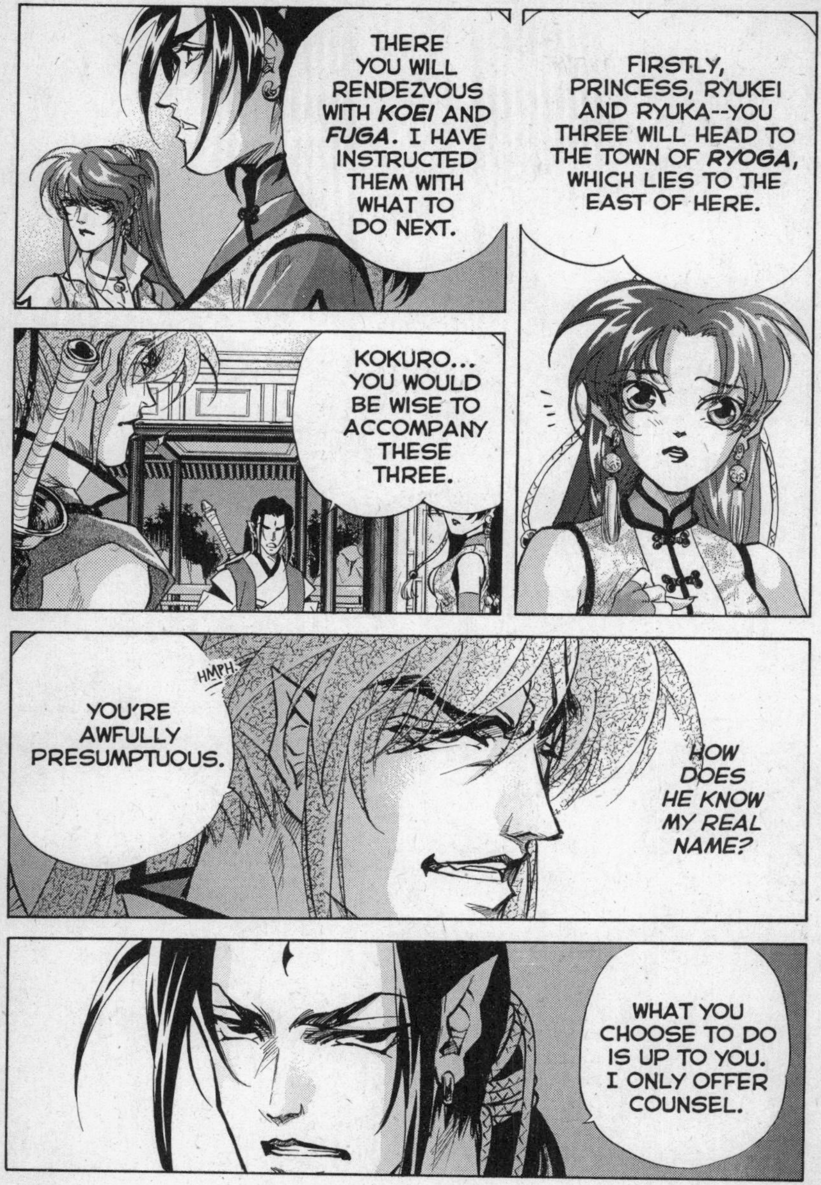
FIRSTLY, PRINCESS, RYUKEI AND RYUKA--YOU THREE WILL HEAD TO THE TOWN OF *RYOGA*, WHICH LIES TO THE EAST OF HERE.
THERE YOU WILL RENDEZVOUS WITH *KOEI* AND *FUGA*. I HAVE INSTRUCTED THEM WITH WHAT TO DO NEXT.
KOKURO... YOU WOULD BE WISE TO ACCOMPANY THESE THREE.
HMPH.
YOU'RE AWFULLY PRESUMPTUOUS.
HOW DOES HE KNOW MY REAL NAME?
WHAT YOU CHOOSE TO DO IS UP TO YOU. I ONLY OFFER COUNSEL.

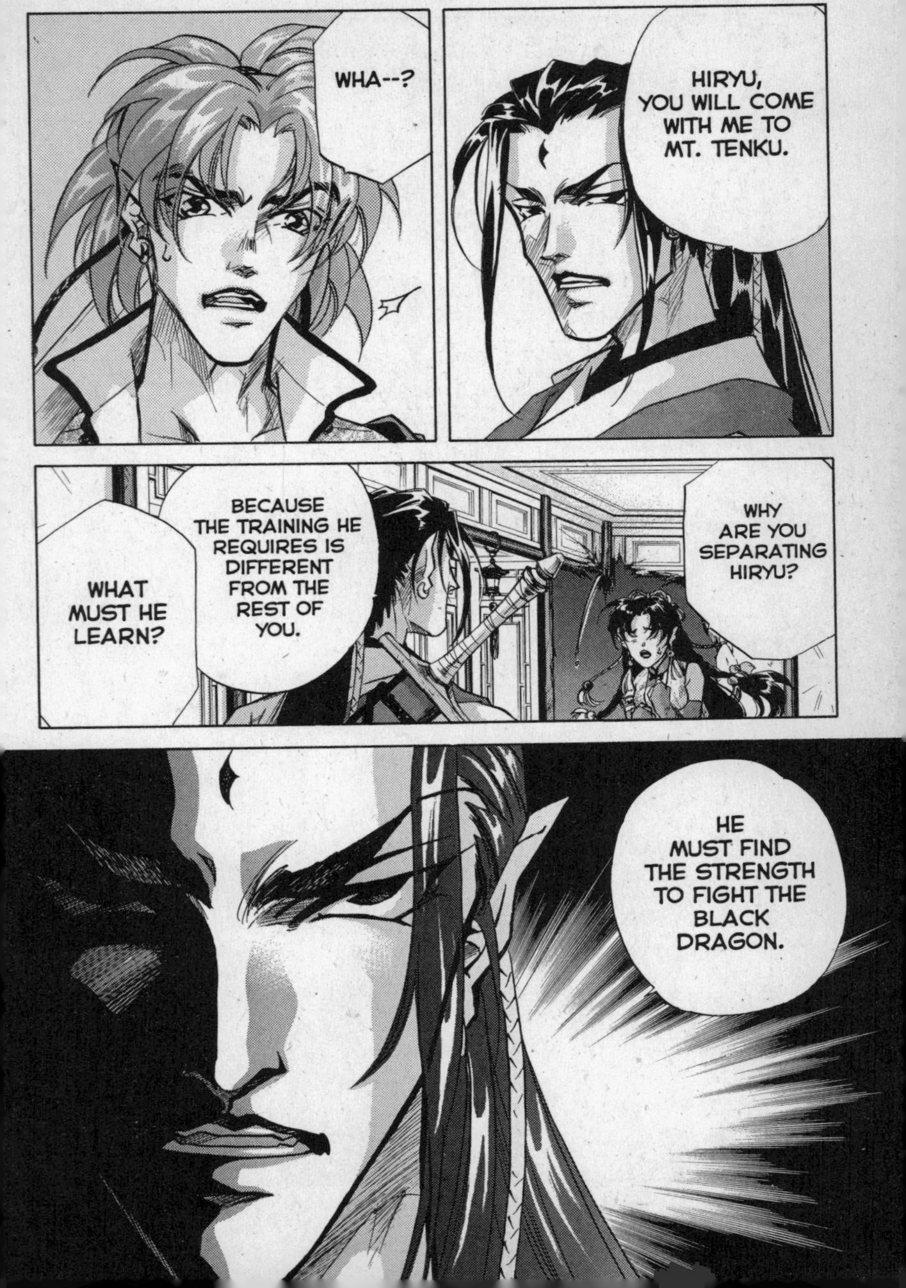
HIRYU, YOU WILL COME WITH ME TO MT. TENKU.
WHA--?
WHY ARE YOU SEPARATING HIRYU?
BECAUSE THE TRAINING HE REQUIRES IS DIFFERENT FROM THE REST OF YOU.
WHAT MUST HE LEARN?
HE MUST FIND THE STRENGTH TO FIGHT THE BLACK DRAGON.

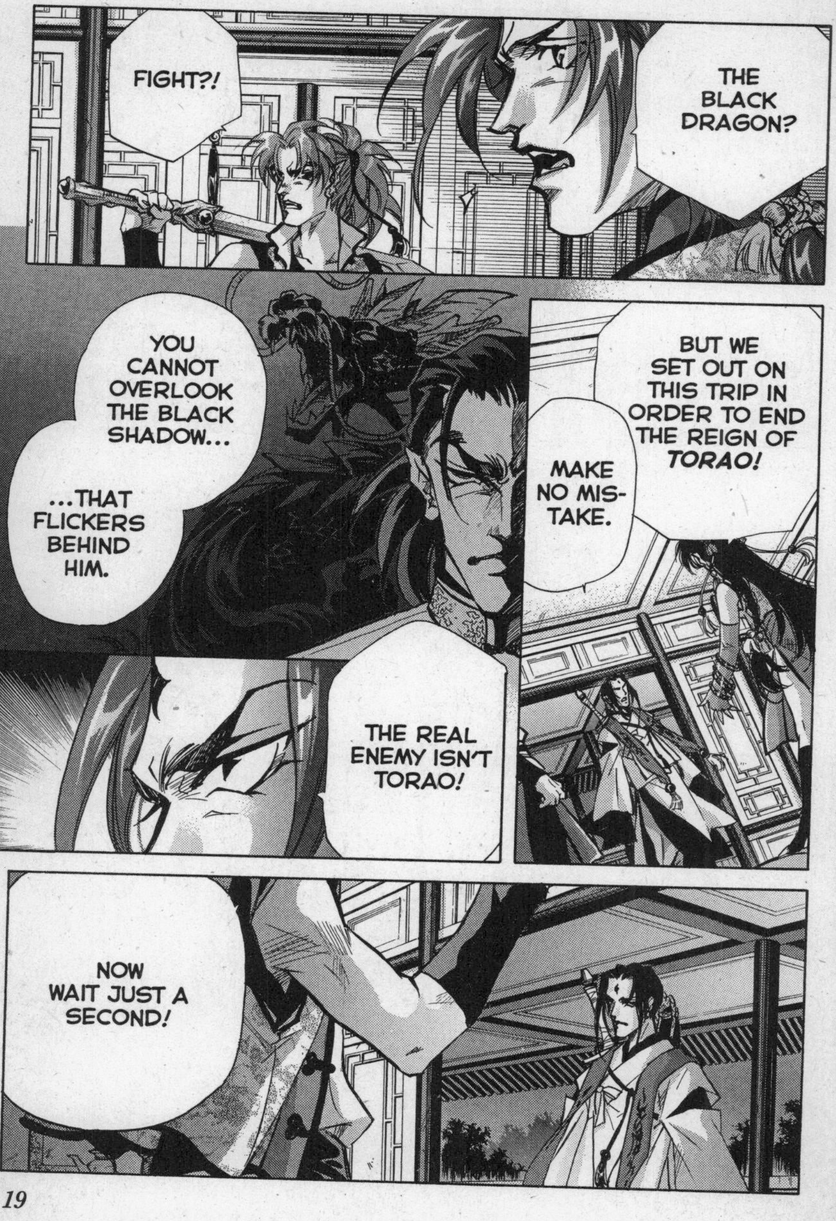
THE BLACK DRAGON?
FIGHT?!
BUT WE SET OUT ON THIS TRIP IN ORDER TO END THE REIGN OF *TORAO!*
MAKE NO MIS-TAKE.
YOU CANNOT OVERLOOK THE BLACK SHADOW...
...THAT FLICKERS BEHIND HIM.
THE REAL ENEMY ISN'T TORAO!
NOW WAIT JUST A SECOND!

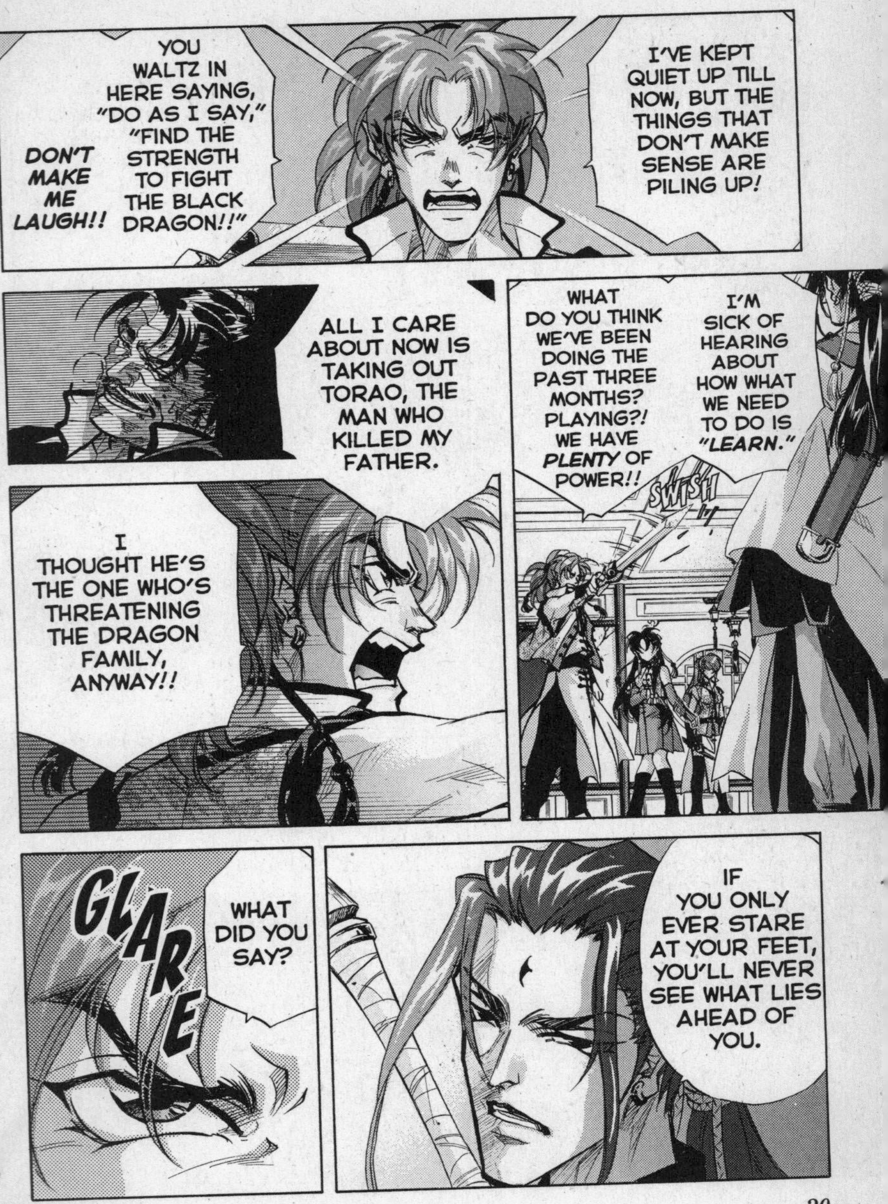
I'VE KEPT QUIET UP TILL NOW, BUT THE THINGS THAT DON'T MAKE SENSE ARE PILING UP!
YOU WALTZ IN HERE SAYING, "DO AS I SAY," "FIND THE STRENGTH TO FIGHT THE BLACK DRAGON!!"
DON'T MAKE ME LAUGH!!
I'M SICK OF HEARING ABOUT HOW WHAT WE NEED TO DO IS "LEARN."
WHAT DO YOU THINK WE'VE BEEN DOING THE PAST THREE MONTHS? PLAYING?! WE HAVE PLENTY OF POWER!!
SWISH
ALL I CARE ABOUT NOW IS TAKING OUT TORAO, THE MAN WHO KILLED MY FATHER.
I THOUGHT HE'S THE ONE WHO'S THREATENING THE DRAGON FAMILY, ANYWAY!!
IF YOU ONLY EVER STARE AT YOUR FEET, YOU'LL NEVER SEE WHAT LIES AHEAD OF YOU.
WHAT DID YOU SAY?
GLARE

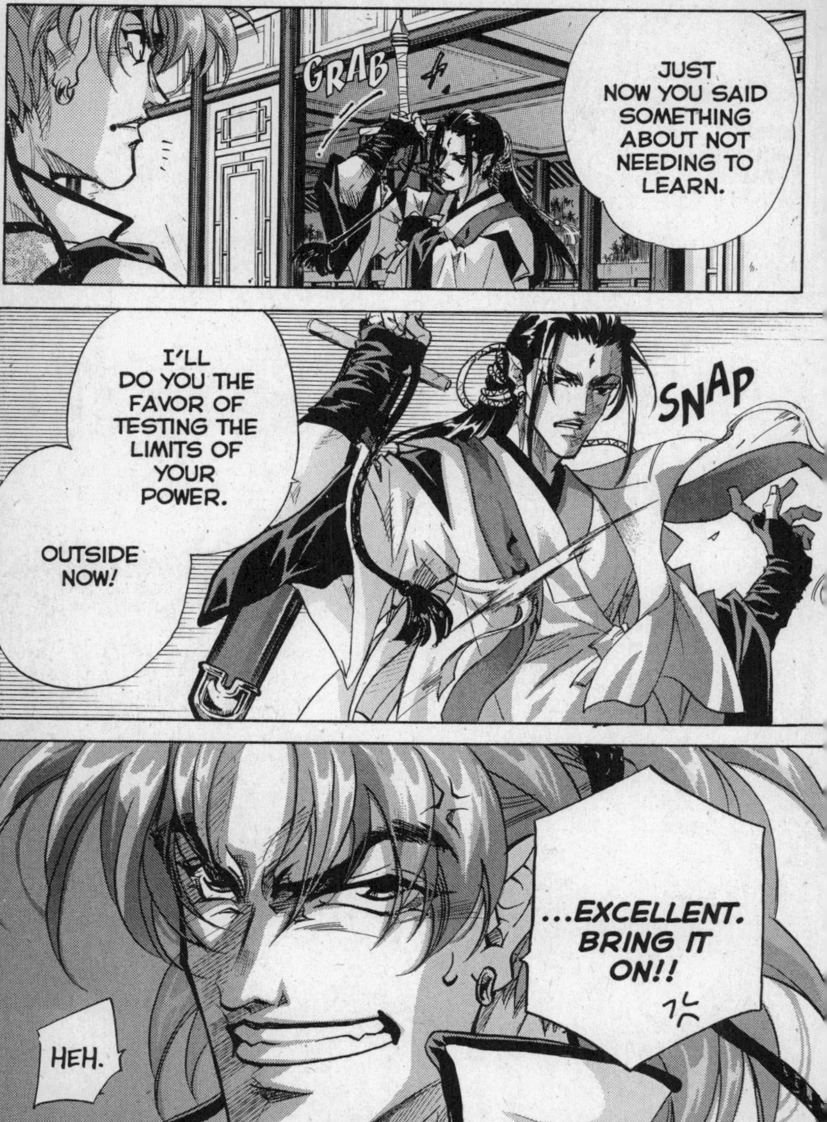
JUST NOW YOU SAID SOMETHING ABOUT NOT NEEDING TO LEARN.
GRAB
SNAP
I'LL DO YOU THE FAVOR OF TESTING THE LIMITS OF YOUR POWER.
OUTSIDE NOW!
...EXCELLENT. BRING IT ON!!
HEH.

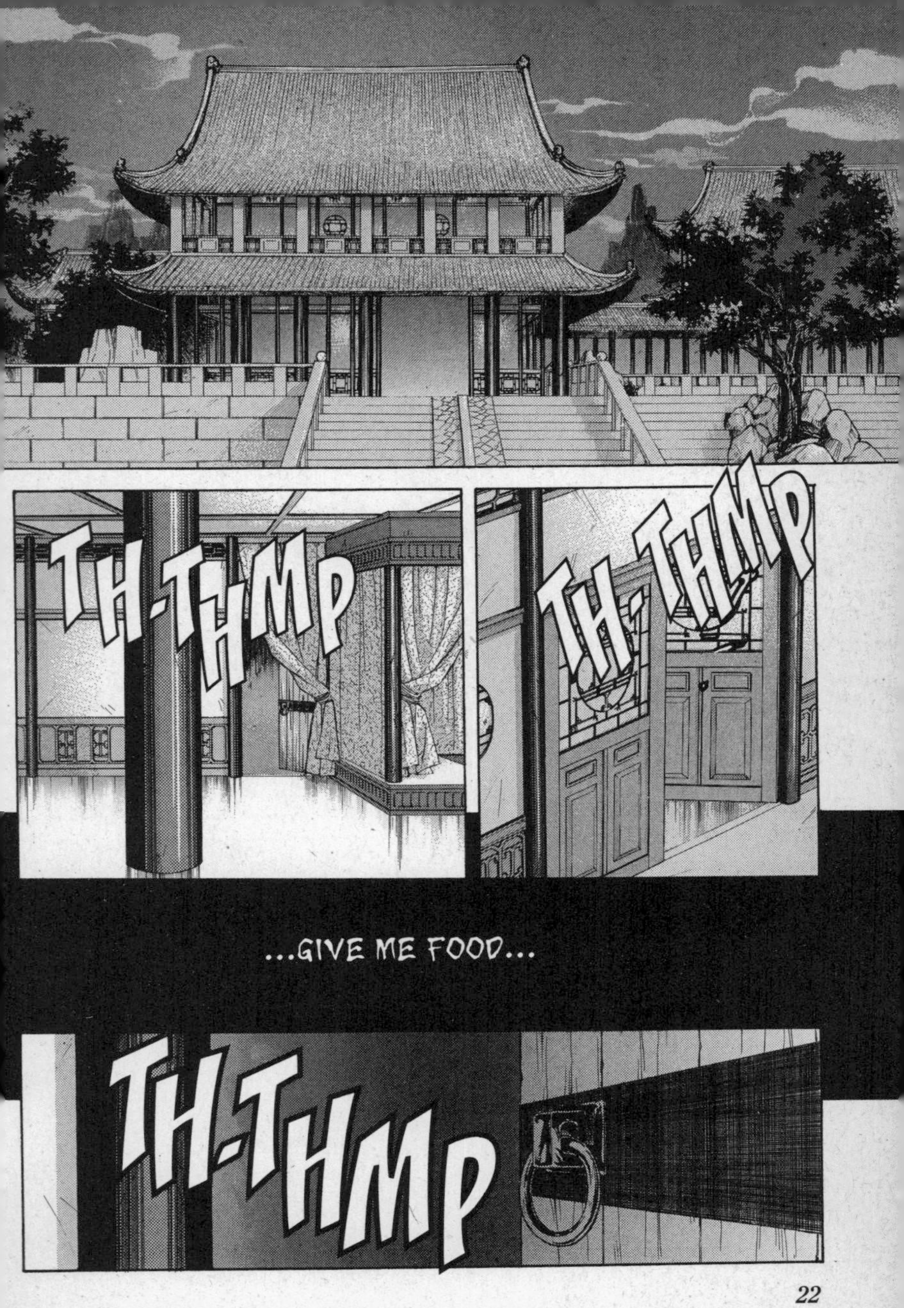
TH-THMP
TH-THMP
...GIVE ME FOOD...
TH-THMP

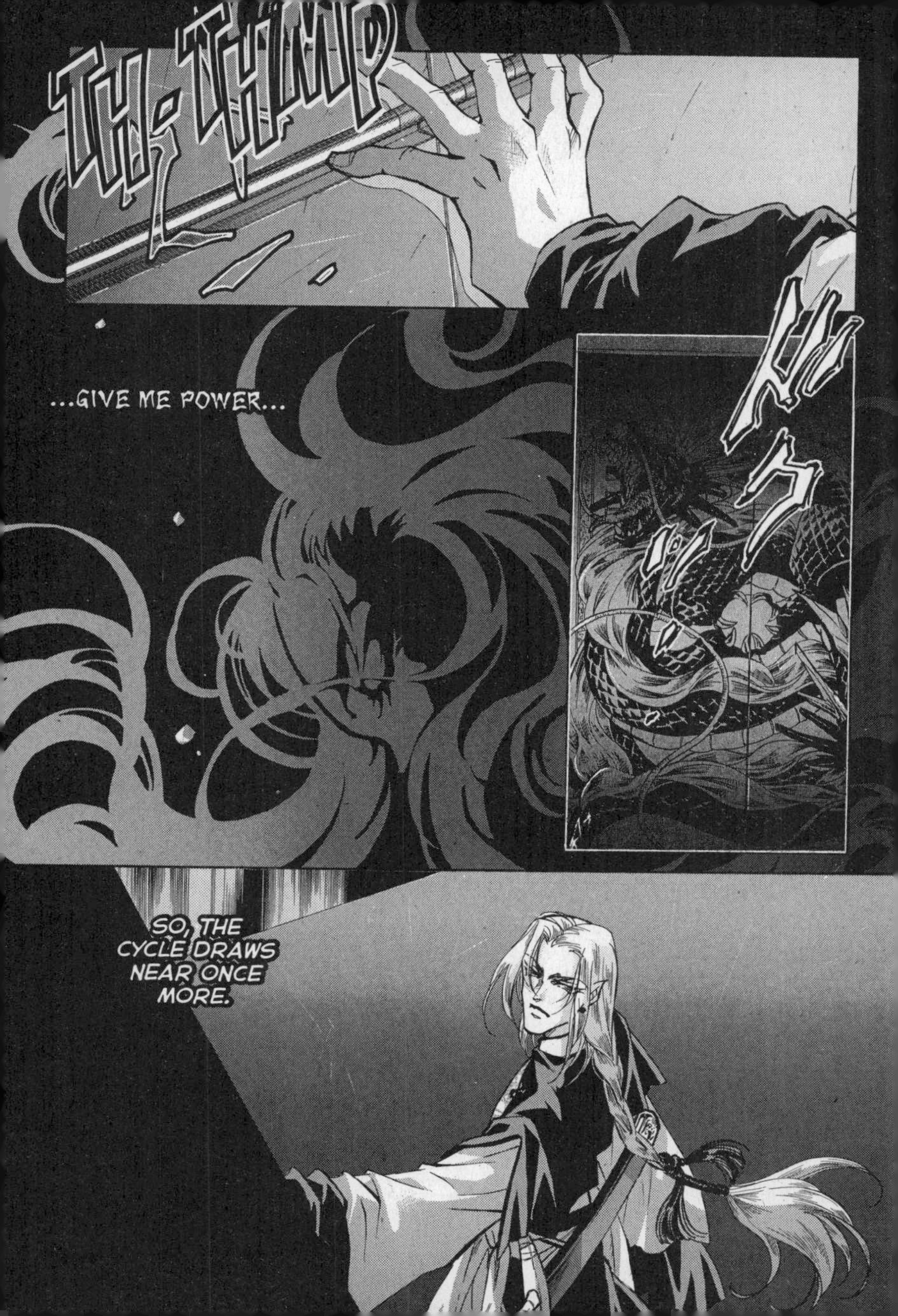
TH-THMP
...GIVE ME POWER...
SO, THE CYCLE DRAWS NEAR ONCE MORE.

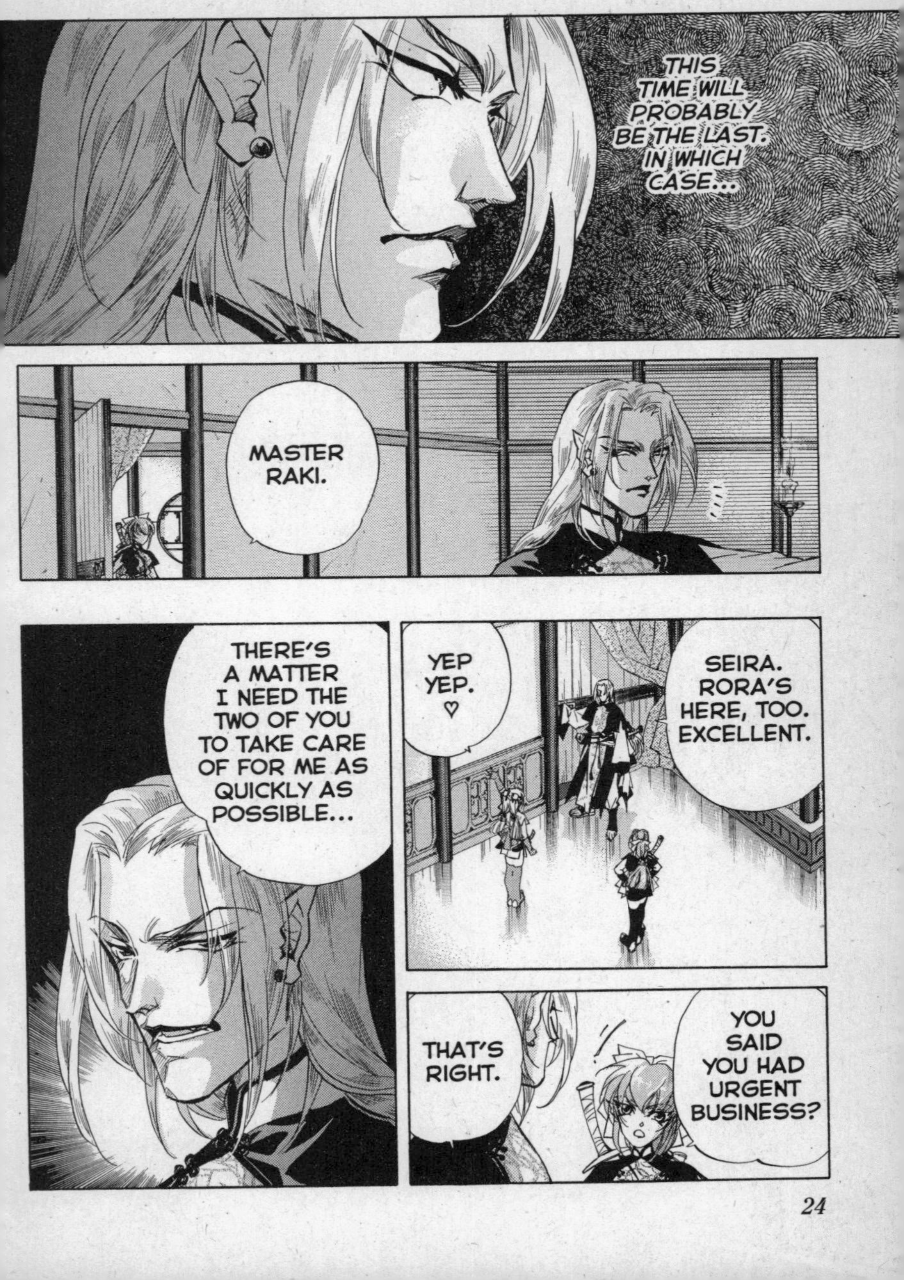
THIS TIME WILL PROBABLY BE THE LAST. IN WHICH CASE...
MASTER RAKI.
SEIRA. RORA'S HERE, TOO. EXCELLENT.
YEP YEP. ♥
YOU SAID YOU HAD URGENT BUSINESS?
THAT'S RIGHT.
THERE'S A MATTER I NEED THE TWO OF YOU TO TAKE CARE OF FOR ME AS QUICKLY AS POSSIBLE...

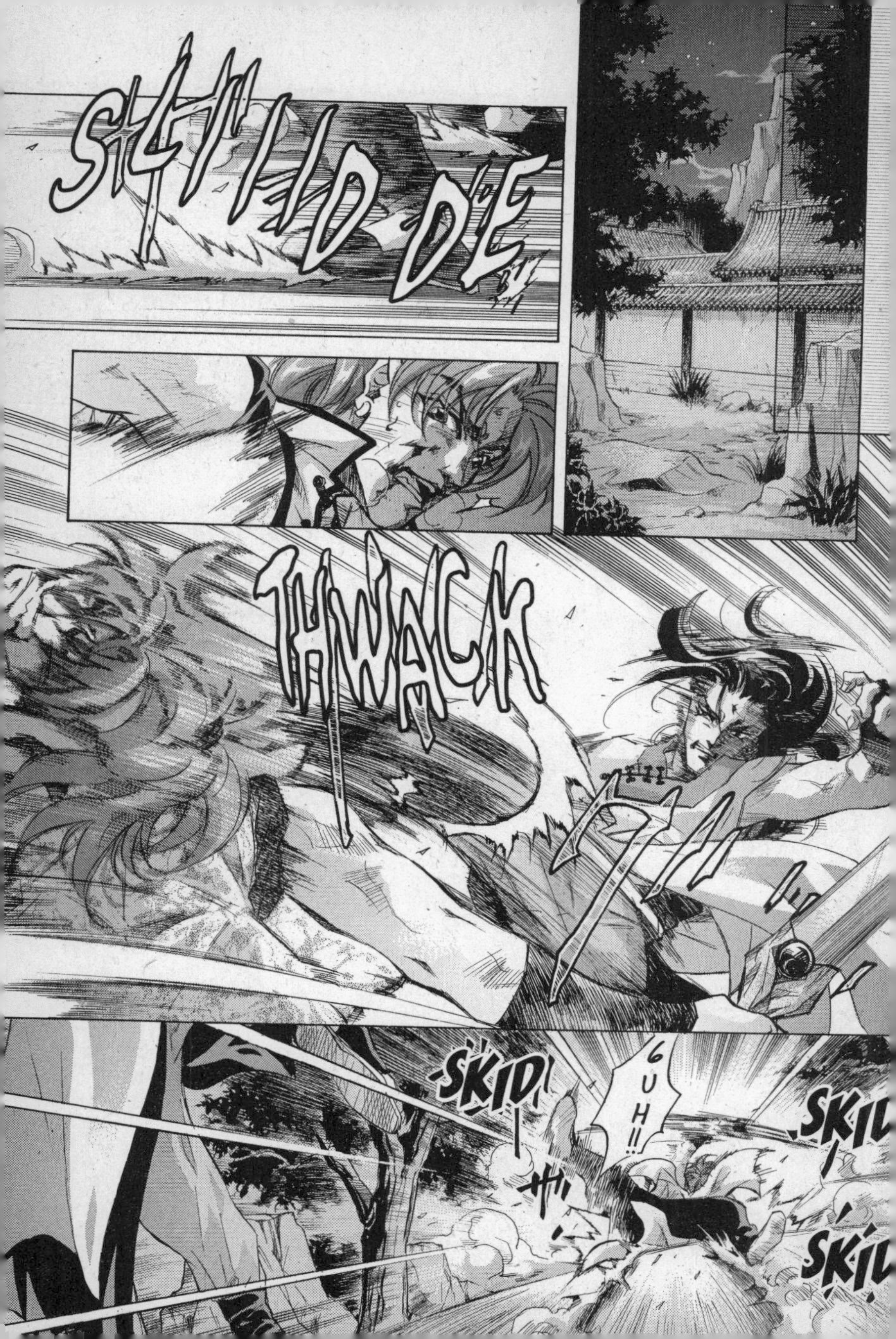
SLIIIDE
THWACK
GUH!!
SKID

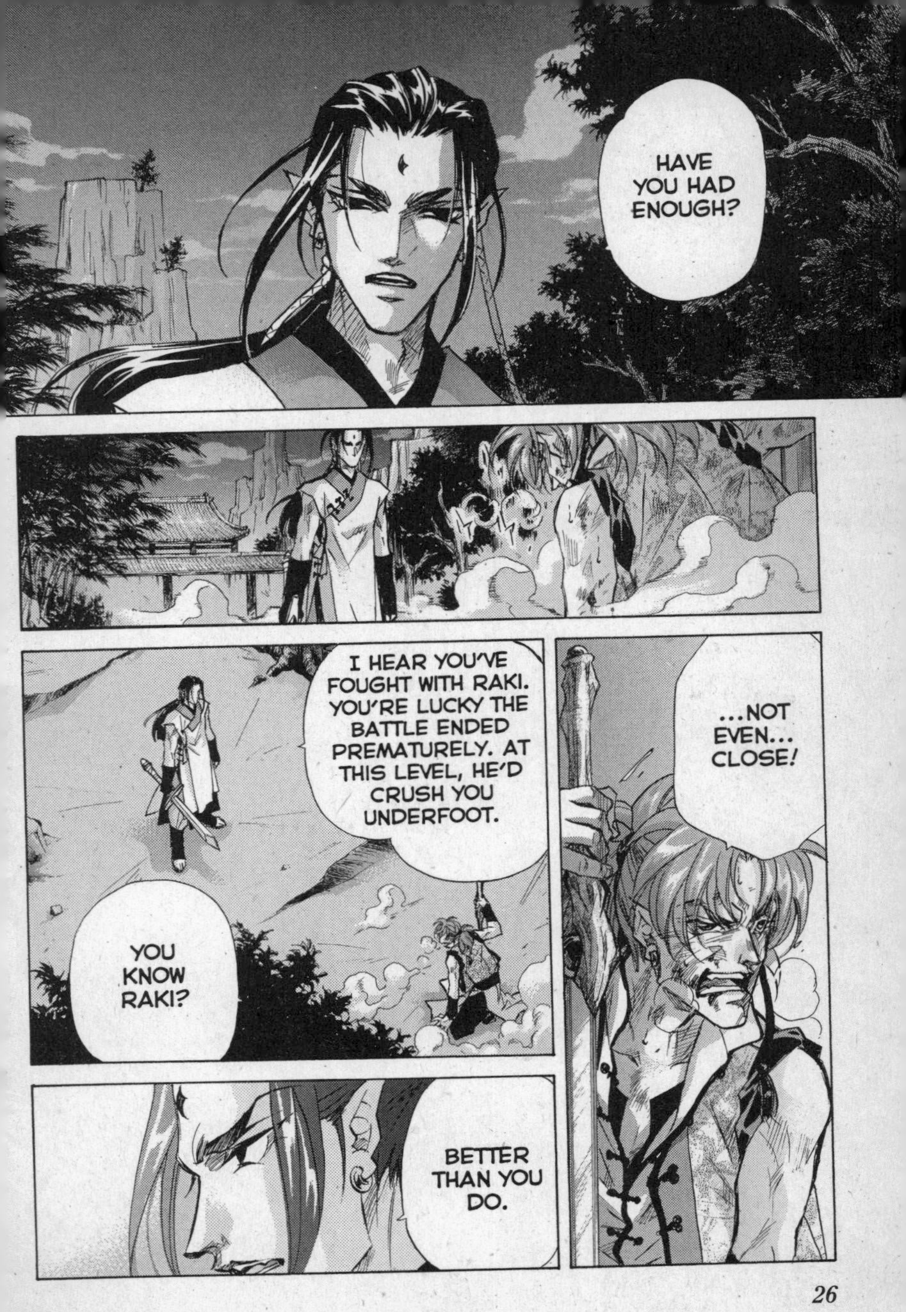
HAVE YOU HAD ENOUGH?
...NOT EVEN... CLOSE!
I HEAR YOU'VE FOUGHT WITH RAKI. YOU'RE LUCKY THE BATTLE ENDED PREMATURELY. AT THIS LEVEL, HE'D CRUSH YOU UNDERFOOT.
YOU KNOW RAKI?
BETTER THAN YOU DO.

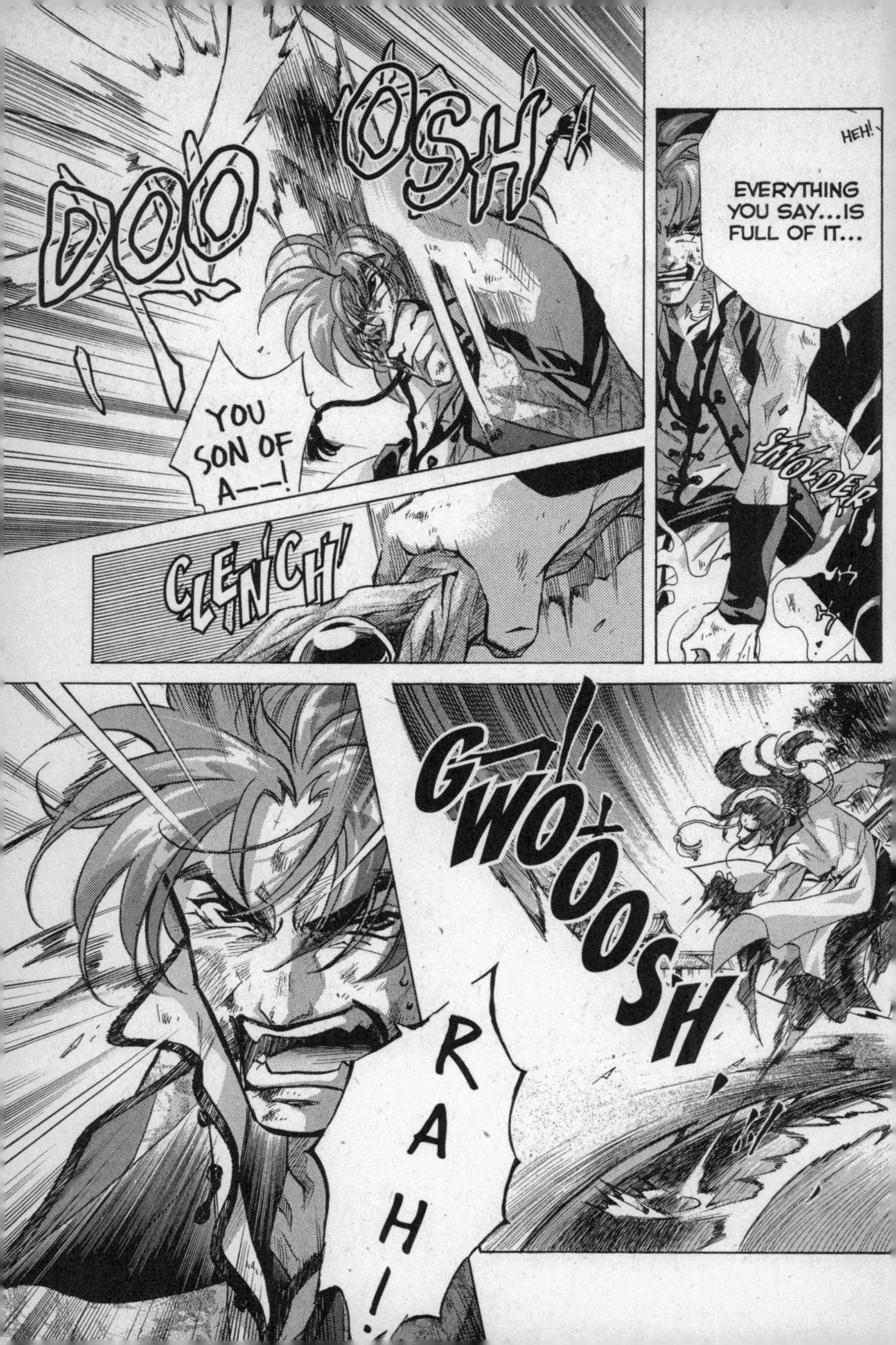
HEH!
EVERYTHING YOU SAY...IS FULL OF IT...
SMOLDER
DOOOSH!
YOU SON OF A--!
CLENCH!
GWOOOOSH!
RAH!

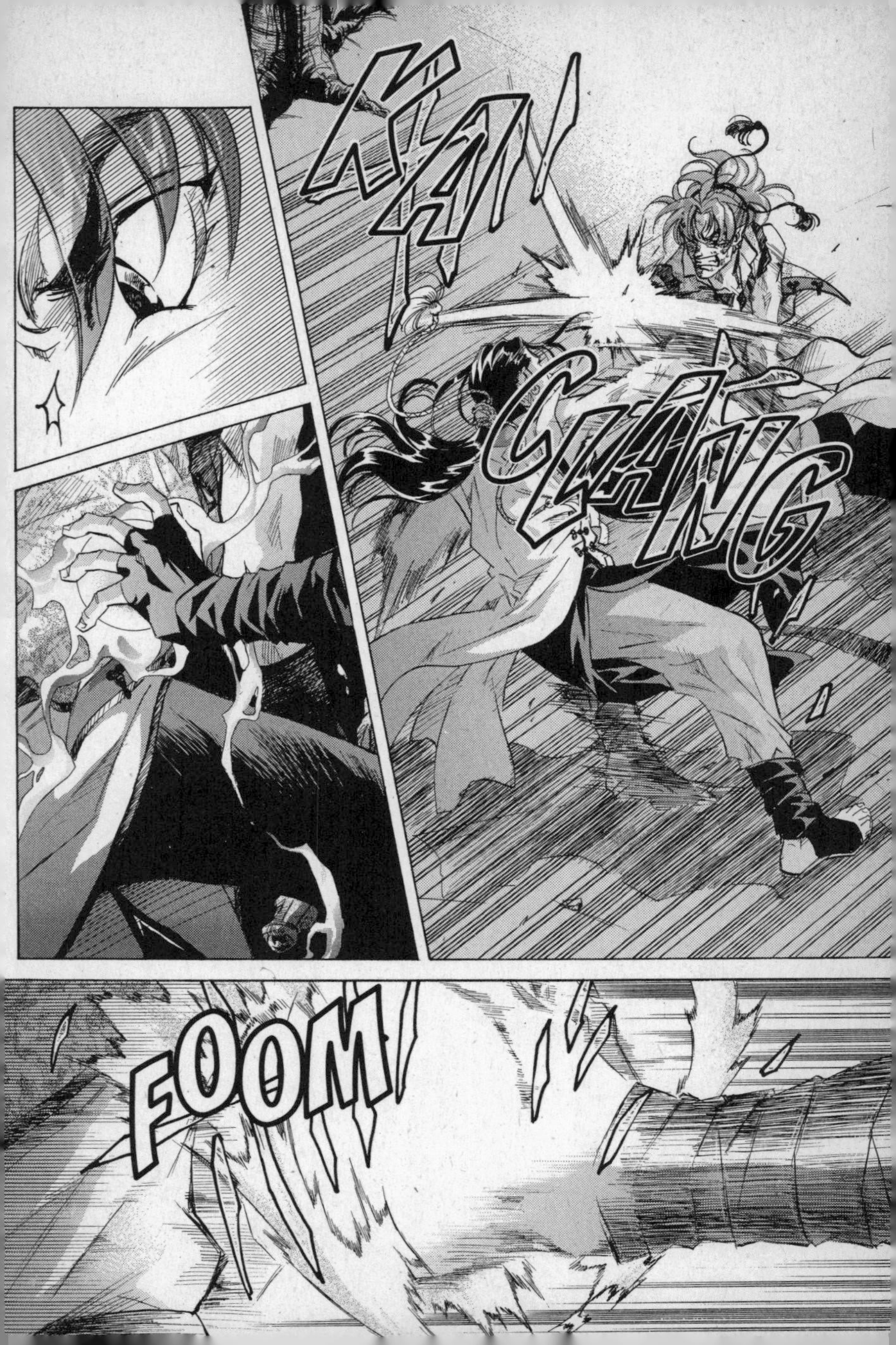
CLANG
FOOM

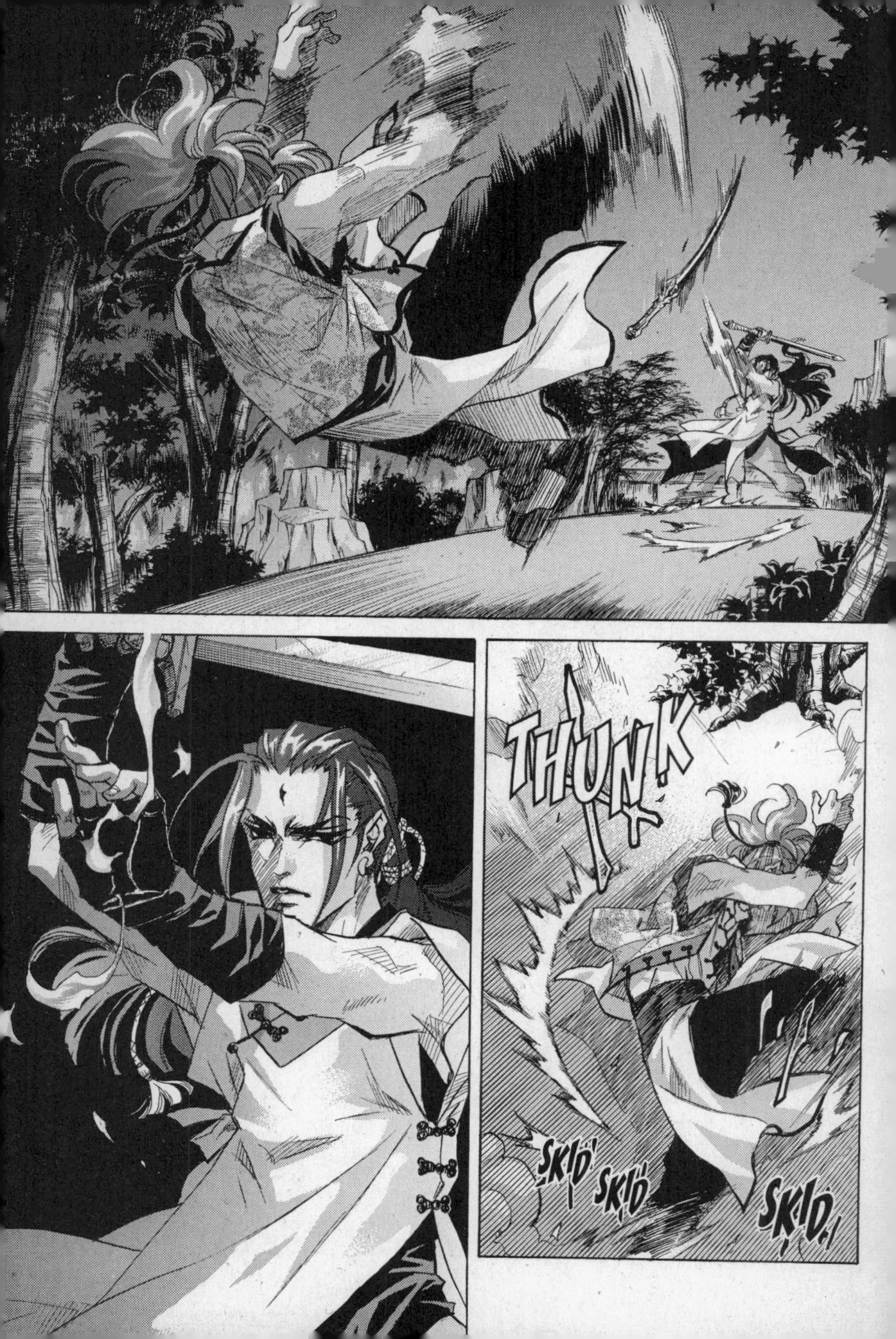
THUNK
SKID
SKID
SKID

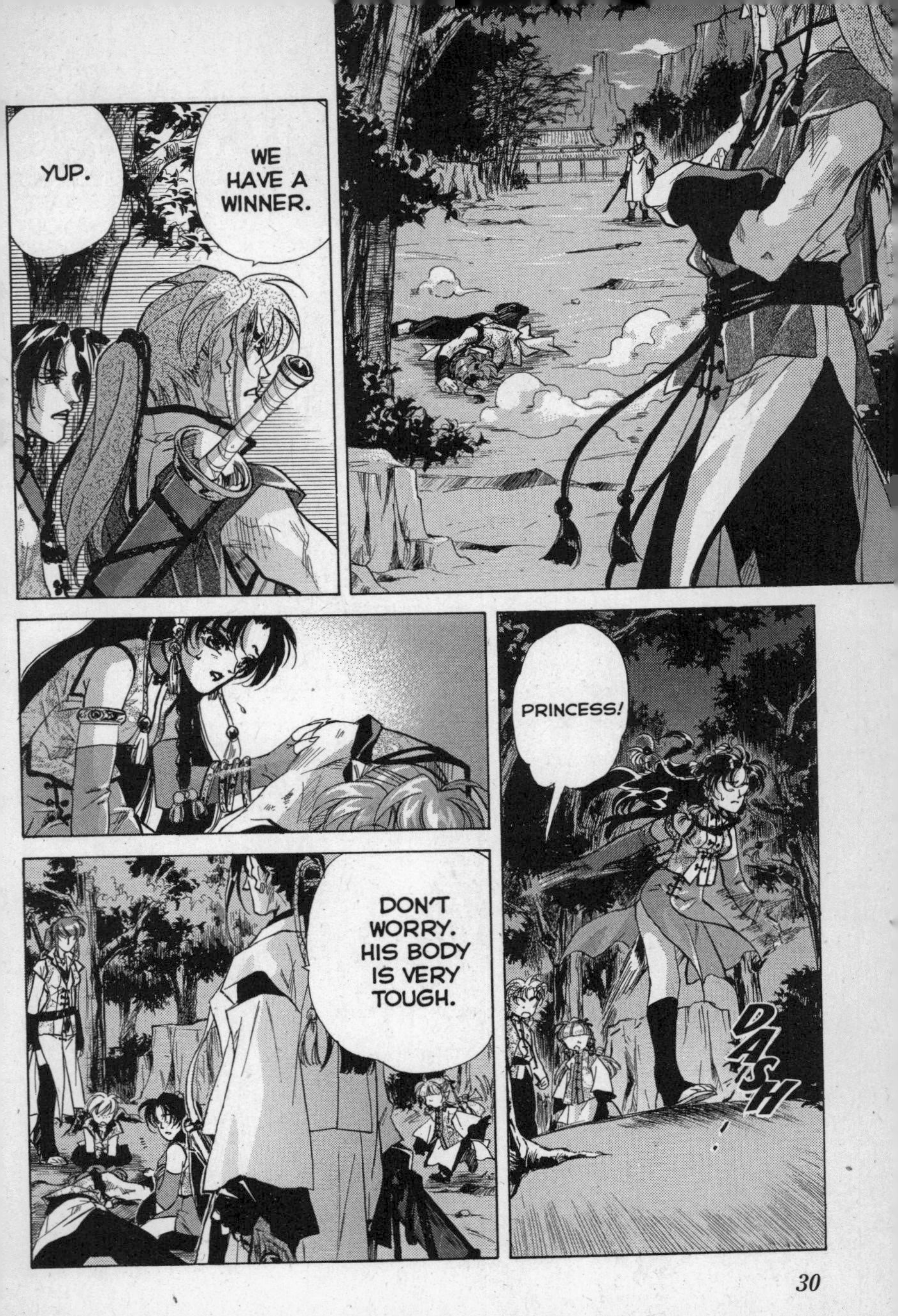
WE HAVE A WINNER.
YUP.
PRINCESS!
DASH
DON'T WORRY. HIS BODY IS VERY TOUGH.

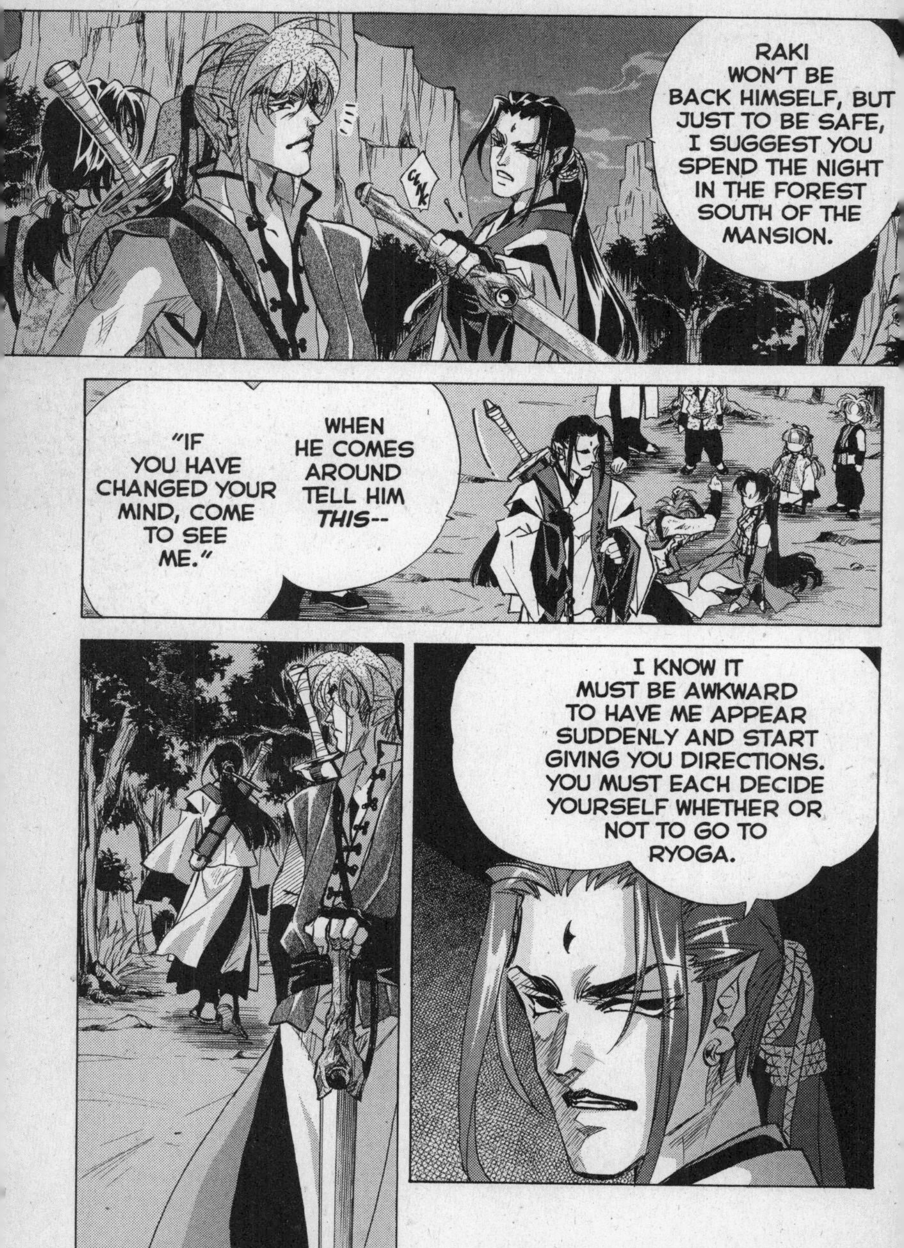
RAKI WON'T BE BACK HIMSELF, BUT JUST TO BE SAFE, I SUGGEST YOU SPEND THE NIGHT IN THE FOREST SOUTH OF THE MANSION.
WHEN HE COMES AROUND TELL HIM *THIS*--
"IF YOU HAVE CHANGED YOUR MIND, COME TO SEE ME."
I KNOW IT MUST BE AWKWARD TO HAVE ME APPEAR SUDDENLY AND START GIVING YOU DIRECTIONS. YOU MUST EACH DECIDE YOURSELF WHETHER OR NOT TO GO TO RYOGA.

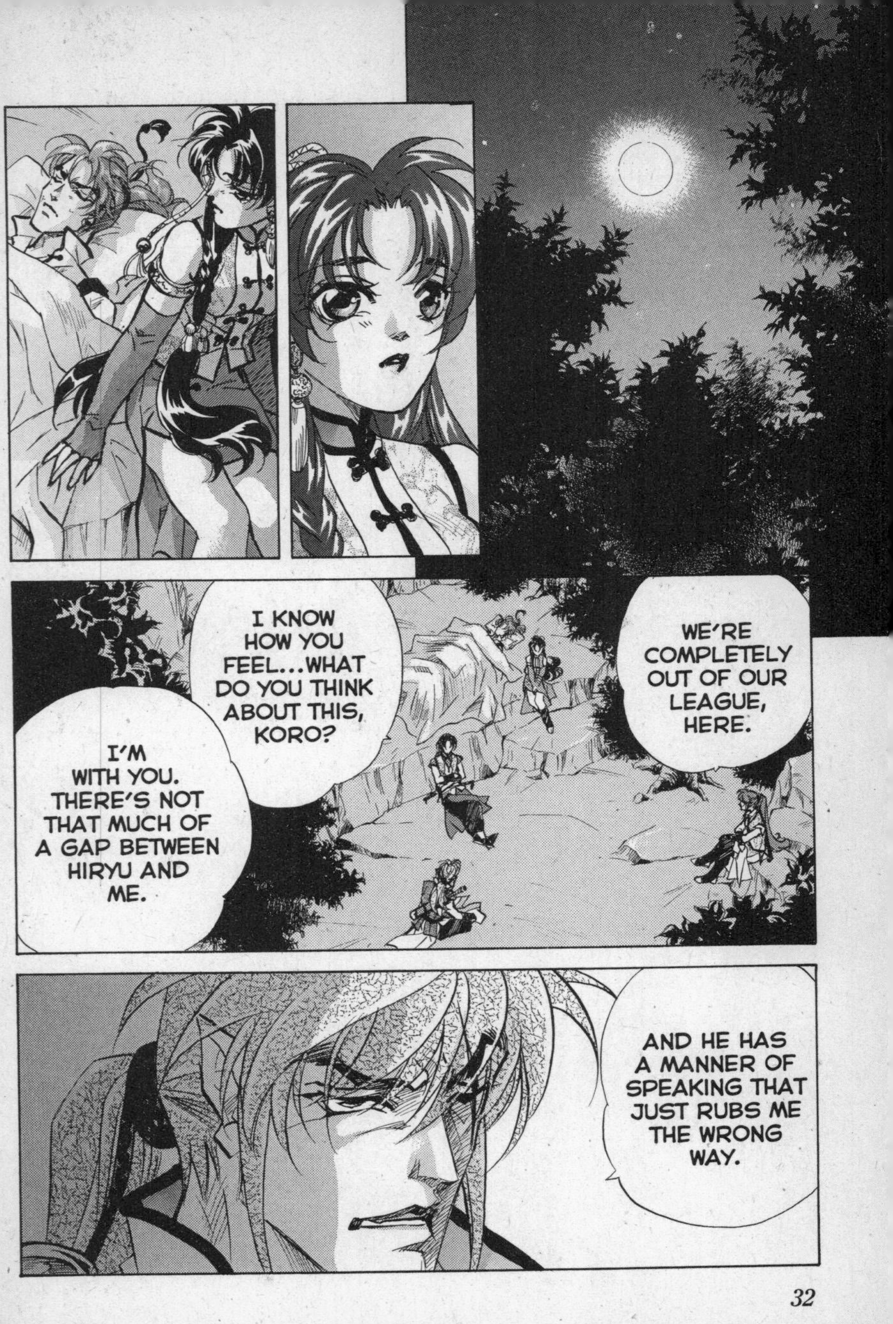
WE'RE COMPLETELY OUT OF OUR LEAGUE, HERE.
I KNOW HOW YOU FEEL...WHAT DO YOU THINK ABOUT THIS, KORO?
I'M WITH YOU. THERE'S NOT THAT MUCH OF A GAP BETWEEN HIRYU AND ME.
AND HE HAS A MANNER OF SPEAKING THAT JUST RUBS ME THE WRONG WAY.

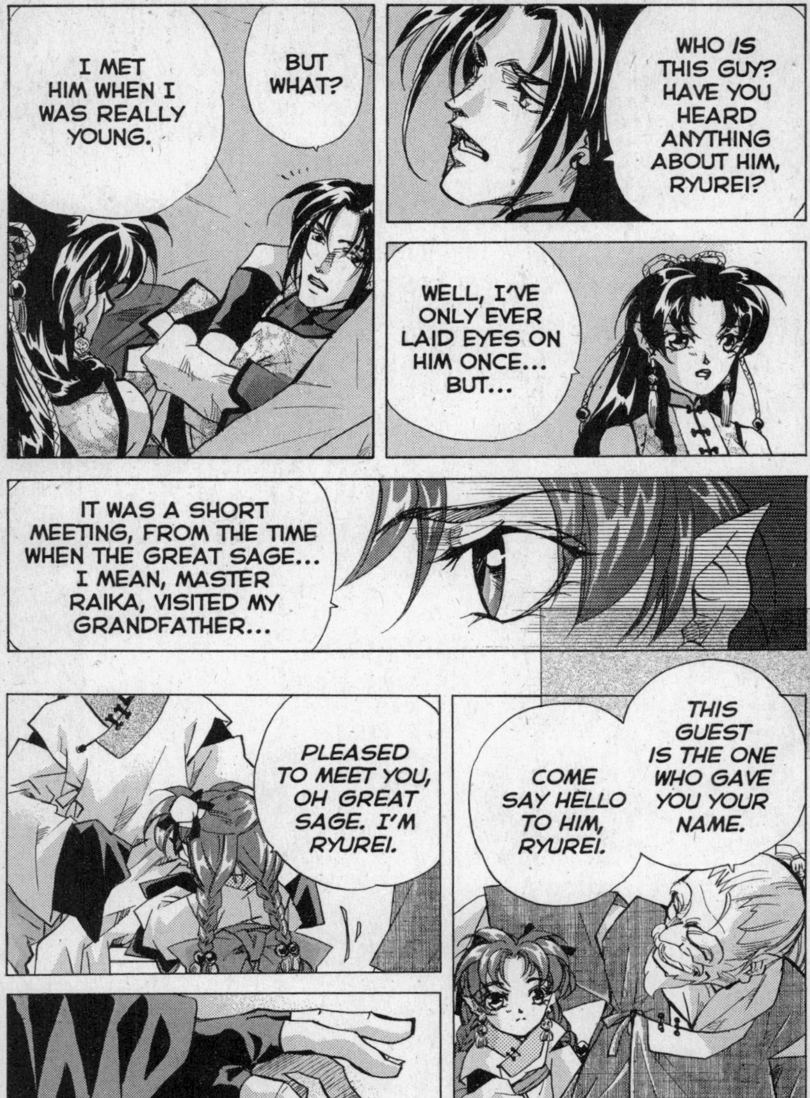
WHO IS THIS GUY? HAVE YOU HEARD ANYTHING ABOUT HIM, RYUREI?
WELL, I'VE ONLY EVER LAID EYES ON HIM ONCE... BUT...
BUT WHAT?
I MET HIM WHEN I WAS REALLY YOUNG.
IT WAS A SHORT MEETING, FROM THE TIME WHEN THE GREAT SAGE... I MEAN, MASTER RAIKA, VISITED MY GRANDFATHER...
THIS GUEST IS THE ONE WHO GAVE YOU YOUR NAME.
COME SAY HELLO TO HIM, RYUREI.
PLEASED TO MEET YOU, OH GREAT SAGE. I'M RYUREI.

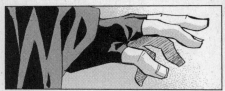

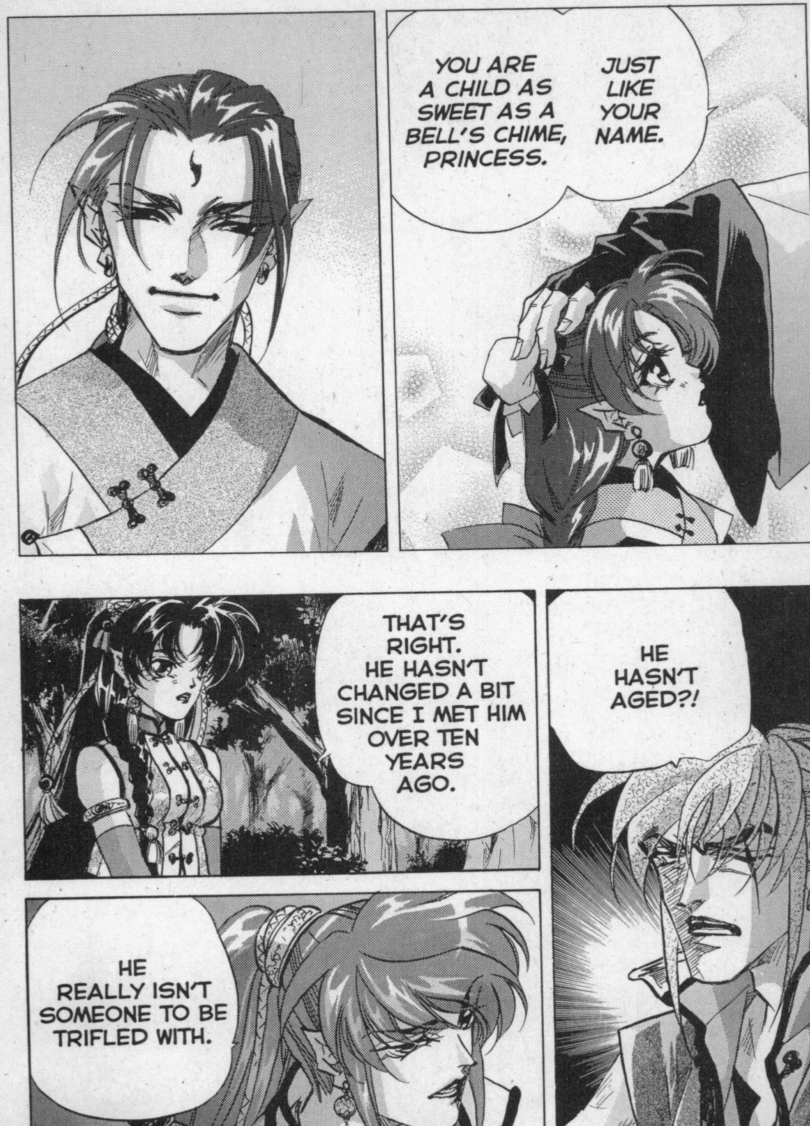
YOU ARE A CHILD AS SWEET AS A BELL'S CHIME, PRINCESS.
JUST LIKE YOUR NAME.
HE HASN'T AGED?!
THAT'S RIGHT. HE HASN'T CHANGED A BIT SINCE I MET HIM OVER TEN YEARS AGO.
HE REALLY ISN'T SOMEONE TO BE TRIFLED WITH.

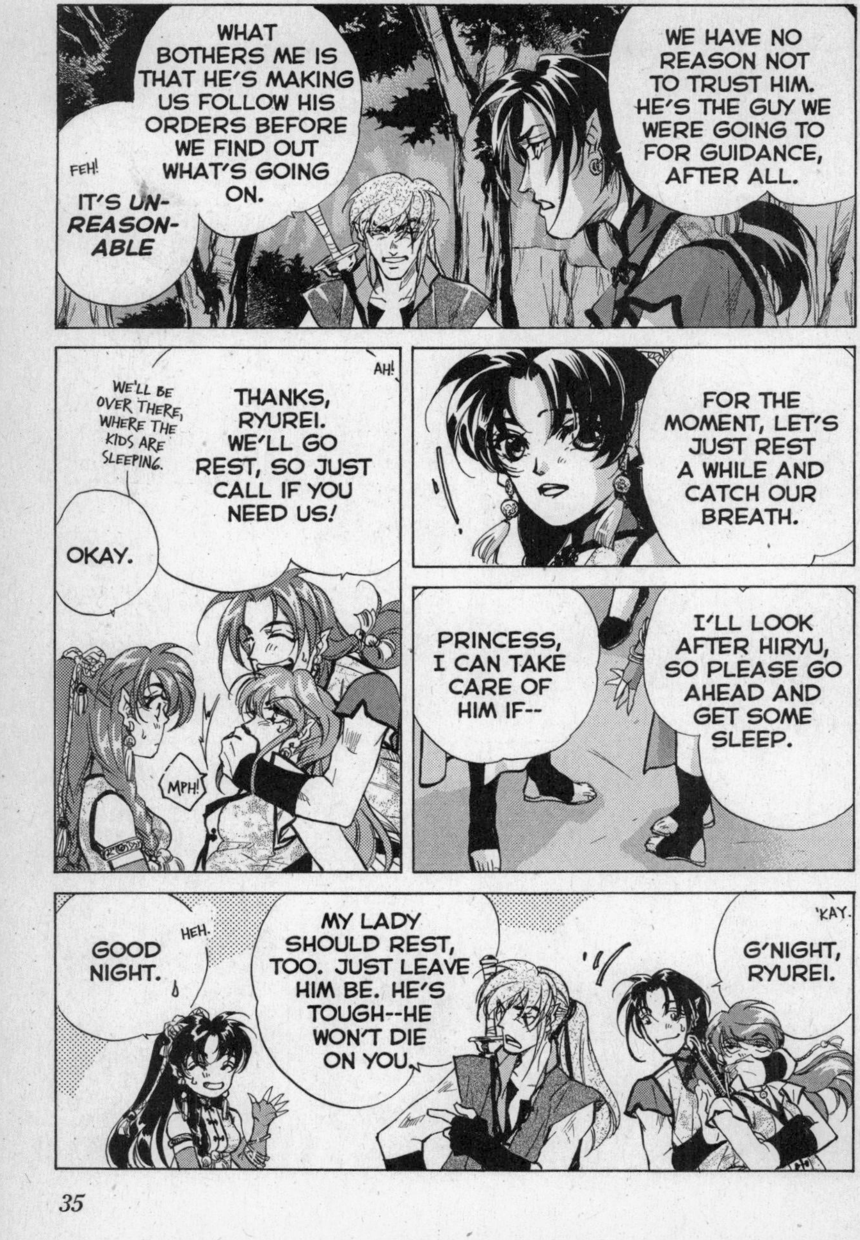
WE HAVE NO REASON NOT TO TRUST HIM. HE'S THE GUY WE WERE GOING TO FOR GUIDANCE, AFTER ALL.
WHAT BOTHERS ME IS THAT HE'S MAKING US FOLLOW HIS ORDERS BEFORE WE FIND OUT WHAT'S GOING ON.
FEH!
IT'S *UN*-*REASON*-*ABLE*
FOR THE MOMENT, LET'S JUST REST A WHILE AND CATCH OUR BREATH.
I'LL LOOK AFTER HIRYU, SO PLEASE GO AHEAD AND GET SOME SLEEP.
PRINCESS, I CAN TAKE CARE OF HIM IF--
AH!
THANKS, RYUREI. WE'LL GO REST, SO JUST CALL IF YOU NEED US!
WE'LL BE OVER THERE, WHERE THE KIDS ARE SLEEPING.
OKAY.
MPH!
'KAY.
G'NIGHT, RYUREI.
MY LADY SHOULD REST, TOO. JUST LEAVE HIM BE. HE'S TOUGH--HE WON'T DIE ON YOU.
HEH.
GOOD NIGHT.

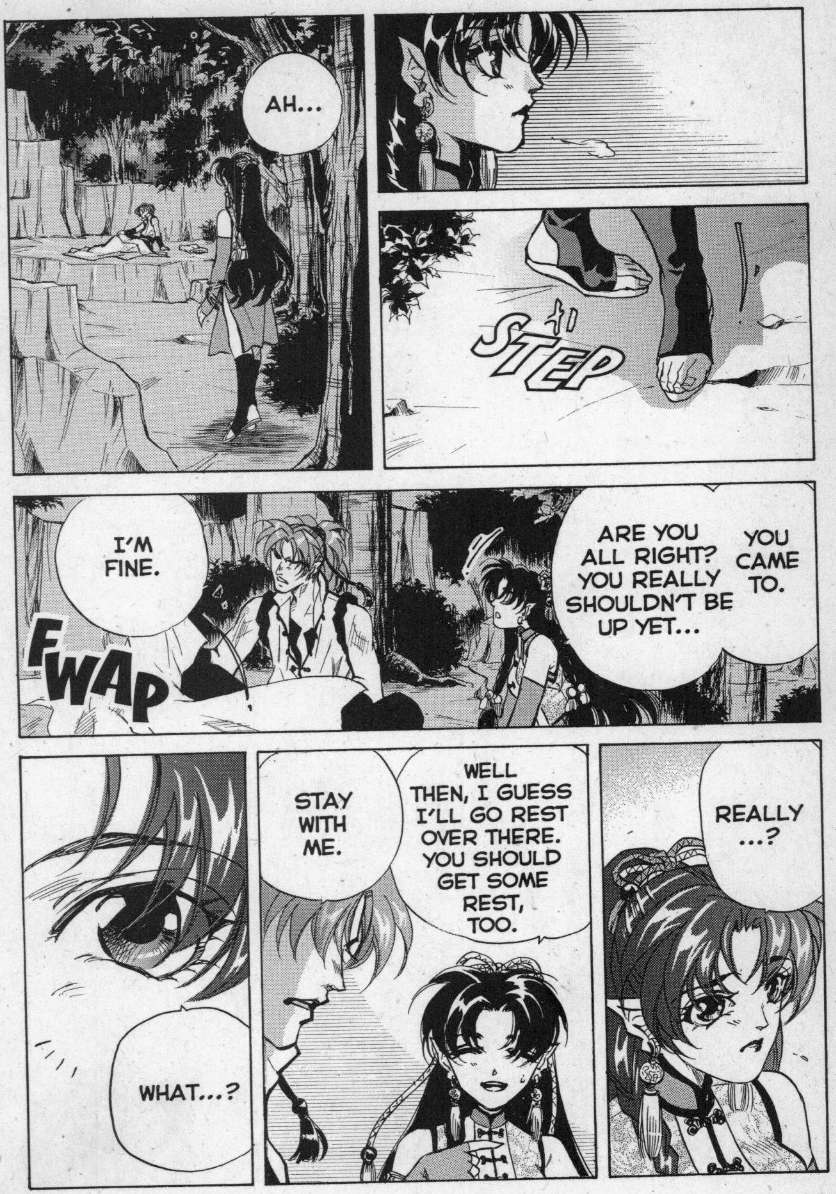
STEP
AH...
YOU CAME TO.
ARE YOU ALL RIGHT? YOU REALLY SHOULDN'T BE UP YET...
I'M FINE.
FWAP
REALLY ...?
WELL THEN, I GUESS I'LL GO REST OVER THERE. YOU SHOULD GET SOME REST, TOO.
STAY WITH ME.
WHAT...?

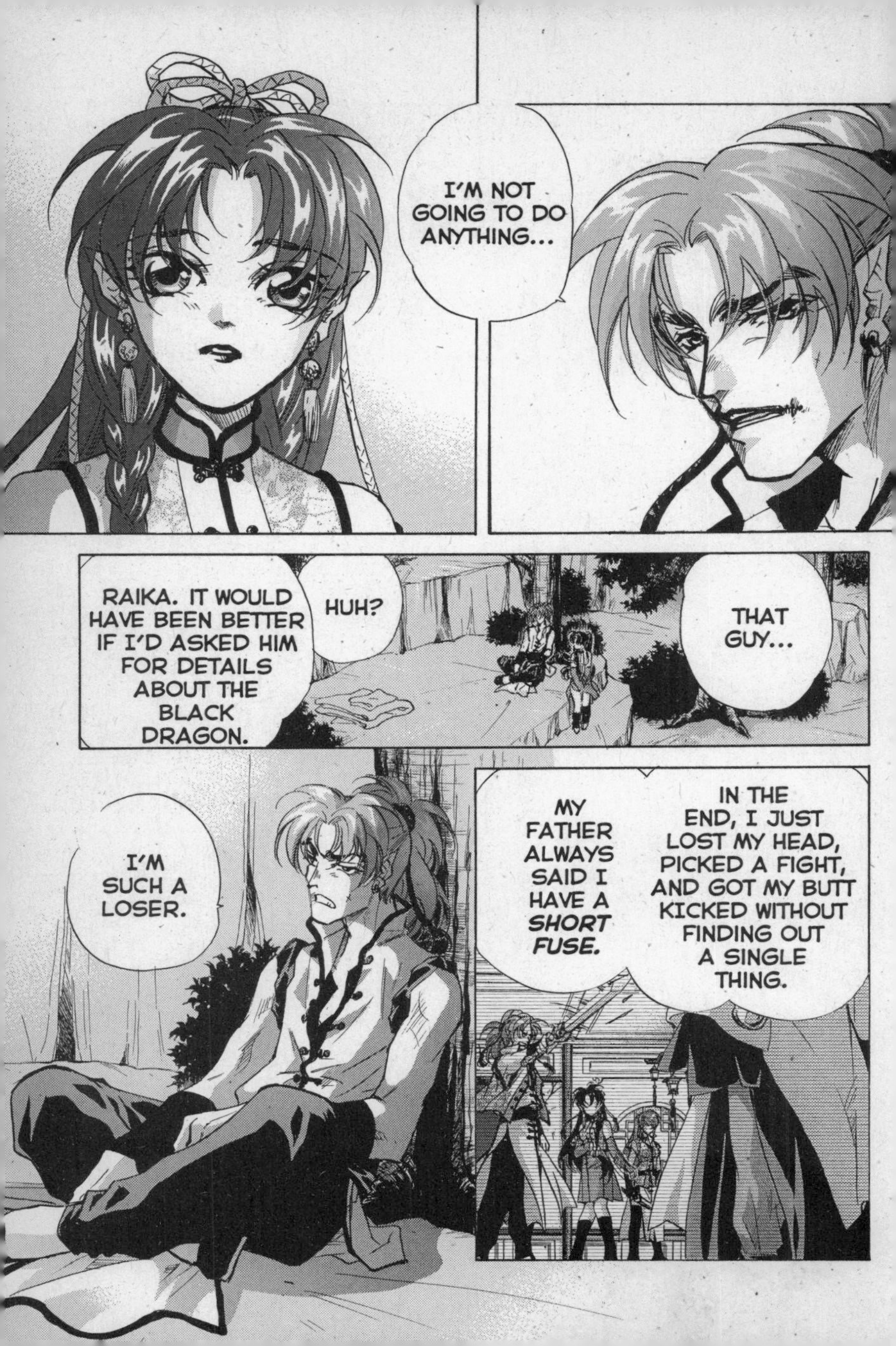
I'M NOT GOING TO DO ANYTHING...
THAT GUY...
HUH?
RAIKA. IT WOULD HAVE BEEN BETTER IF I'D ASKED HIM FOR DETAILS ABOUT THE BLACK DRAGON.
IN THE END, I JUST LOST MY HEAD, PICKED A FIGHT, AND GOT MY BUTT KICKED WITHOUT FINDING OUT A SINGLE THING.
MY FATHER ALWAYS SAID I HAVE A *SHORT FUSE.*
I'M SUCH A LOSER.

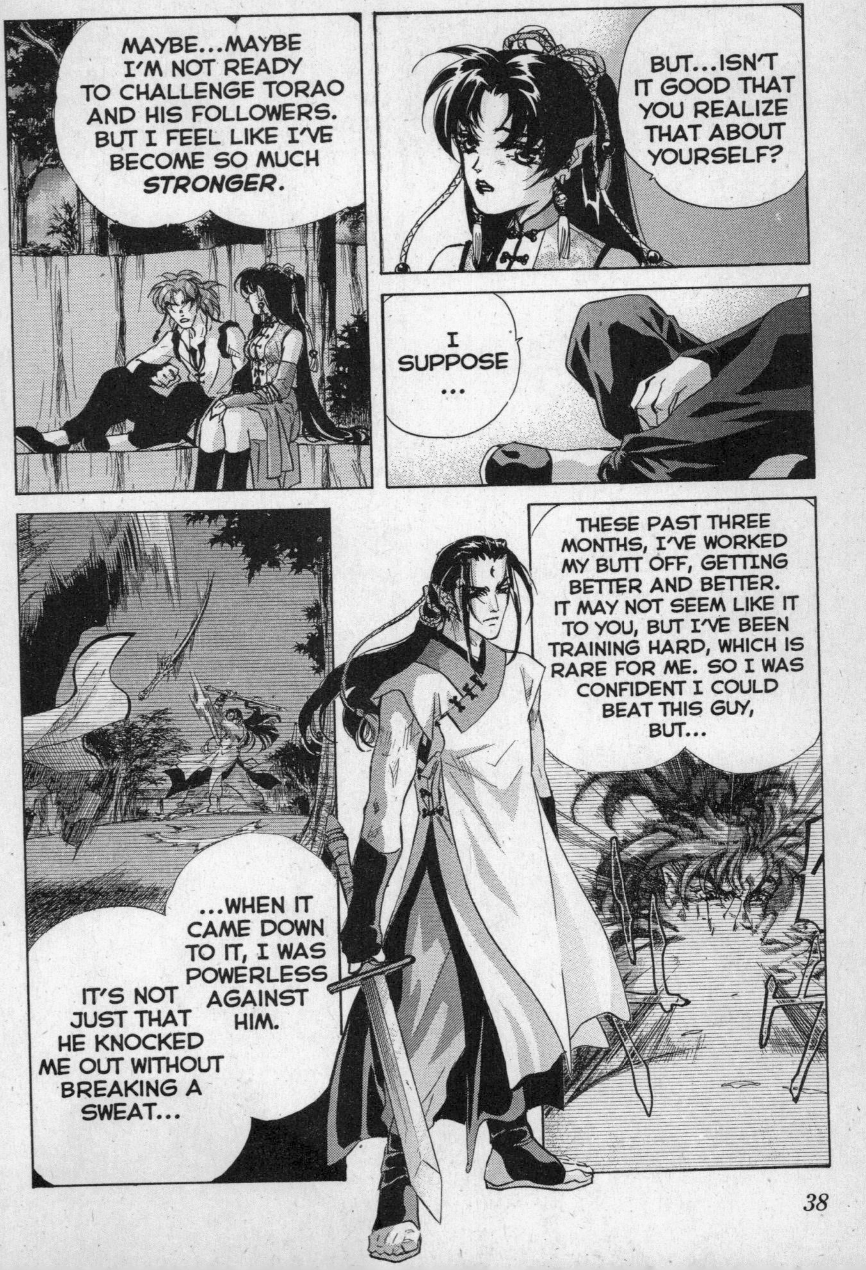
MAYBE...MAYBE I'M NOT READY TO CHALLENGE TORAO AND HIS FOLLOWERS. BUT I FEEL LIKE I'VE BECOME SO MUCH STRONGER.
BUT...ISN'T IT GOOD THAT YOU REALIZE THAT ABOUT YOURSELF?
I SUPPOSE ...
THESE PAST THREE MONTHS, I'VE WORKED MY BUTT OFF, GETTING BETTER AND BETTER. IT MAY NOT SEEM LIKE IT TO YOU, BUT I'VE BEEN TRAINING HARD, WHICH IS RARE FOR ME. SO I WAS CONFIDENT I COULD BEAT THIS GUY, BUT...
...WHEN IT CAME DOWN TO IT, I WAS POWERLESS AGAINST HIM.
IT'S NOT JUST THAT HE KNOCKED ME OUT WITHOUT BREAKING A SWEAT...

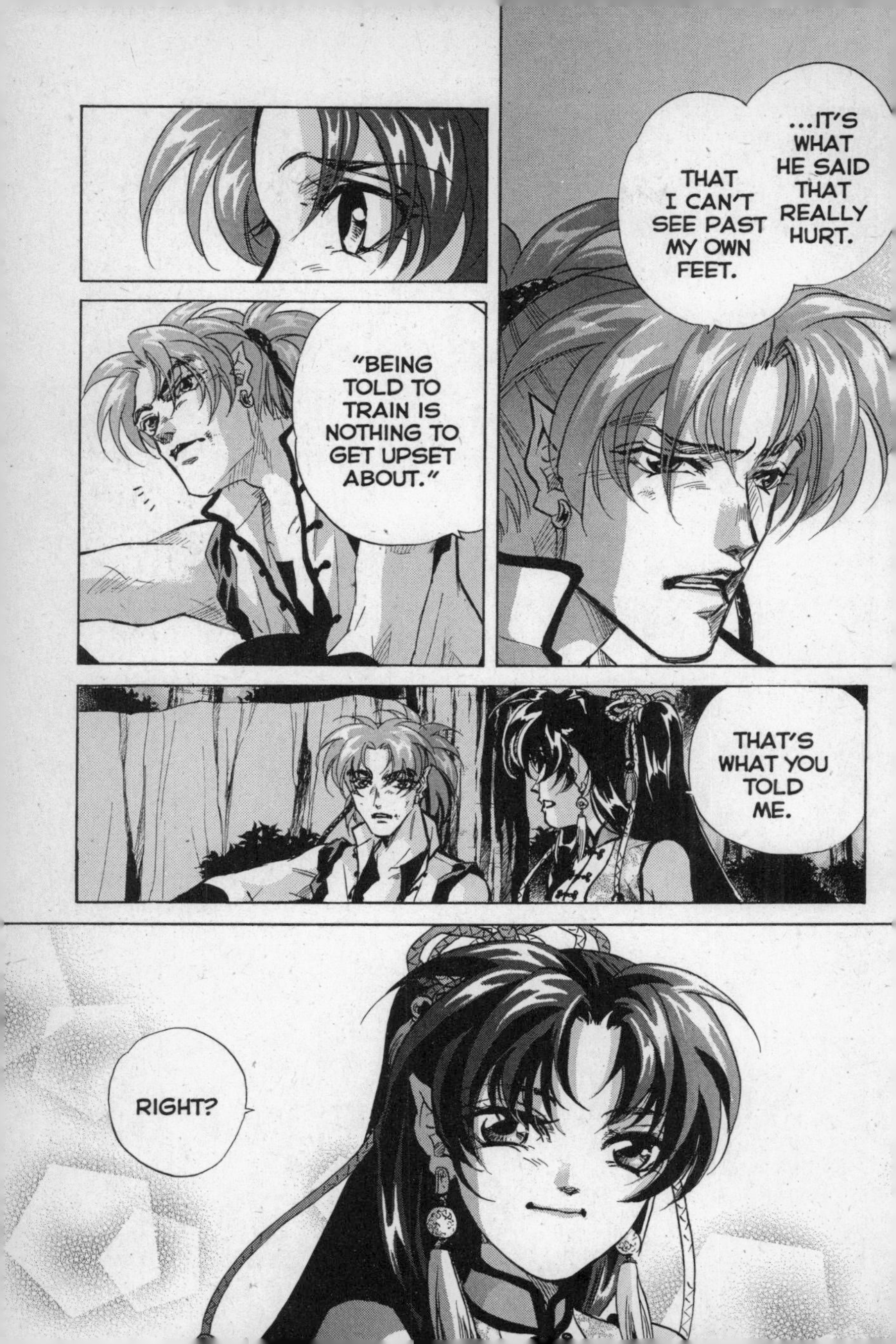
...IT'S WHAT HE SAID THAT REALLY HURT.
THAT I CAN'T SEE PAST MY OWN FEET.
"BEING TOLD TO TRAIN IS NOTHING TO GET UPSET ABOUT."
THAT'S WHAT YOU TOLD ME.
RIGHT?

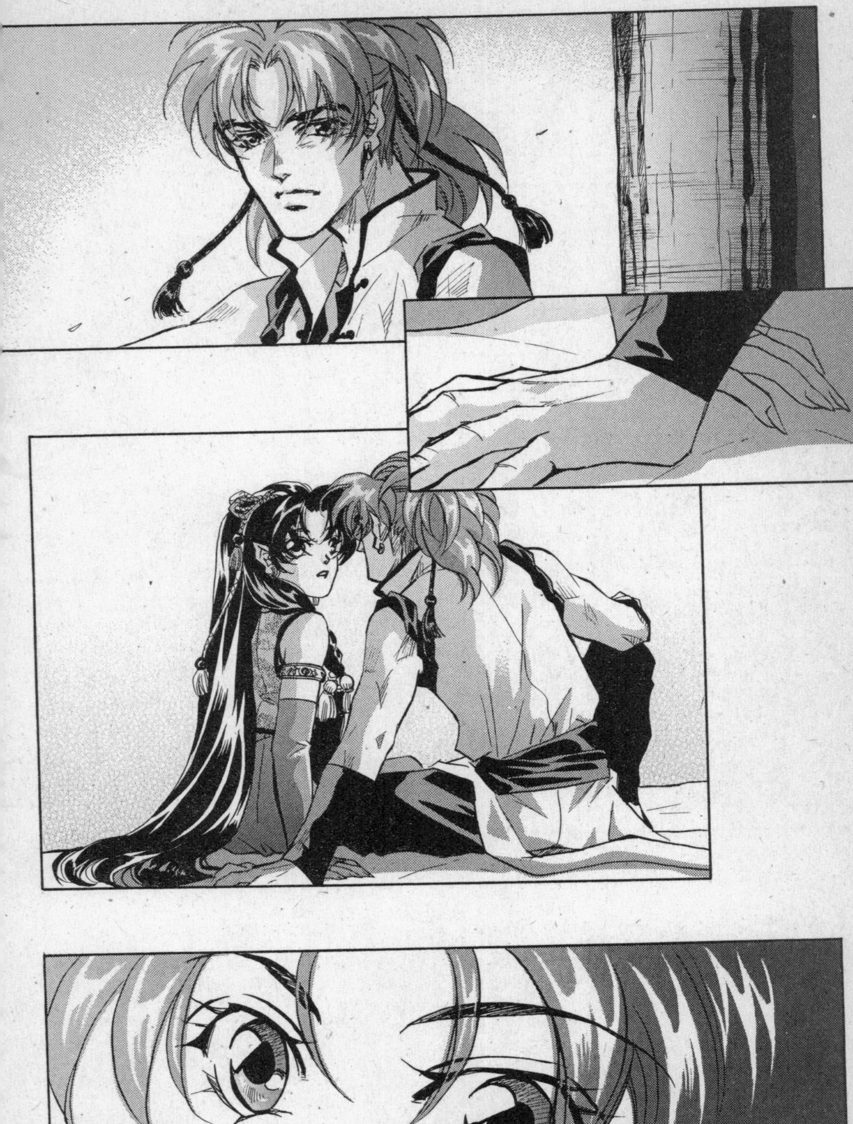

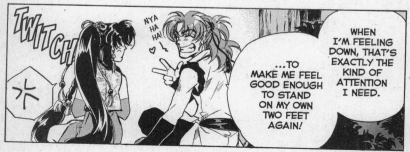

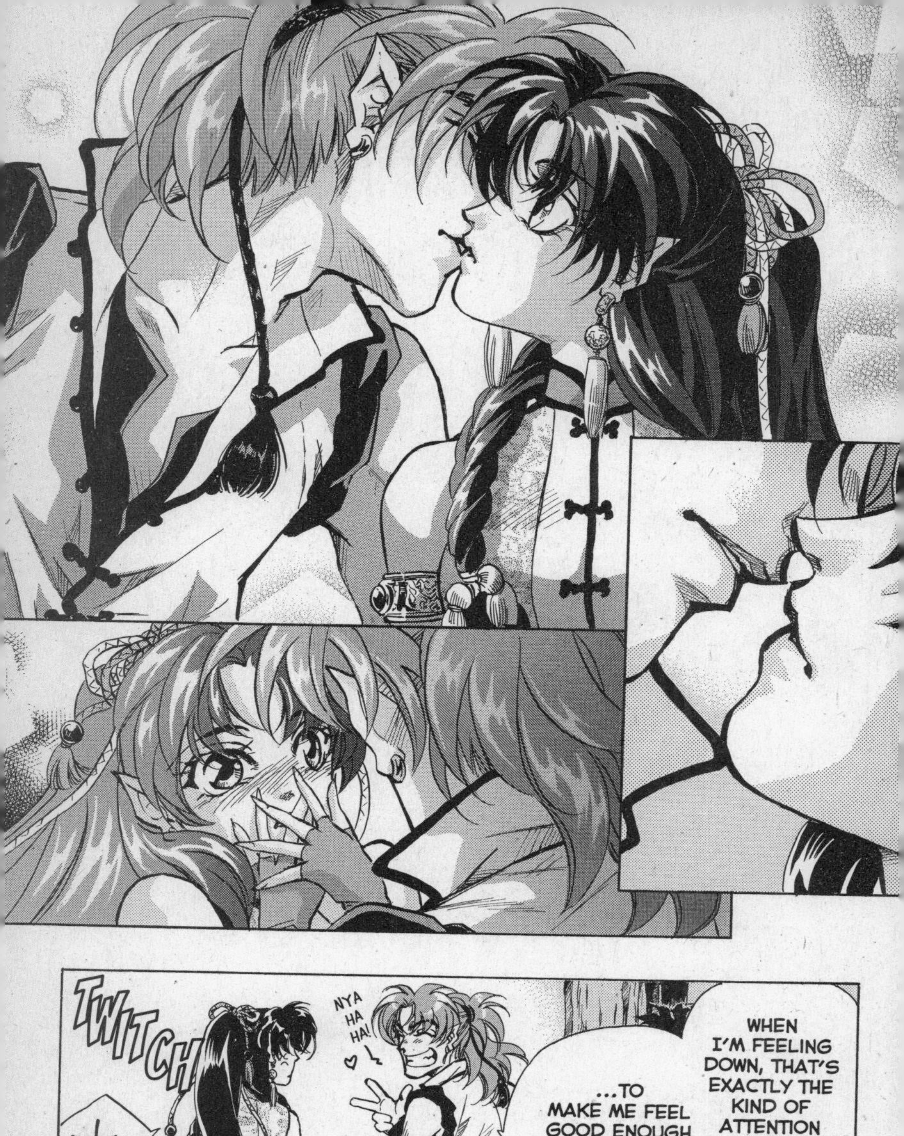
WHEN I'M FEELING DOWN, THAT'S EXACTLY THE KIND OF ATTENTION I NEED.
...TO MAKE ME FEEL GOOD ENOUGH TO STAND ON MY OWN TWO FEET AGAIN!
NYA HA HA!
TWITCH

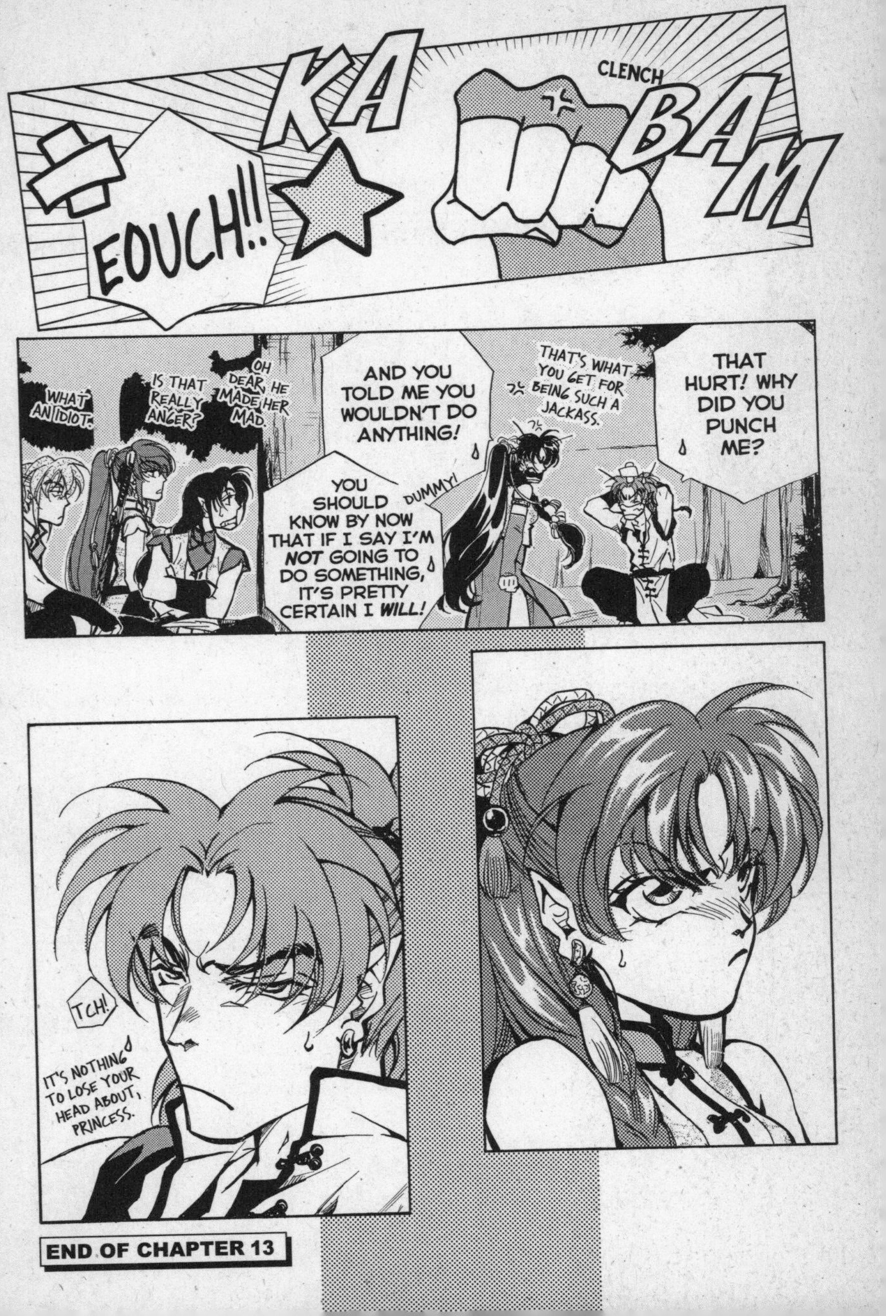
CLENCH
BAM
KA
EOUCH!!
THAT HURT! WHY DID YOU PUNCH ME?
THAT'S WHAT YOU GET FOR BEING SUCH A JACKASS.
AND YOU TOLD ME YOU WOULDN'T DO ANYTHING!
DUMMY!
YOU SHOULD KNOW BY NOW THAT IF I SAY I'M *NOT* GOING TO DO SOMETHING, IT'S PRETTY CERTAIN I *WILL*!
OH DEAR, HE MADE HER MAD.
IS THAT REALLY ANGER?
WHAT AN IDIOT.
TCH!
IT'S NOTHING TO LOSE YOUR HEAD ABOUT, PRINCESS.

END OF CHAPTER 13

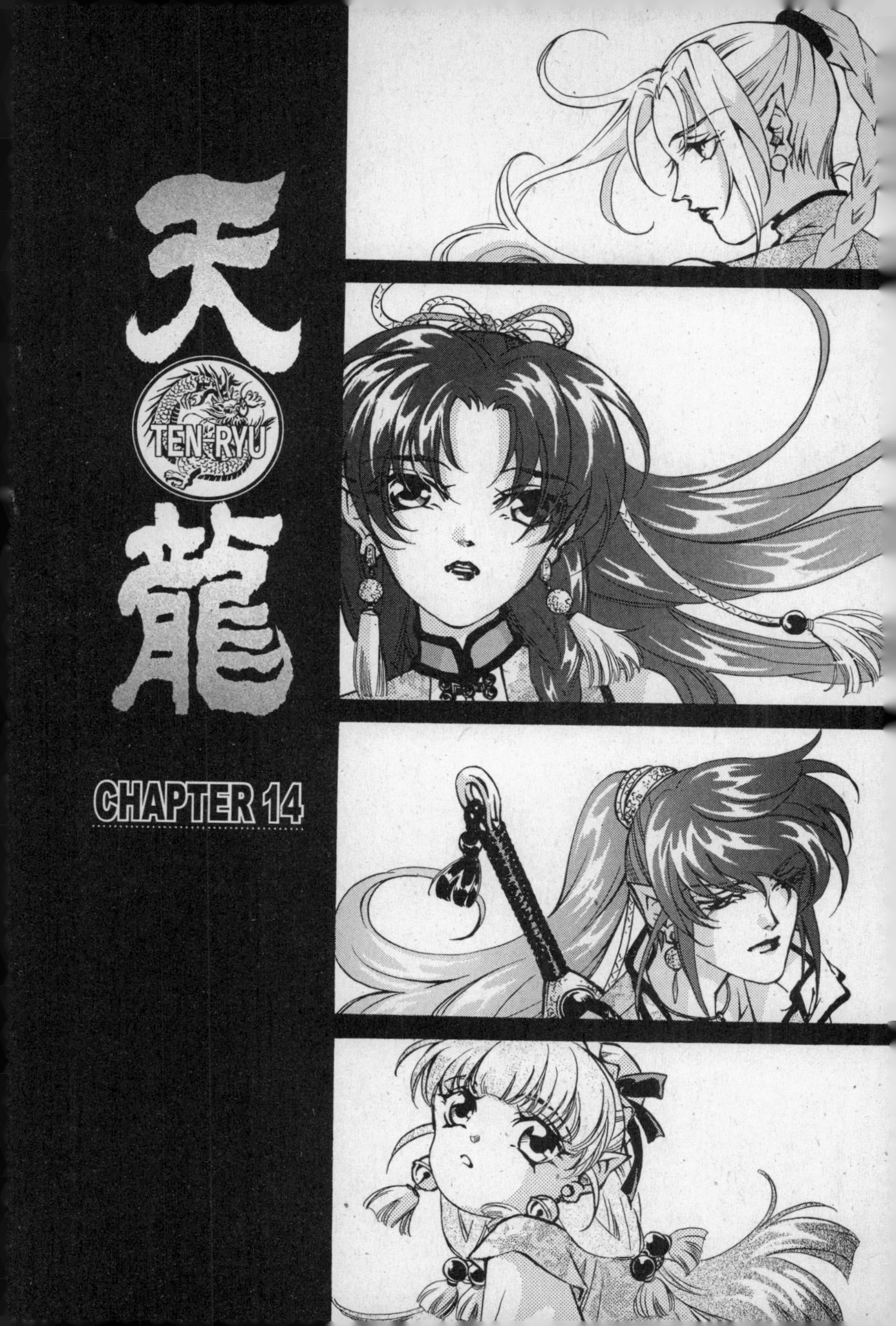
天龍
TEN RYU
CHAPTER 14

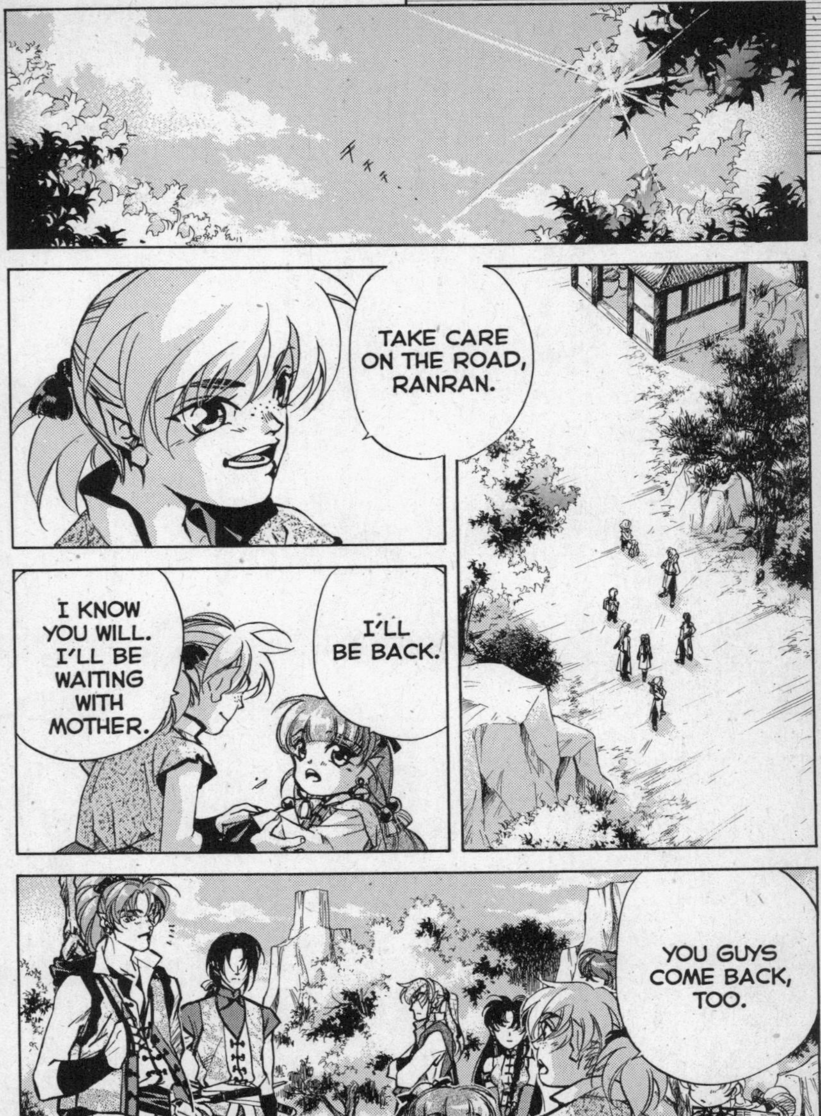
TAKE CARE ON THE ROAD, RANRAN.
I'LL BE BACK.
I KNOW YOU WILL. I'LL BE WAITING WITH MOTHER.
YOU GUYS COME BACK, TOO.

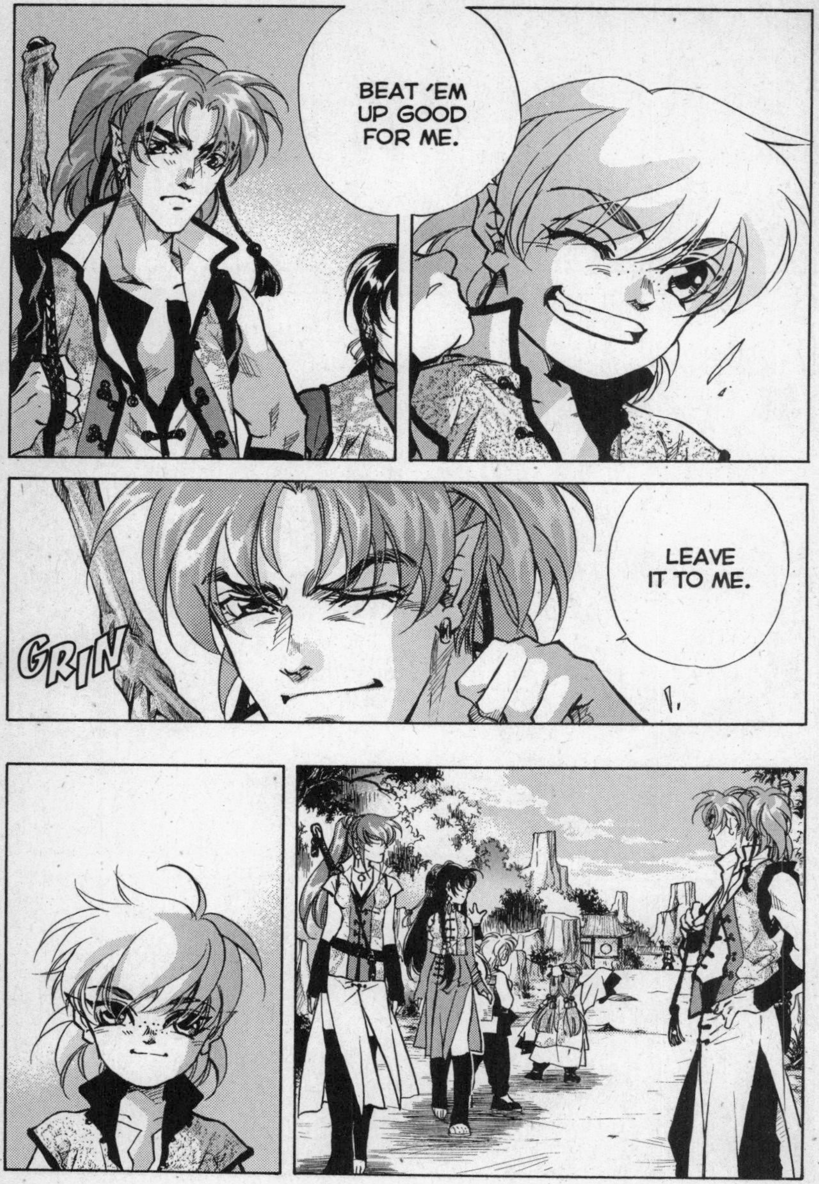
BEAT 'EM UP GOOD FOR ME.
LEAVE IT TO ME.
GRIN

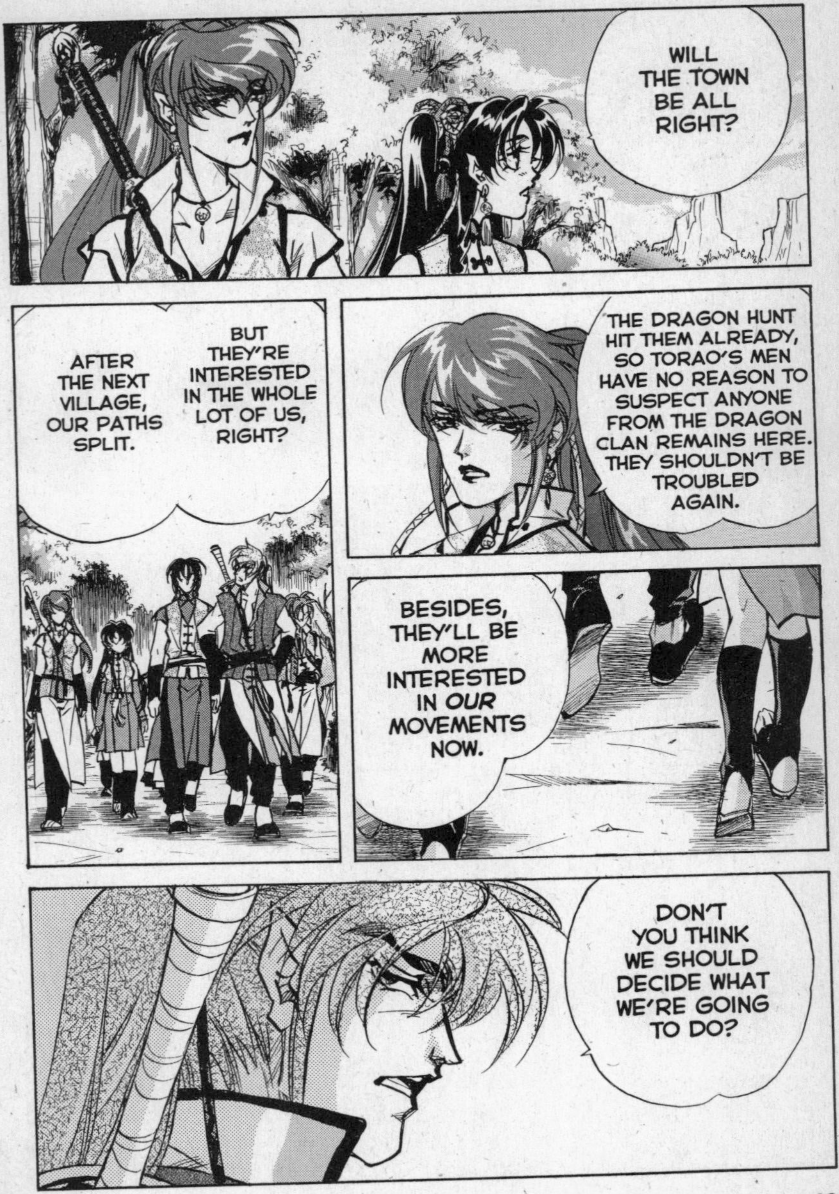
WILL THE TOWN BE ALL RIGHT?
THE DRAGON HUNT HIT THEM ALREADY, SO TORAO'S MEN HAVE NO REASON TO SUSPECT ANYONE FROM THE DRAGON CLAN REMAINS HERE. THEY SHOULDN'T BE TROUBLED AGAIN.
BESIDES, THEY'LL BE MORE INTERESTED IN *OUR* MOVEMENTS NOW.
BUT THEY'RE INTERESTED IN THE WHOLE LOT OF US, RIGHT?
AFTER THE NEXT VILLAGE, OUR PATHS SPLIT.
DON'T YOU THINK WE SHOULD DECIDE WHAT WE'RE GOING TO DO?

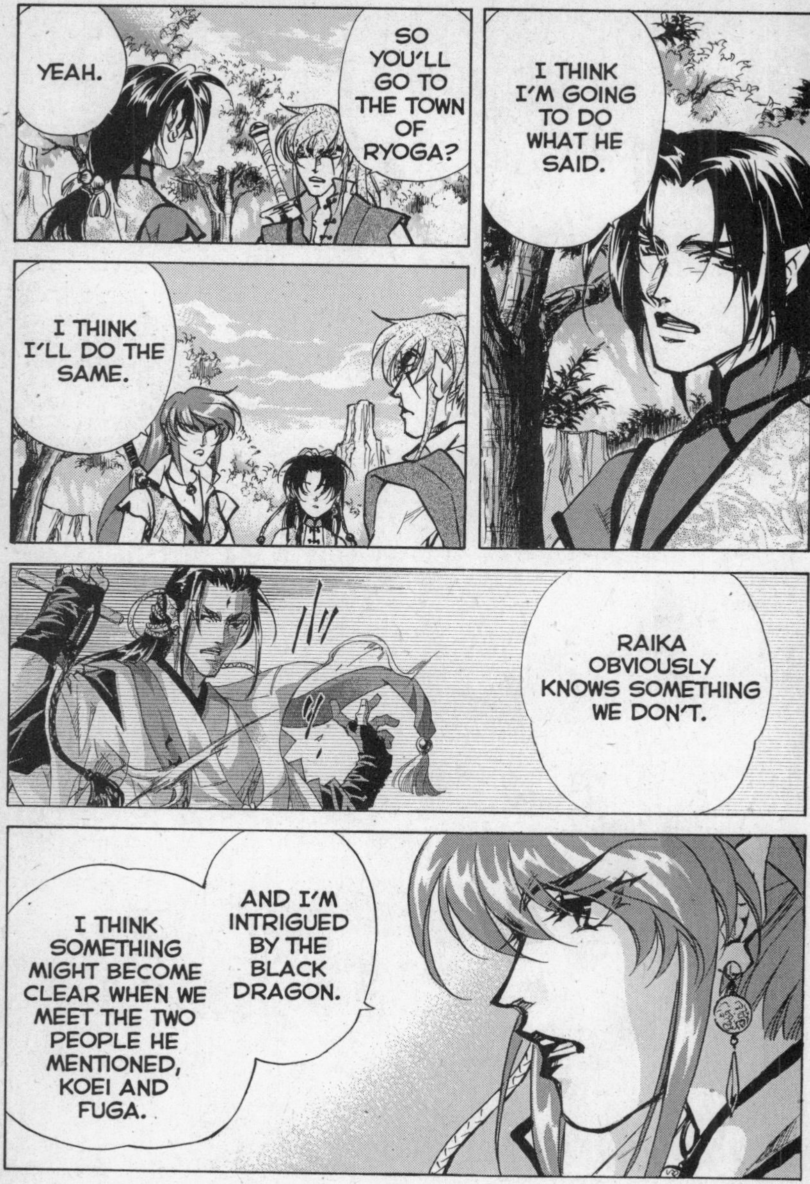
I THINK I'M GOING TO DO WHAT HE SAID.
SO YOU'LL GO TO THE TOWN OF RYOGA?
YEAH.
I THINK I'LL DO THE SAME.
RAIKA OBVIOUSLY KNOWS SOMETHING WE DON'T.
AND I'M INTRIGUED BY THE BLACK DRAGON.
I THINK SOMETHING MIGHT BECOME CLEAR WHEN WE MEET THE TWO PEOPLE HE MENTIONED, KOEI AND FUGA.

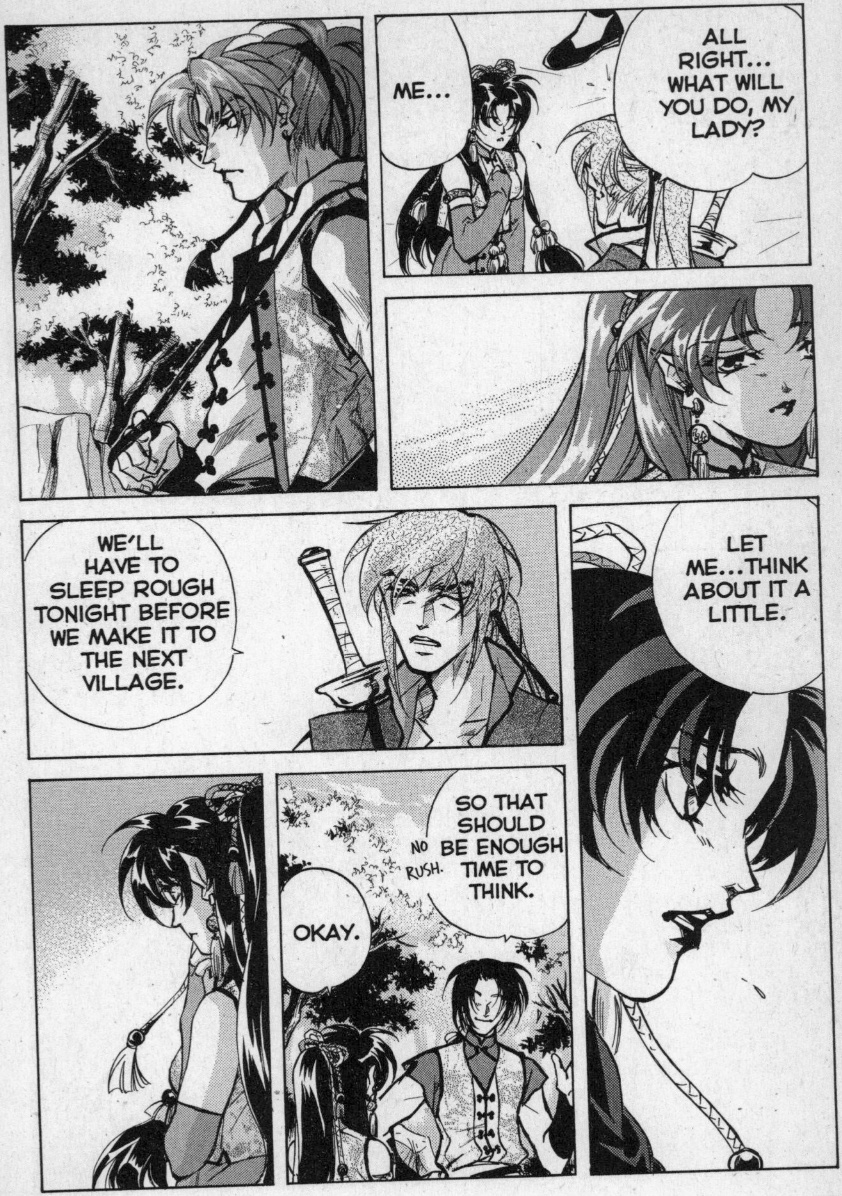
ALL RIGHT... WHAT WILL YOU DO, MY LADY?
ME...
LET ME...THINK ABOUT IT A LITTLE.
WE'LL HAVE TO SLEEP ROUGH TONIGHT BEFORE WE MAKE IT TO THE NEXT VILLAGE.
SO THAT SHOULD BE ENOUGH TIME TO THINK.
NO RUSH.
OKAY.

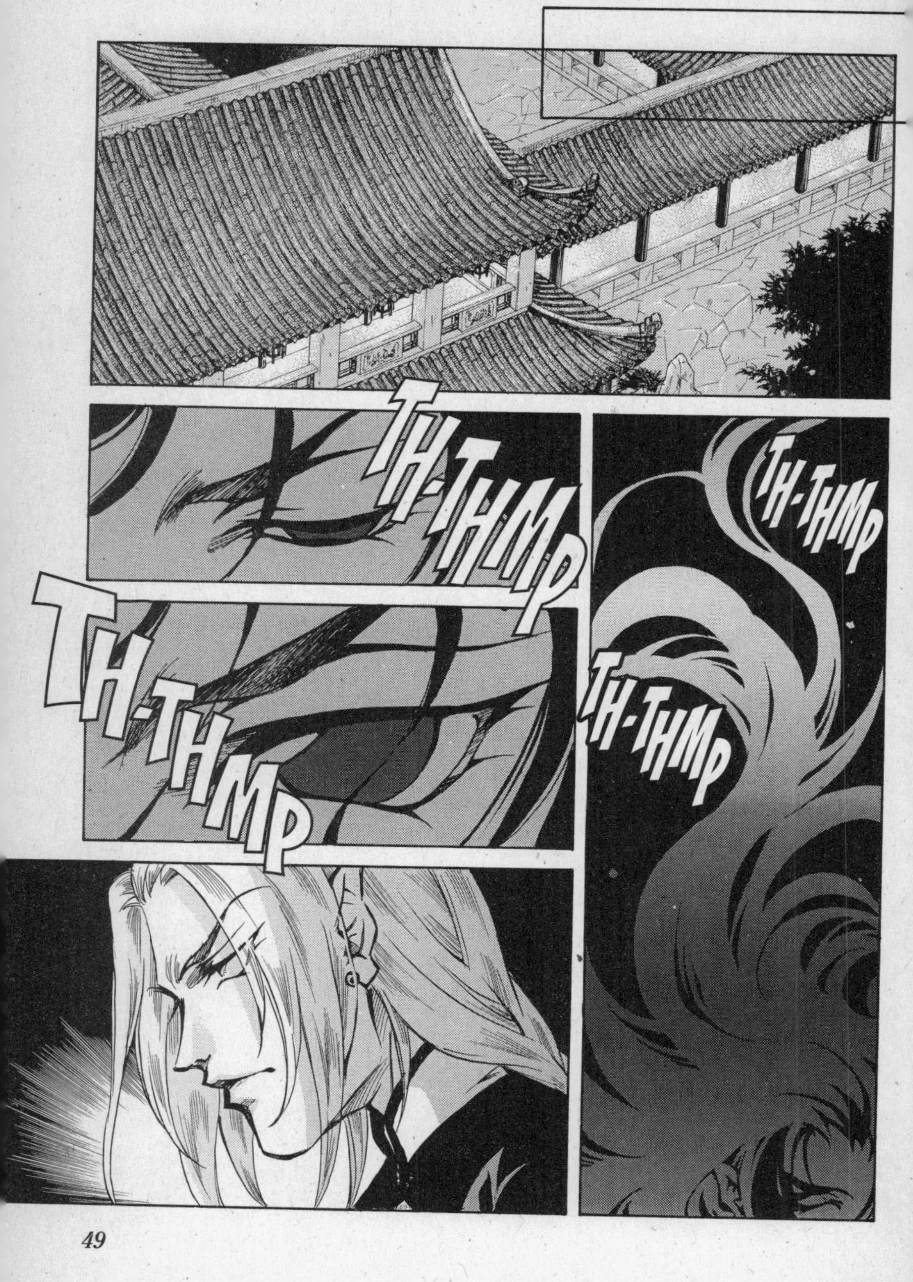
TH-THMP
TH-THMP
TH-THMP
TH-THMP

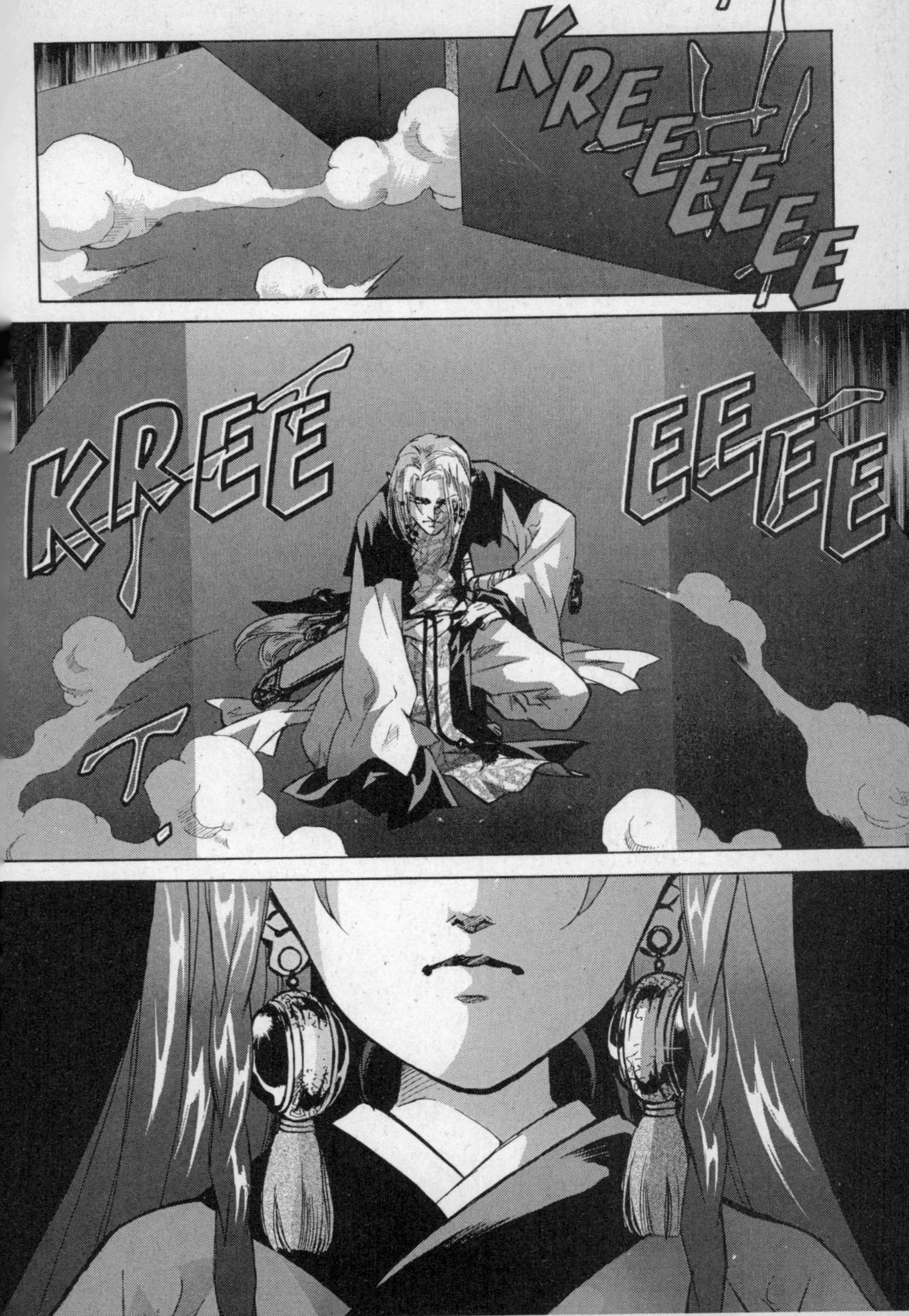
KREEEEEEE
KREEEEEEE

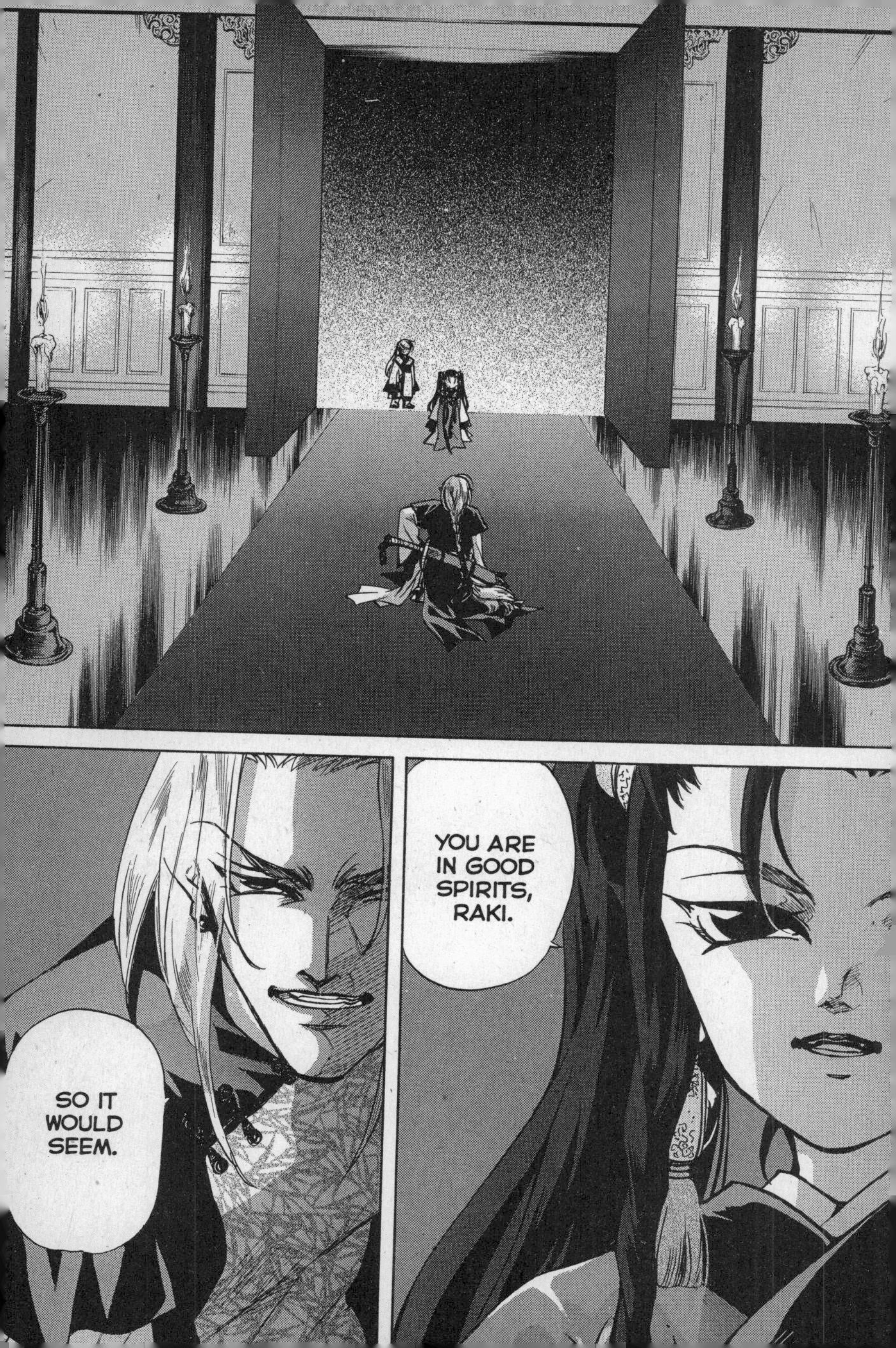
YOU ARE IN GOOD SPIRITS, RAKI.
SO IT WOULD SEEM.

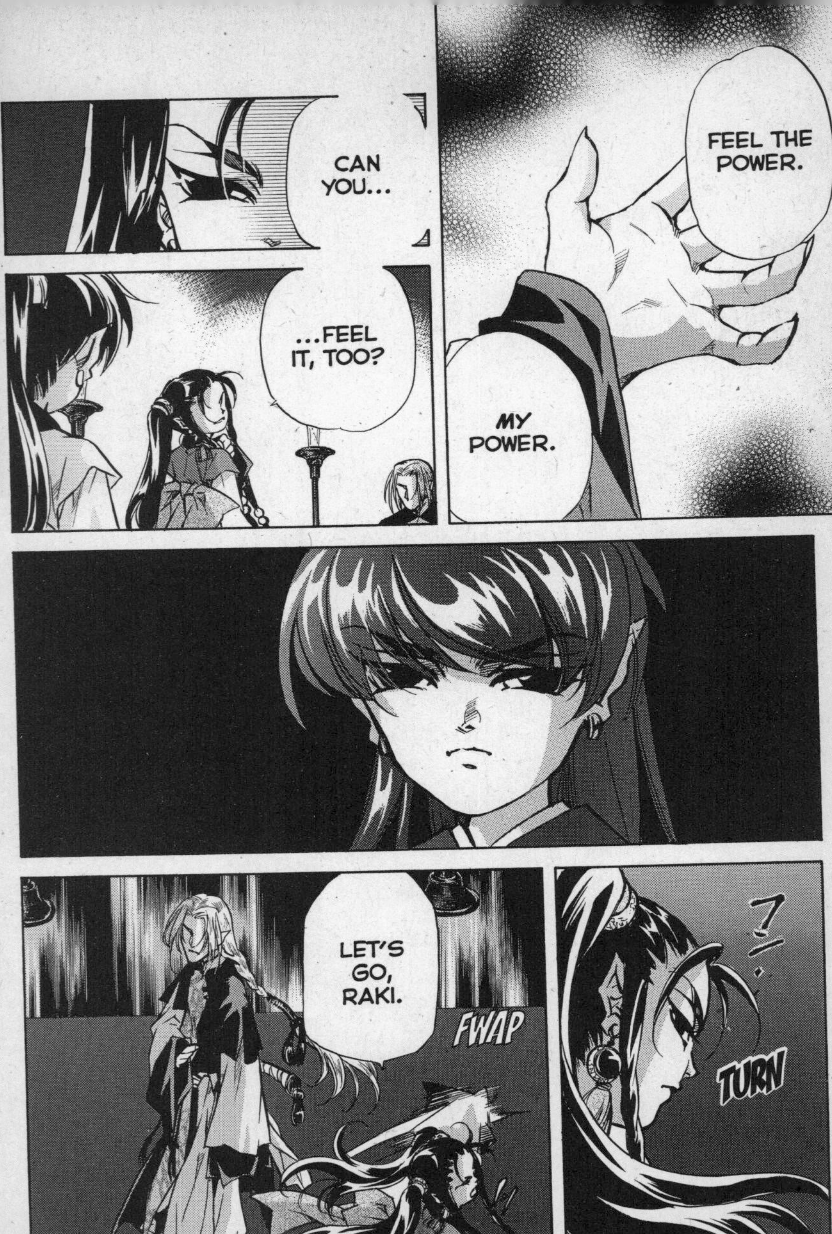
FEEL THE POWER.
MY POWER.
CAN YOU...
...FEEL IT, TOO?
TURN
LET'S GO, RAKI.
FWAP

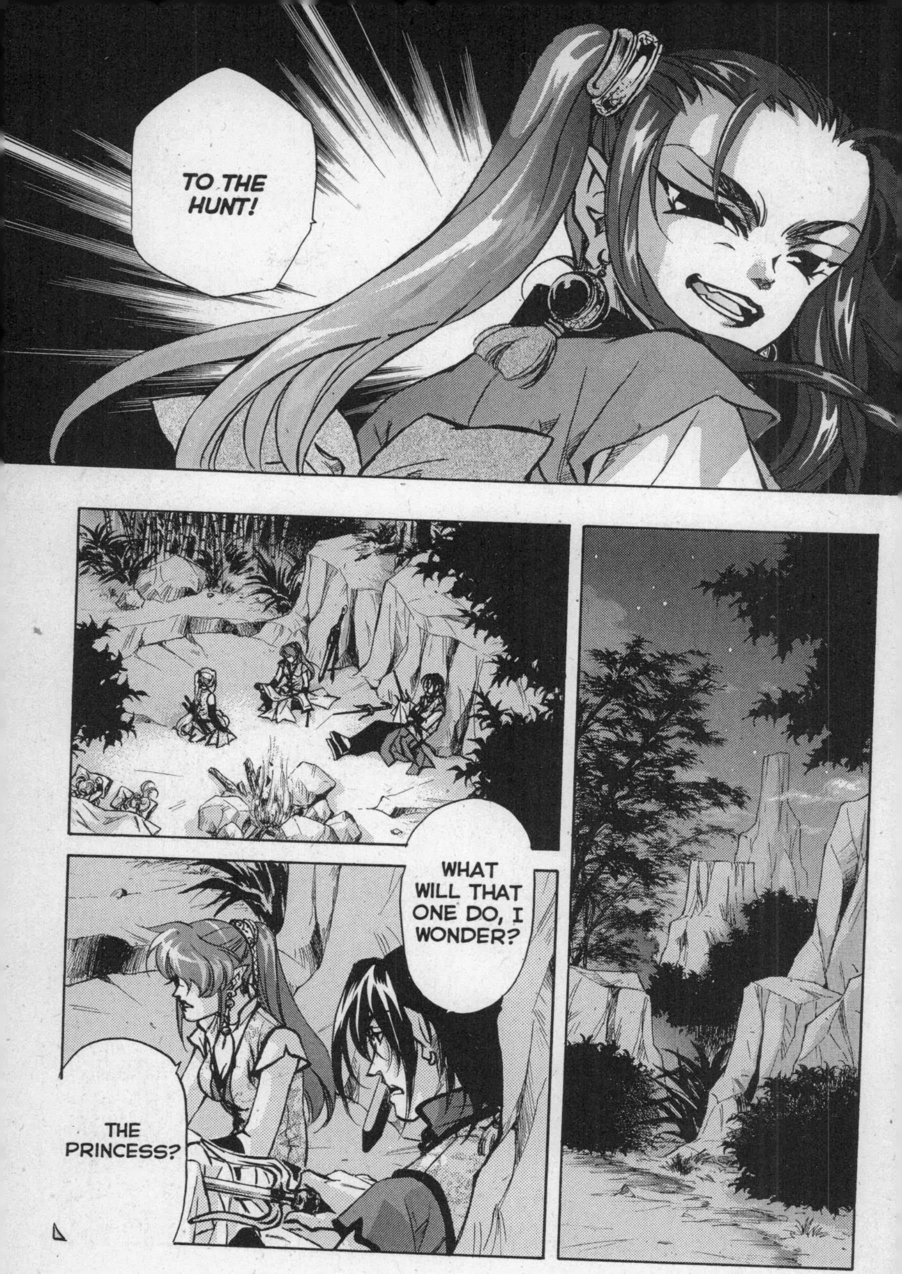
TO THE HUNT!
WHAT WILL THAT ONE DO, I WONDER?
THE PRINCESS?

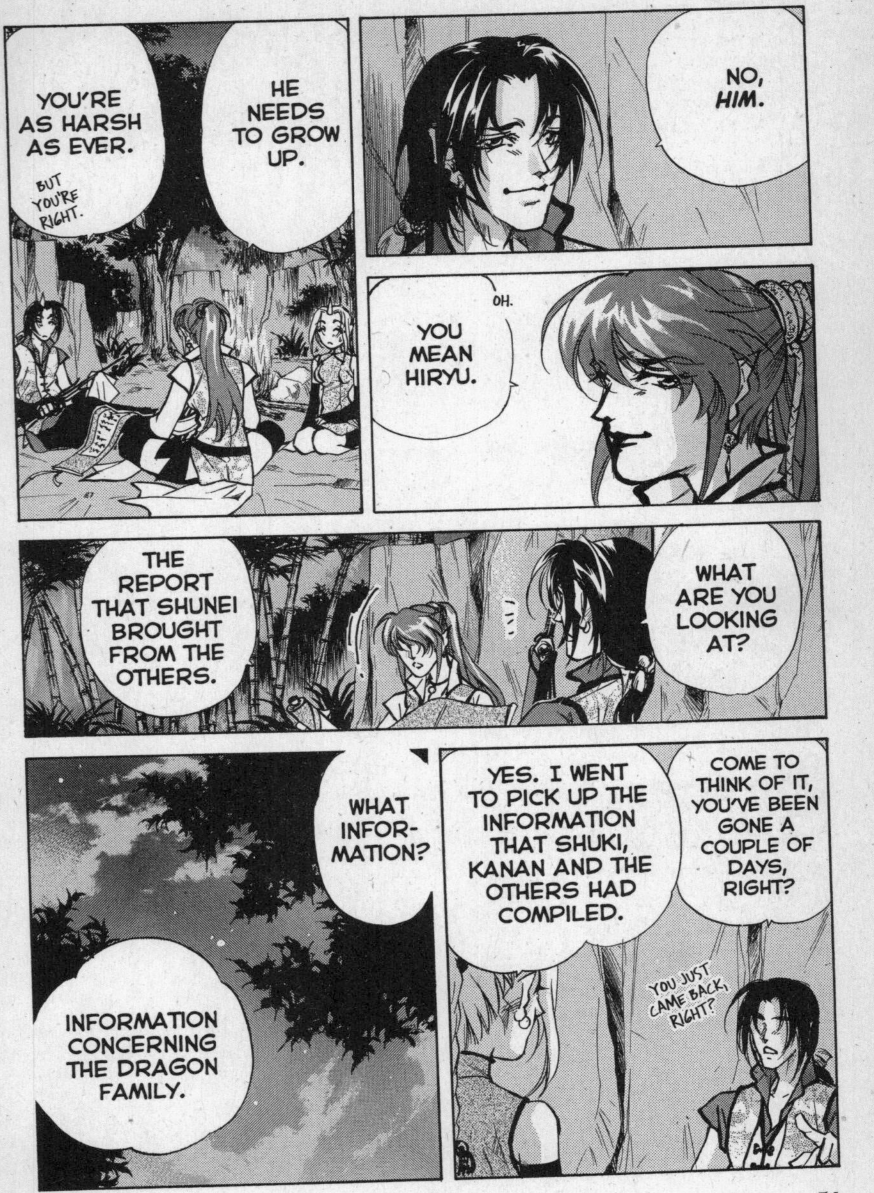
NO, HIM.
OH.
YOU MEAN HIRYU.
HE NEEDS TO GROW UP.
YOU'RE AS HARSH AS EVER.
BUT YOU'RE RIGHT.
WHAT ARE YOU LOOKING AT?
THE REPORT THAT SHUNEI BROUGHT FROM THE OTHERS.
COME TO THINK OF IT, YOU'VE BEEN GONE A COUPLE OF DAYS, RIGHT?
YOU JUST CAME BACK, RIGHT?
YES. I WENT TO PICK UP THE INFORMATION THAT SHUKI, KANAN AND THE OTHERS HAD COMPILED.
WHAT INFOR-MATION?
INFORMATION CONCERNING THE DRAGON FAMILY.

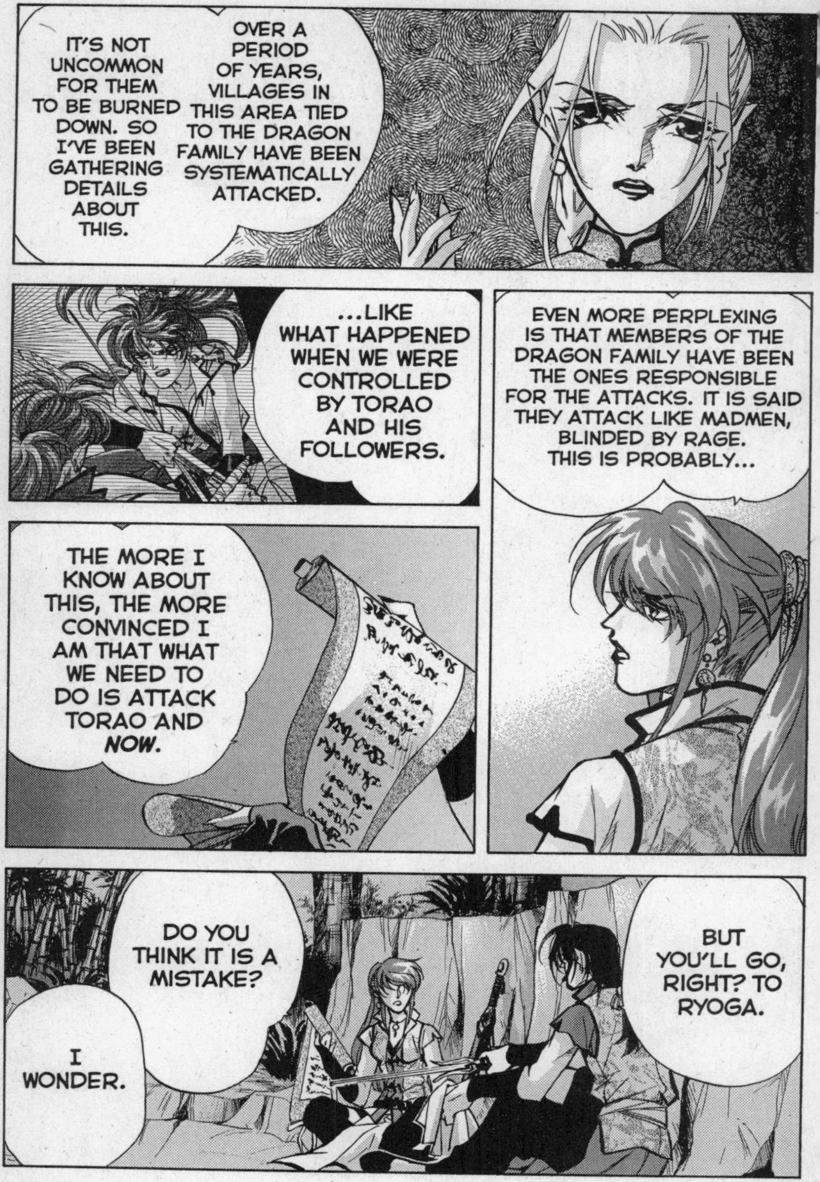
OVER A PERIOD OF YEARS, VILLAGES IN THIS AREA TIED TO THE DRAGON FAMILY HAVE BEEN SYSTEMATICALLY ATTACKED.
IT'S NOT UNCOMMON FOR THEM TO BE BURNED DOWN. SO I'VE BEEN GATHERING DETAILS ABOUT THIS.
EVEN MORE PERPLEXING IS THAT MEMBERS OF THE DRAGON FAMILY HAVE BEEN THE ONES RESPONSIBLE FOR THE ATTACKS. IT IS SAID THEY ATTACK LIKE MADMEN, BLINDED BY RAGE. THIS IS PROBABLY...
...LIKE WHAT HAPPENED WHEN WE WERE CONTROLLED BY TORAO AND HIS FOLLOWERS.
THE MORE I KNOW ABOUT THIS, THE MORE CONVINCED I AM THAT WHAT WE NEED TO DO IS ATTACK TORAO AND *NOW*.
BUT YOU'LL GO, RIGHT? TO RYOGA.
DO YOU THINK IT IS A MISTAKE?
I WONDER.

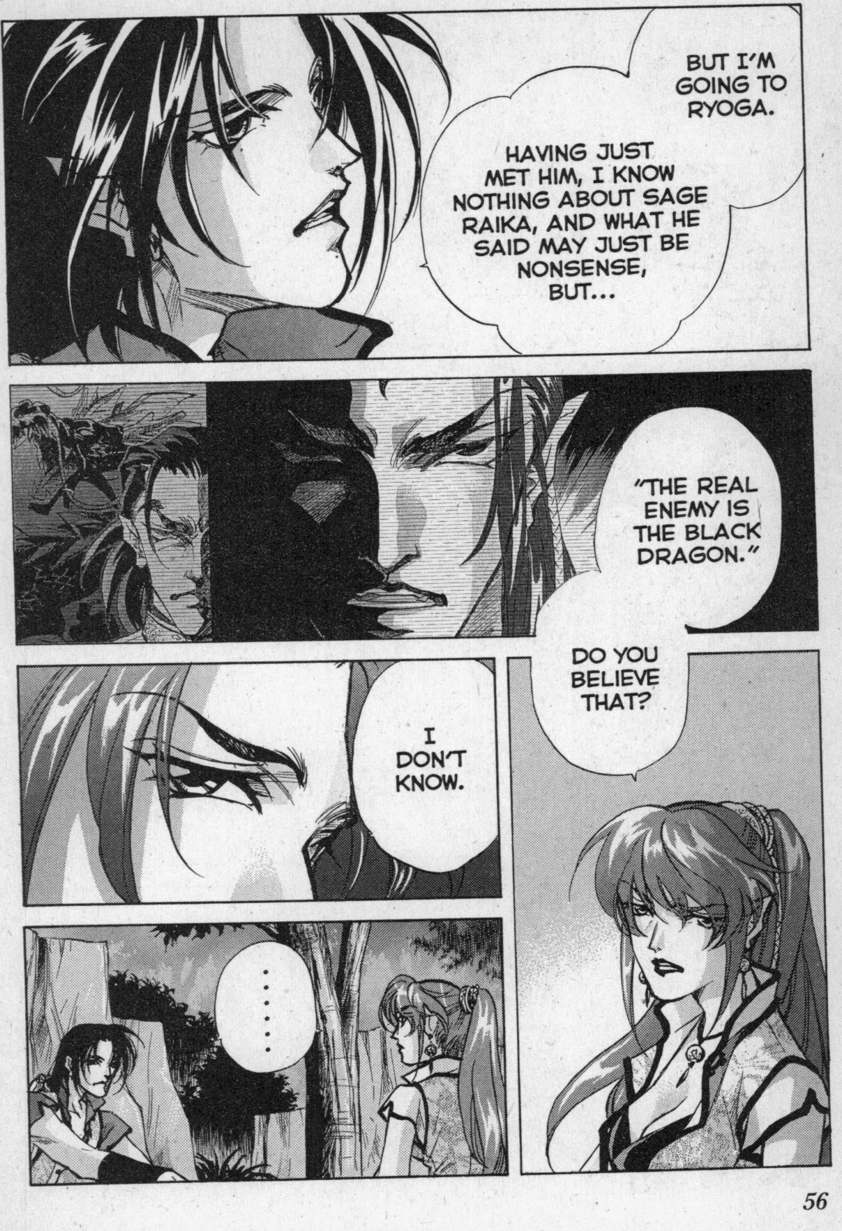
BUT I'M GOING TO RYOGA.
HAVING JUST MET HIM, I KNOW NOTHING ABOUT SAGE RAIKA, AND WHAT HE SAID MAY JUST BE NONSENSE, BUT...
"THE REAL ENEMY IS THE BLACK DRAGON."
DO YOU BELIEVE THAT?
I DON'T KNOW.
......

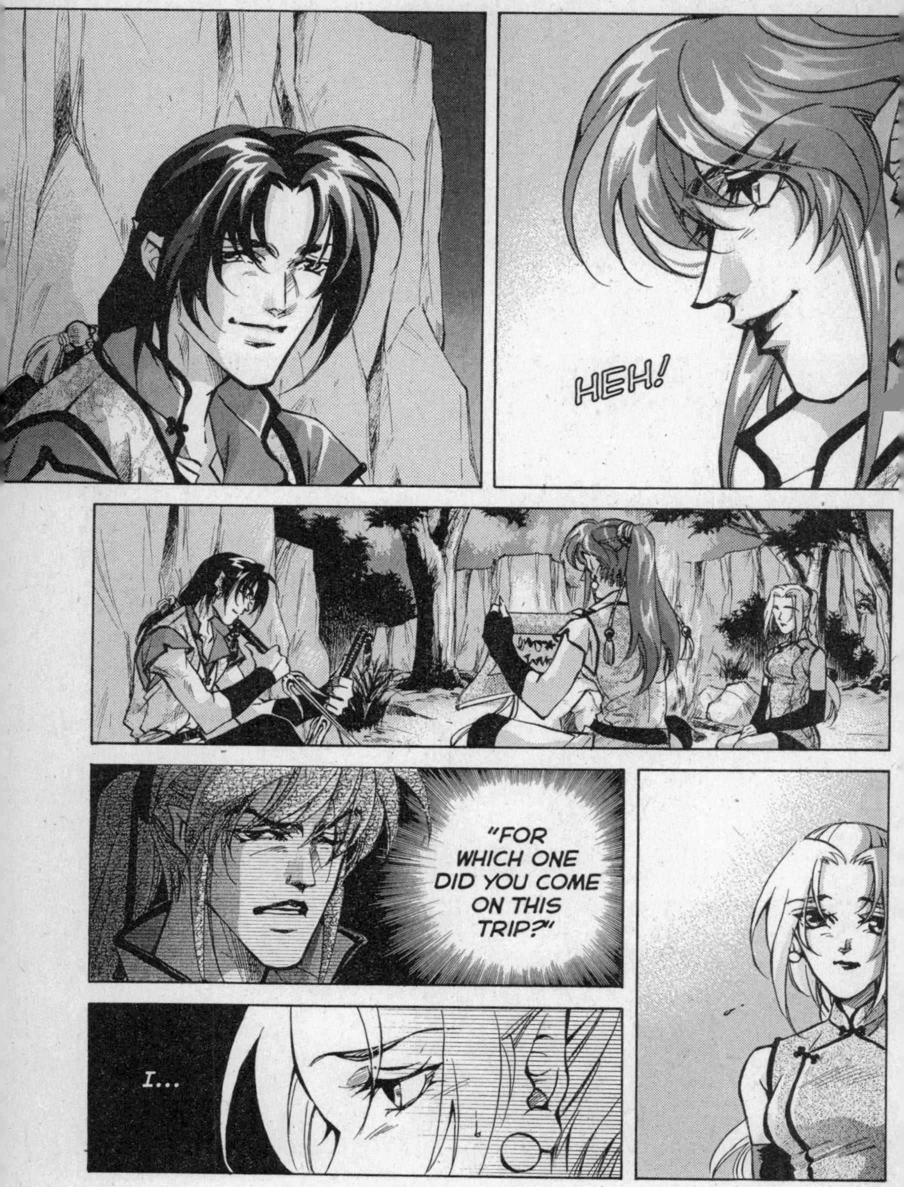
HEH!
"FOR WHICH ONE DID YOU COME ON THIS TRIP?"
I...

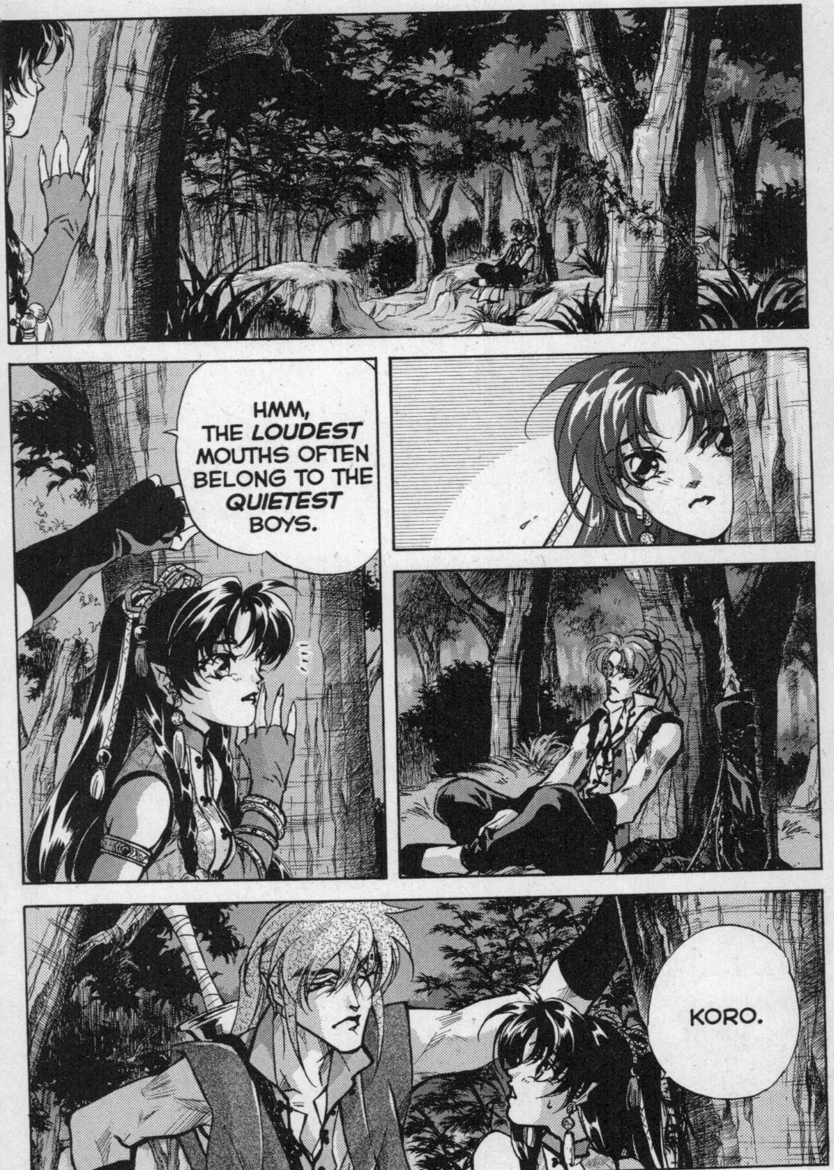
HMM, THE LOUDEST MOUTHS OFTEN BELONG TO THE QUIETEST BOYS.
KORO.

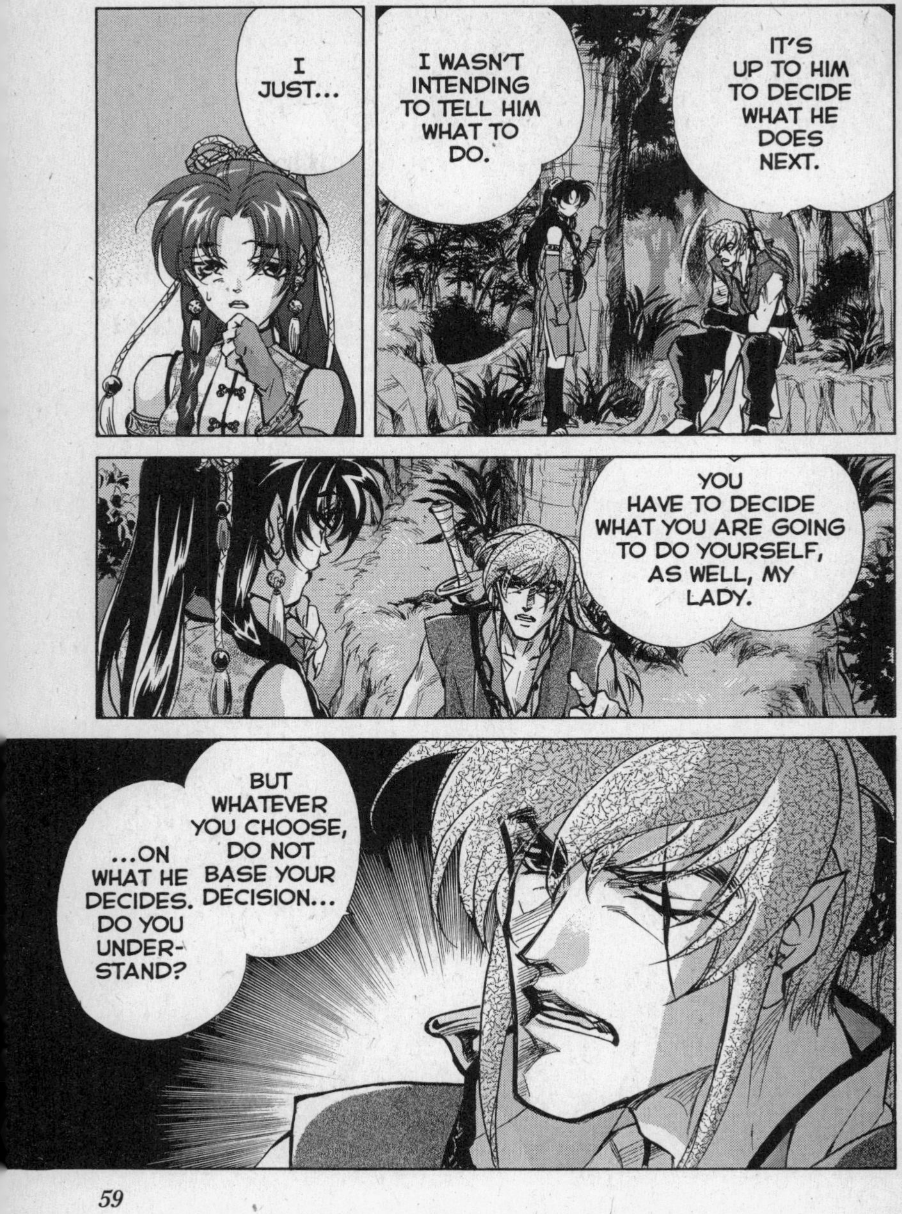
IT'S UP TO HIM TO DECIDE WHAT HE DOES NEXT.
I WASN'T INTENDING TO TELL HIM WHAT TO DO.
I JUST...
YOU HAVE TO DECIDE WHAT YOU ARE GOING TO DO YOURSELF, AS WELL, MY LADY.
BUT WHATEVER YOU CHOOSE, DO NOT BASE YOUR DECISION...
...ON WHAT HE DECIDES. DO YOU UNDER-STAND?

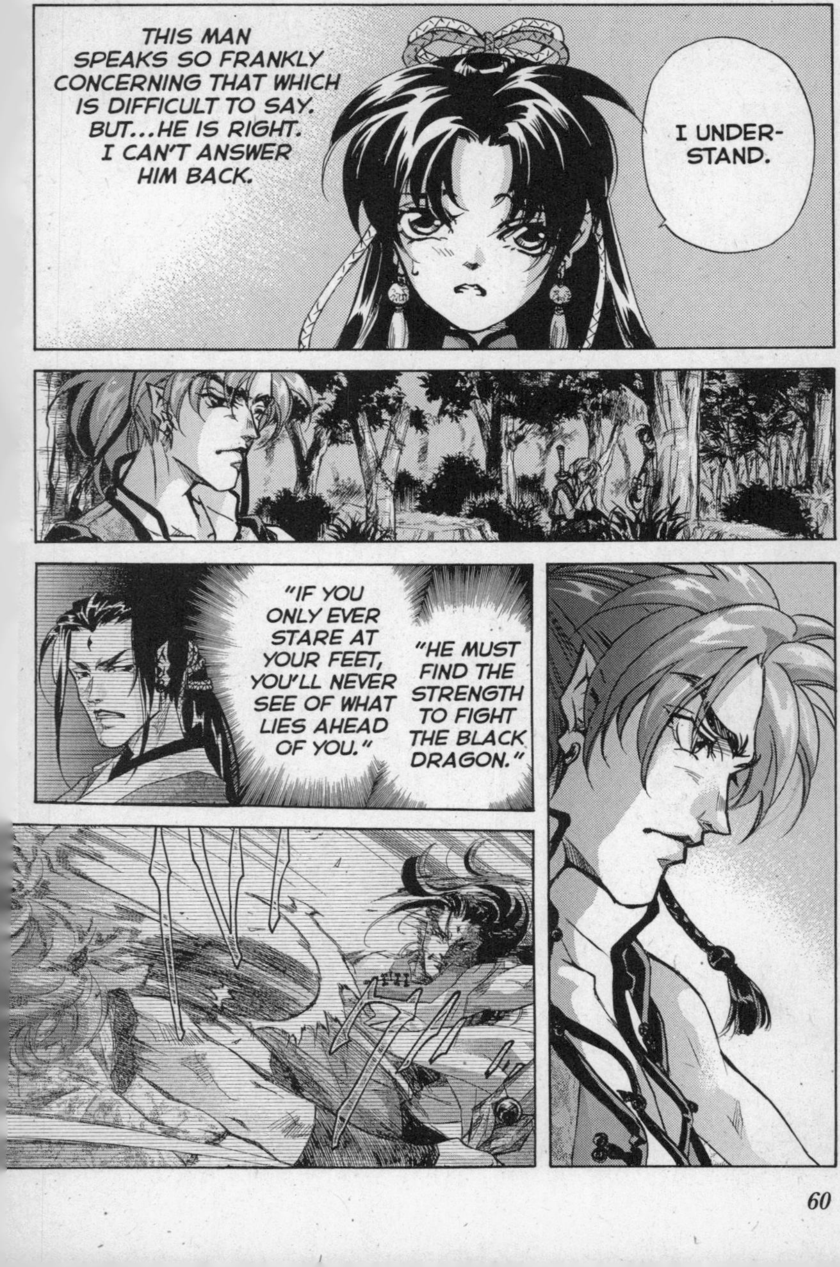
I UNDER-
STAND.
THIS MAN SPEAKS SO FRANKLY CONCERNING THAT WHICH IS DIFFICULT TO SAY. BUT...HE IS RIGHT. I CAN'T ANSWER HIM BACK.
"HE MUST FIND THE STRENGTH TO FIGHT THE BLACK DRAGON."
"IF YOU ONLY EVER STARE AT YOUR FEET, YOU'LL NEVER SEE OF WHAT LIES AHEAD OF YOU."

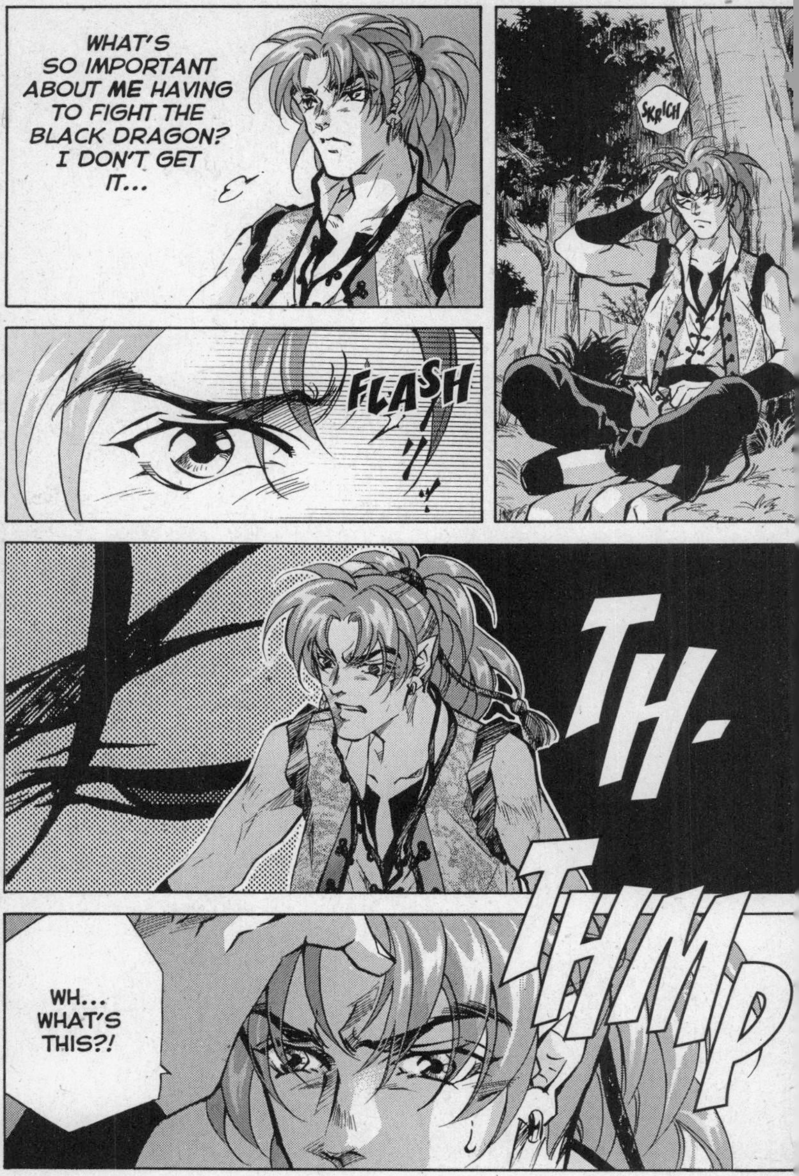
SKRICH
WHAT'S SO IMPORTANT ABOUT ME HAVING TO FIGHT THE BLACK DRAGON? I DON'T GET IT...
FLASH
TH-THMP
WH... WHAT'S THIS?!

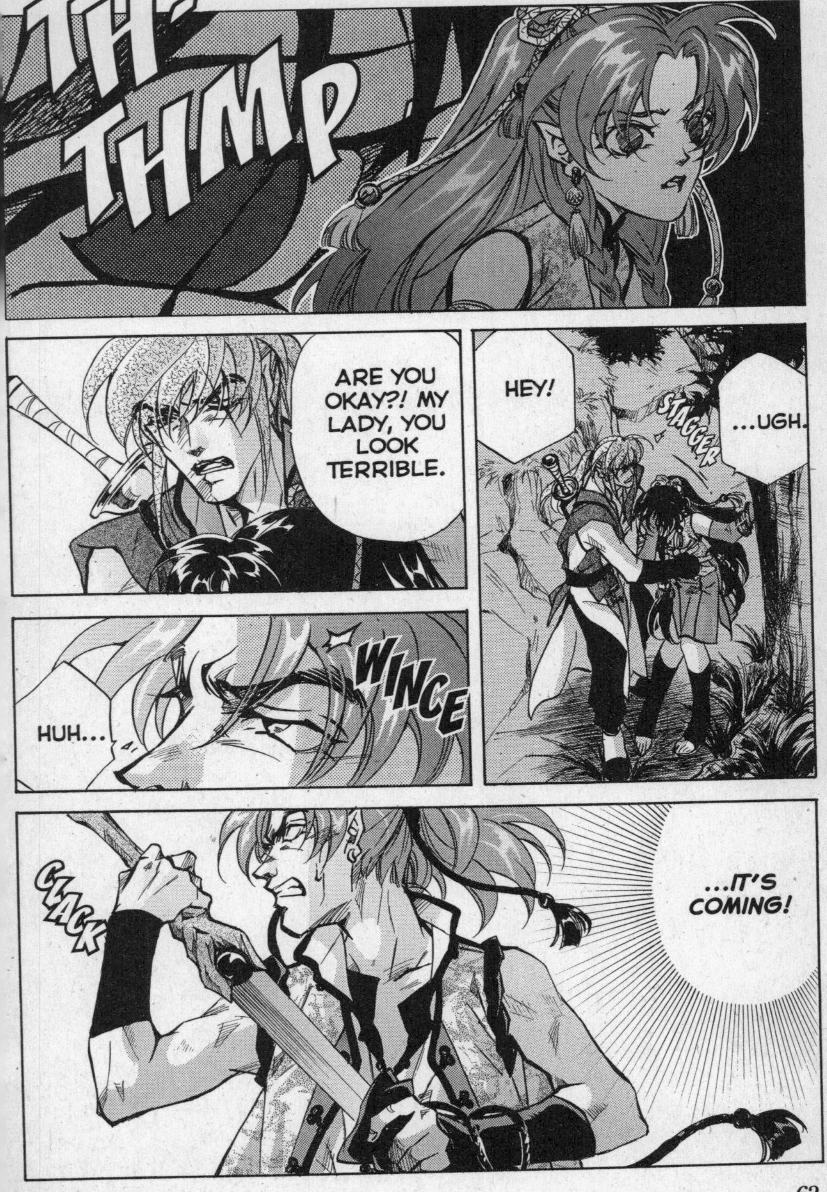
TH-THMP
...UGH.
STAGGER
HEY!
ARE YOU OKAY?! MY LADY, YOU LOOK TERRIBLE.
WINCE
HUH...
...IT'S COMING!
CLACK

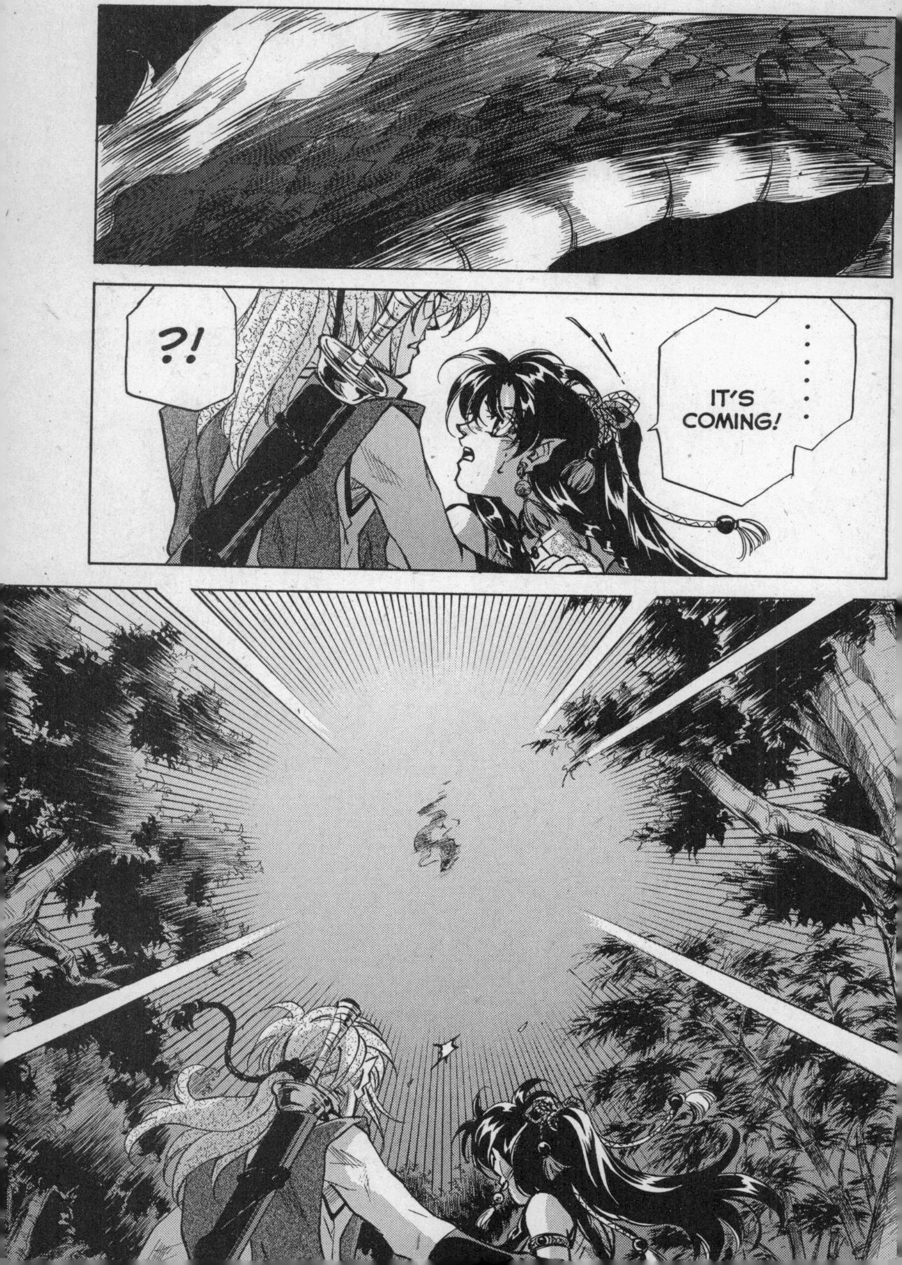

...... IT'S COMING!
?!

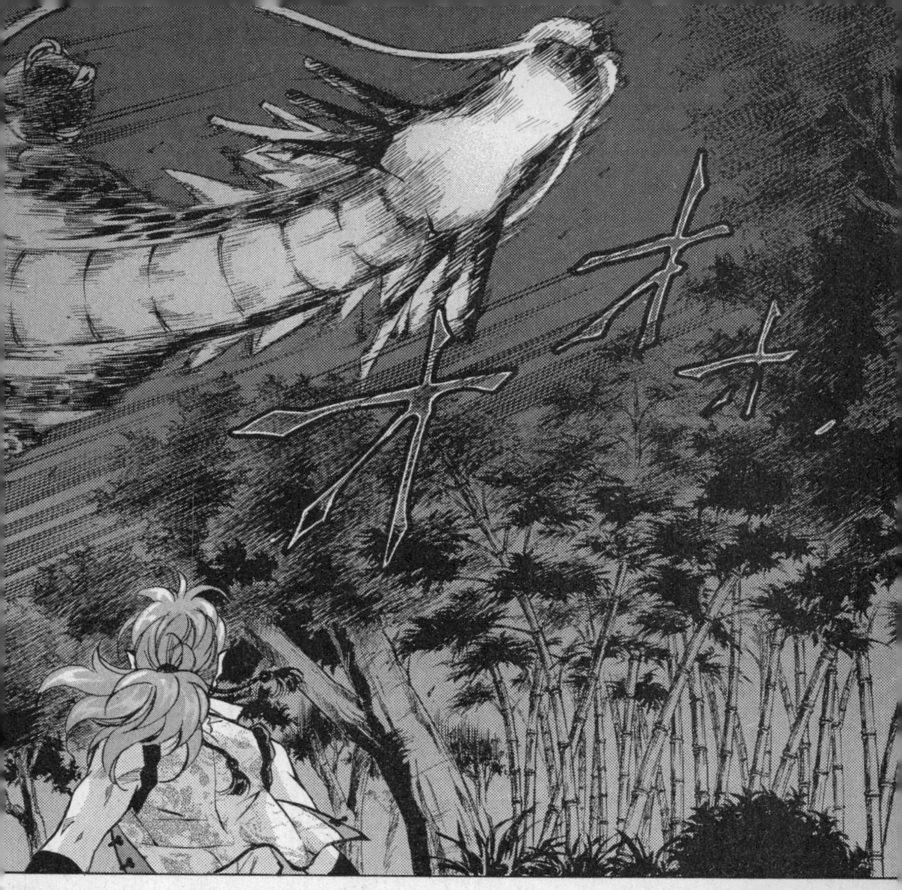
オオォ
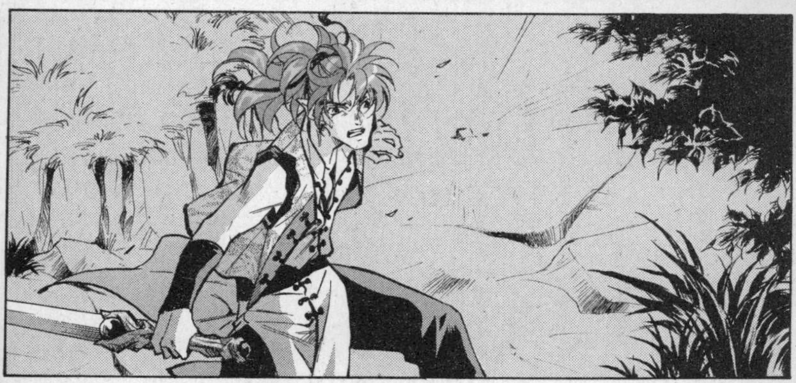

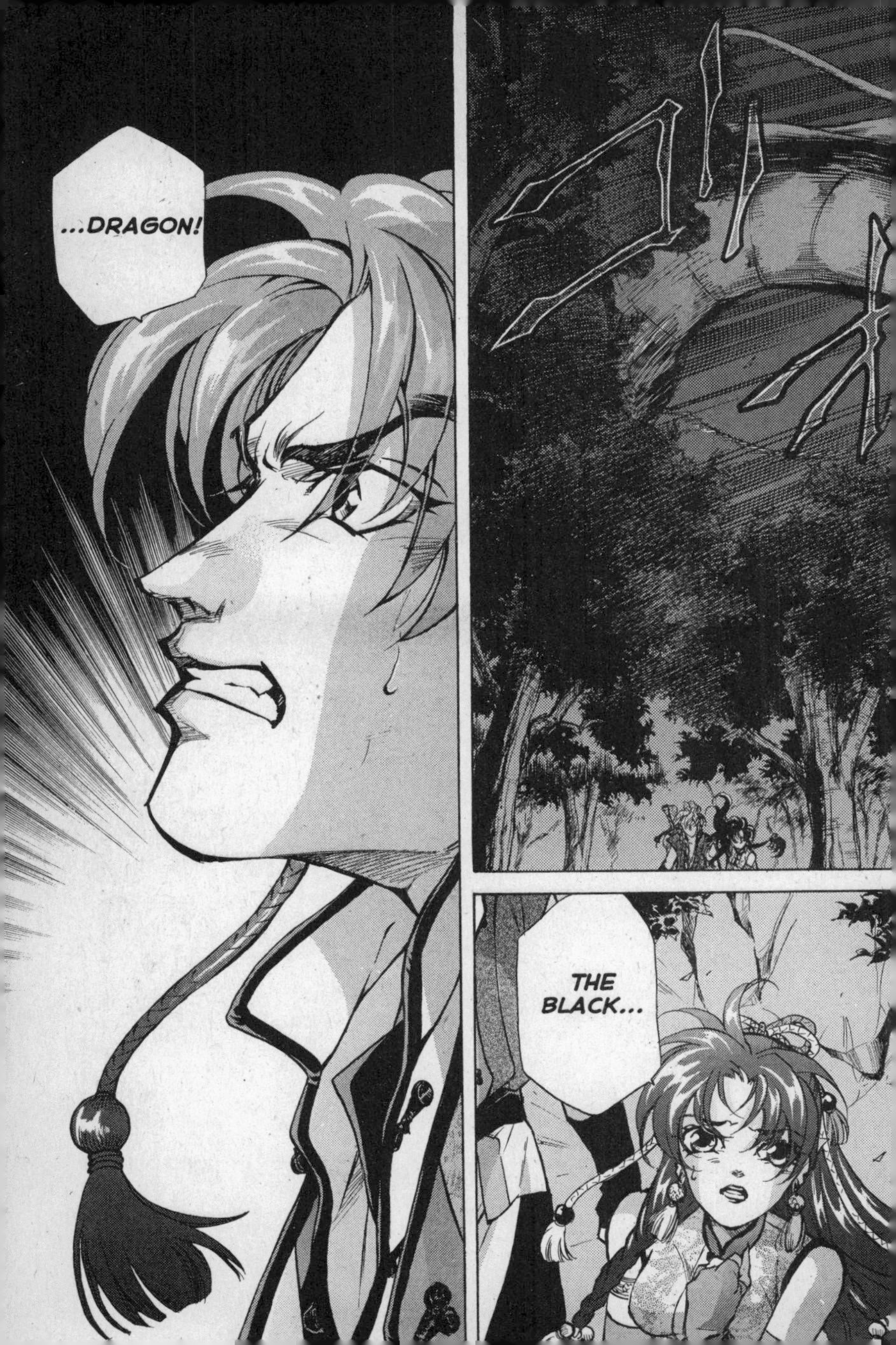
THE BLACK...
...DRAGON!

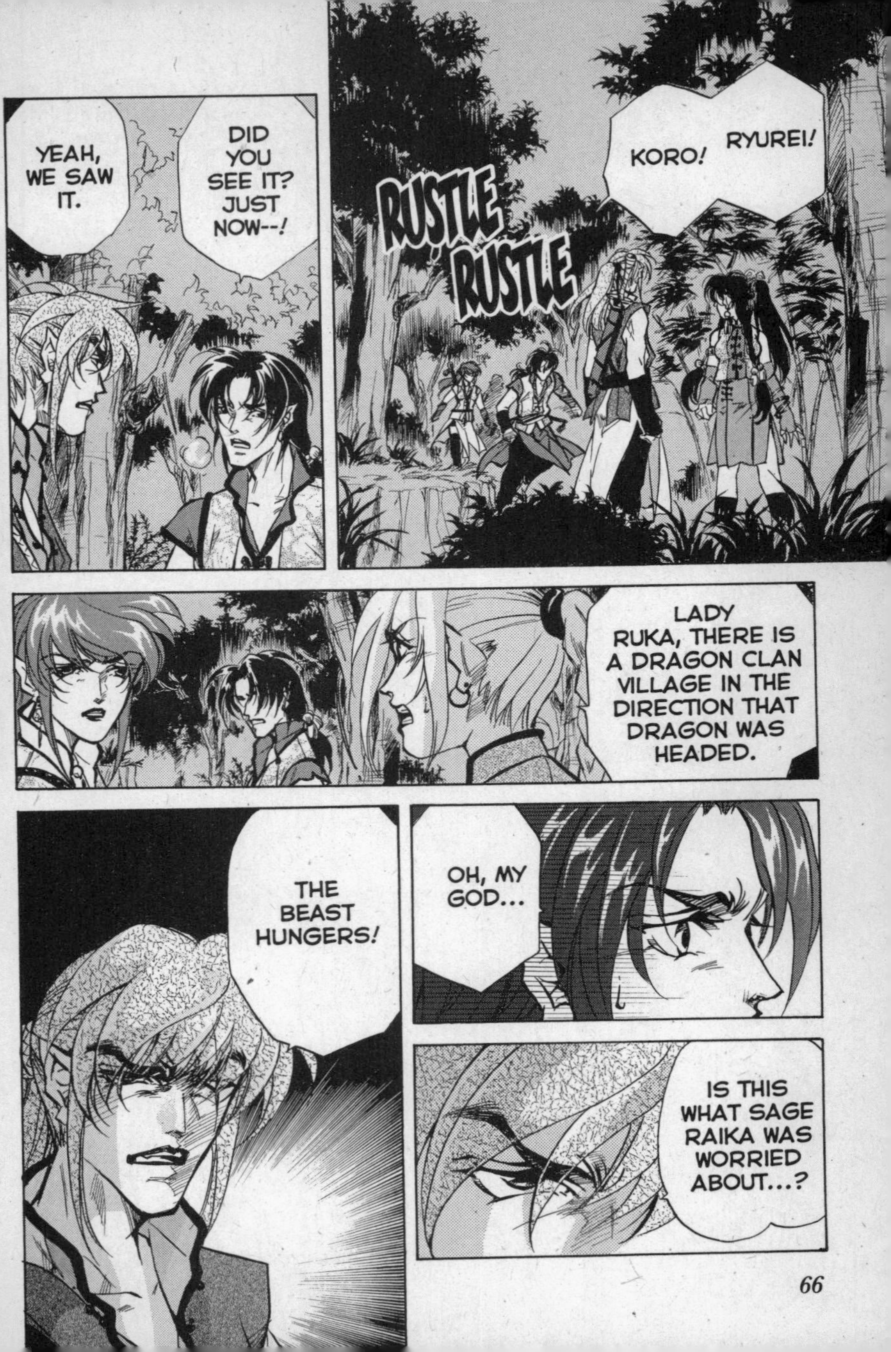
RYUREI! KORO!
RUSTLE RUSTLE
DID YOU SEE IT? JUST NOW--!
YEAH, WE SAW IT.
LADY RUKA, THERE IS A DRAGON CLAN VILLAGE IN THE DIRECTION THAT DRAGON WAS HEADED.
OH, MY GOD...
IS THIS WHAT SAGE RAIKA WAS WORRIED ABOUT...?
THE BEAST HUNGERS!

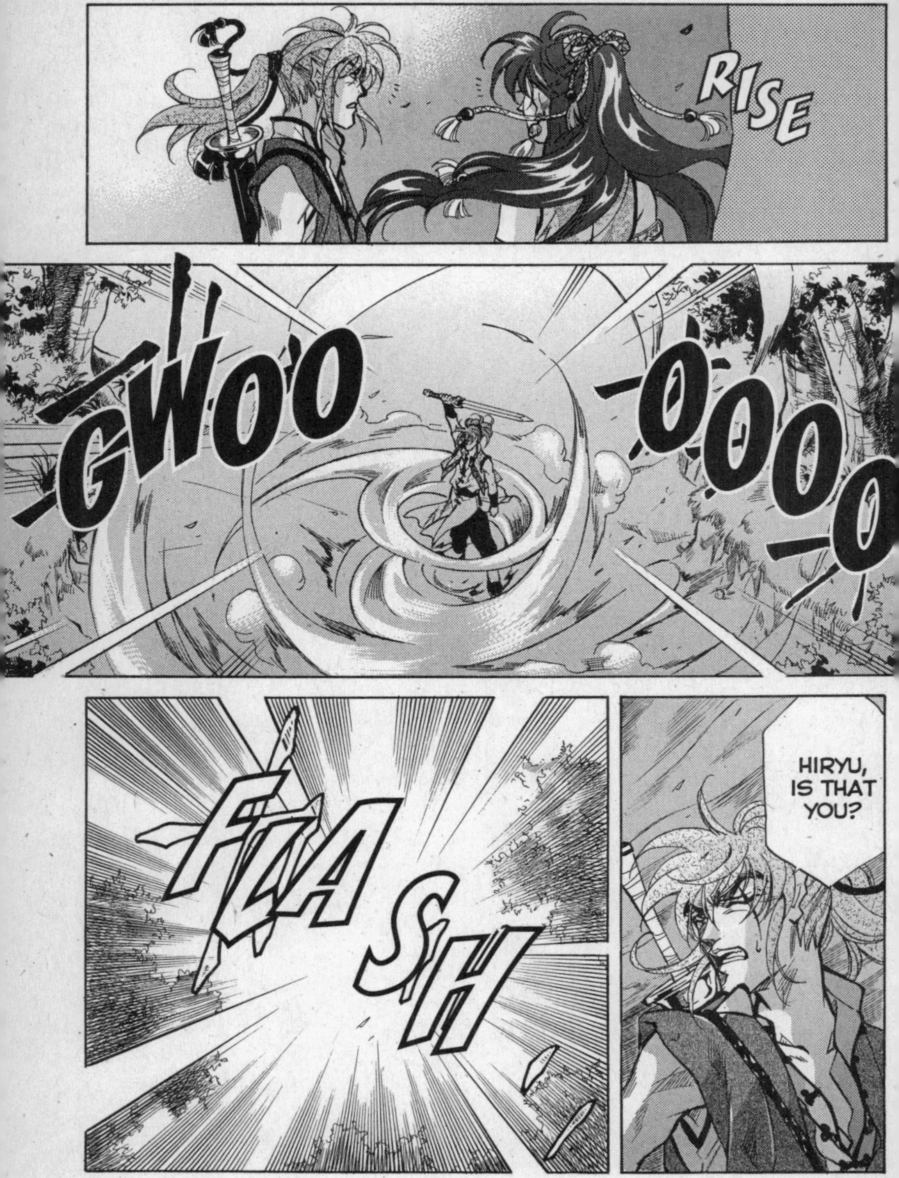
RISE
GWOOO-OOOO
HIRYU, IS THAT YOU?
FLASH

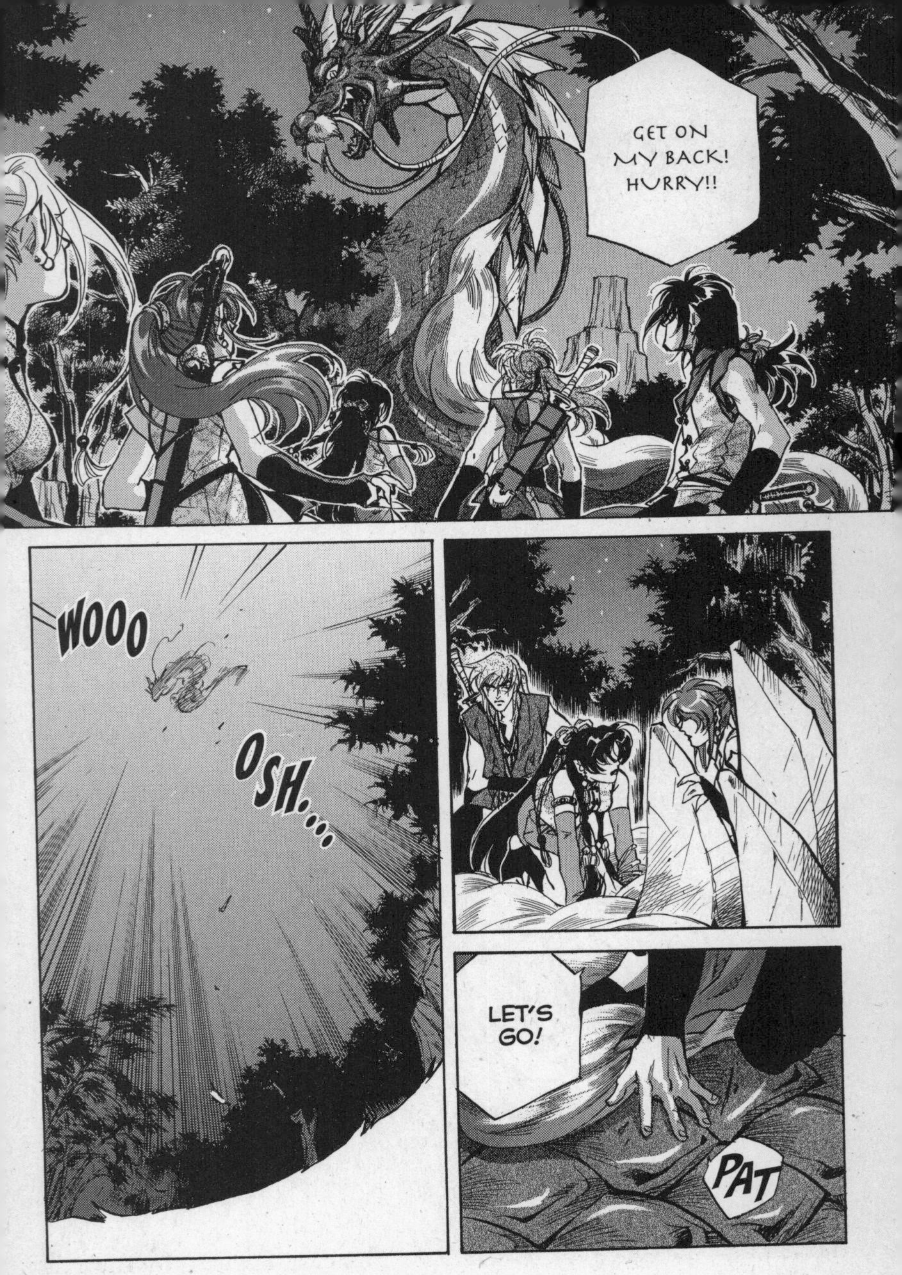
GET ON MY BACK! HURRY!!
LET'S GO!
PAT
WOOO
OSH....

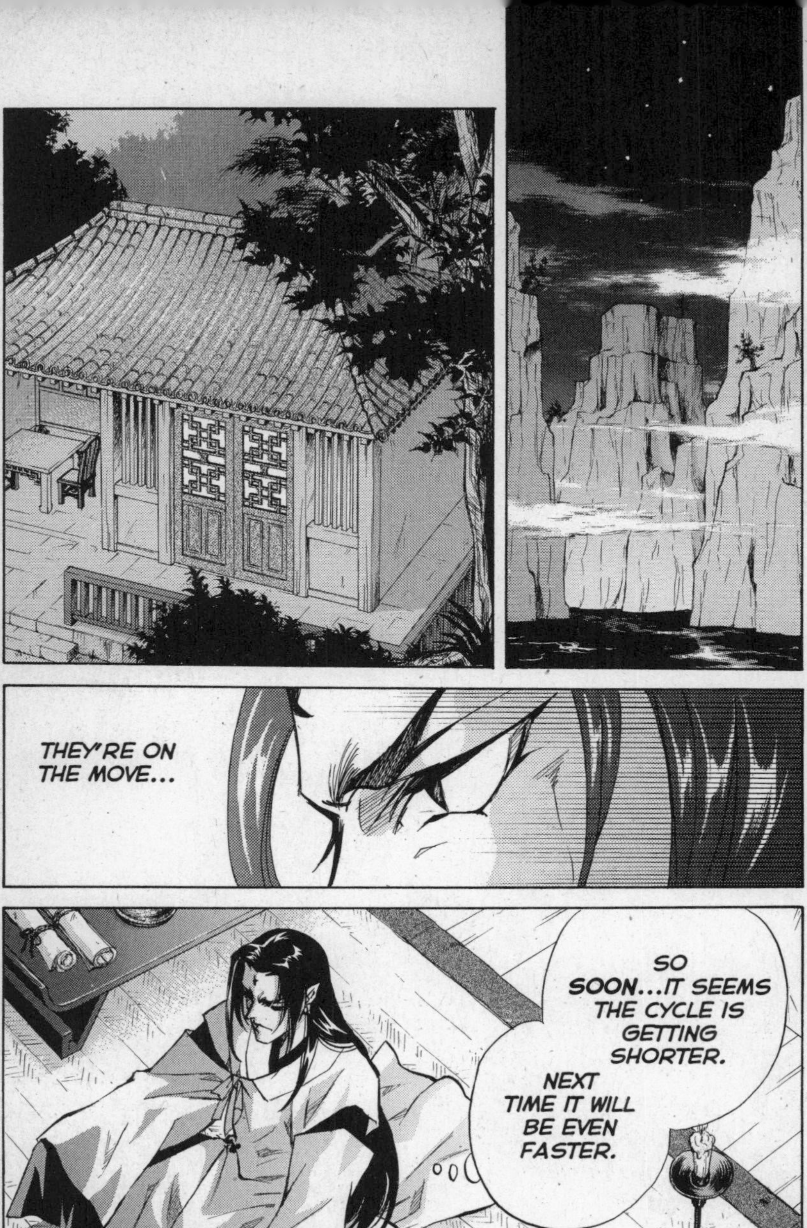
THEY'RE ON THE MOVE...
SO SOON...IT SEEMS THE CYCLE IS GETTING SHORTER.
NEXT TIME IT WILL BE EVEN FASTER.

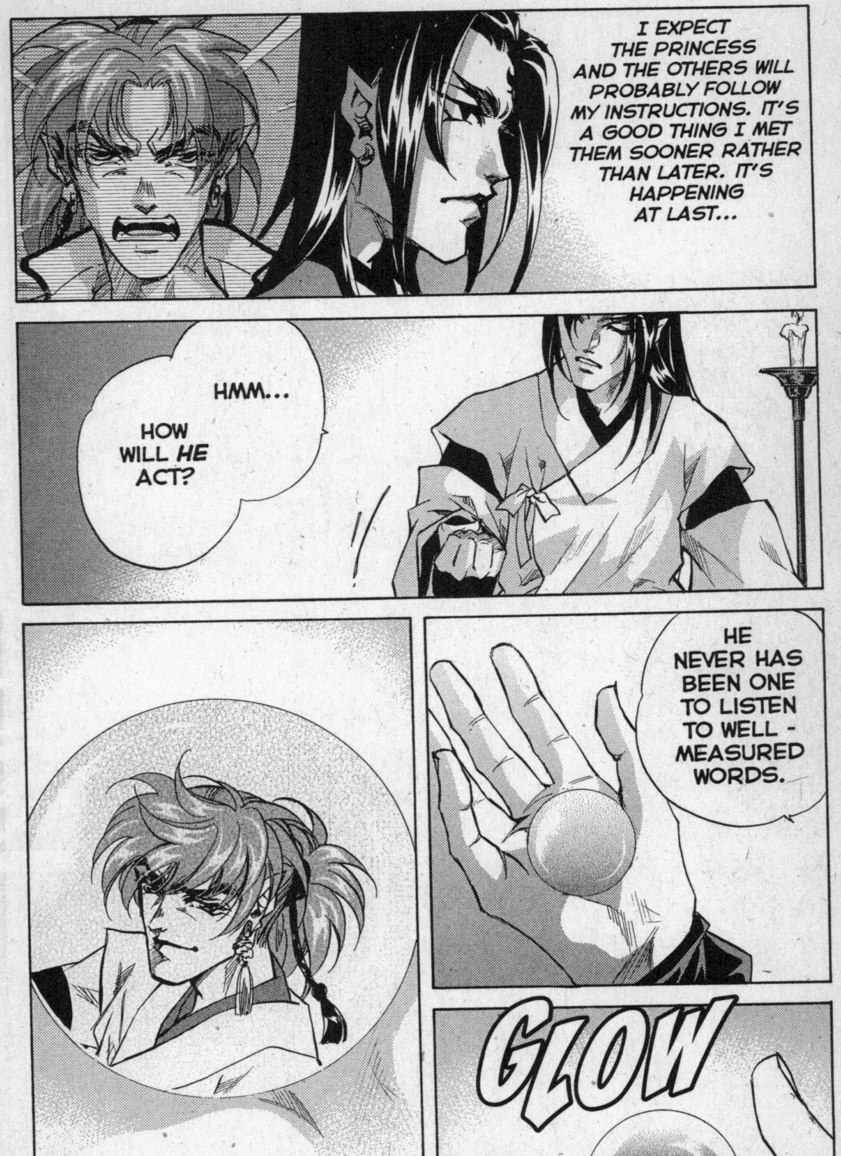
I EXPECT THE PRINCESS AND THE OTHERS WILL PROBABLY FOLLOW MY INSTRUCTIONS. IT'S A GOOD THING I MET THEM SOONER RATHER THAN LATER. IT'S HAPPENING AT LAST...
HMM...
HOW WILL *HE* ACT?
HE NEVER HAS BEEN ONE TO LISTEN TO WELL-MEASURED WORDS.
GLOW

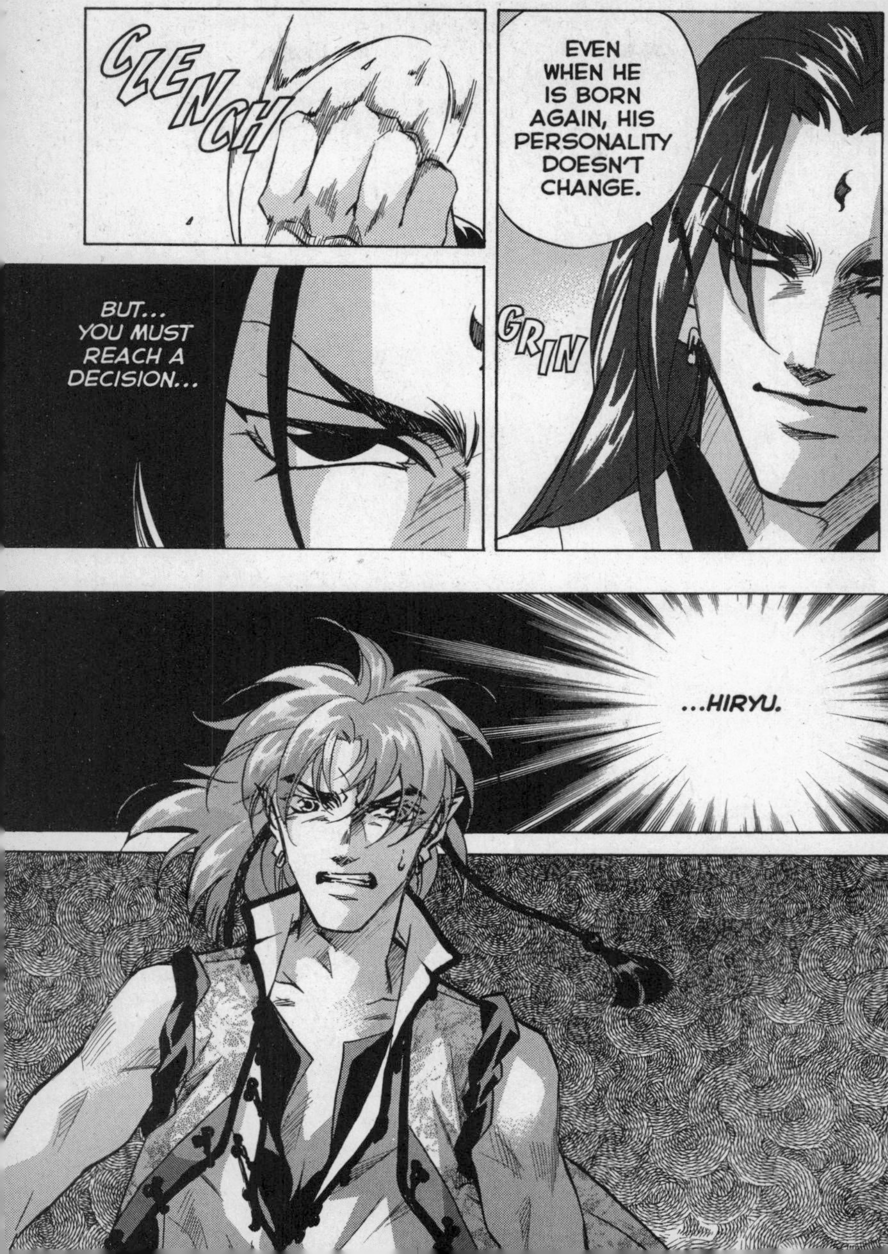
EVEN WHEN HE IS BORN AGAIN, HIS PERSONALITY DOESN'T CHANGE.
GRIN
CLENCH
BUT... YOU MUST REACH A DECISION...
...HIRYU.

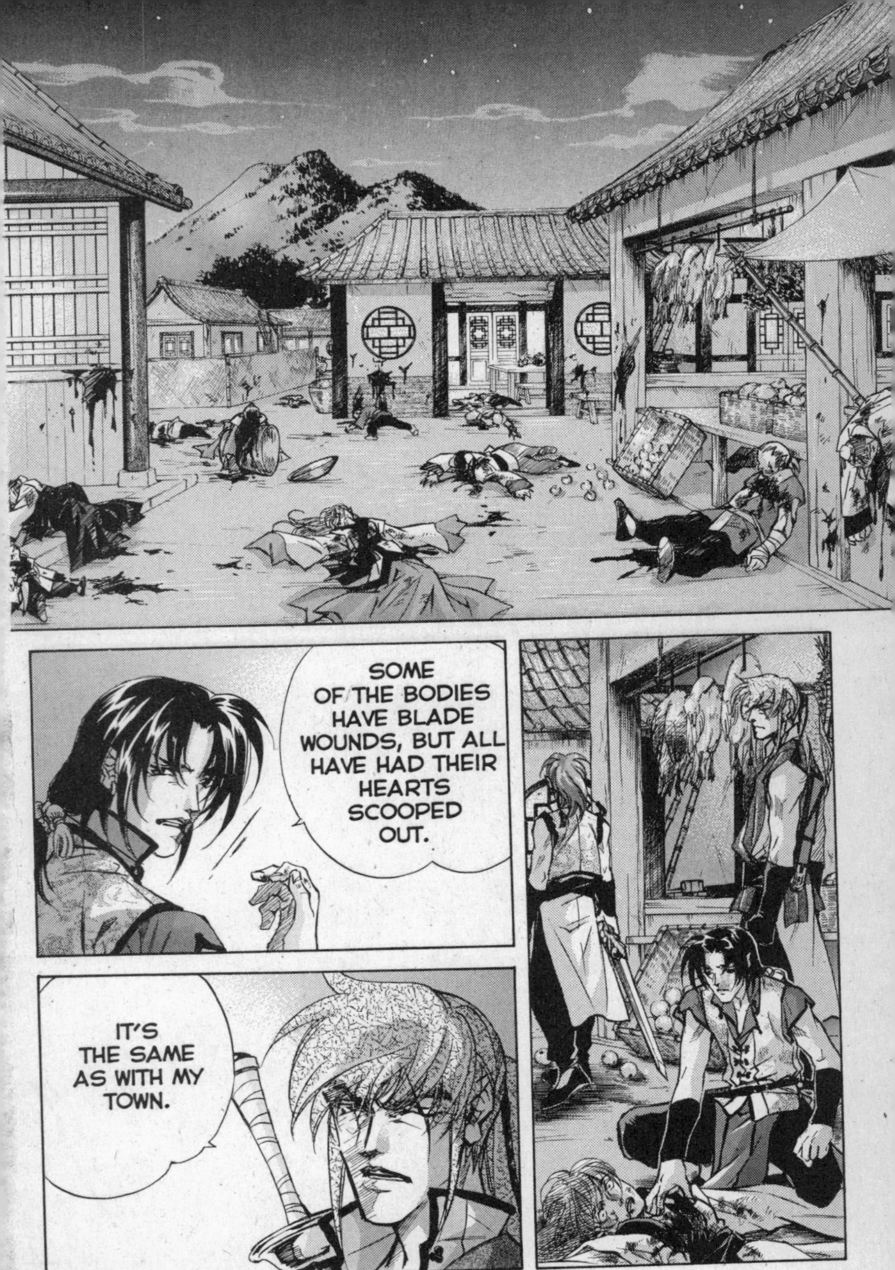
SOME OF THE BODIES HAVE BLADE WOUNDS, BUT ALL HAVE HAD THEIR HEARTS SCOOPED OUT.
IT'S THE SAME AS WITH MY TOWN.

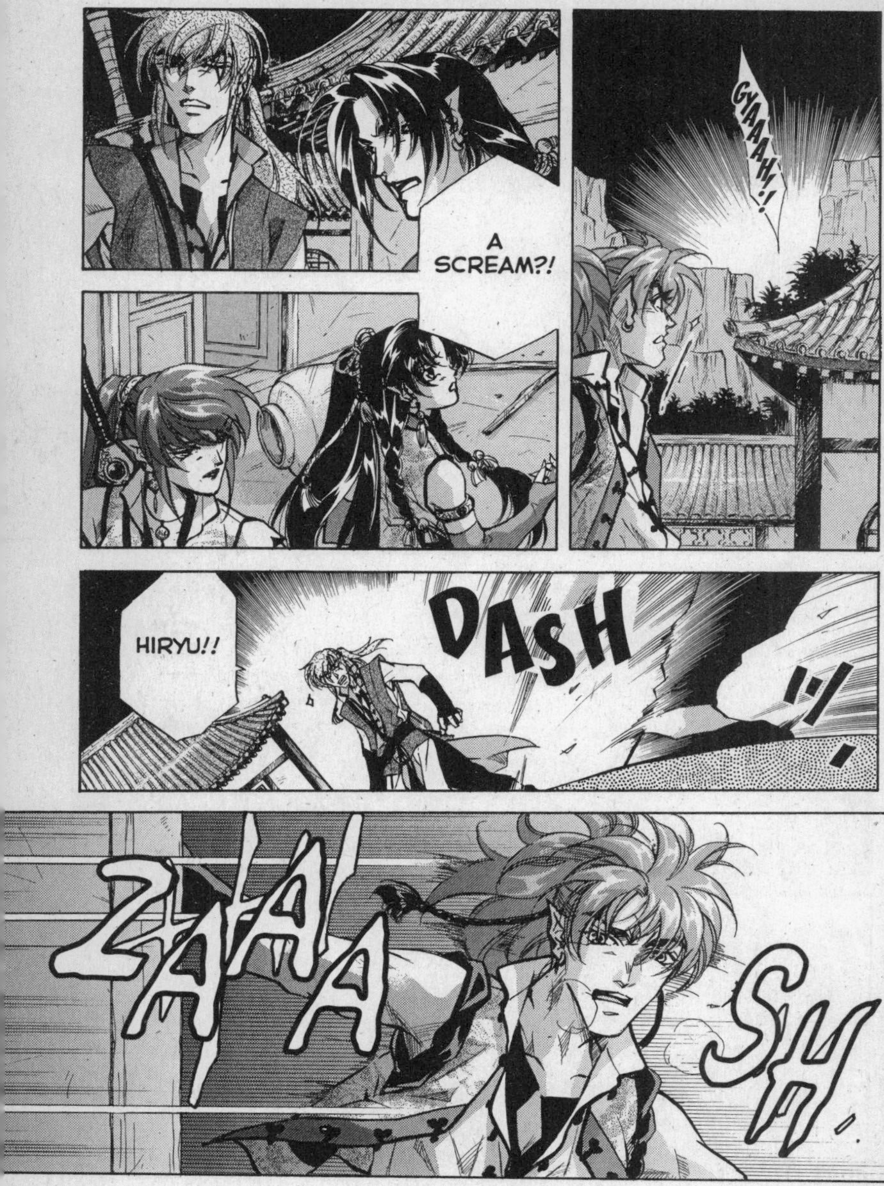
GYAAAH!!
A SCREAM?!
HIRYU!!
DASH
ZAAAASH

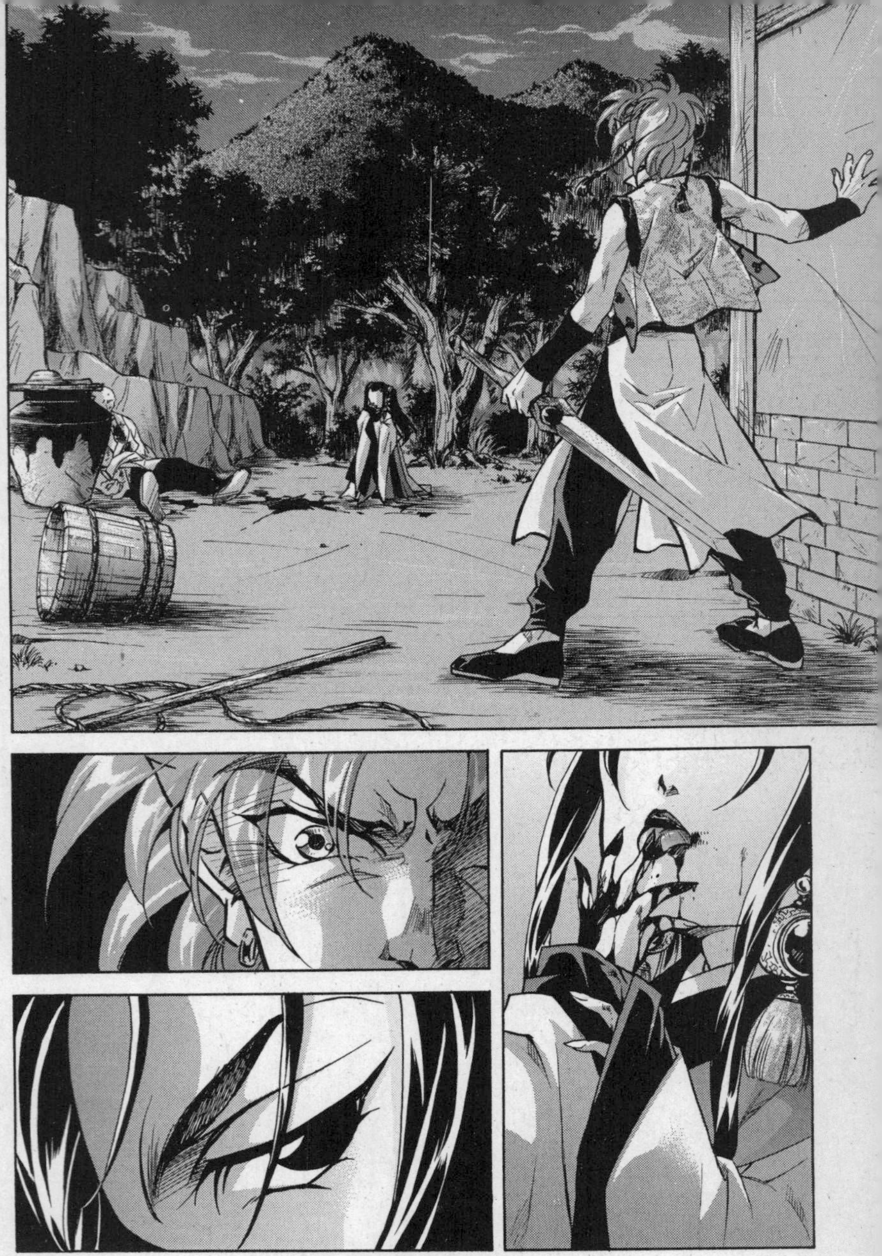

END OF CHAPTER 14

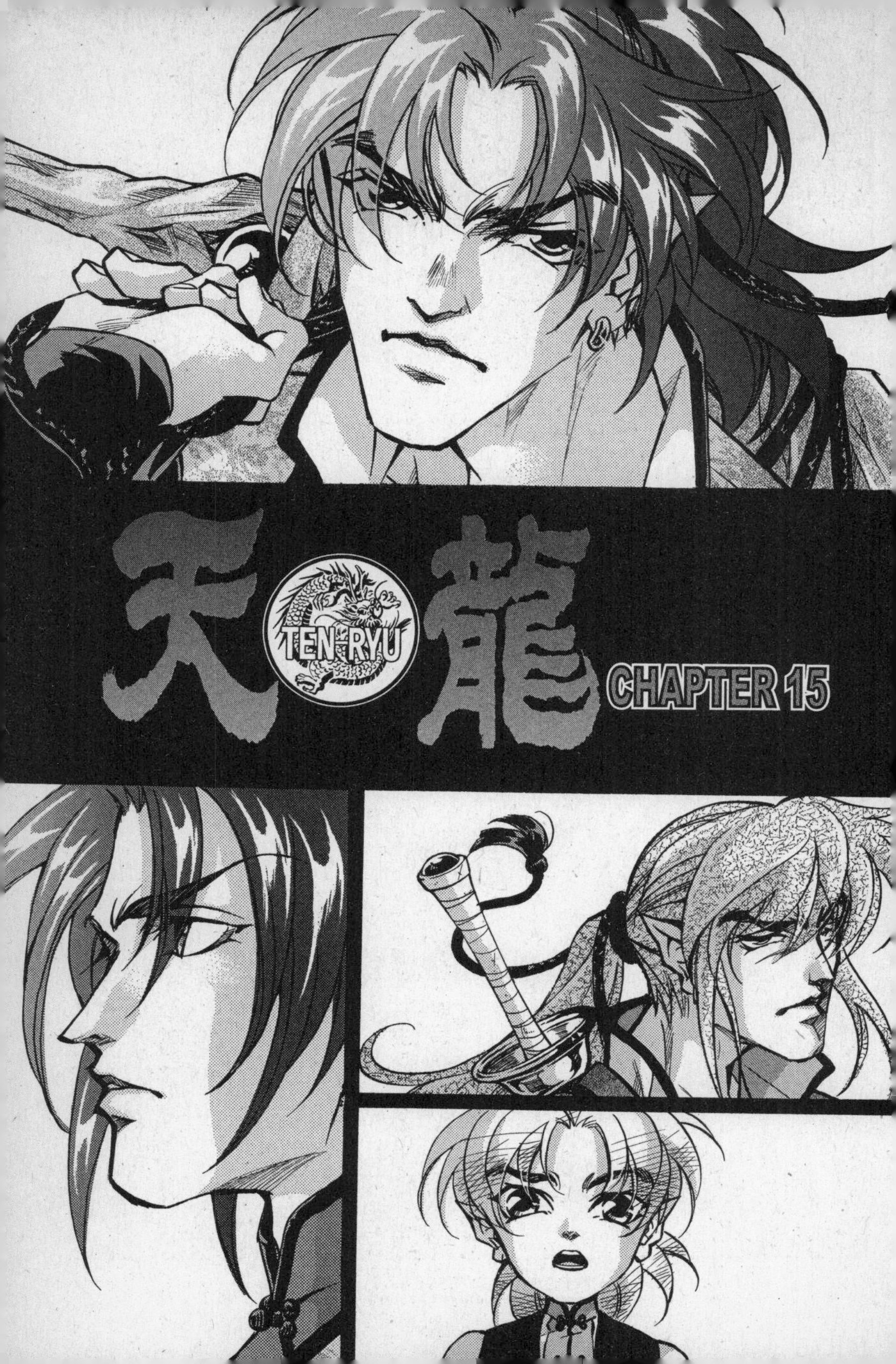
天龍
TEN-RYU
CHAPTER 15

THE DRAGON CYCLE

TEN-RYU 4th STORY

sanami-matoh presents

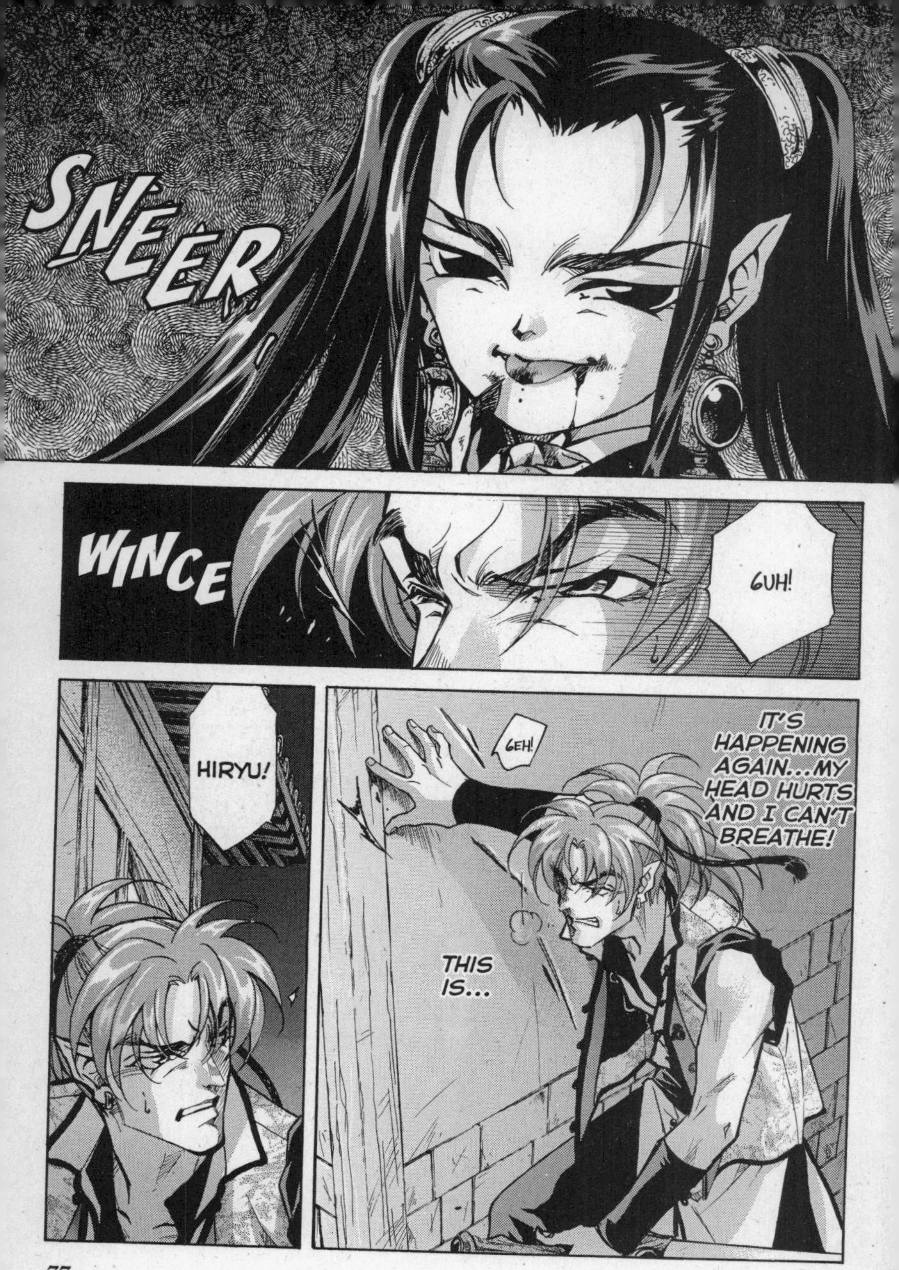
SNEER.
GUH!
WINCE
IT'S HAPPENING AGAIN...MY HEAD HURTS AND I CAN'T BREATHE!
GEH!
THIS IS...
HIRYU!

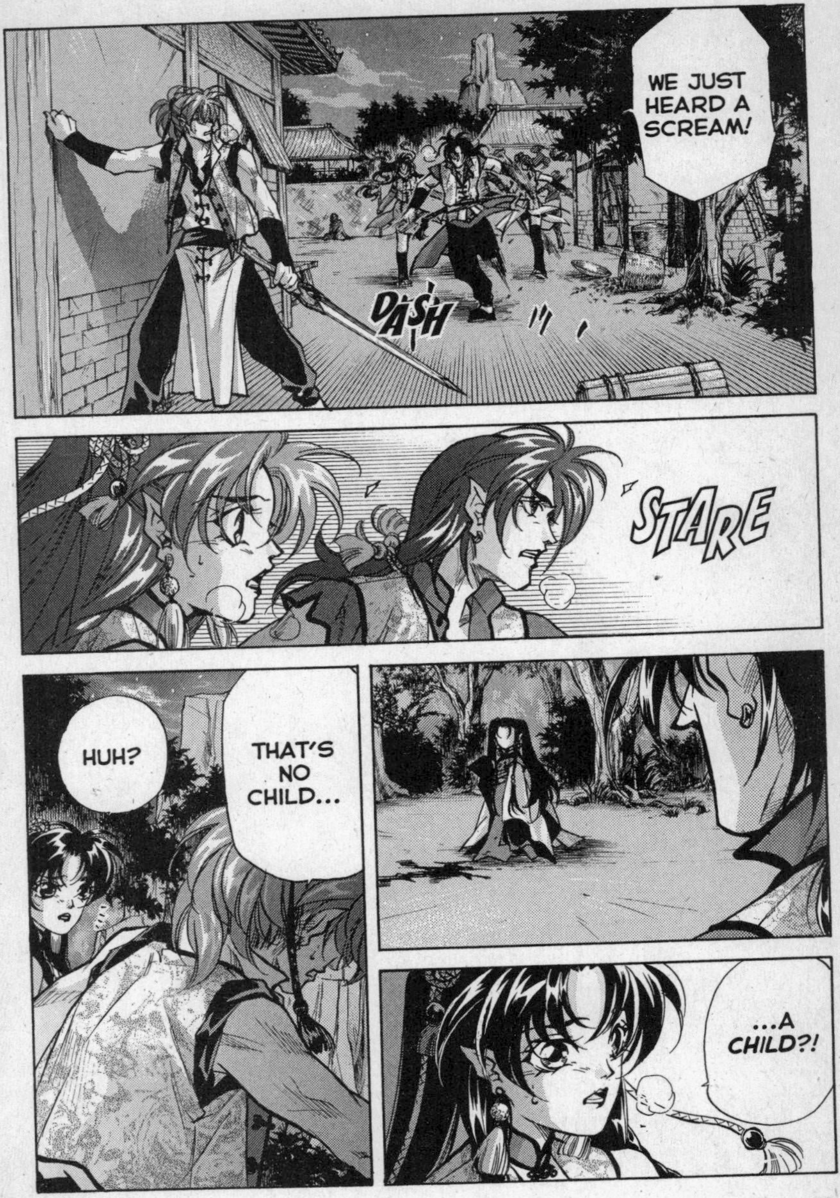
WE JUST HEARD A SCREAM!
DASH
STARE
...A CHILD?!
THAT'S NO CHILD...
HUH?

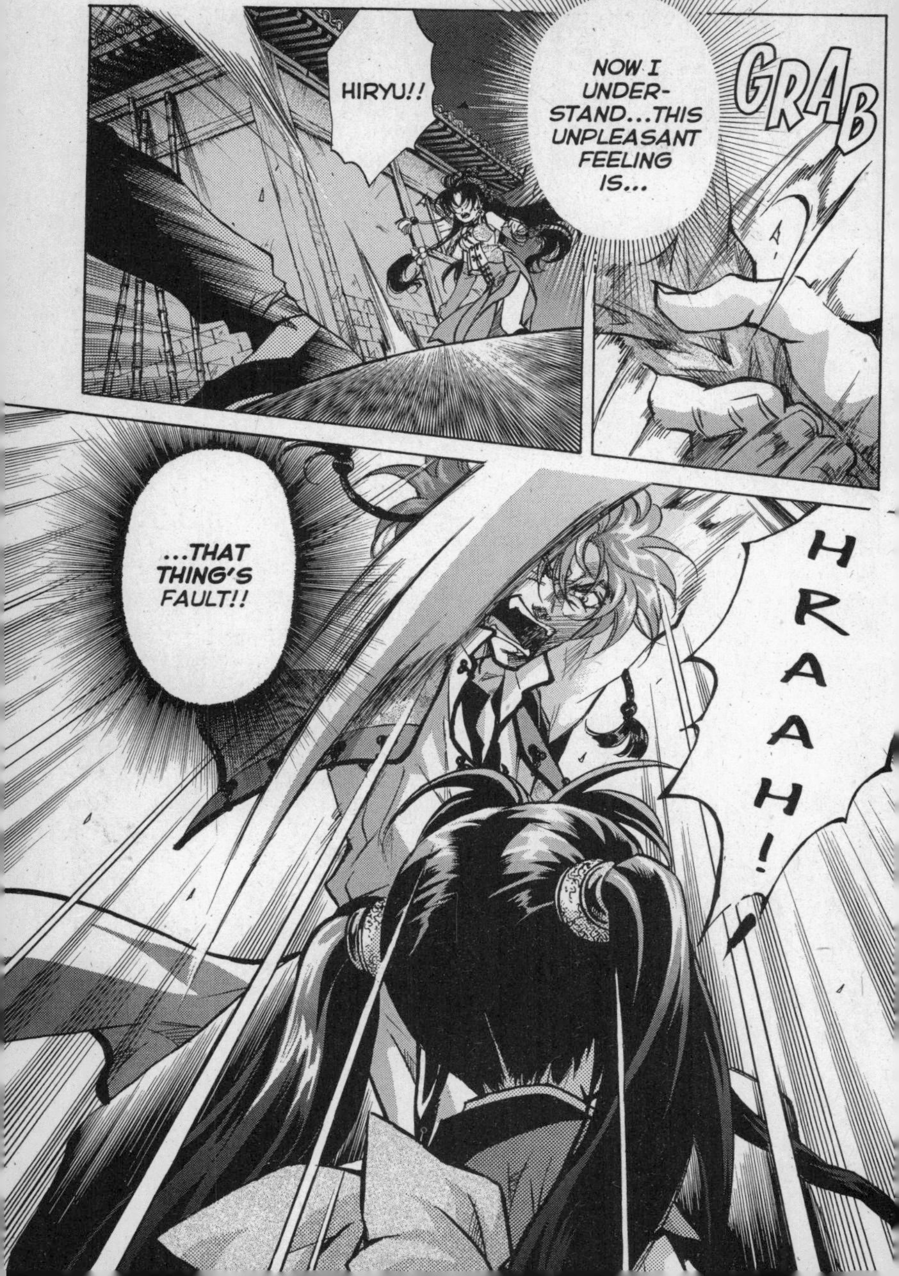
GRAB
NOW I UNDERSTAND...THIS UNPLEASANT FEELING IS...
HIRYU!!
HRAAH!!
...THAT THING'S FAULT!!

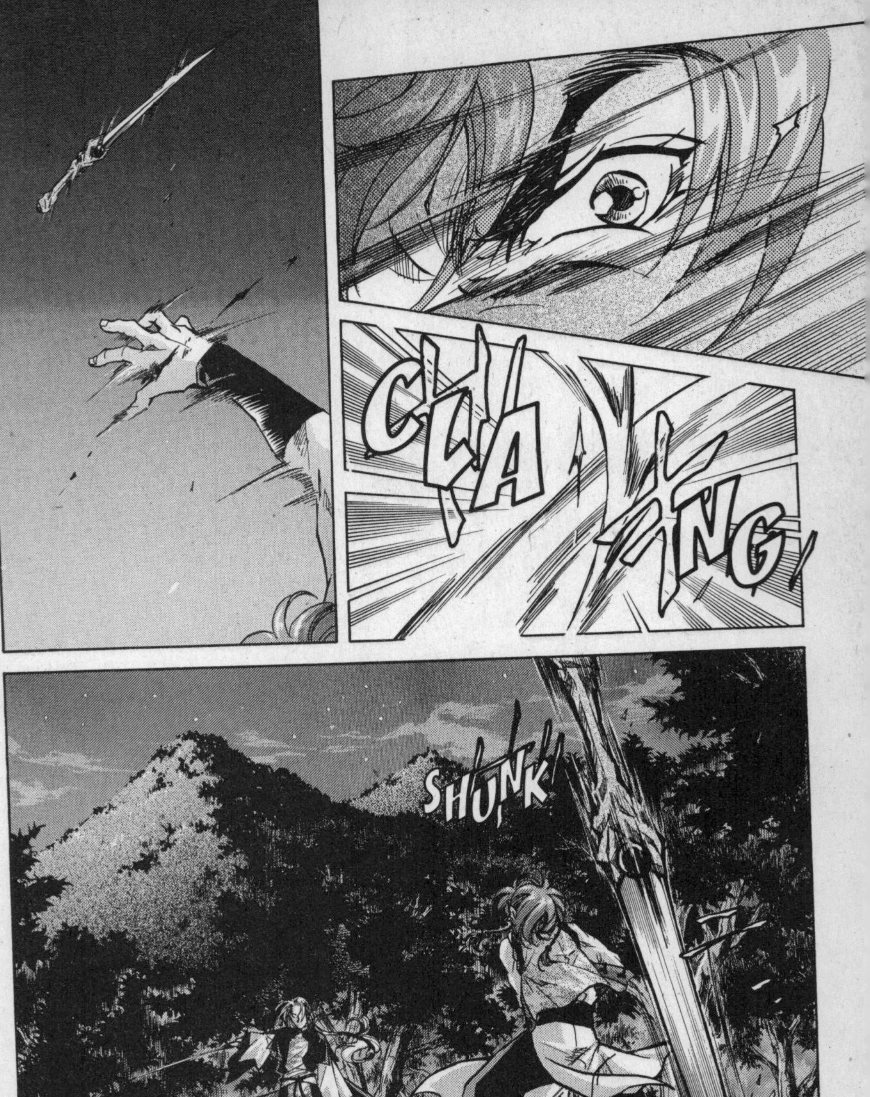
CLAANG!
SHUNK!

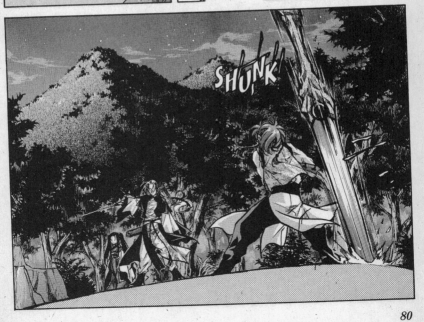

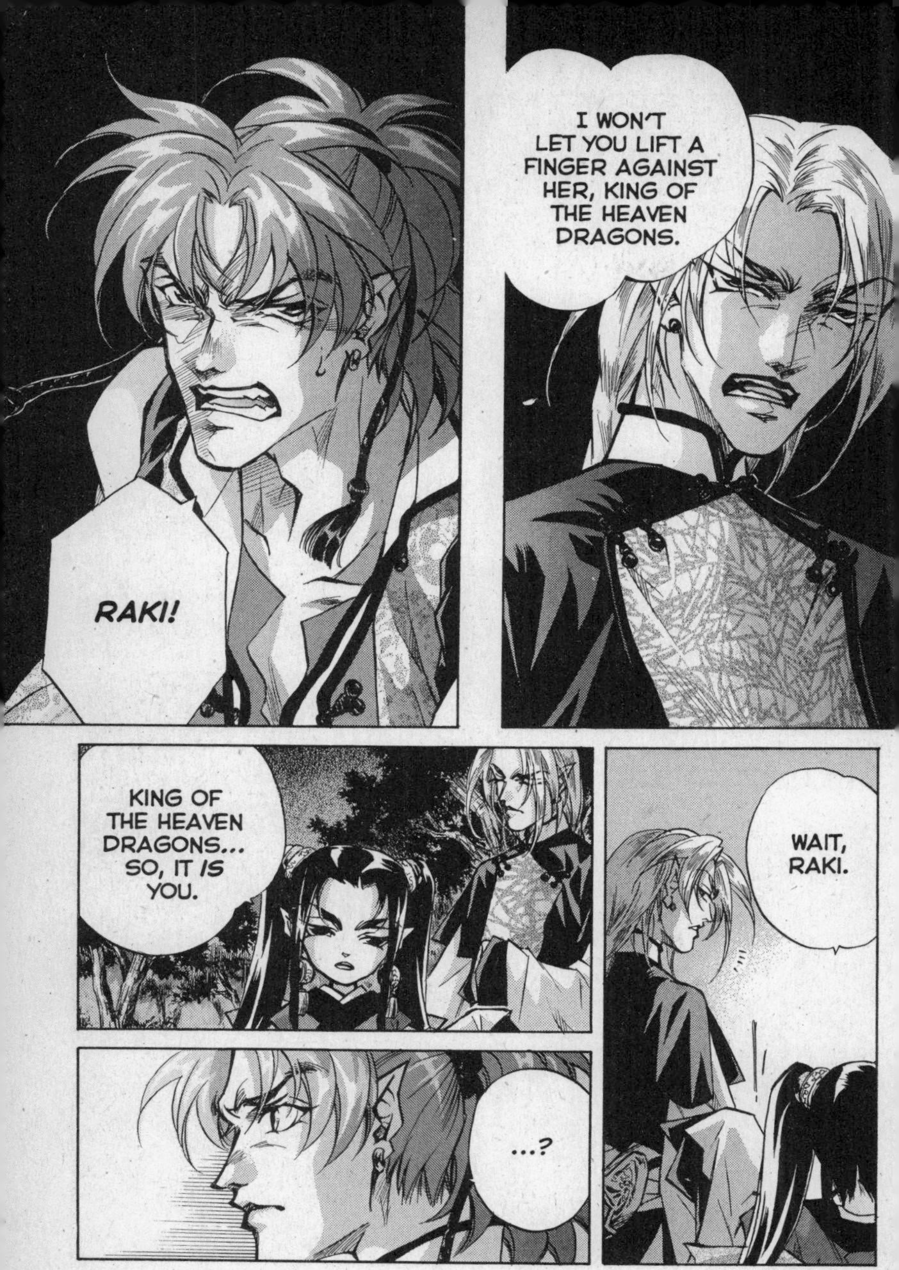
I WON'T LET YOU LIFT A FINGER AGAINST HER, KING OF THE HEAVEN DRAGONS.
RAKI!
WAIT, RAKI.
KING OF THE HEAVEN DRAGONS... SO, IT *IS* YOU.
...?

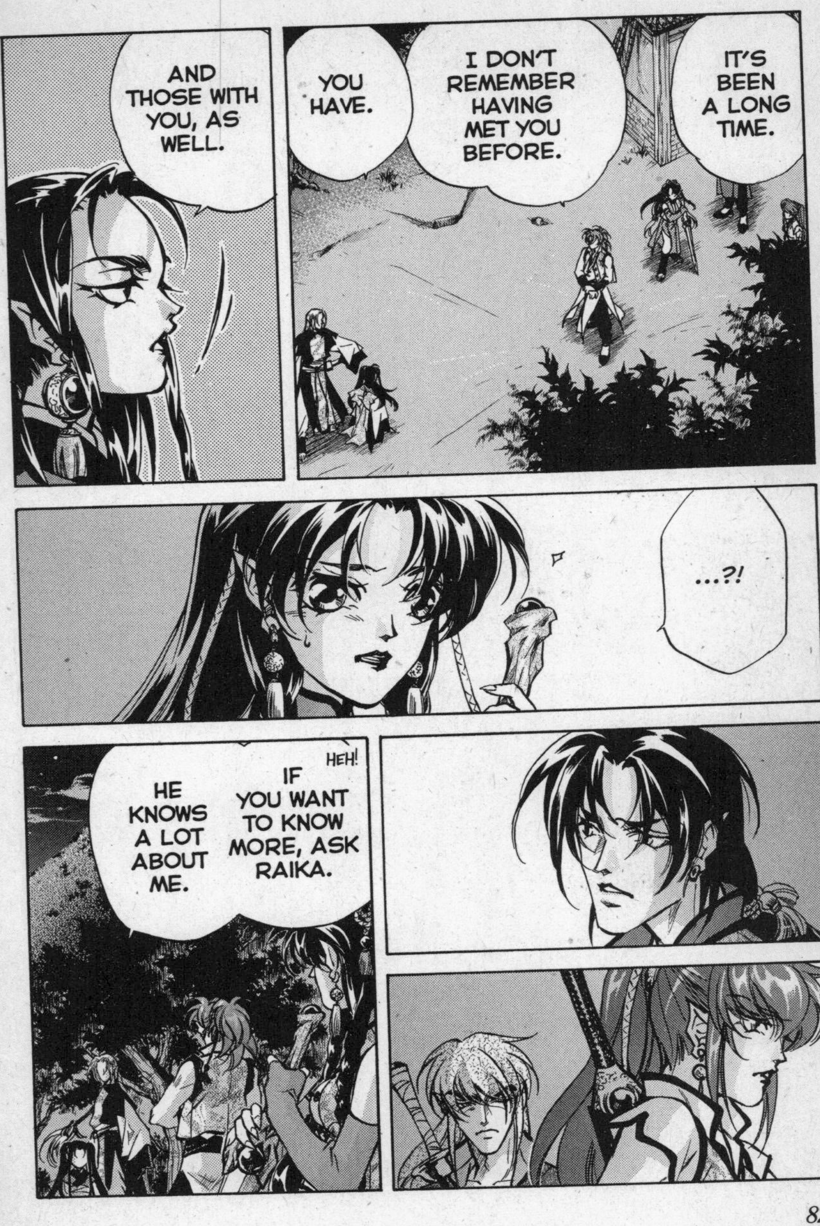
IT'S BEEN A LONG TIME.
I DON'T REMEMBER HAVING MET YOU BEFORE.
YOU HAVE.
AND THOSE WITH YOU, AS WELL.
...?!
HEH!
IF YOU WANT TO KNOW MORE, ASK RAIKA.
HE KNOWS A LOT ABOUT ME.

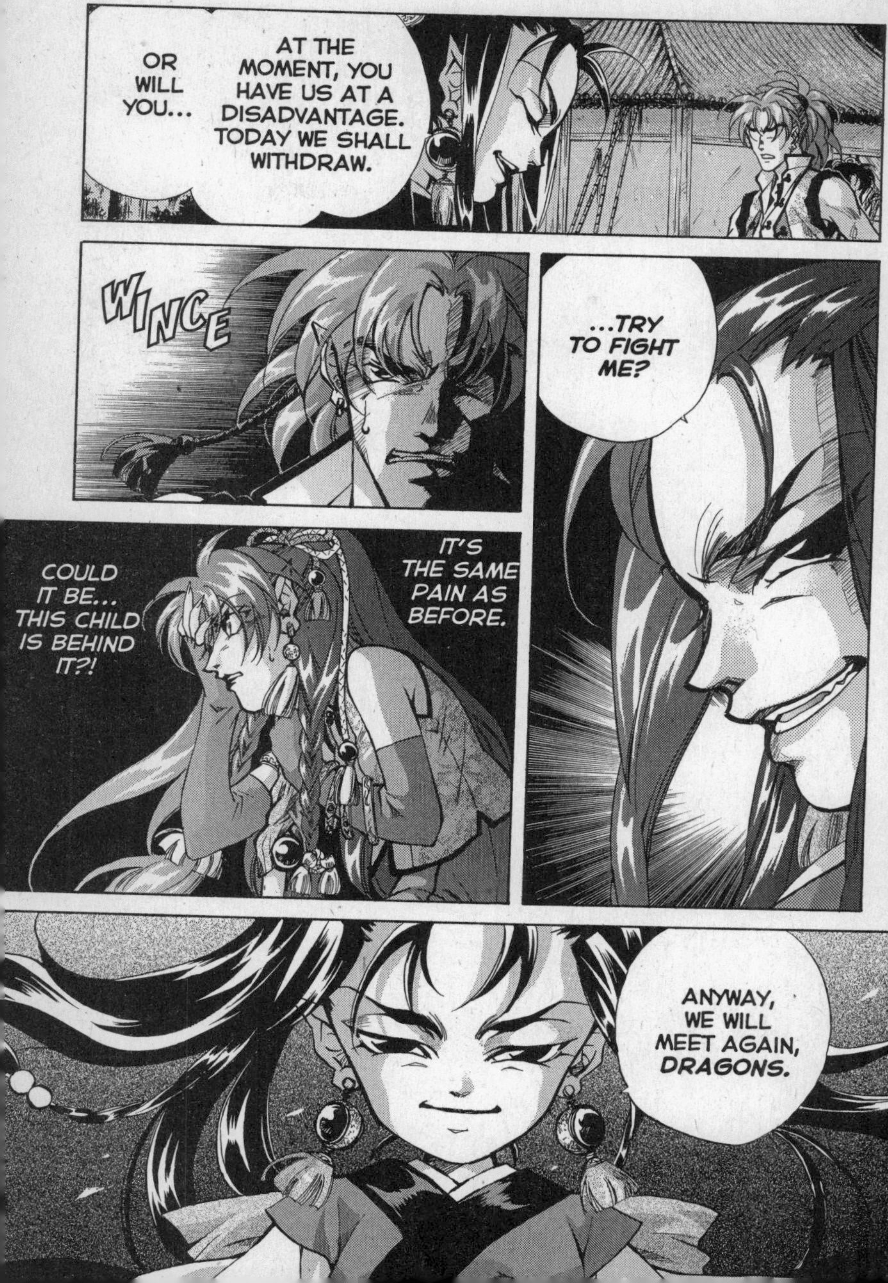
AT THE MOMENT, YOU HAVE US AT A DISADVANTAGE. TODAY WE SHALL WITHDRAW.
OR WILL YOU...
...TRY TO FIGHT ME?
WINCE
IT'S THE SAME PAIN AS BEFORE.
COULD IT BE... THIS CHILD IS BEHIND IT?!
ANYWAY, WE WILL MEET AGAIN, DRAGONS.

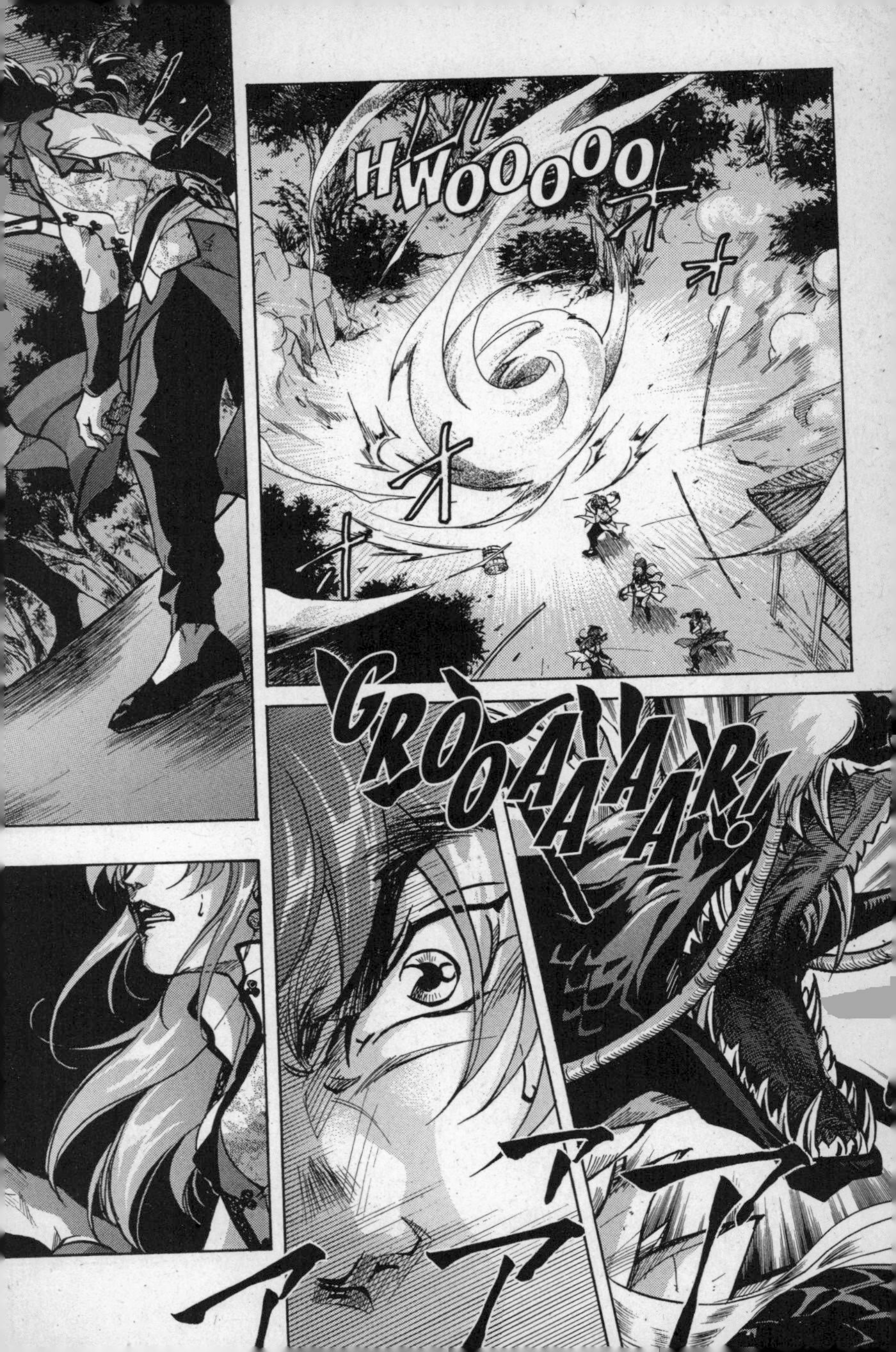
HWOOOOO
オオオオ
GROOAAAAR!
アアアアア

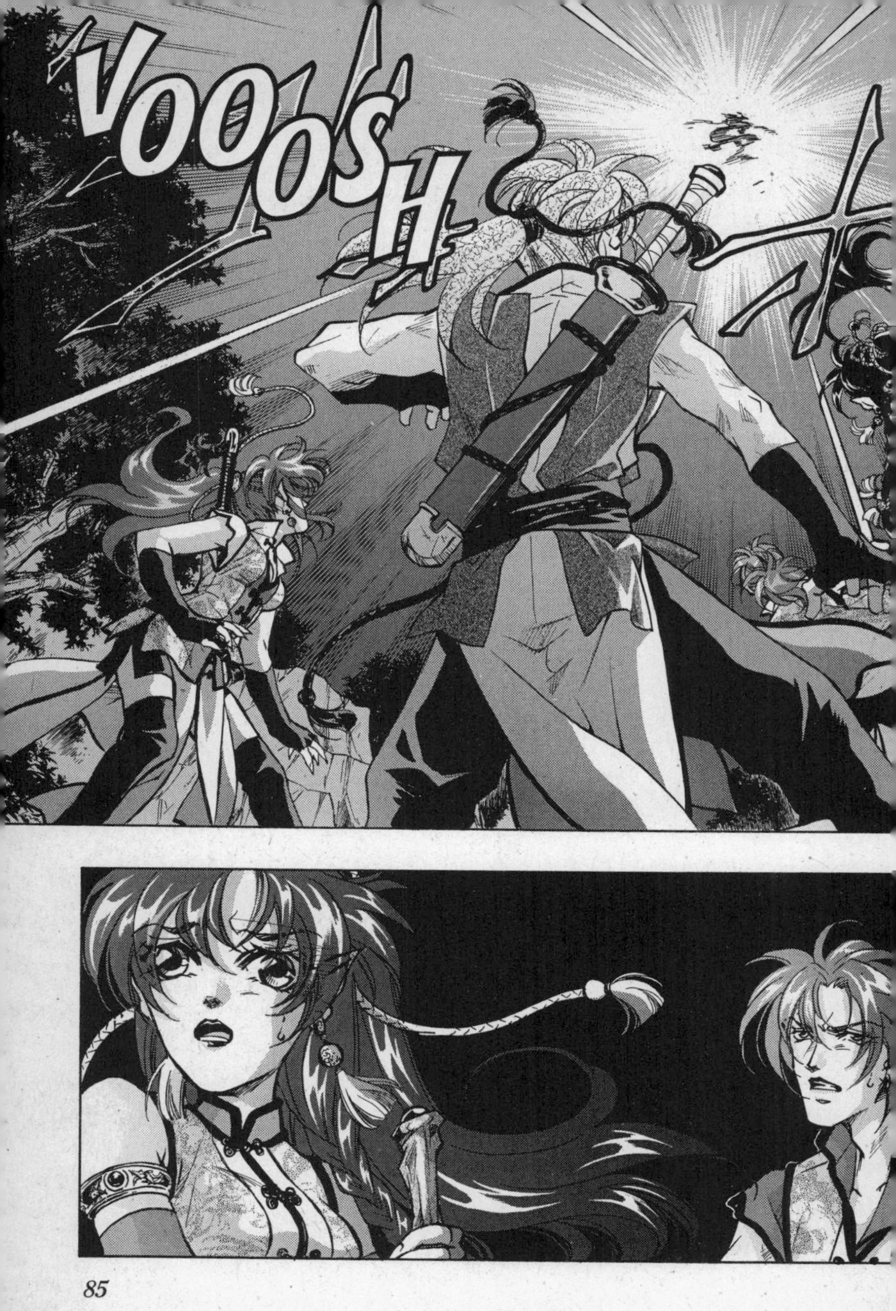
VOOOSH

A DIS-ADVANTAGE, THEY SAID? I DON'T SEE HOW.

THAT SON OF A--!

CLENCH

. . . . .

IT WON'T STOP...

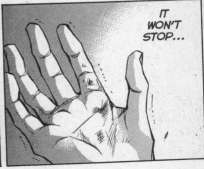

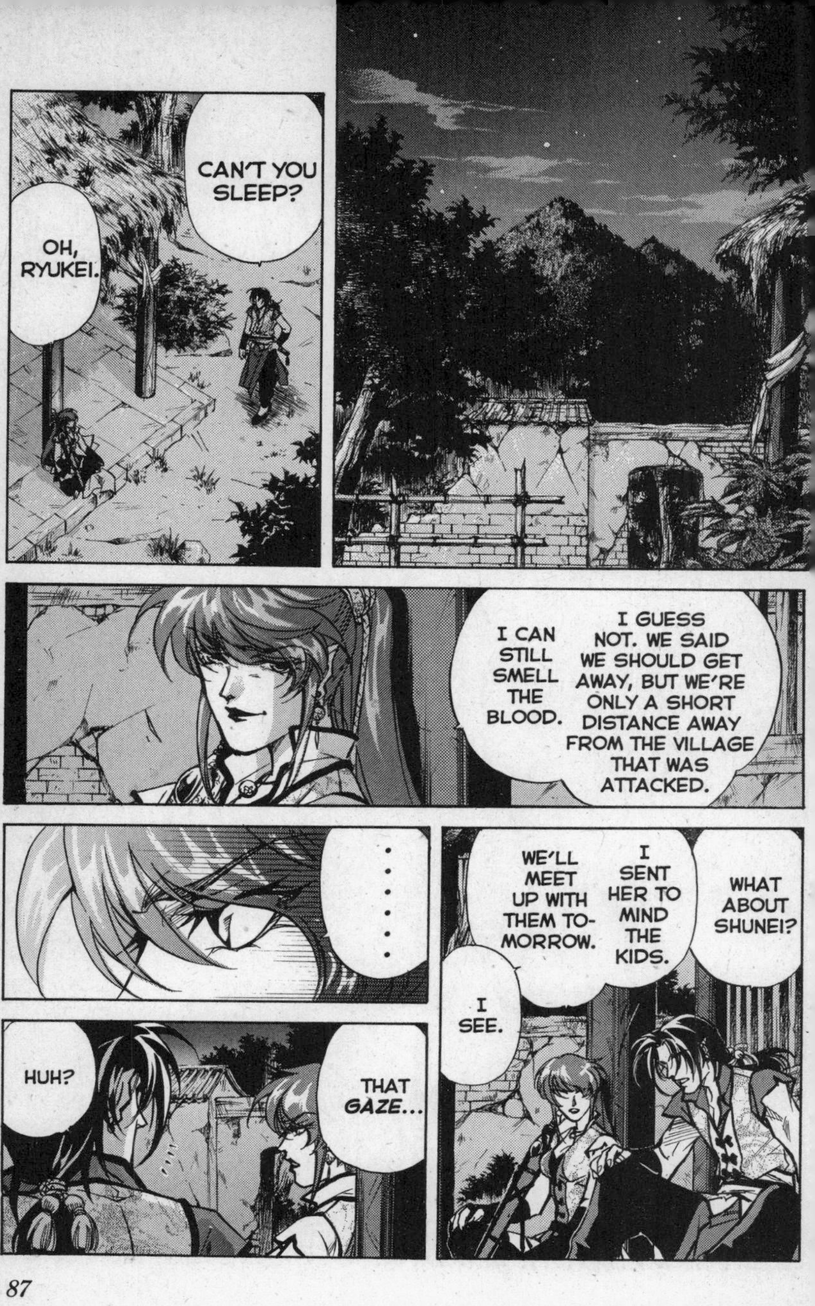
CAN'T YOU SLEEP?
OH, RYUKEI.
I GUESS NOT. WE SAID WE SHOULD GET AWAY, BUT WE'RE ONLY A SHORT DISTANCE AWAY FROM THE VILLAGE THAT WAS ATTACKED.
I CAN STILL SMELL THE BLOOD.
WHAT ABOUT SHUNEI?
I SENT HER TO MIND THE KIDS.
WE'LL MEET UP WITH THEM TO-MORROW.
I SEE.
......
THAT *GAZE*...
HUH?

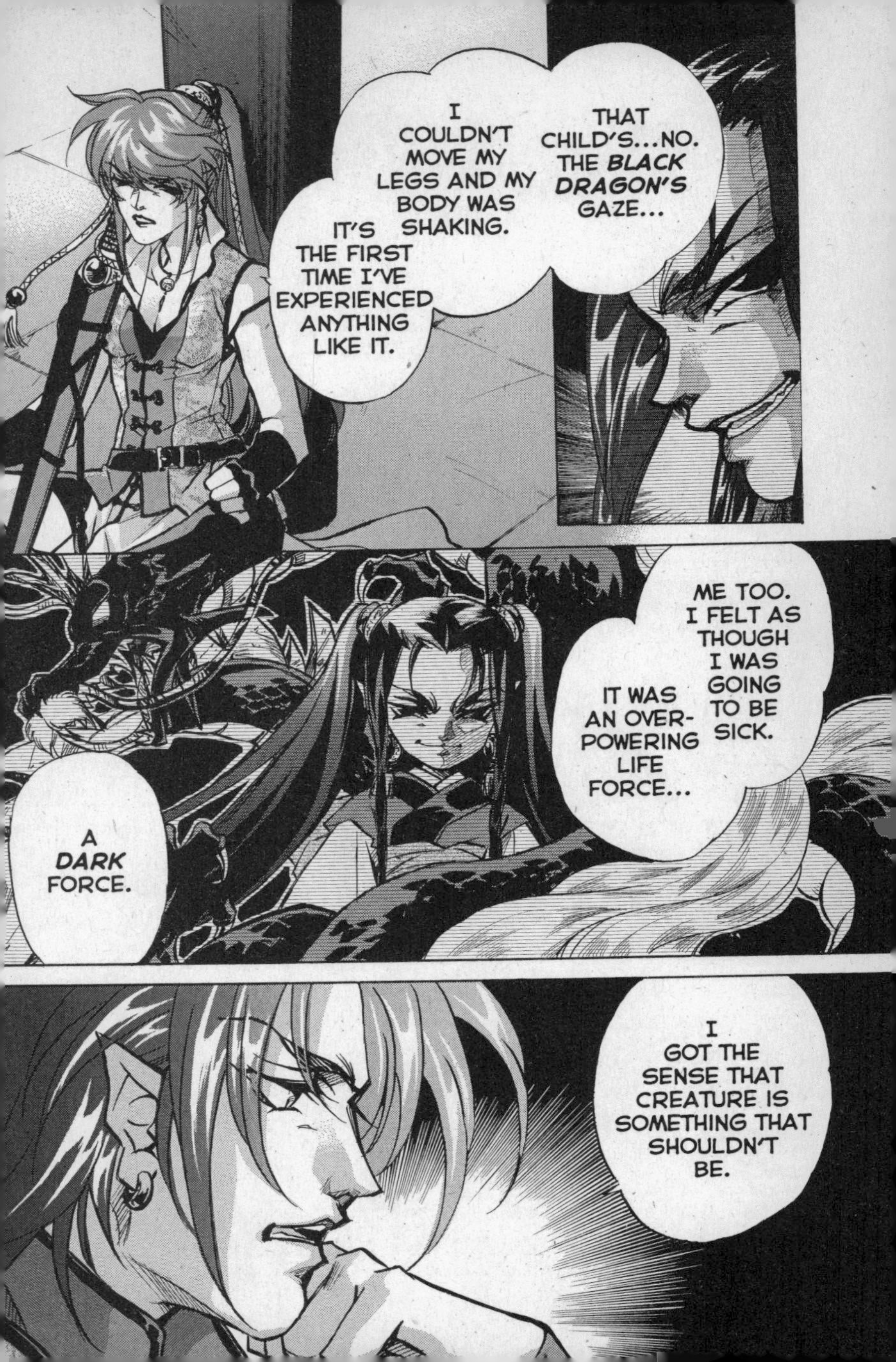
THAT CHILD'S...NO. THE *BLACK DRAGON'S* GAZE...
I COULDN'T MOVE MY LEGS AND MY BODY WAS SHAKING.
IT'S THE FIRST TIME I'VE EXPERIENCED ANYTHING LIKE IT.
ME TOO. I FELT AS THOUGH I WAS GOING TO BE SICK.
IT WAS AN OVER-POWERING LIFE FORCE...
A *DARK* FORCE.
I GOT THE SENSE THAT CREATURE IS SOMETHING THAT SHOULDN'T BE.

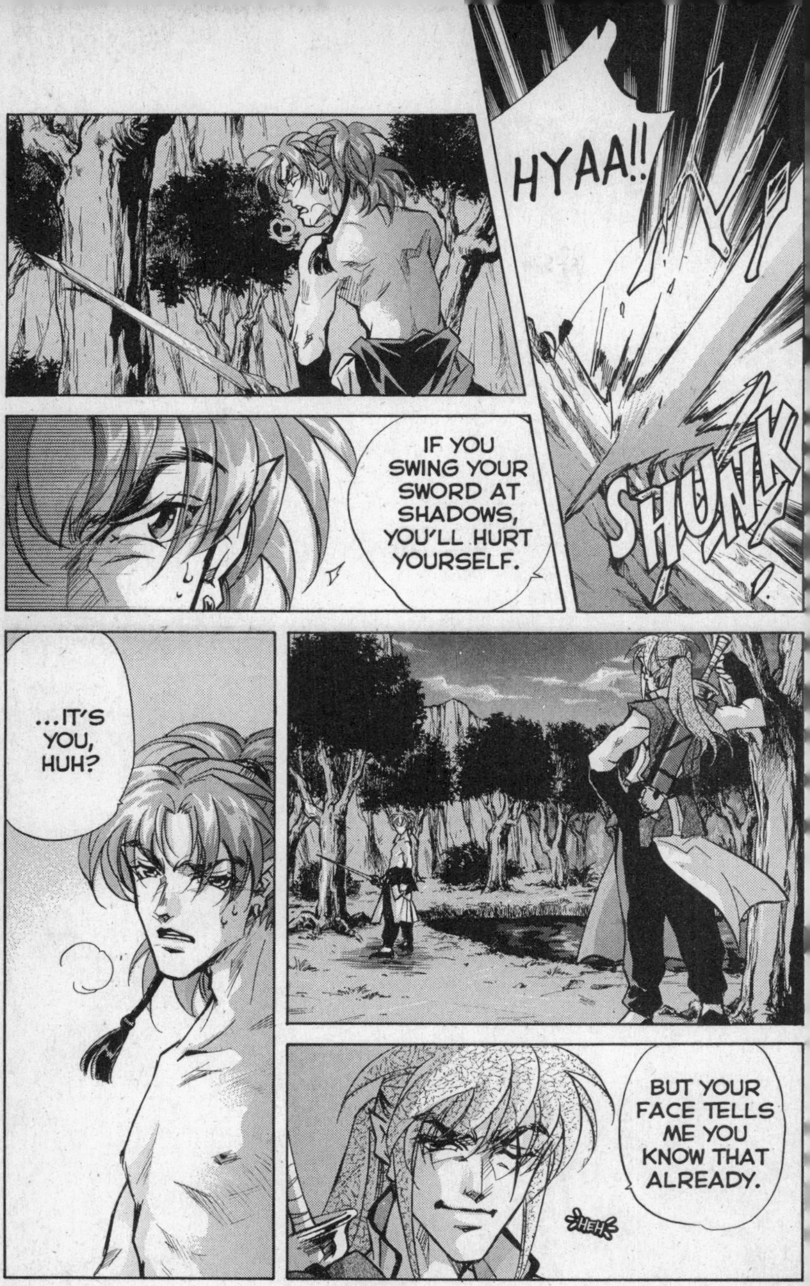
HYAA!!
SHUNK
IF YOU SWING YOUR SWORD AT SHADOWS, YOU'LL HURT YOURSELF.
BUT YOUR FACE TELLS ME YOU KNOW THAT ALREADY.
HEH
...IT'S YOU, HUH?

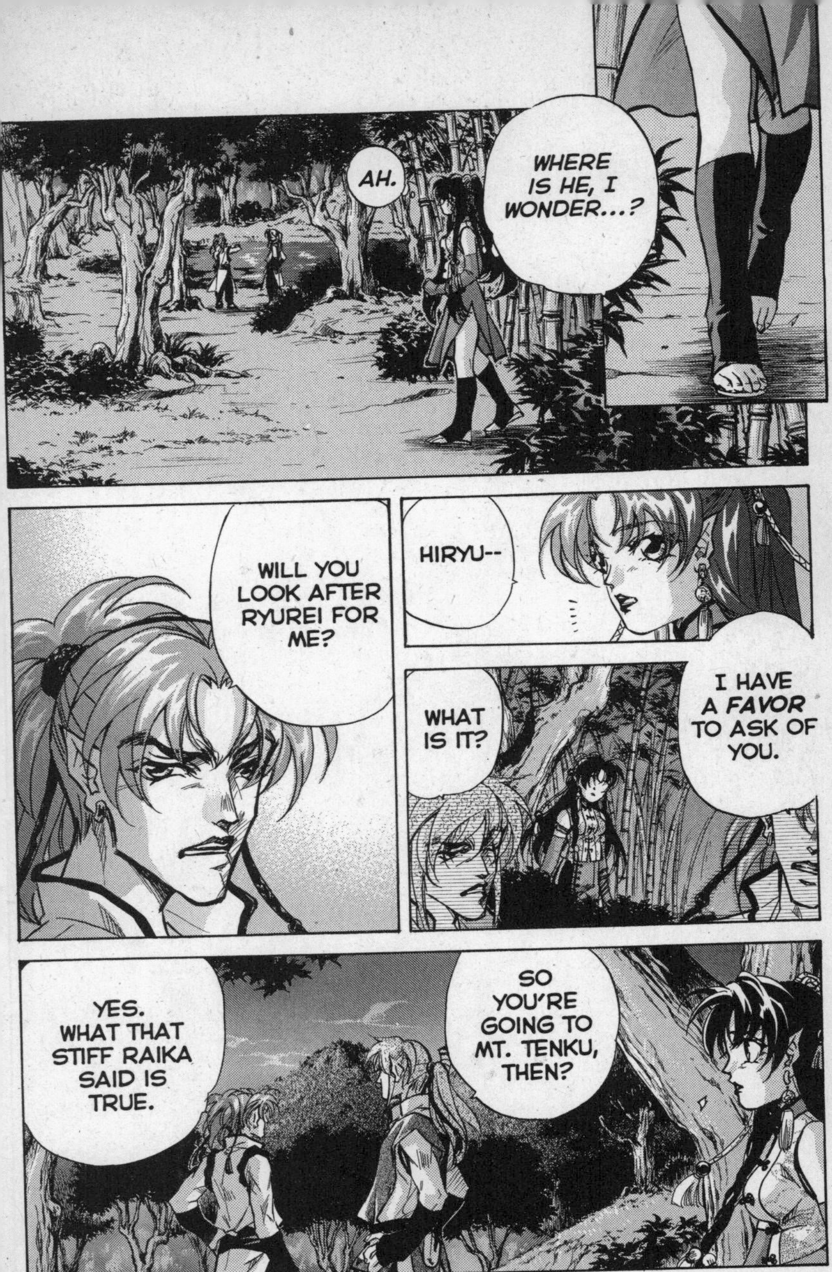
WHERE IS HE, I WONDER...?
AH.
HIRYU--
I HAVE A *FAVOR* TO ASK OF YOU.
WHAT IS IT?
WILL YOU LOOK AFTER RYUREI FOR ME?
SO YOU'RE GOING TO MT. TENKU, THEN?
YES. WHAT THAT STIFF RAIKA SAID IS TRUE.

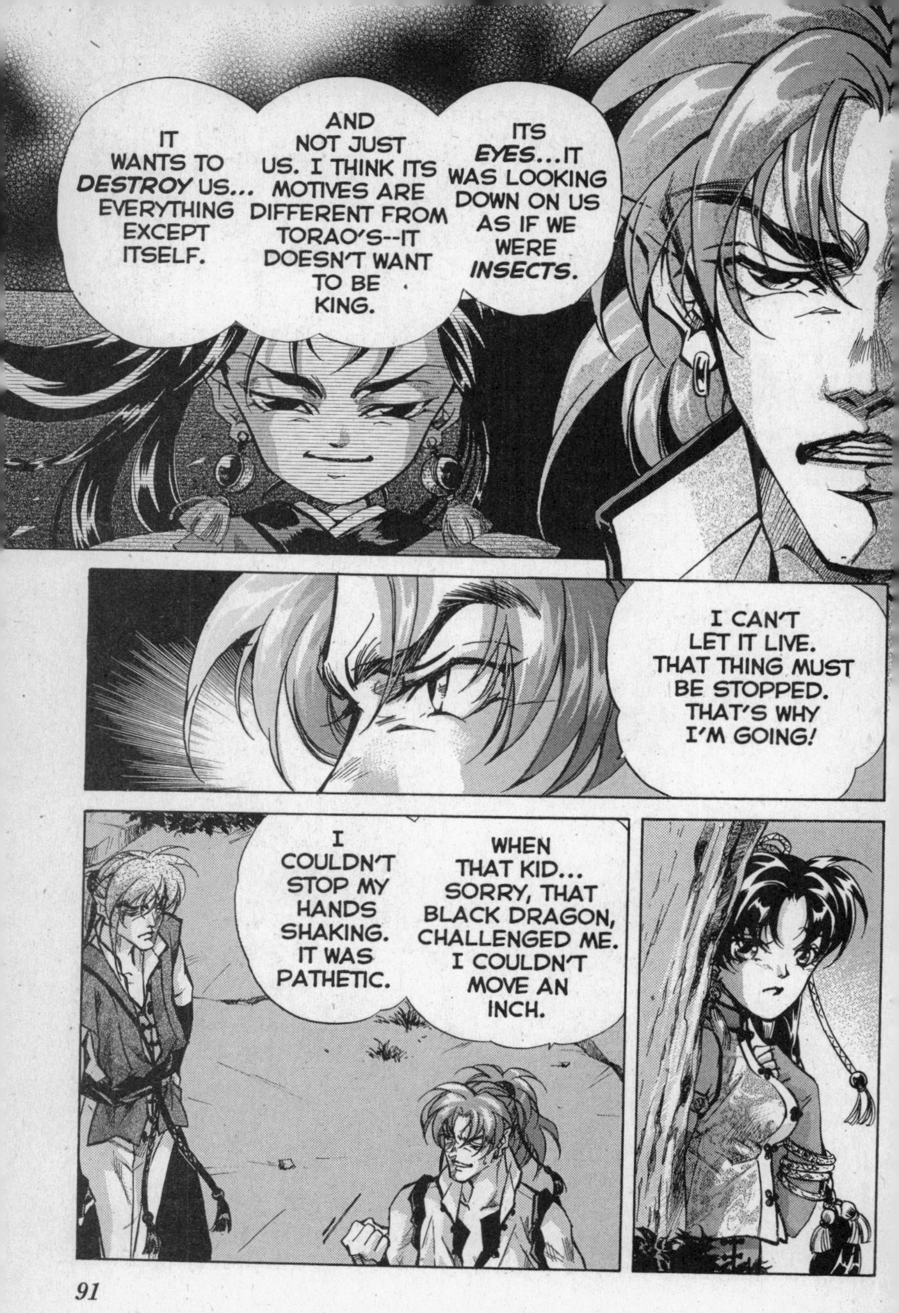
ITS EYES...IT WAS LOOKING DOWN ON US AS IF WE WERE INSECTS.
AND NOT JUST US. I THINK ITS MOTIVES ARE DIFFERENT FROM TORAO'S--IT DOESN'T WANT TO BE KING.
IT WANTS TO DESTROY US... EVERYTHING EXCEPT ITSELF.
I CAN'T LET IT LIVE. THAT THING MUST BE STOPPED. THAT'S WHY I'M GOING!
WHEN THAT KID... SORRY, THAT BLACK DRAGON, CHALLENGED ME. I COULDN'T MOVE AN INCH.
I COULDN'T STOP MY HANDS SHAKING. IT WAS PATHETIC.

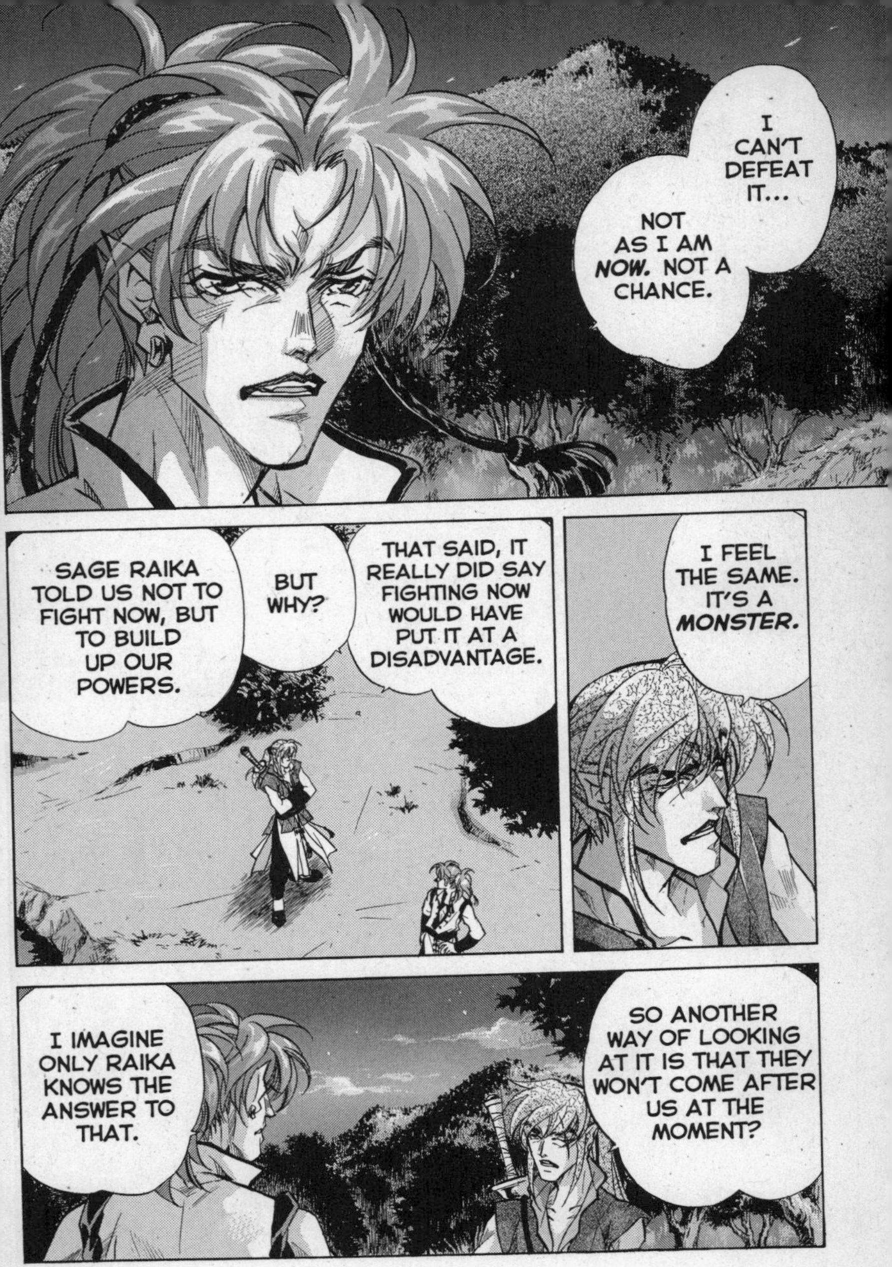
I CAN'T DEFEAT IT...
NOT AS I AM *NOW.* NOT A CHANCE.
I FEEL THE SAME. IT'S A *MONSTER.*
THAT SAID, IT REALLY DID SAY FIGHTING NOW WOULD HAVE PUT IT AT A DISADVANTAGE.
BUT WHY?
SAGE RAIKA TOLD US NOT TO FIGHT NOW, BUT TO BUILD UP OUR POWERS.
SO ANOTHER WAY OF LOOKING AT IT IS THAT THEY WON'T COME AFTER US AT THE MOMENT?
I IMAGINE ONLY RAIKA KNOWS THE ANSWER TO THAT.

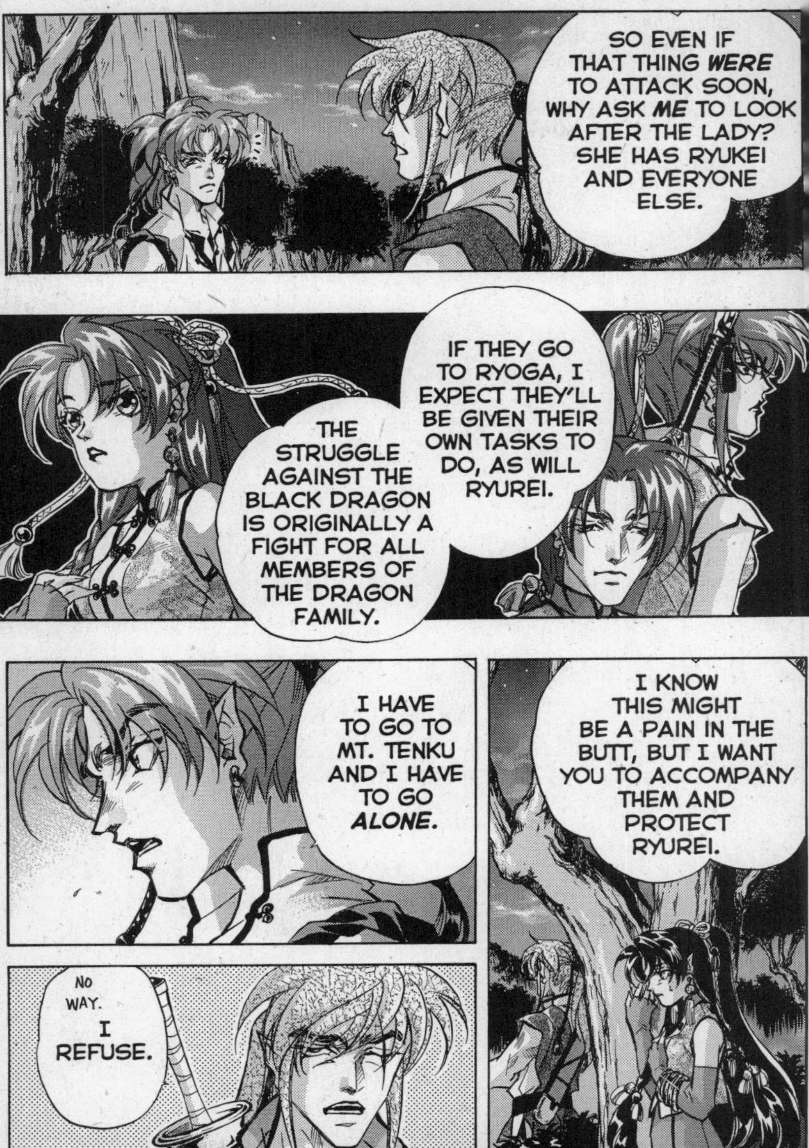
SO EVEN IF THAT THING *WERE* TO ATTACK SOON, WHY ASK *ME* TO LOOK AFTER THE LADY? SHE HAS RYUKEI AND EVERYONE ELSE.
IF THEY GO TO RYOGA, I EXPECT THEY'LL BE GIVEN THEIR OWN TASKS TO DO, AS WILL RYUREI.
THE STRUGGLE AGAINST THE BLACK DRAGON IS ORIGINALLY A FIGHT FOR ALL MEMBERS OF THE DRAGON FAMILY.
I KNOW THIS MIGHT BE A PAIN IN THE BUTT, BUT I WANT YOU TO ACCOMPANY THEM AND PROTECT RYUREI.
I HAVE TO GO TO MT. TENKU AND I HAVE TO GO *ALONE*.
NO WAY.
I REFUSE.

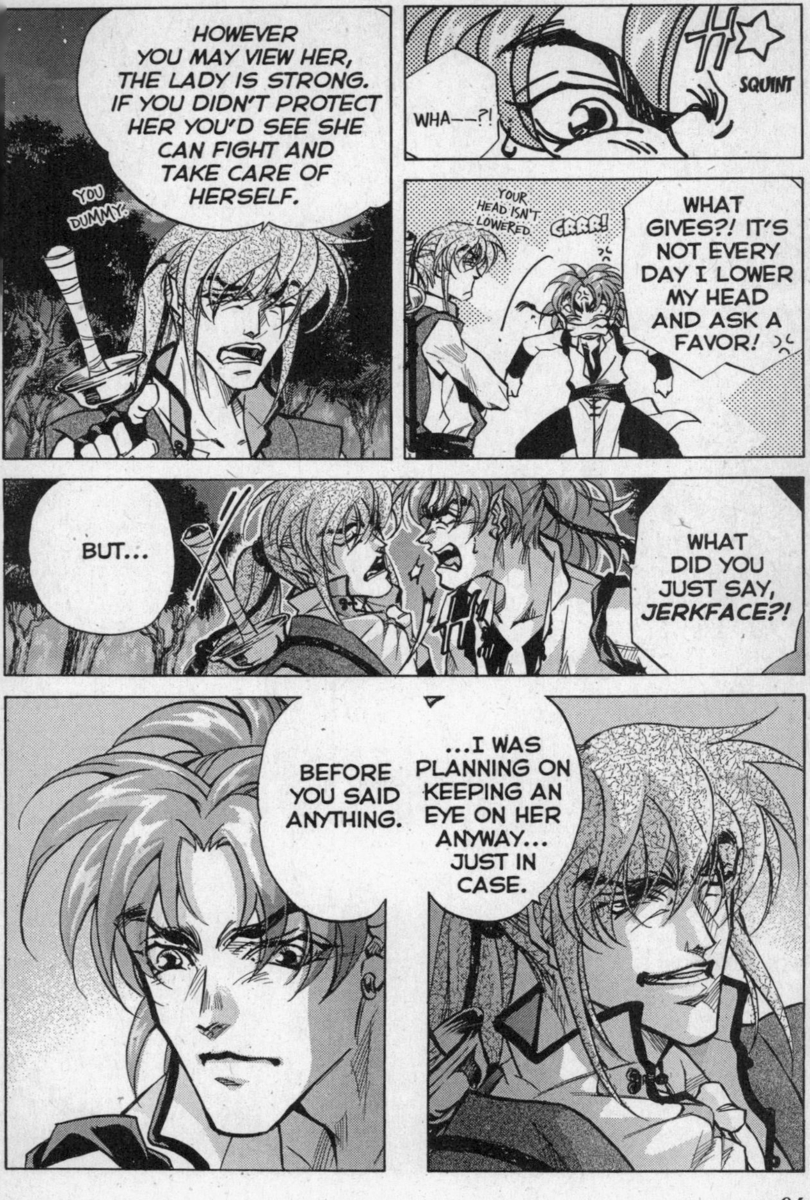
SQUINT
WHA--?!
WHAT GIVES?! IT'S NOT EVERY DAY I LOWER MY HEAD AND ASK A FAVOR!
GRRR!
YOUR HEAD ISN'T LOWERED.
HOWEVER YOU MAY VIEW HER, THE LADY IS STRONG. IF YOU DIDN'T PROTECT HER YOU'D SEE SHE CAN FIGHT AND TAKE CARE OF HERSELF.
YOU DUMMY.
WHAT DID YOU JUST SAY, *JERKFACE?!*
BUT...
...I WAS PLANNING ON KEEPING AN EYE ON HER ANYWAY... JUST IN CASE.
BEFORE YOU SAID ANYTHING.

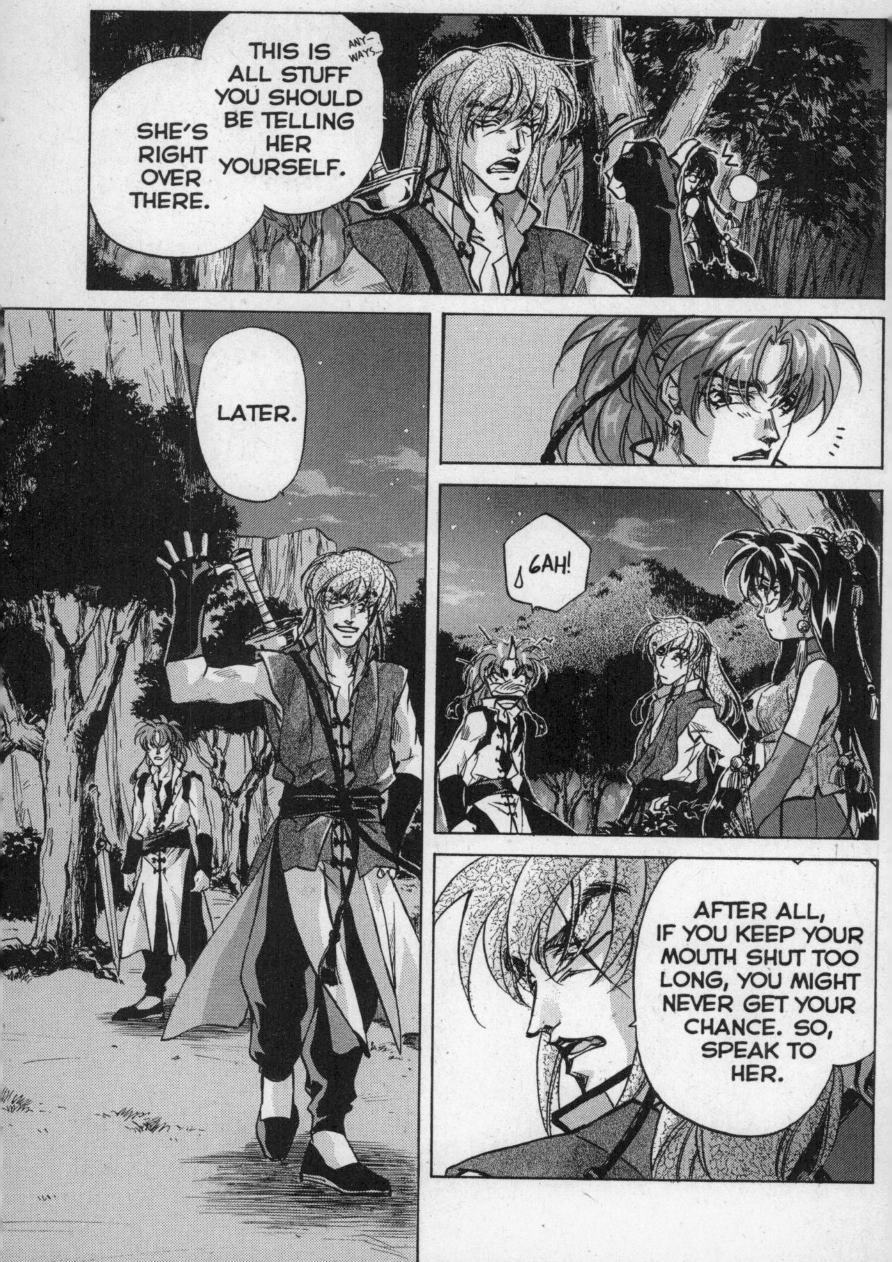
ANY-WAYS...
THIS IS ALL STUFF YOU SHOULD BE TELLING HER YOURSELF.
SHE'S RIGHT OVER THERE.
...
GAH!
AFTER ALL, IF YOU KEEP YOUR MOUTH SHUT TOO LONG, YOU MIGHT NEVER GET YOUR CHANCE. SO, SPEAK TO HER.
LATER.

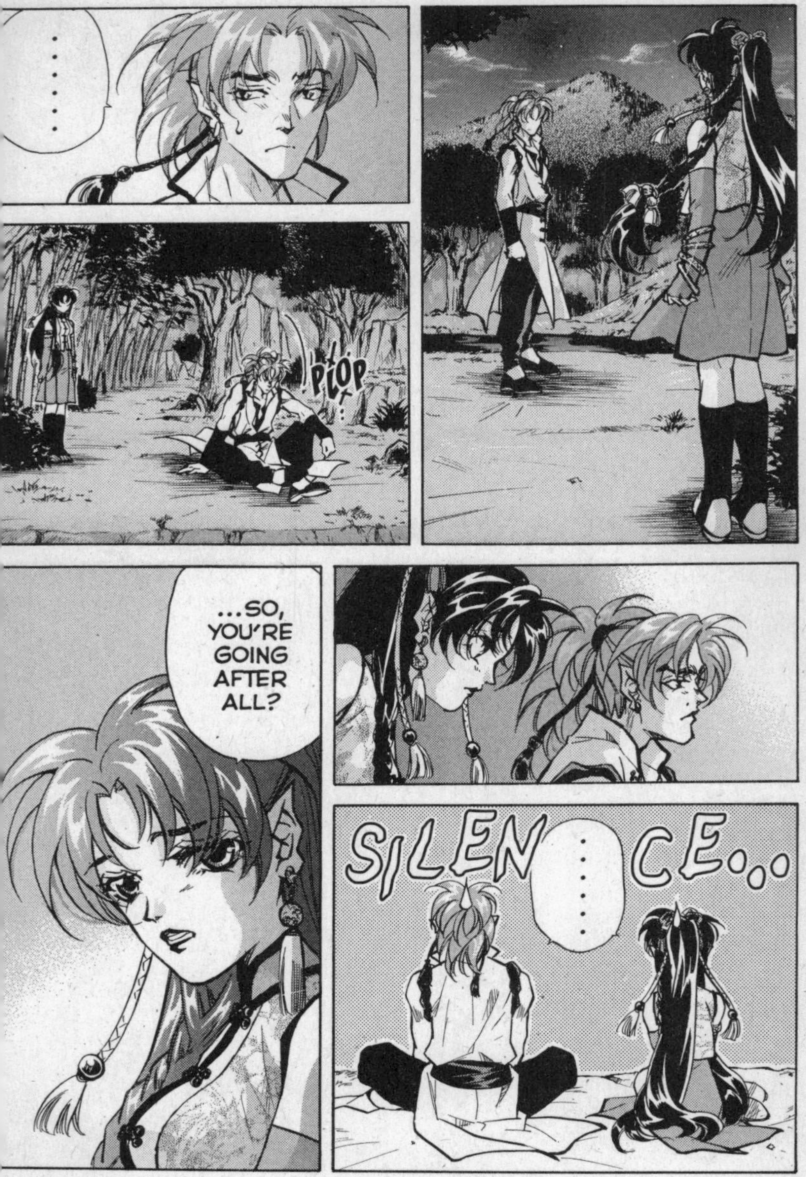
......
PLOP
SILENCE...
.....
...SO, YOU'RE GOING AFTER ALL?

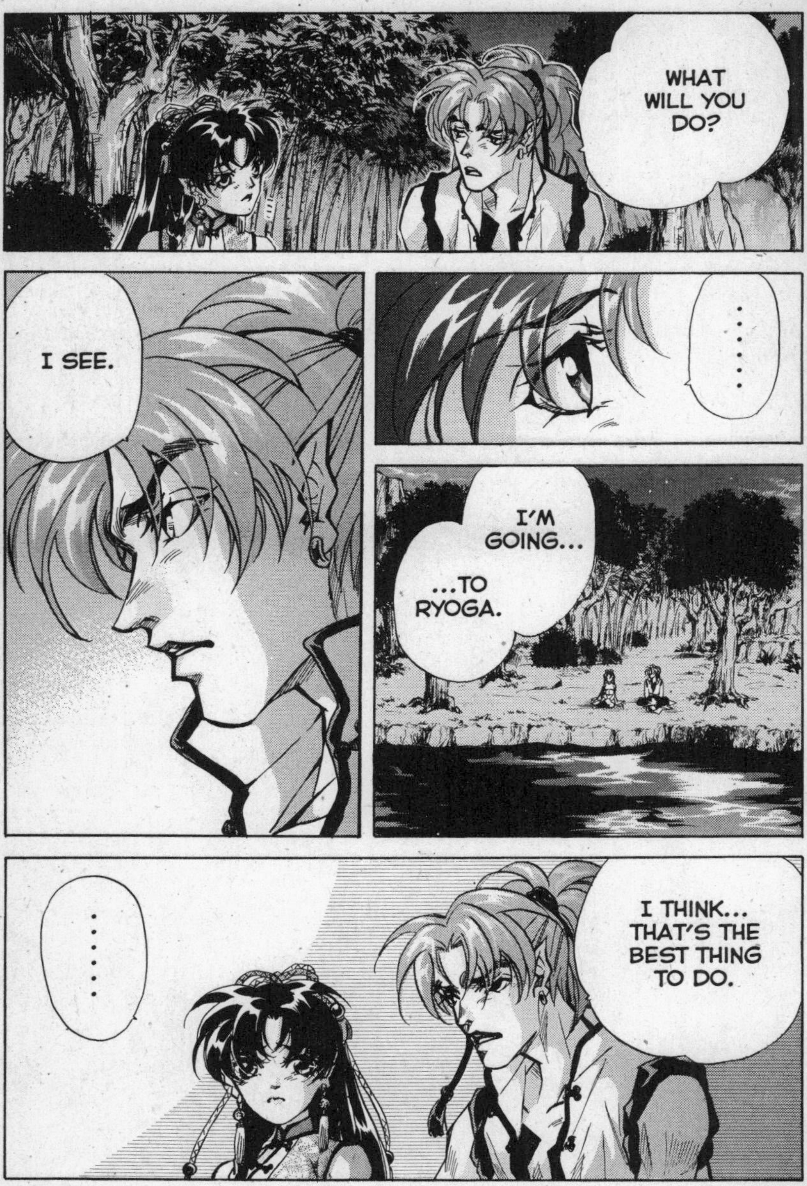
WHAT WILL YOU DO?
......
I'M GOING...
...TO RYOGA.
I SEE.
I THINK... THAT'S THE BEST THING TO DO.
......

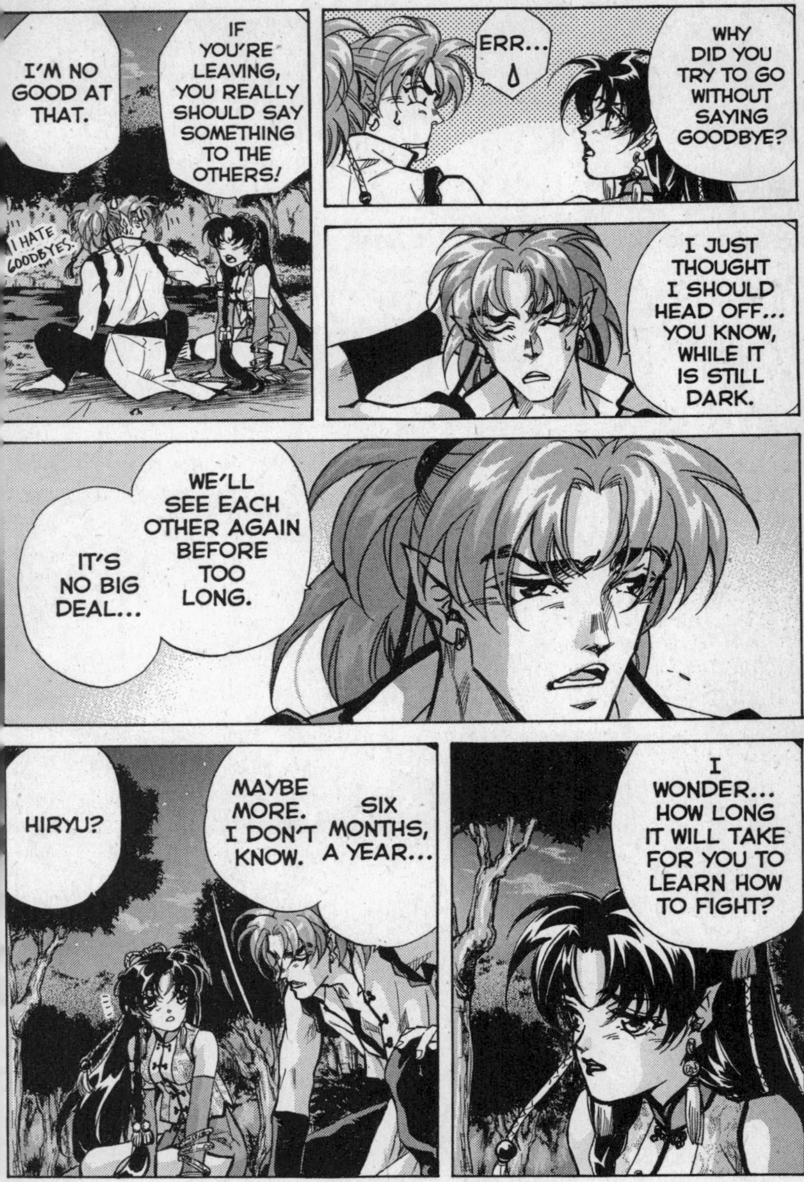
WHY DID YOU TRY TO GO WITHOUT SAYING GOODBYE?
ERR...
I JUST THOUGHT I SHOULD HEAD OFF... YOU KNOW, WHILE IT IS STILL DARK.
IF YOU'RE LEAVING, YOU REALLY SHOULD SAY SOMETHING TO THE OTHERS!
I'M NO GOOD AT THAT.
I HATE GOODBYES.
WE'LL SEE EACH OTHER AGAIN BEFORE TOO LONG.
IT'S NO BIG DEAL...
I WONDER... HOW LONG IT WILL TAKE FOR YOU TO LEARN HOW TO FIGHT?
SIX MONTHS, A YEAR...
MAYBE MORE. I DON'T KNOW.
HIRYU?

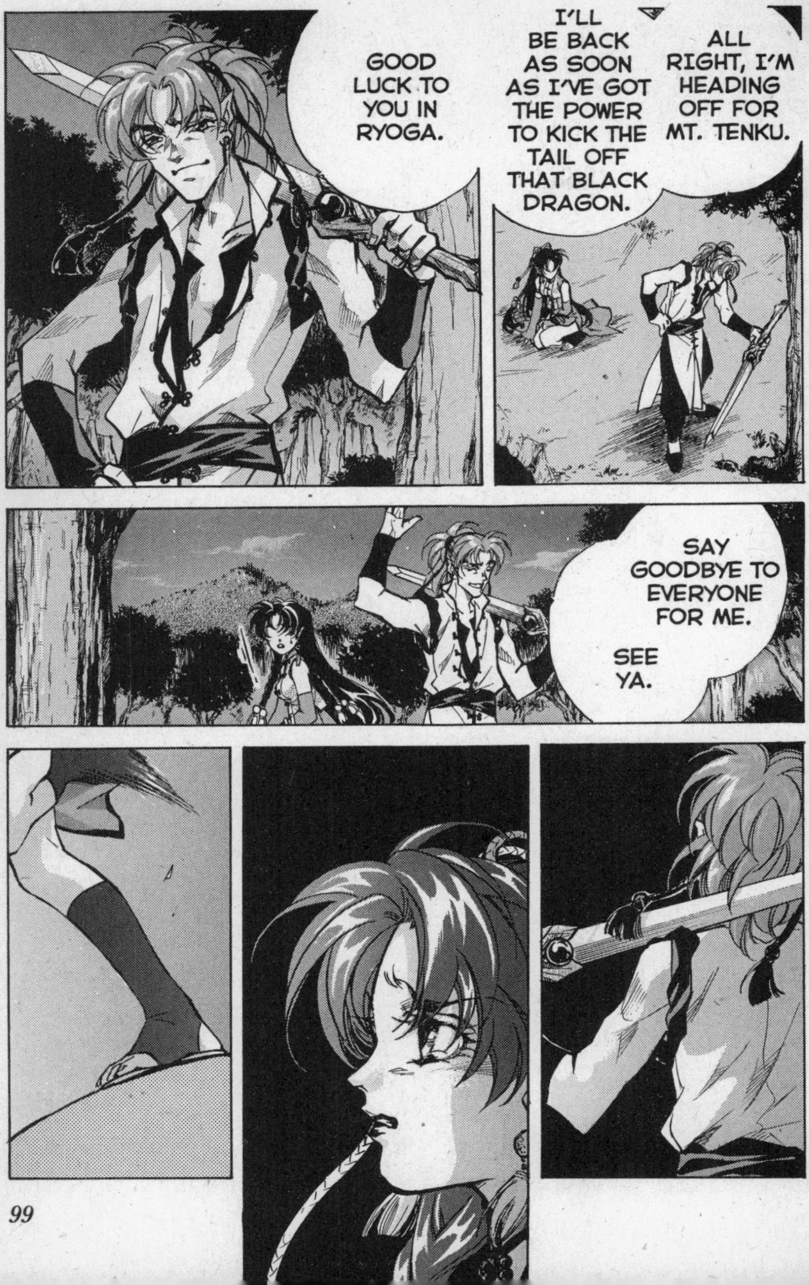
ALL RIGHT, I'M HEADING OFF FOR MT. TENKU.
I'LL BE BACK AS SOON AS I'VE GOT THE POWER TO KICK THE TAIL OFF THAT BLACK DRAGON.
GOOD LUCK TO YOU IN RYOGA.
SAY GOODBYE TO EVERYONE FOR ME.
SEE YA.

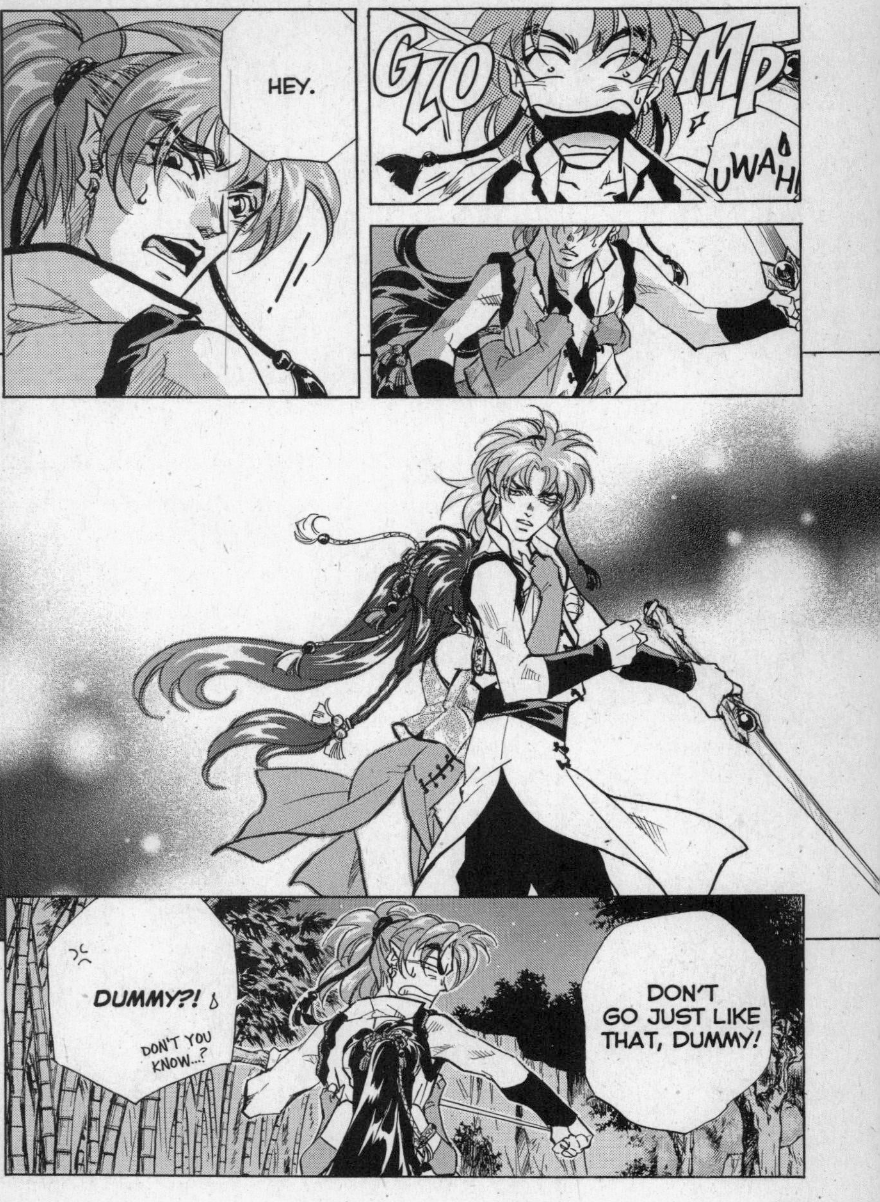
GZOMP
UWAH!
HEY.
DON'T GO JUST LIKE THAT, DUMMY!
DUMMY?!
DON'T YOU KNOW...?

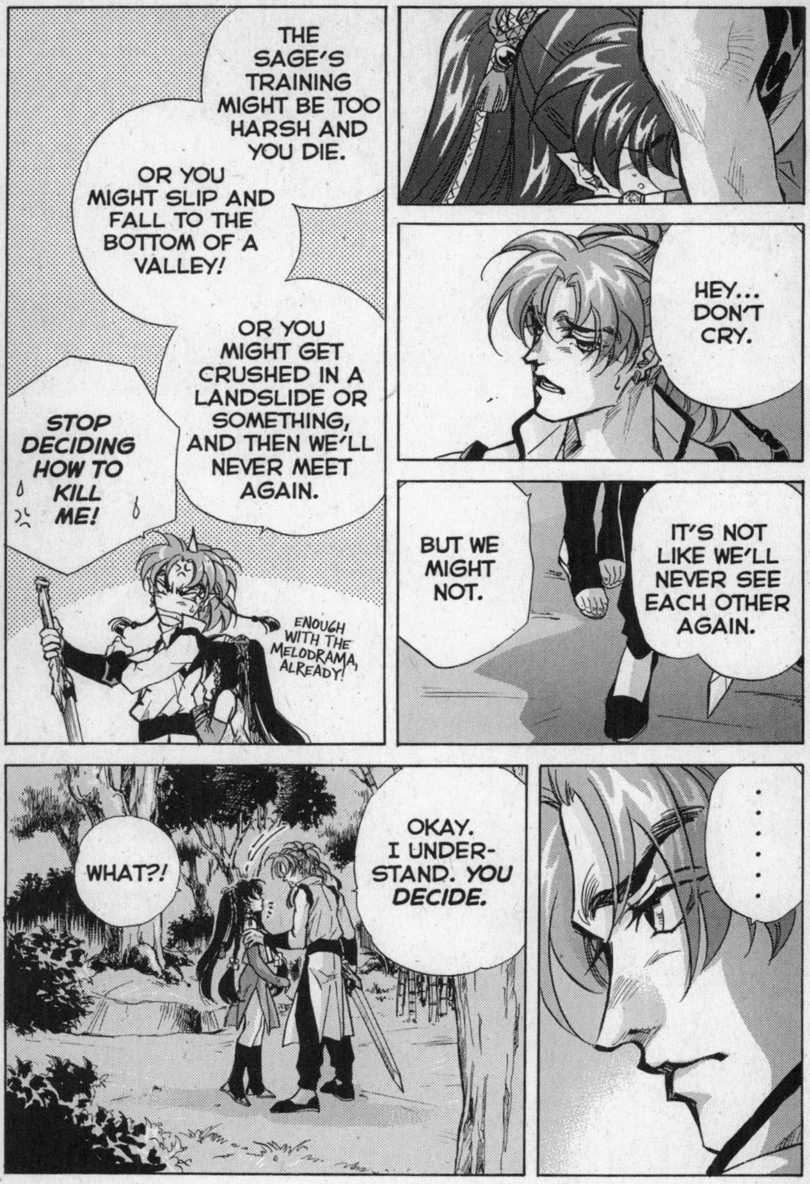
HEY... DON'T CRY.
IT'S NOT LIKE WE'LL NEVER SEE EACH OTHER AGAIN.
BUT WE MIGHT NOT.
THE SAGE'S TRAINING MIGHT BE TOO HARSH AND YOU DIE.
OR YOU MIGHT SLIP AND FALL TO THE BOTTOM OF A VALLEY!
OR YOU MIGHT GET CRUSHED IN A LANDSLIDE OR SOMETHING, AND THEN WE'LL NEVER MEET AGAIN.
STOP DECIDING HOW TO KILL ME!
ENOUGH WITH THE MELODRAMA, ALREADY!
......
OKAY. I UNDERSTAND. *YOU DECIDE.*
WHAT?!

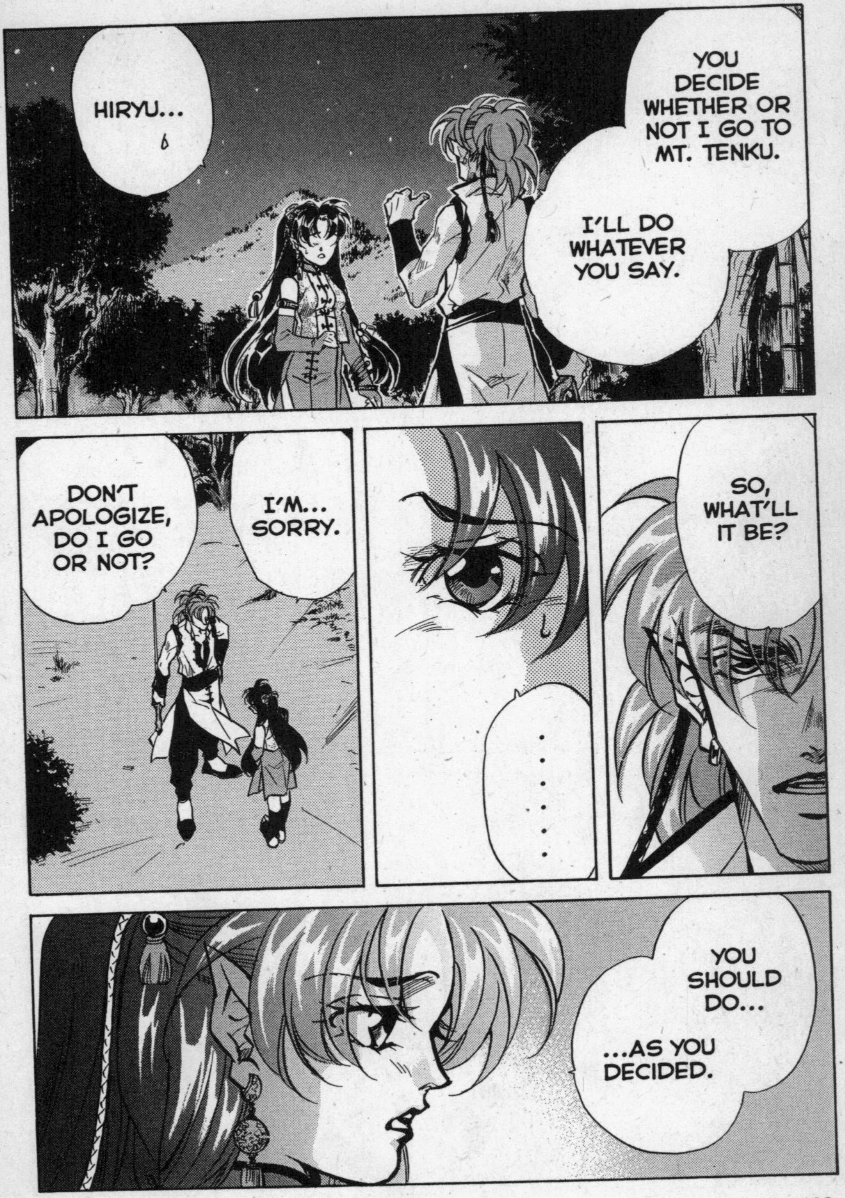
YOU DECIDE WHETHER OR NOT I GO TO MT. TENKU.
I'LL DO WHATEVER YOU SAY.
HIRYU...
SO, WHAT'LL IT BE?
......
I'M... SORRY.
DON'T APOLOGIZE, DO I GO OR NOT?
YOU SHOULD DO...
...AS YOU DECIDED.

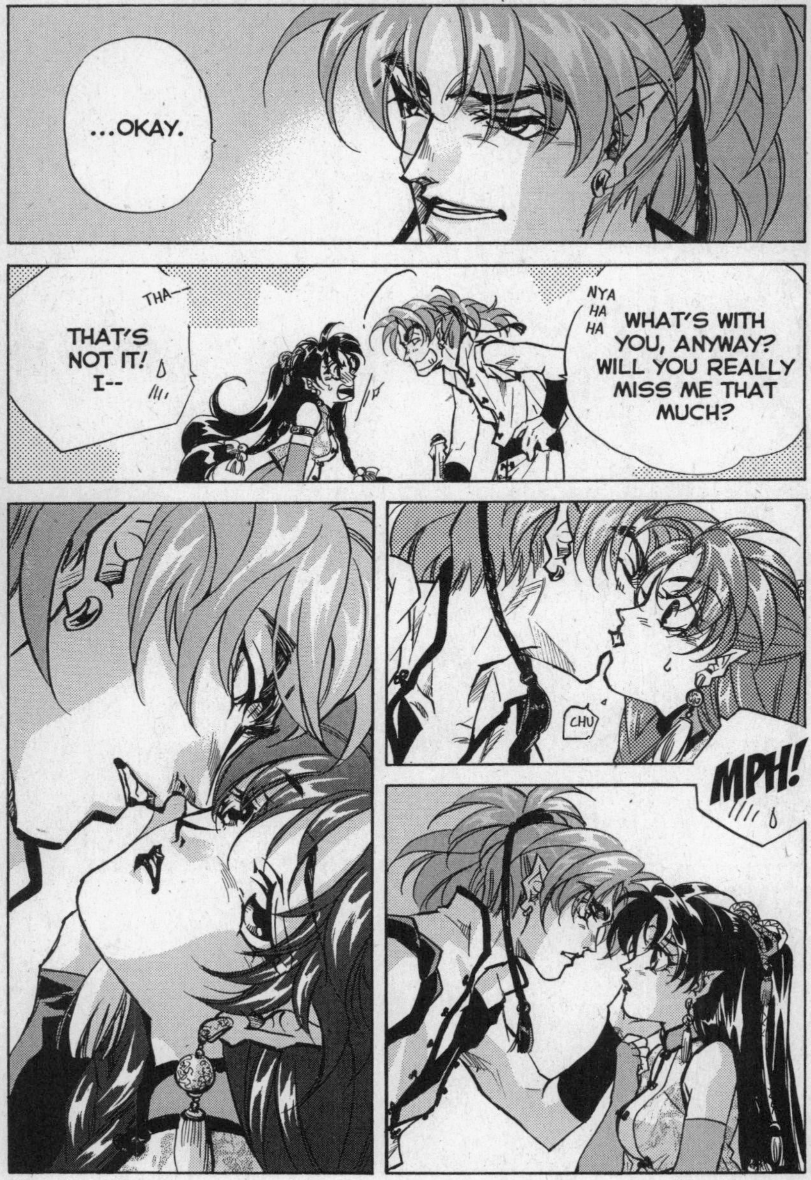
...OKAY.
NYA HA HA
WHAT'S WITH YOU, ANYWAY? WILL YOU REALLY MISS ME THAT MUCH?
THA--
THAT'S NOT IT! I--
CHU
MPH!

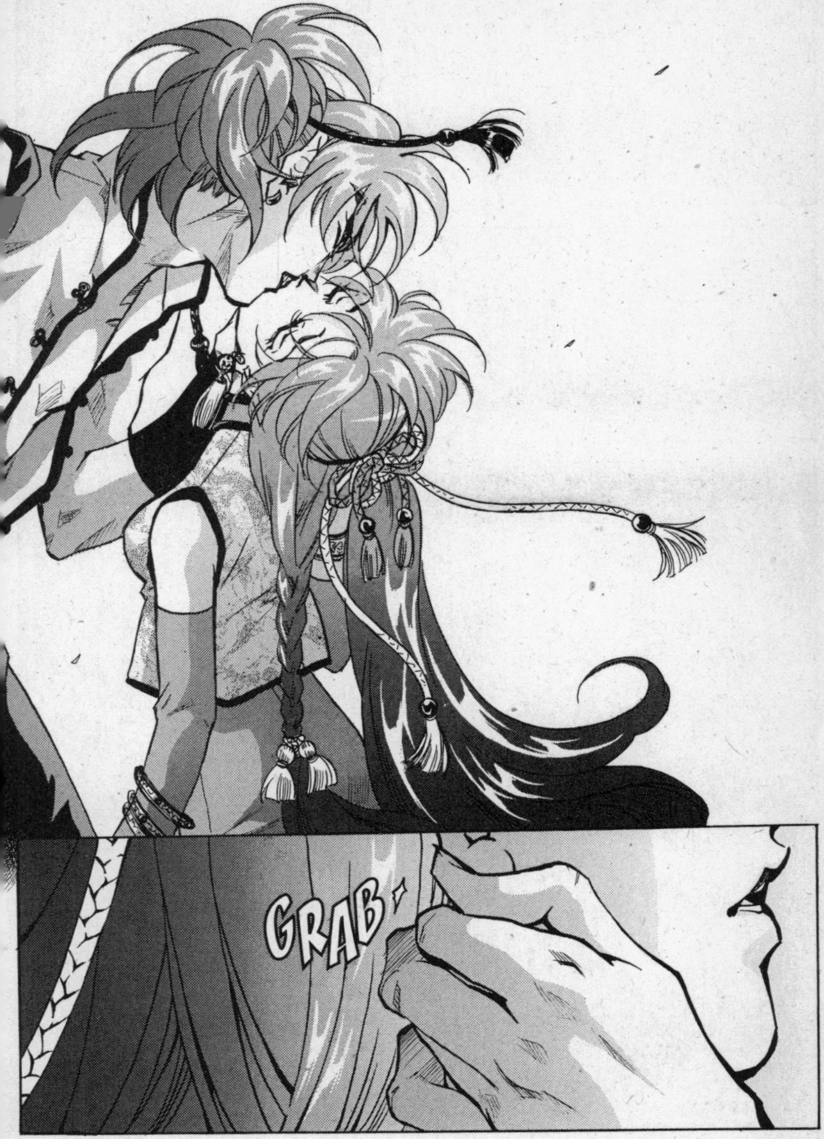
GRAB

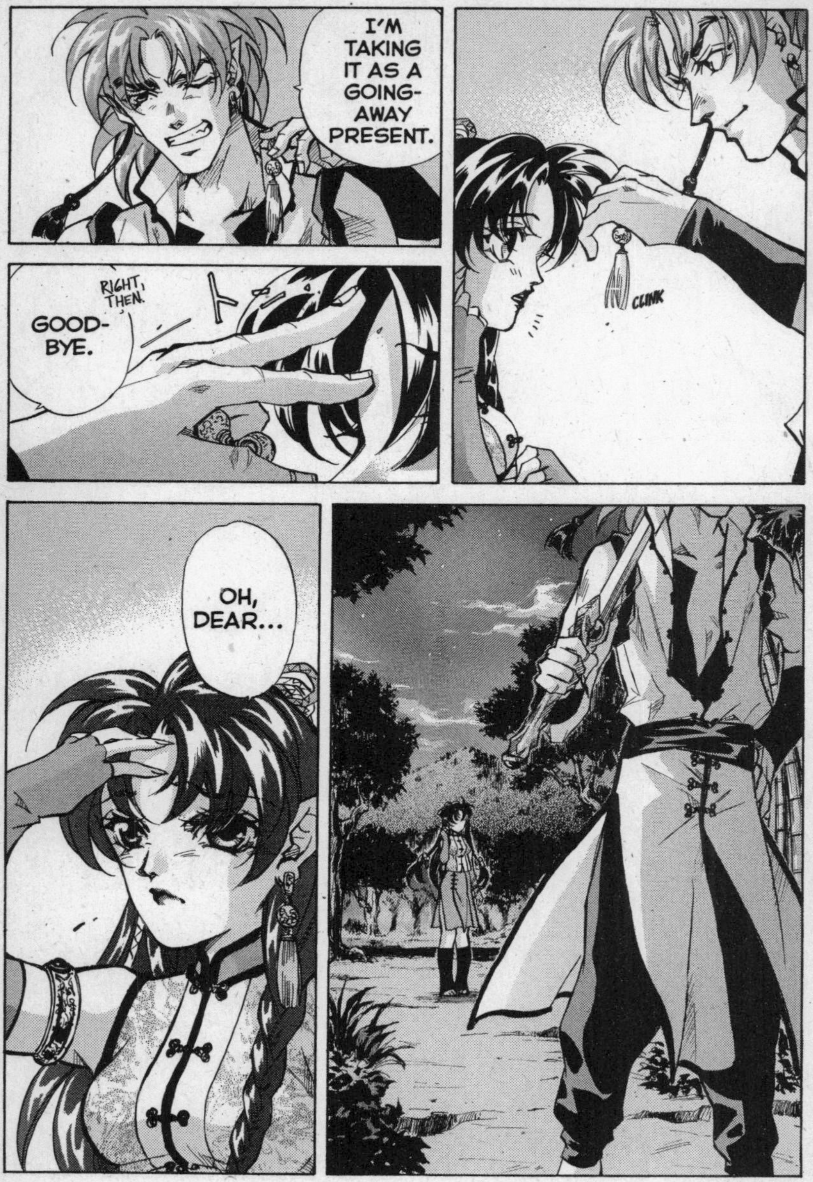
CLINK
I'M TAKING IT AS A GOING-AWAY PRESENT.
RIGHT, THEN.
GOOD-BYE.
OH, DEAR...

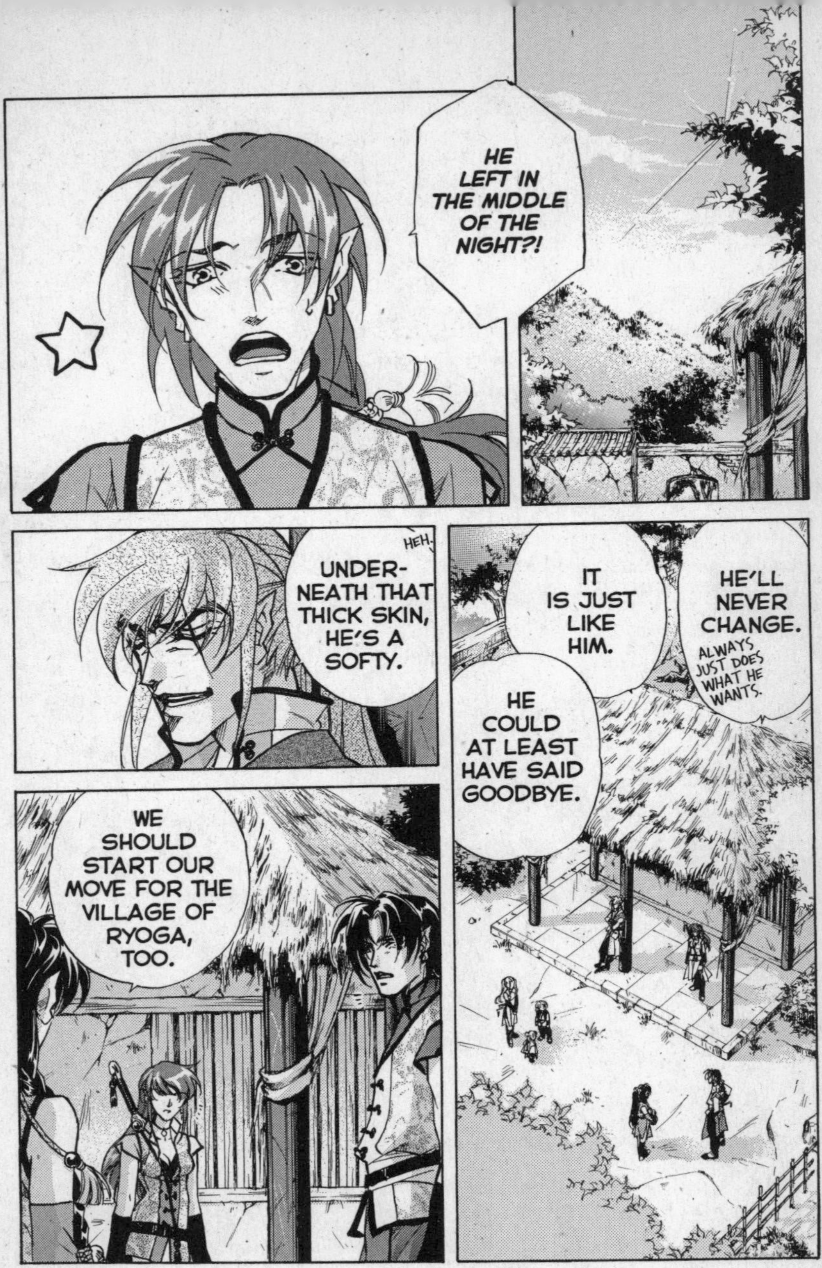
HE LEFT IN THE MIDDLE OF THE NIGHT?!
HE'LL NEVER CHANGE.
ALWAYS JUST DOES WHAT HE WANTS.
IT IS JUST LIKE HIM.
HE COULD AT LEAST HAVE SAID GOODBYE.
HEH.
UNDER-NEATH THAT THICK SKIN, HE'S A SOFTY.
WE SHOULD START OUR MOVE FOR THE VILLAGE OF RYOGA, TOO.

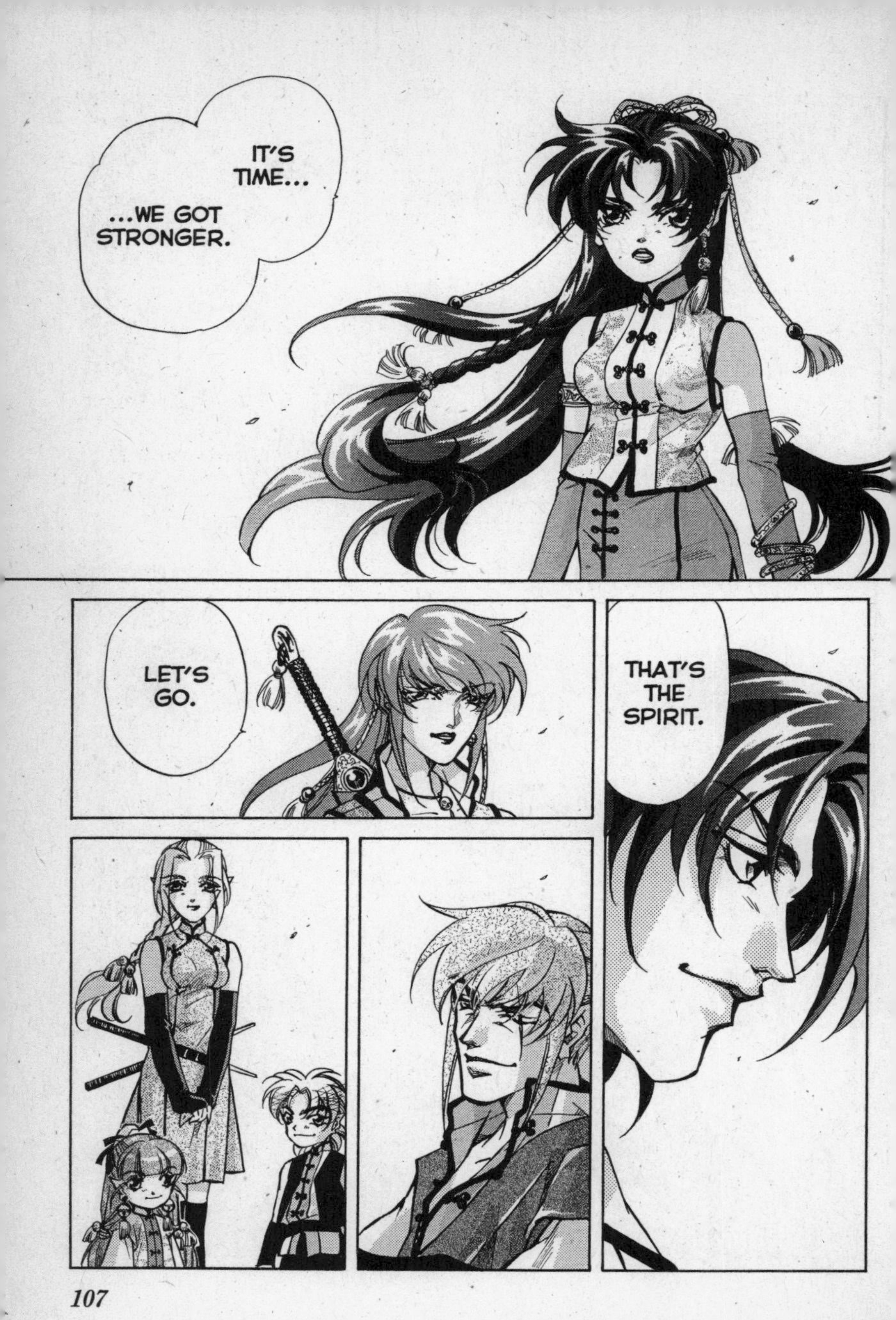
IT'S TIME...
...WE GOT STRONGER.
THAT'S THE SPIRIT.
LET'S GO.

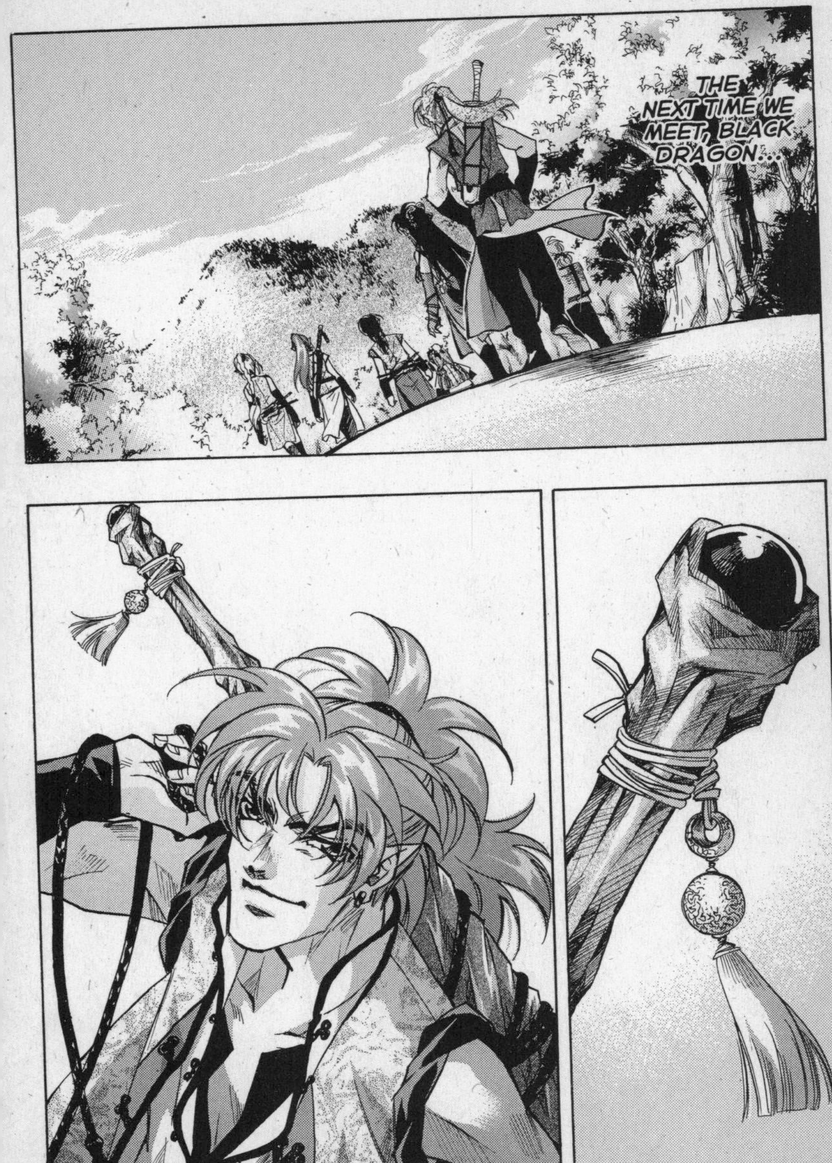
THE NEXT TIME WE MEET, BLACK DRAGON...

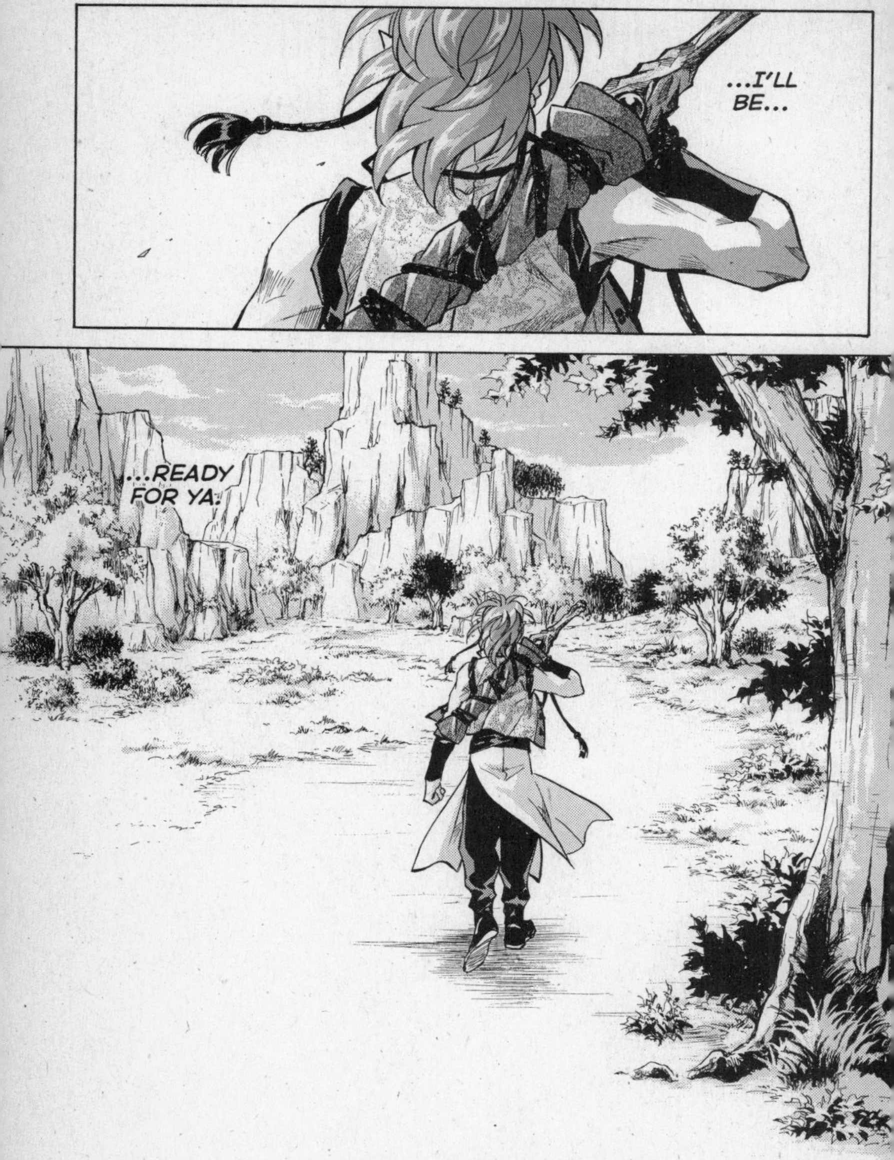
...I'LL BE...
...READY FOR YA.

END OF CHAPTER 15

THE DRAGON CYCLE

TEN-RYU 4th STORY

sanami-matoh presents

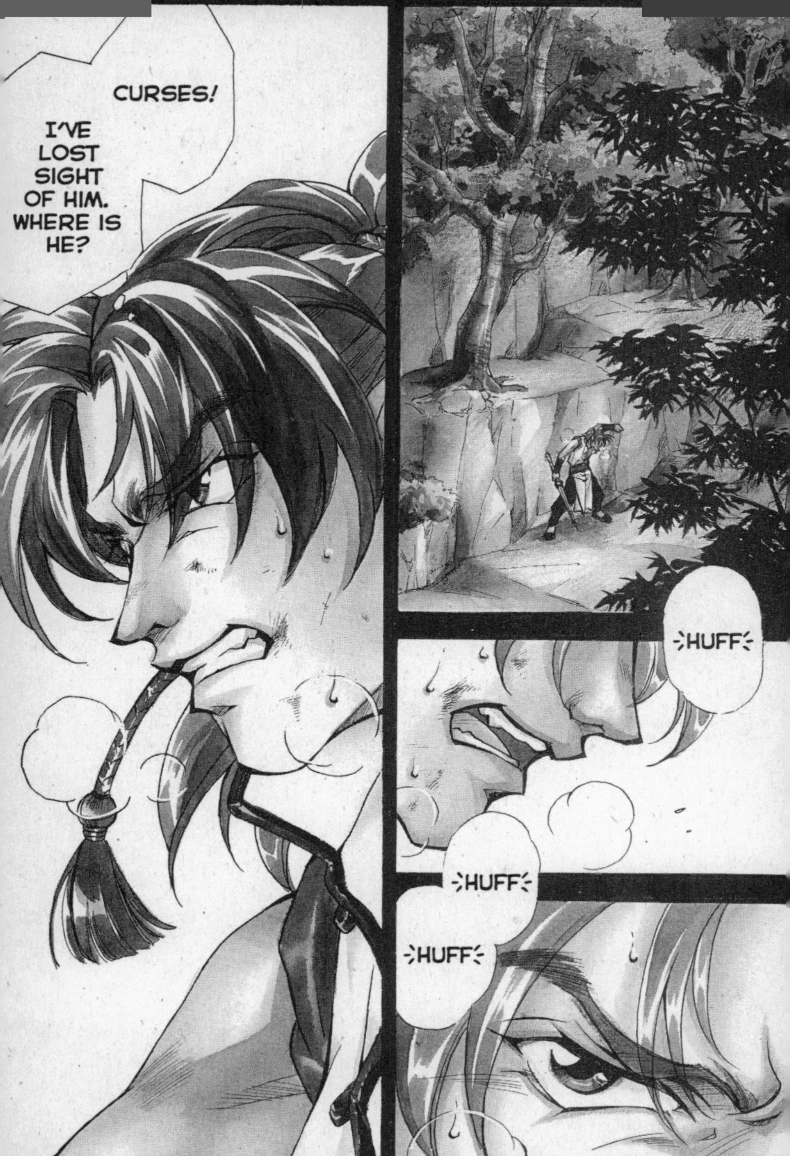
HUFF
HUFF
HUFF
CURSES!
I'VE LOST SIGHT OF HIM. WHERE IS HE?

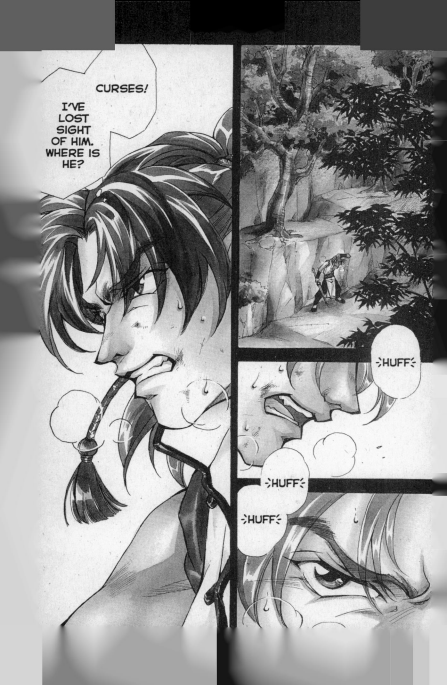

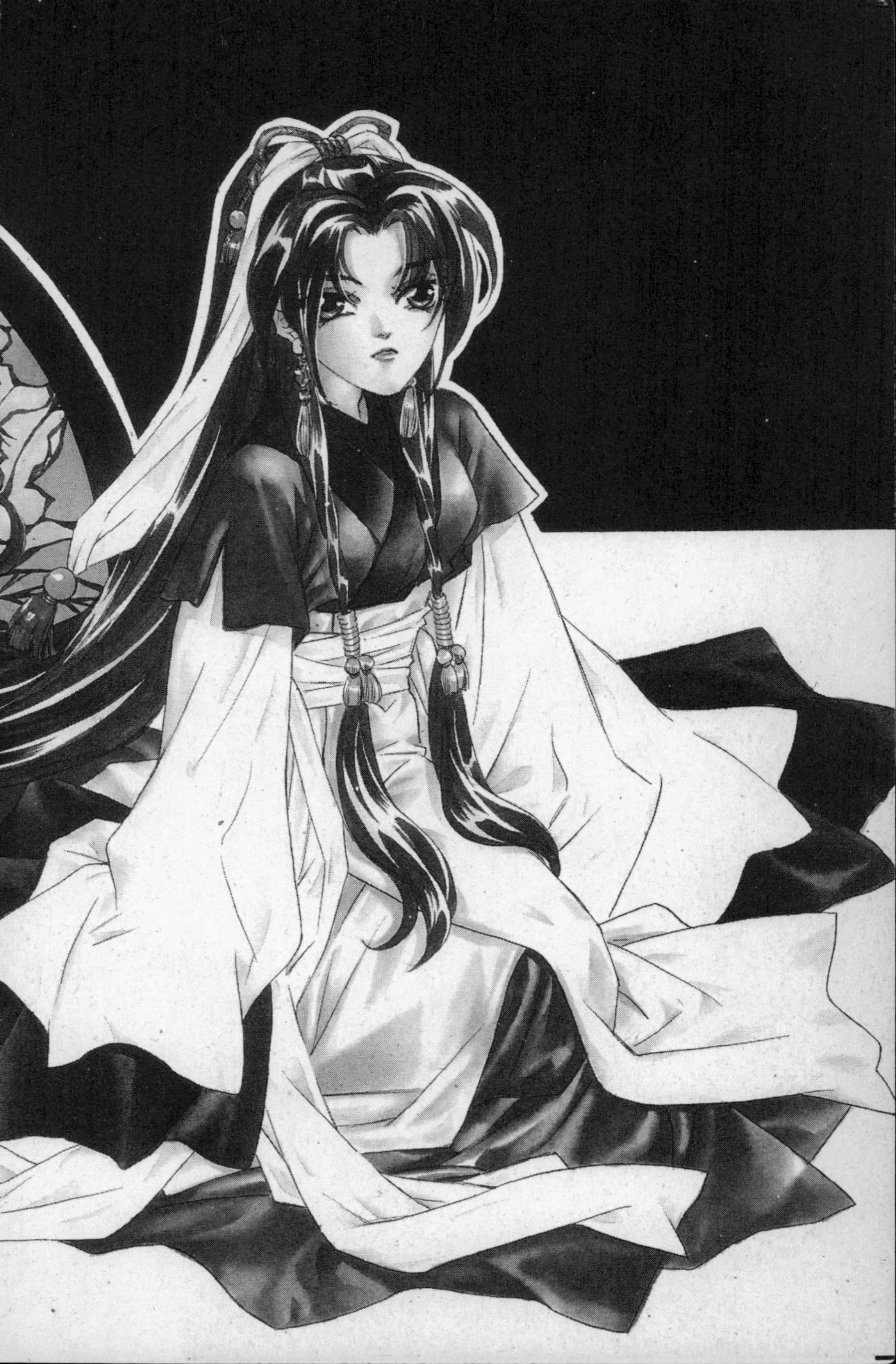

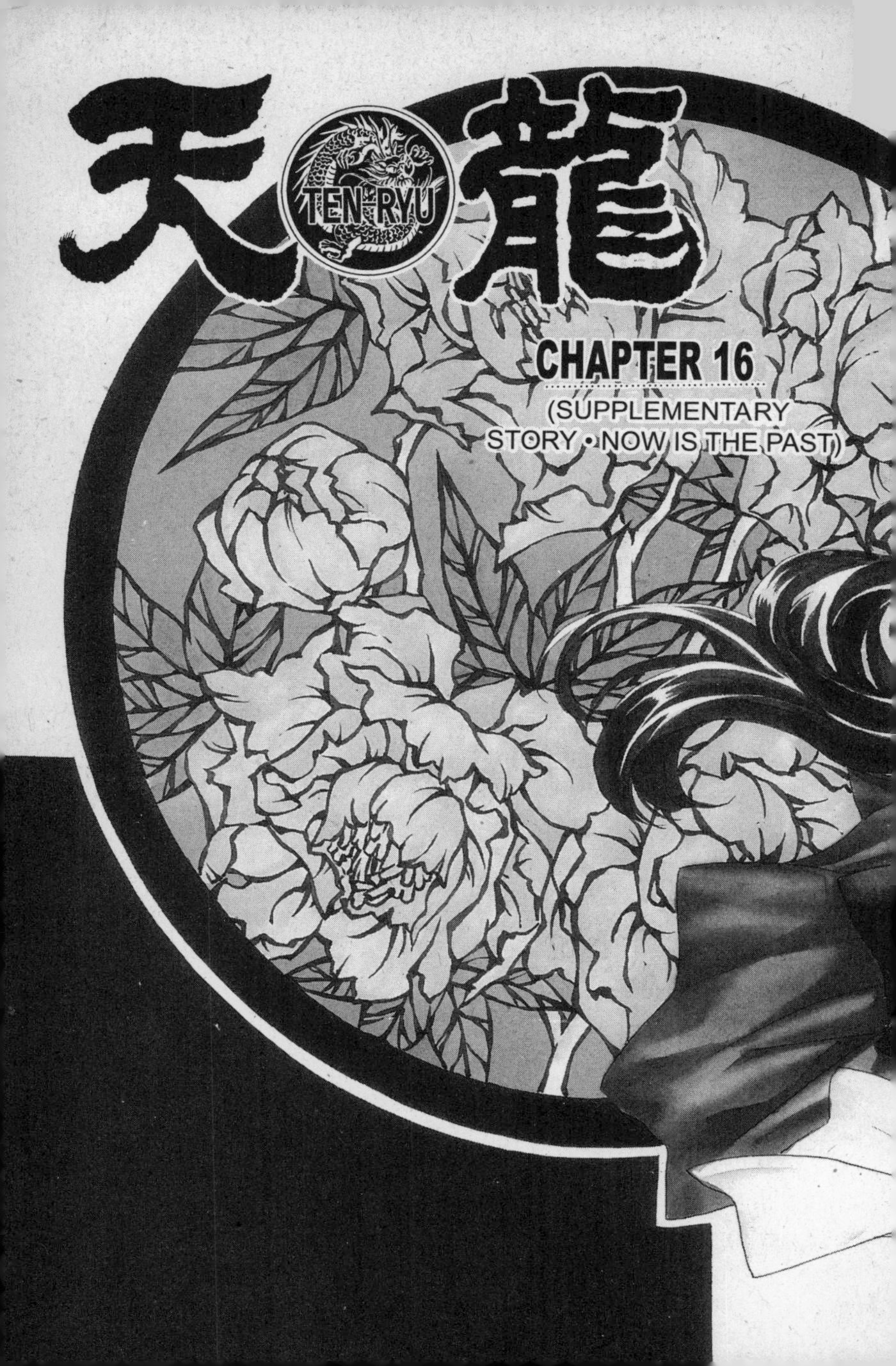
天龍
TEN-RYU
CHAPTER 16
(SUPPLEMENTARY STORY • NOW IS THE PAST)

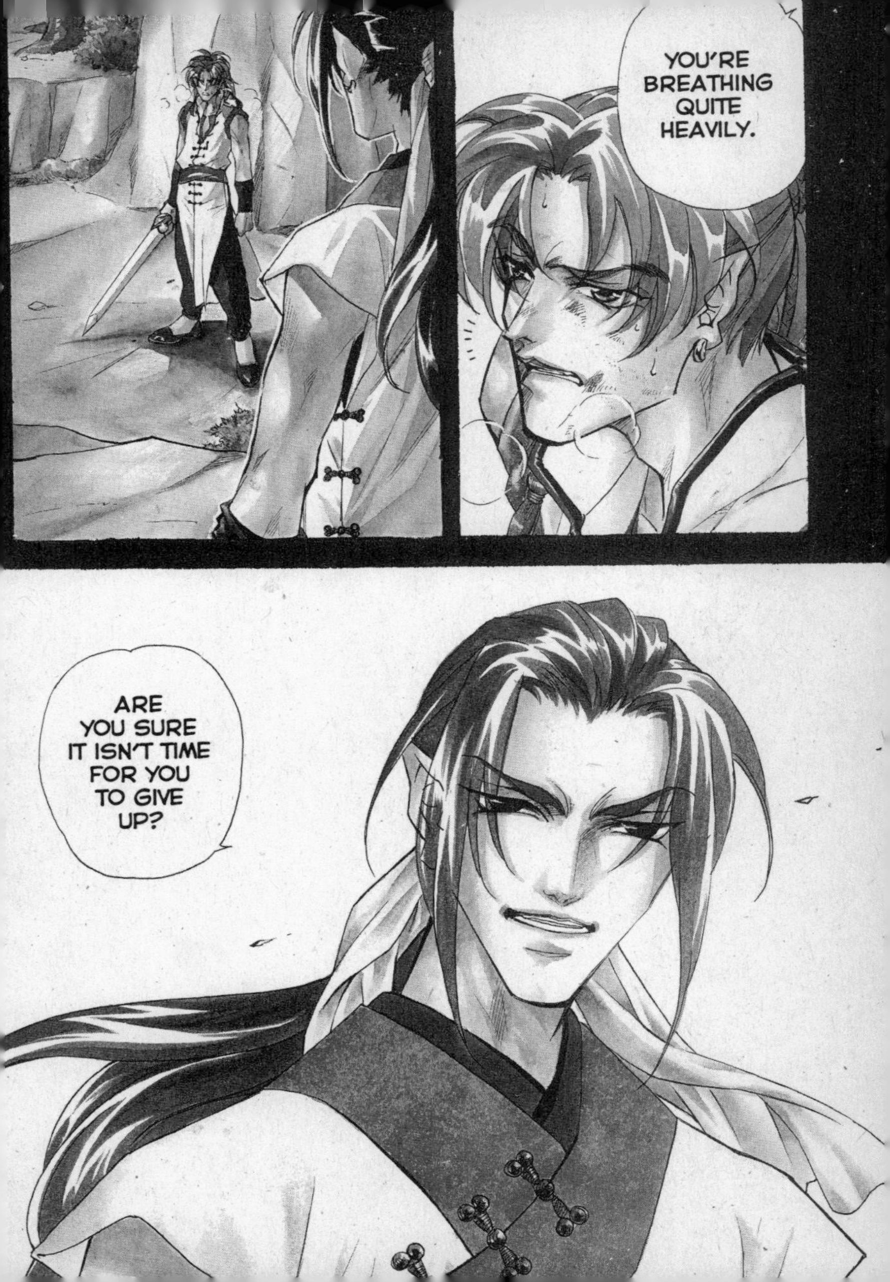
YOU'RE BREATHING QUITE HEAVILY.
ARE YOU SURE IT ISN'T TIME FOR YOU TO GIVE UP?

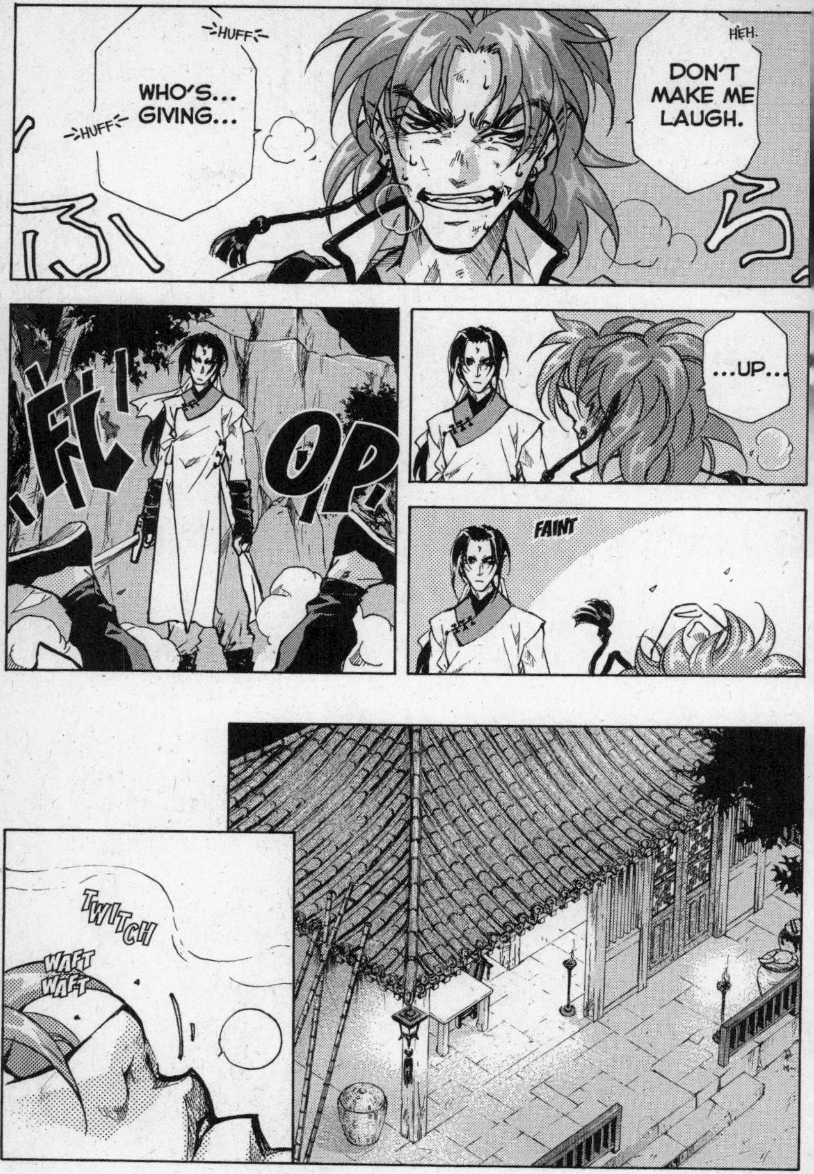

HEH.
DON'T MAKE ME LAUGH.
HUFF
WHO'S... GIVING...
HUFF
...UP...
FAINT
FLOP
TWITCH
WAFT WAFT

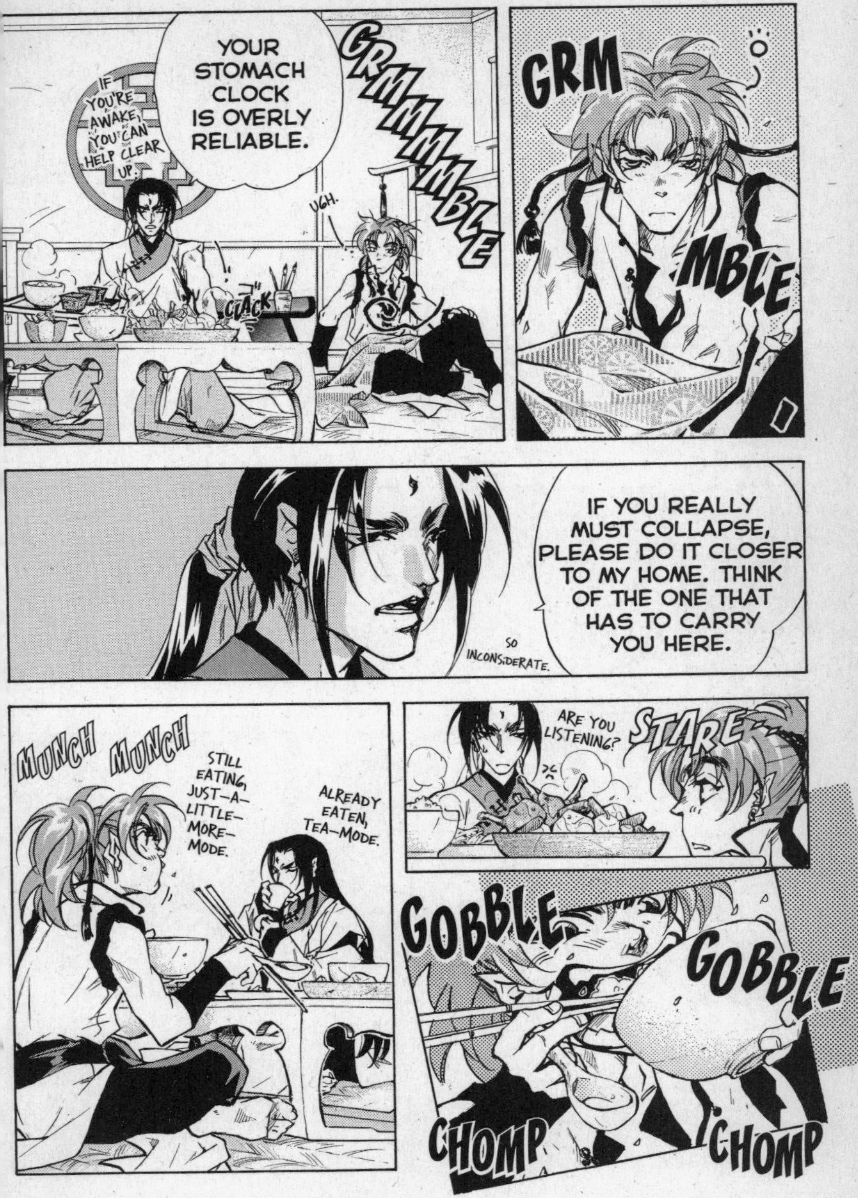
GRM
MBLE
GRMMMMBLE
YOUR STOMACH CLOCK IS OVERLY RELIABLE.
IF YOU'RE AWAKE, YOU CAN HELP CLEAR UP.
UGH.
CLACK
IF YOU REALLY MUST COLLAPSE, PLEASE DO IT CLOSER TO MY HOME. THINK OF THE ONE THAT HAS TO CARRY YOU HERE.
SO INCONSIDERATE.
STARE
ARE YOU LISTENING?
GOBBLE
GOBBLE
CHOMP
CHOMP
MUNCH
MUNCH
ALREADY EATEN, TEA-MODE.
STILL EATING, JUST-A-LITTLE-MORE-MODE.

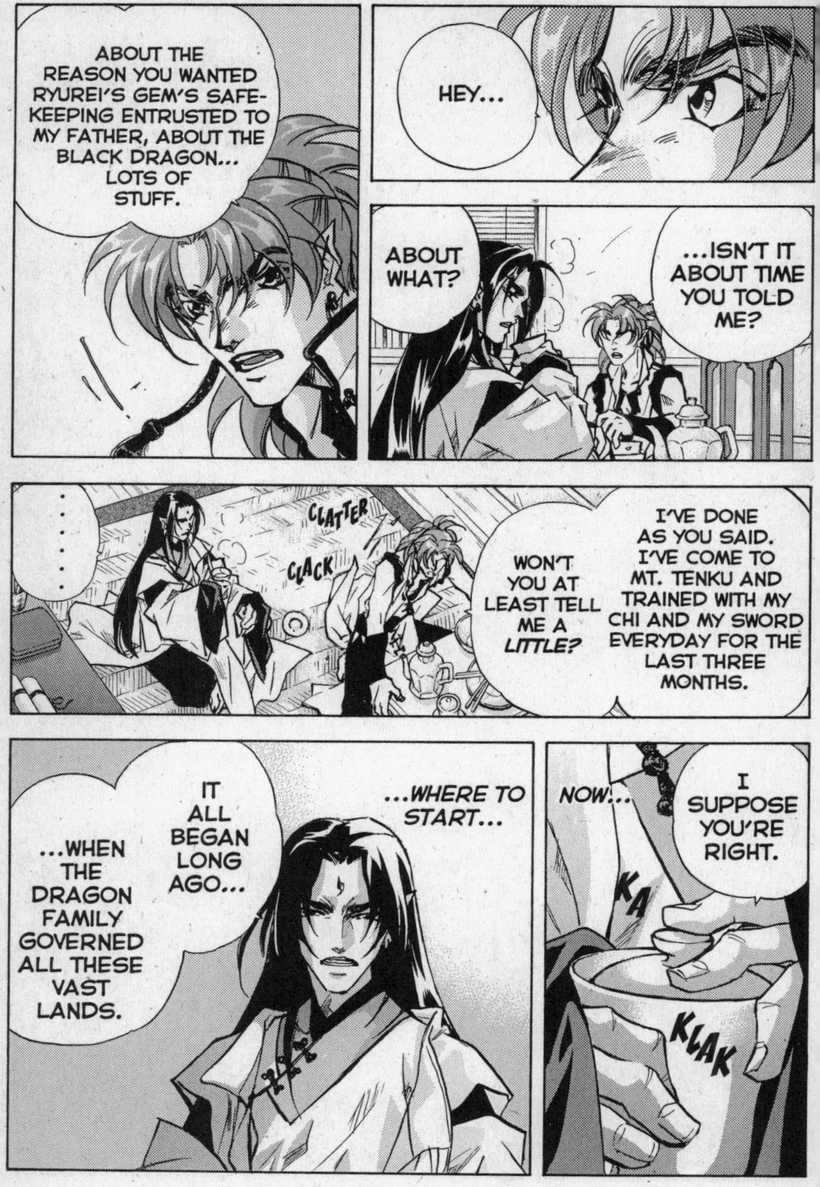
HEY...
...ISN'T IT ABOUT TIME YOU TOLD ME?
ABOUT WHAT?
ABOUT THE REASON YOU WANTED RYUREI'S GEM'S SAFE-KEEPING ENTRUSTED TO MY FATHER, ABOUT THE BLACK DRAGON... LOTS OF STUFF.
I'VE DONE AS YOU SAID. I'VE COME TO MT. TENKU AND TRAINED WITH MY CHI AND MY SWORD EVERYDAY FOR THE LAST THREE MONTHS.
WON'T YOU AT LEAST TELL ME A *LITTLE?*
CLATTER
CLACK
. . . .
I SUPPOSE YOU'RE RIGHT.
KA
KLAK
NOW...
...WHERE TO START...
IT ALL BEGAN LONG AGO...
...WHEN THE DRAGON FAMILY GOVERNED ALL THESE VAST LANDS.

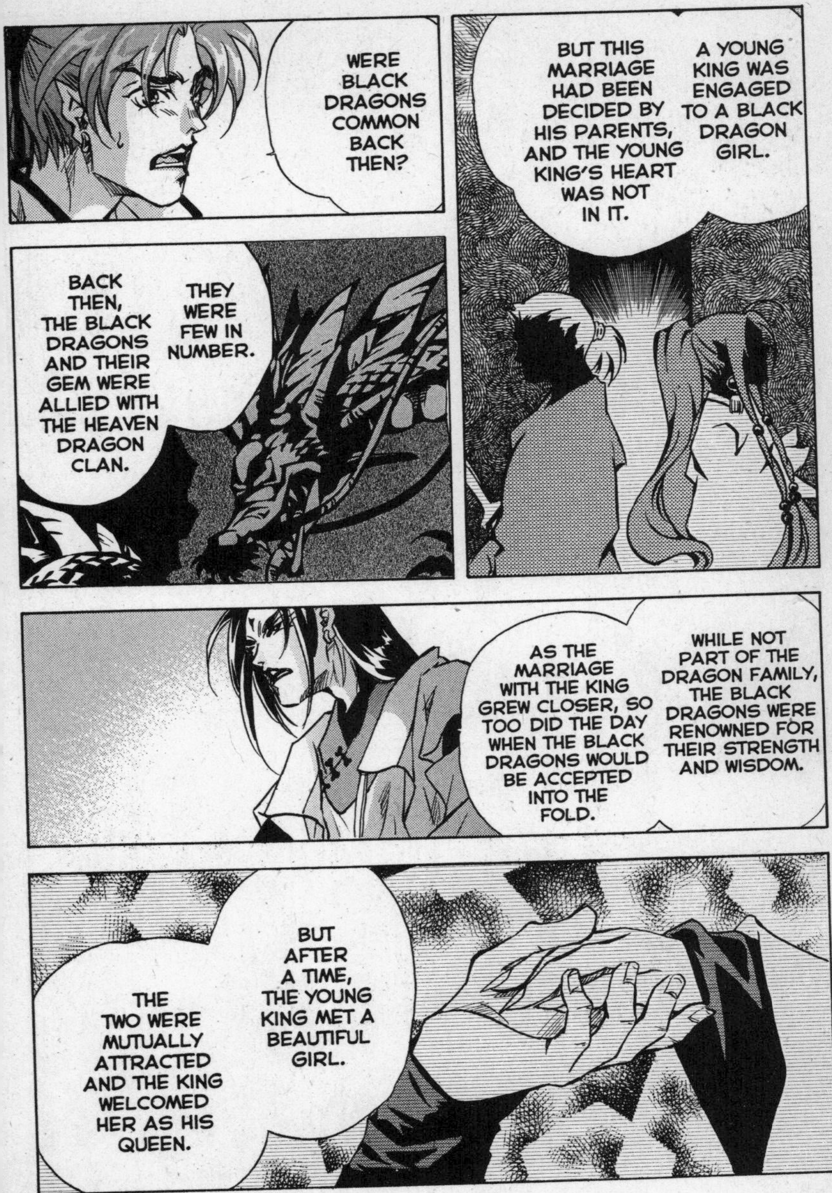
A YOUNG KING WAS ENGAGED TO A BLACK DRAGON GIRL.
BUT THIS MARRIAGE HAD BEEN DECIDED BY HIS PARENTS, AND THE YOUNG KING'S HEART WAS NOT IN IT.
WERE BLACK DRAGONS COMMON BACK THEN?
THEY WERE FEW IN NUMBER.
BACK THEN, THE BLACK DRAGONS AND THEIR GEM WERE ALLIED WITH THE HEAVEN DRAGON CLAN.
WHILE NOT PART OF THE DRAGON FAMILY, THE BLACK DRAGONS WERE RENOWNED FOR THEIR STRENGTH AND WISDOM.
AS THE MARRIAGE WITH THE KING GREW CLOSER, SO TOO DID THE DAY WHEN THE BLACK DRAGONS WOULD BE ACCEPTED INTO THE FOLD.
BUT AFTER A TIME, THE YOUNG KING MET A BEAUTIFUL GIRL.
THE TWO WERE MUTUALLY ATTRACTED AND THE KING WELCOMED HER AS HIS QUEEN.

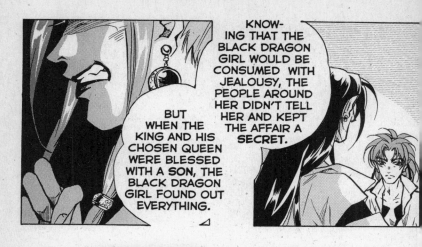

KNOWING THAT THE BLACK DRAGON GIRL WOULD BE CONSUMED WITH JEALOUSY, THE PEOPLE AROUND HER DIDN'T TELL HER AND KEPT THE AFFAIR A SECRET.

BUT WHEN THE KING AND HIS CHOSEN QUEEN WERE BLESSED WITH A SON, THE BLACK DRAGON GIRL FOUND OUT EVERYTHING.

RANJU!!

EEEEK!

DASH

RANJU, WHERE ARE YOU? WHAT'S HAPPENING...?

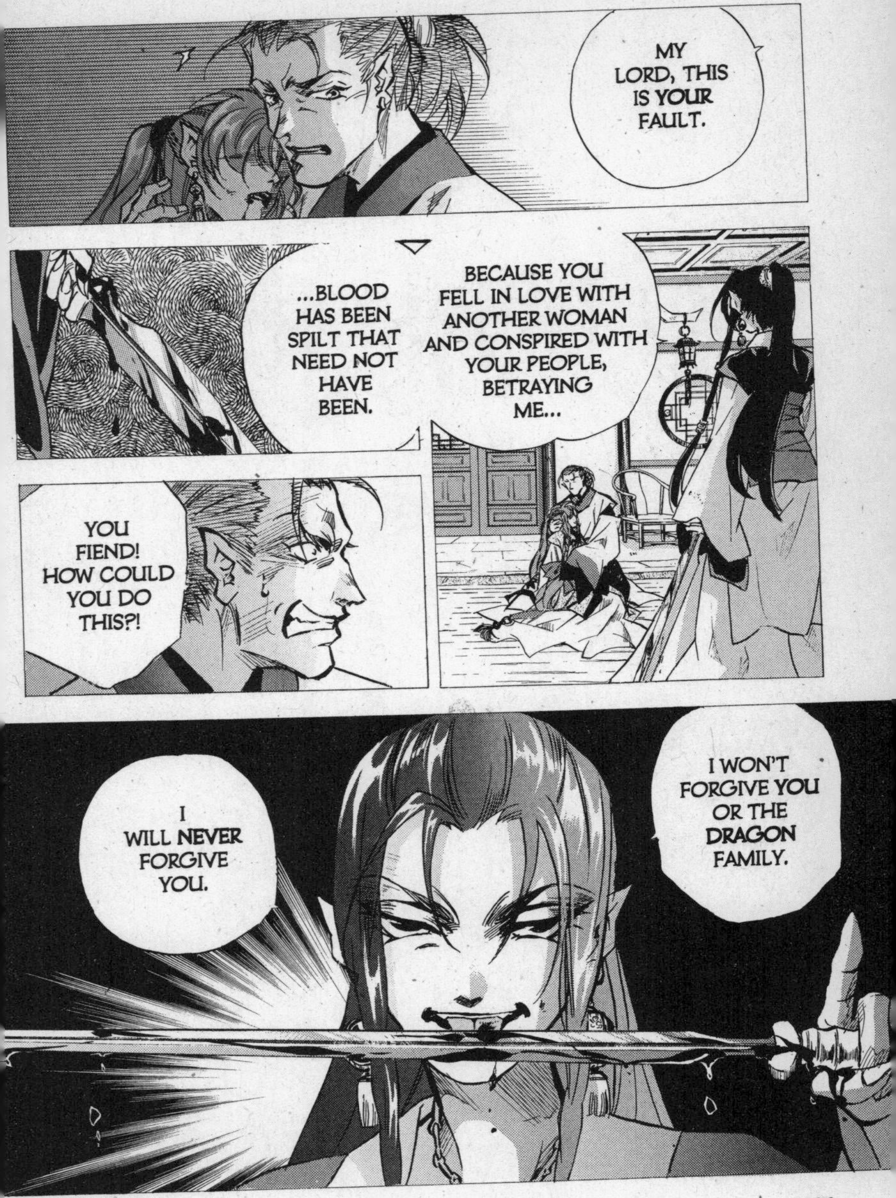
MY LORD, THIS IS YOUR FAULT.
BECAUSE YOU FELL IN LOVE WITH ANOTHER WOMAN AND CONSPIRED WITH YOUR PEOPLE, BETRAYING ME...
...BLOOD HAS BEEN SPILT THAT NEED NOT HAVE BEEN.
YOU FIEND! HOW COULD YOU DO THIS?!
I WON'T FORGIVE YOU OR THE DRAGON FAMILY.
I WILL NEVER FORGIVE YOU.

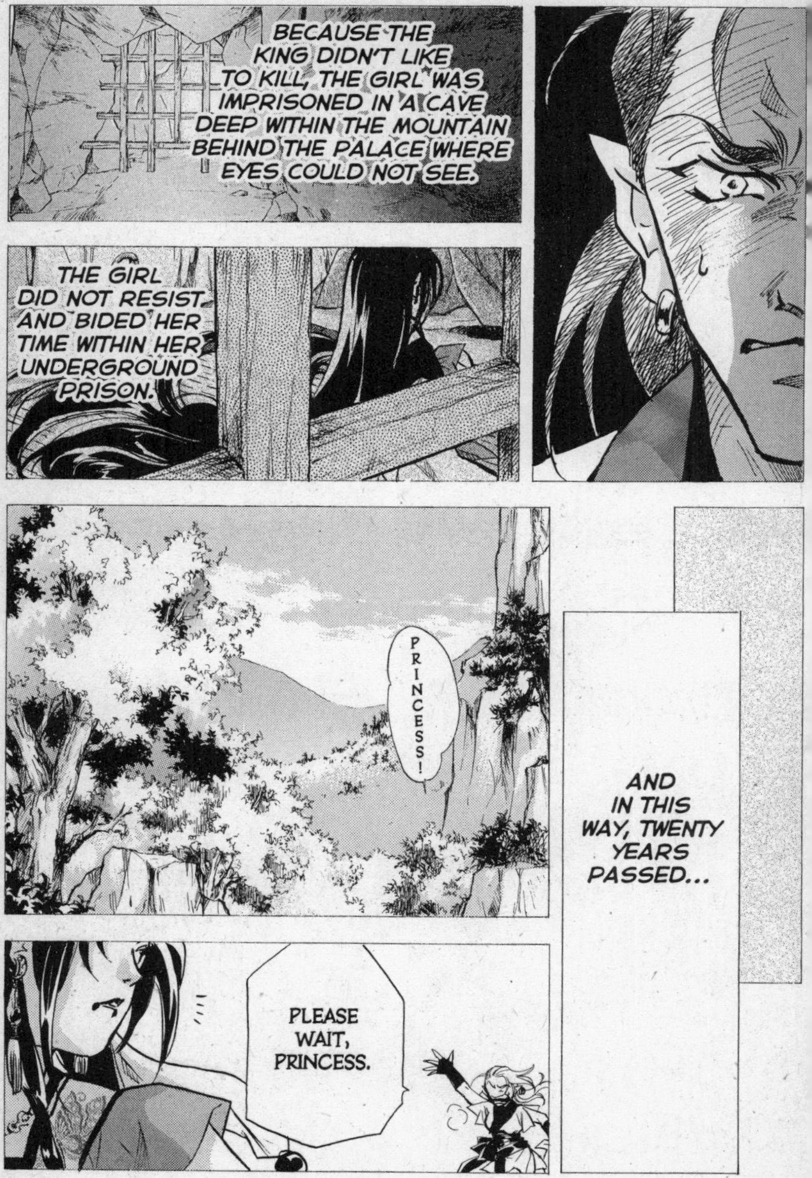
BECAUSE THE KING DIDN'T LIKE TO KILL, THE GIRL WAS IMPRISONED IN A CAVE DEEP WITHIN THE MOUNTAIN BEHIND THE PALACE WHERE EYES COULD NOT SEE.
THE GIRL DID NOT RESIST AND BIDED HER TIME WITHIN HER UNDERGROUND PRISON.
AND IN THIS WAY, TWENTY YEARS PASSED...
PRINCESS!
PLEASE WAIT, PRINCESS.

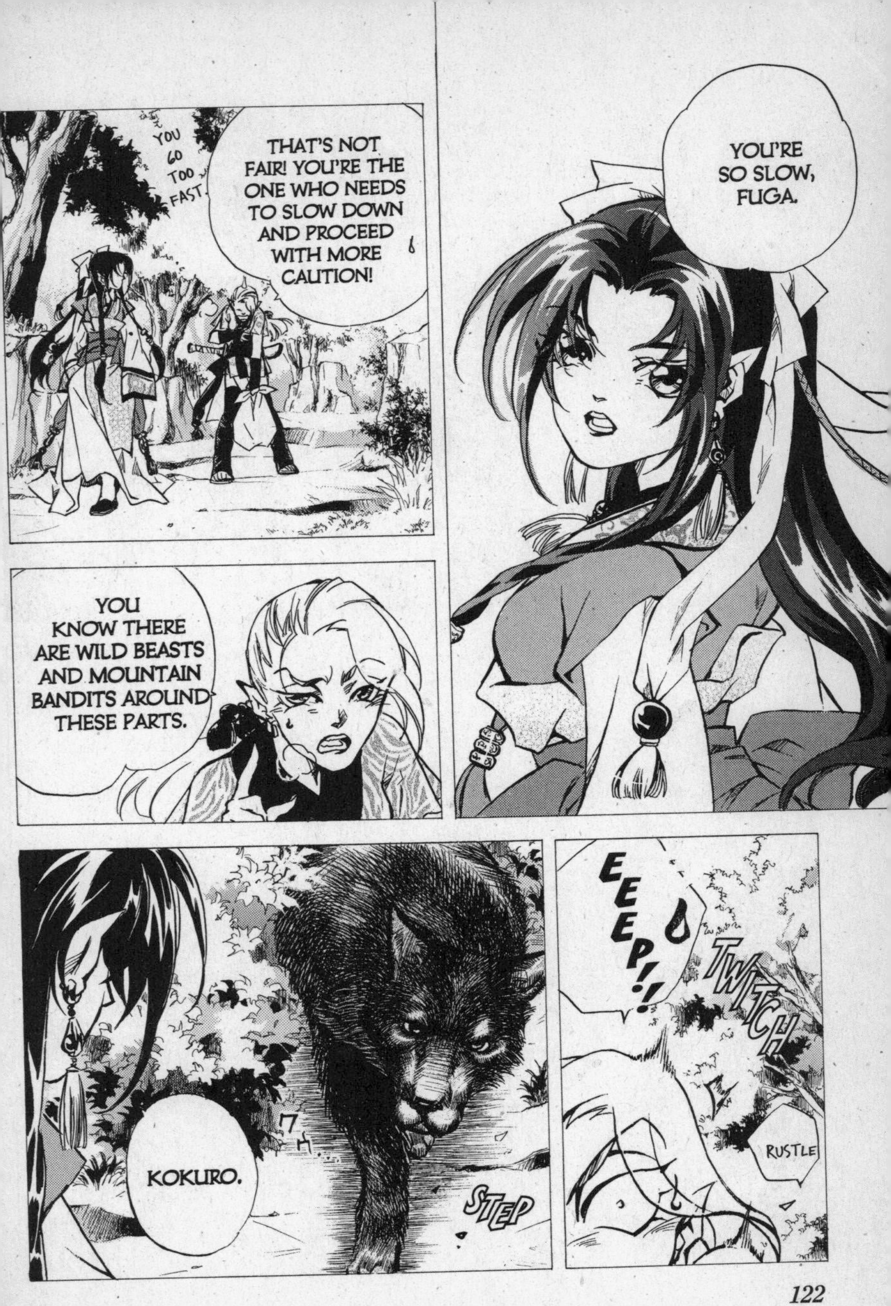
YOU'RE SO SLOW, FUGA.
THAT'S NOT FAIR! YOU'RE THE ONE WHO NEEDS TO SLOW DOWN AND PROCEED WITH MORE CAUTION!
YOU GO TOO FAST.
YOU KNOW THERE ARE WILD BEASTS AND MOUNTAIN BANDITS AROUND THESE PARTS.
EEEP!!
TWITCH
RUSTLE
KOKURO.
STEP

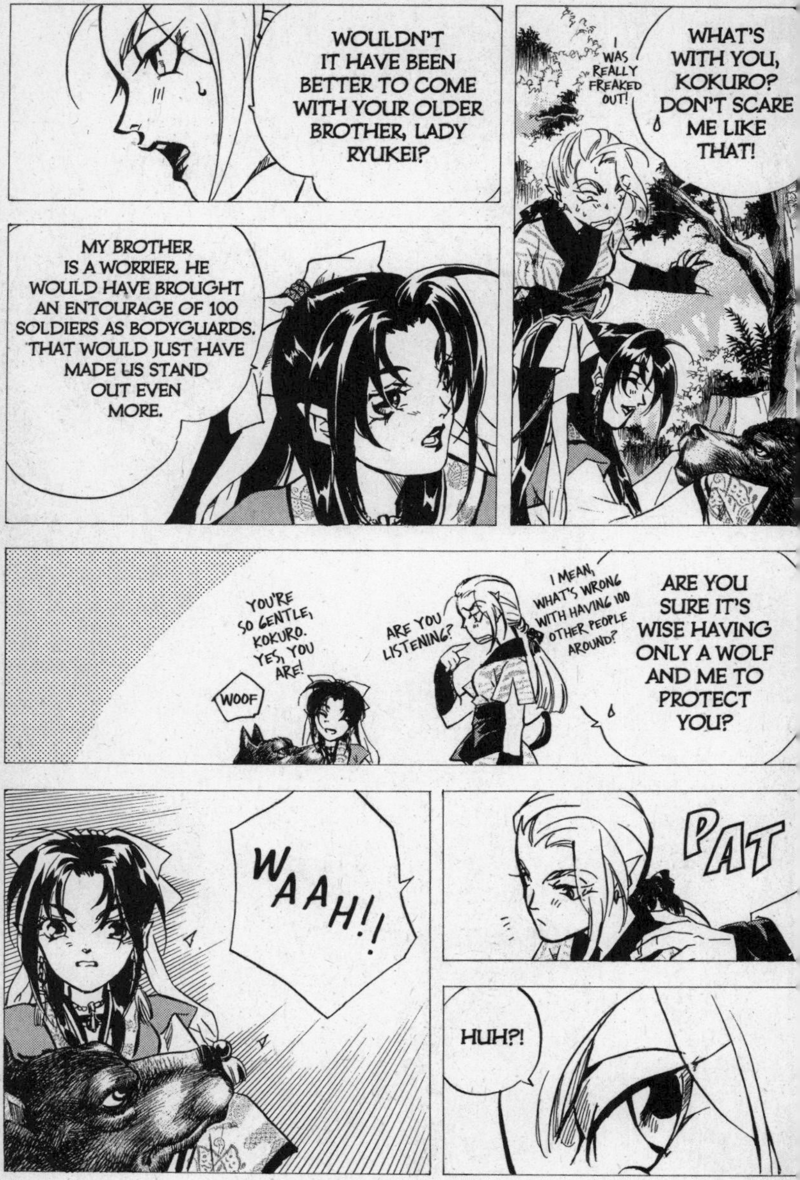
WHAT'S WITH YOU, KOKURO? DON'T SCARE ME LIKE THAT!
I WAS REALLY FREAKED OUT!
WOULDN'T IT HAVE BEEN BETTER TO COME WITH YOUR OLDER BROTHER, LADY RYUKEI?
MY BROTHER IS A WORRIER. HE WOULD HAVE BROUGHT AN ENTOURAGE OF 100 SOLDIERS AS BODYGUARDS. THAT WOULD JUST HAVE MADE US STAND OUT EVEN MORE.
ARE YOU SURE IT'S WISE HAVING ONLY A WOLF AND ME TO PROTECT YOU?
I MEAN, WHAT'S WRONG WITH HAVING 100 OTHER PEOPLE AROUND?
ARE YOU LISTENING?
YOU'RE SO GENTLE, KOKURO. YES, YOU ARE!
WOOF
PAT
HUH?!
WAAH!!

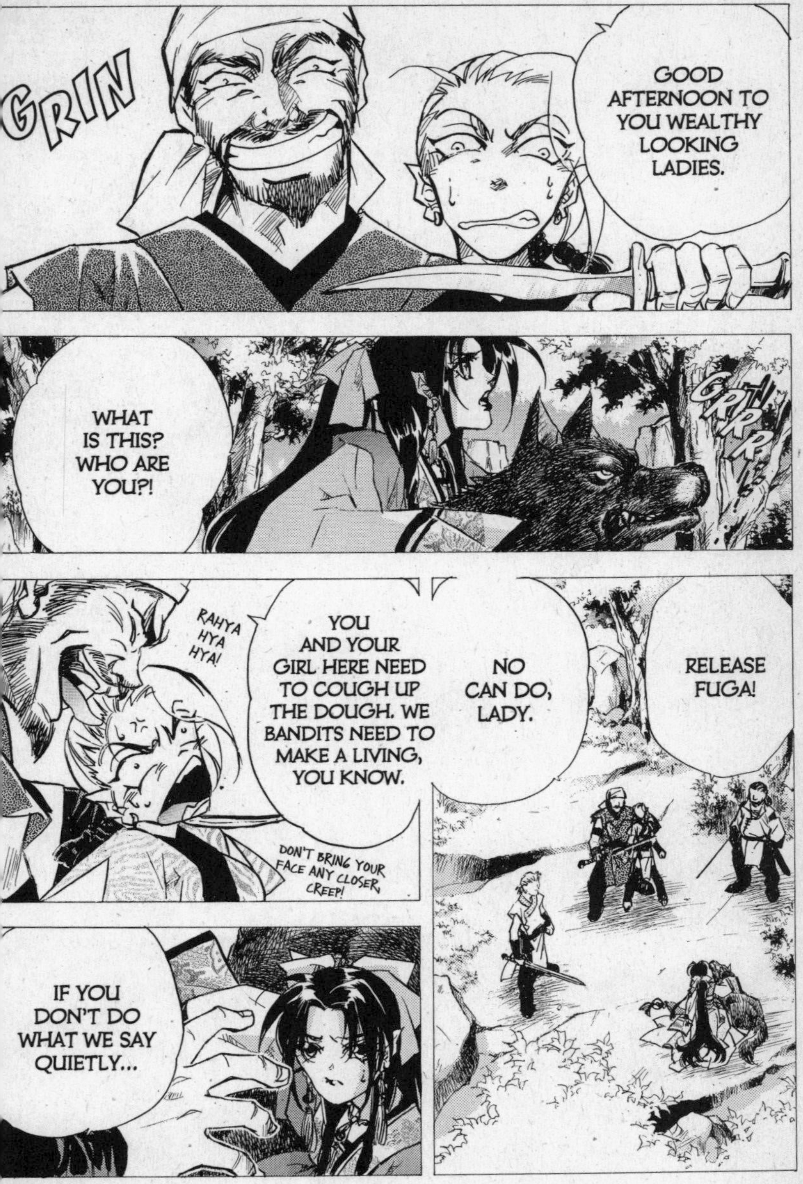
GOOD AFTERNOON TO YOU WEALTHY LOOKING LADIES.
GRIN
GRRR
WHAT IS THIS? WHO ARE YOU?!
RELEASE FUGA!
NO CAN DO, LADY.
YOU AND YOUR GIRL HERE NEED TO COUGH UP THE DOUGH. WE BANDITS NEED TO MAKE A LIVING, YOU KNOW.
RAHYA HYA HYA!
DON'T BRING YOUR FACE ANY CLOSER, CREEP!
IF YOU DON'T DO WHAT WE SAY QUIETLY...

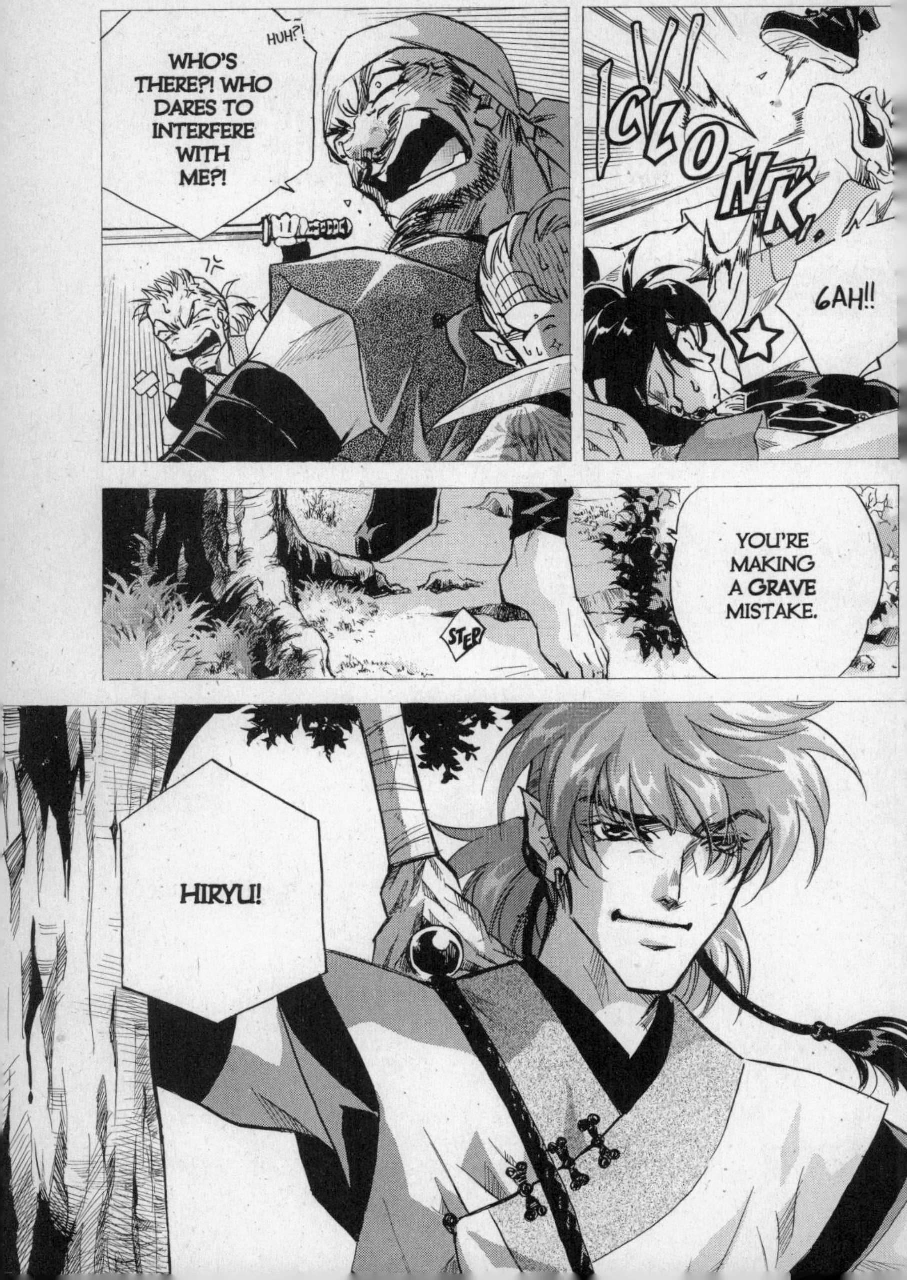
CLONK
GAH!!
HUH?!
WHO'S THERE?! WHO DARES TO INTERFERE WITH ME?!
YOU'RE MAKING A GRAVE MISTAKE.
STEP
HIRYU!

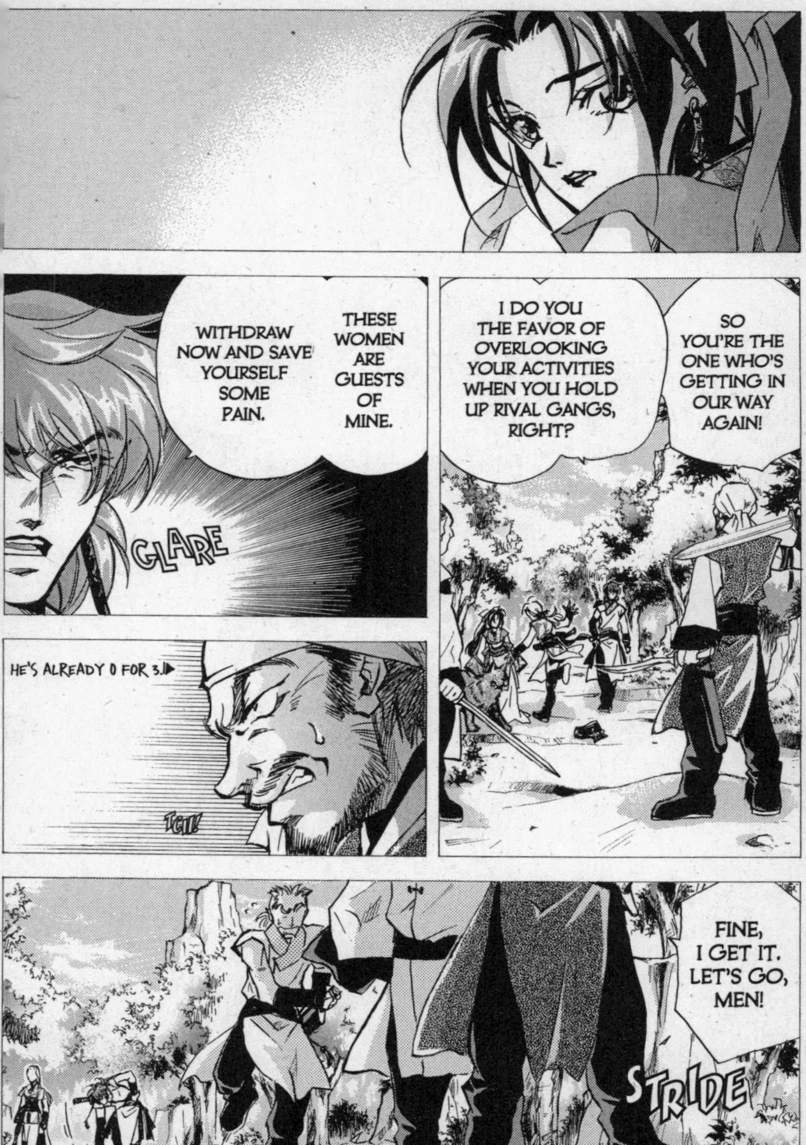
SO YOU'RE THE ONE WHO'S GETTING IN OUR WAY AGAIN!
I DO YOU THE FAVOR OF OVERLOOKING YOUR ACTIVITIES WHEN YOU HOLD UP RIVAL GANGS, RIGHT?
THESE WOMEN ARE GUESTS OF MINE.
WITHDRAW NOW AND SAVE YOURSELF SOME PAIN.
GLARE
HE'S ALREADY 0 FOR 3.
TCH!
FINE, I GET IT. LET'S GO, MEN!
STRIDE

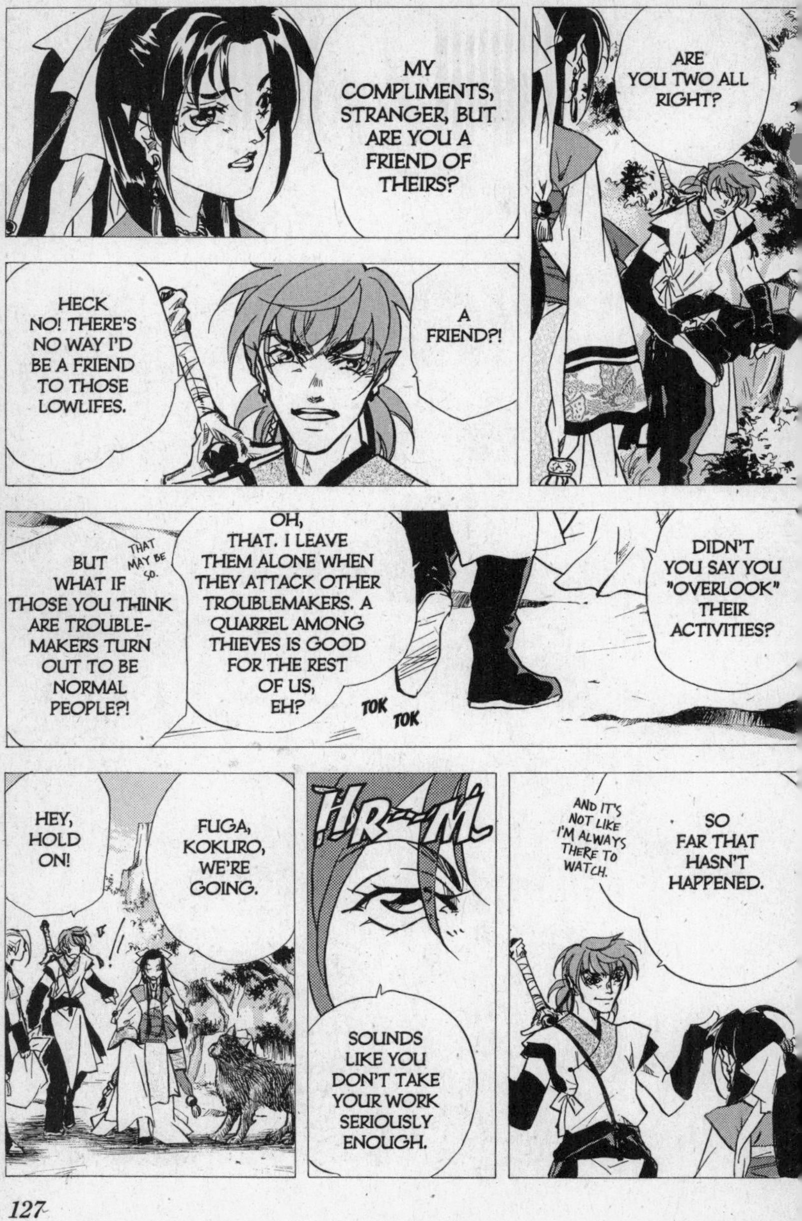
ARE YOU TWO ALL RIGHT?
MY COMPLIMENTS, STRANGER, BUT ARE YOU A FRIEND OF THEIRS?
A FRIEND?!
HECK NO! THERE'S NO WAY I'D BE A FRIEND TO THOSE LOWLIFES.
DIDN'T YOU SAY YOU "OVERLOOK" THEIR ACTIVITIES?
OH, THAT. I LEAVE THEM ALONE WHEN THEY ATTACK OTHER TROUBLEMAKERS. A QUARREL AMONG THIEVES IS GOOD FOR THE REST OF US, EH?
TOK TOK
THAT MAY BE SO.
BUT WHAT IF THOSE YOU THINK ARE TROUBLE-MAKERS TURN OUT TO BE NORMAL PEOPLE?!
SO FAR THAT HASN'T HAPPENED.
AND IT'S NOT LIKE I'M ALWAYS THERE TO WATCH.
HR-M
SOUNDS LIKE YOU DON'T TAKE YOUR WORK SERIOUSLY ENOUGH.
FUGA, KOKURO, WE'RE GOING.
HEY, HOLD ON!

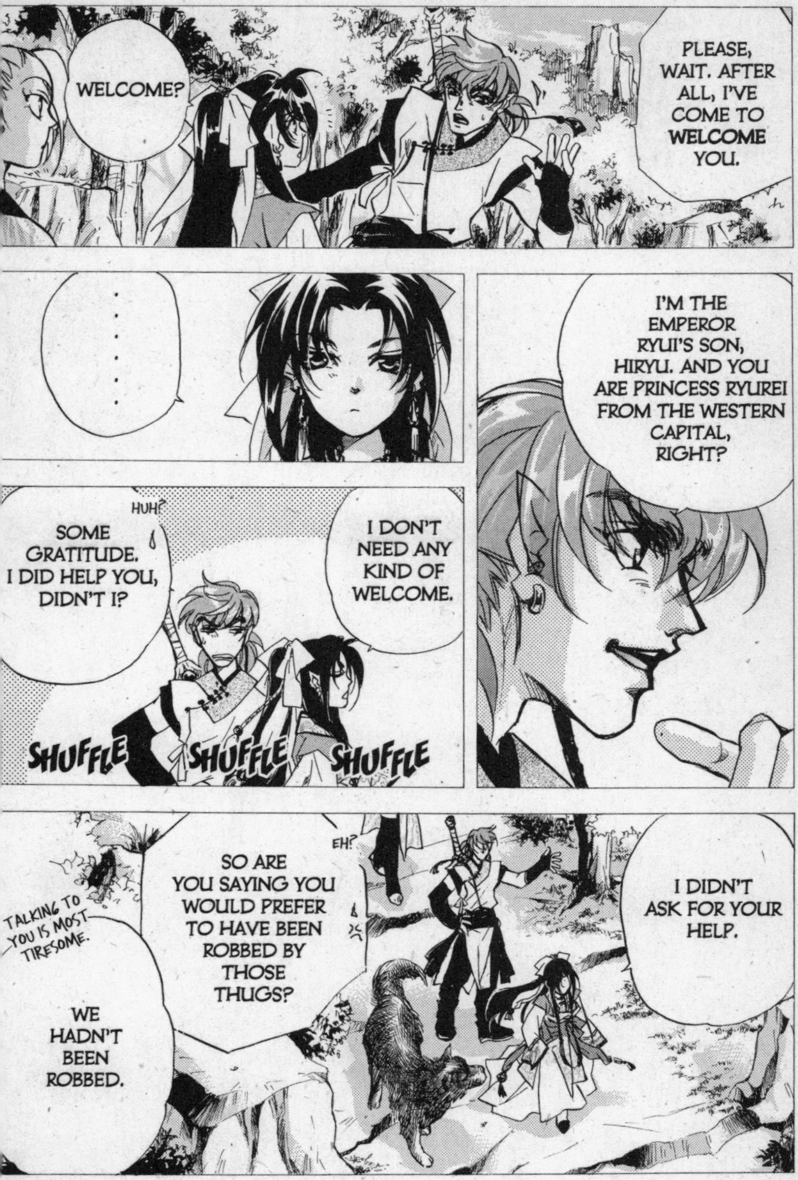
PLEASE, WAIT. AFTER ALL, I'VE COME TO WELCOME YOU.
WELCOME?
I'M THE EMPEROR RYUI'S SON, HIRYU. AND YOU ARE PRINCESS RYUREI FROM THE WESTERN CAPITAL, RIGHT?
......
I DON'T NEED ANY KIND OF WELCOME.
HUH?
SOME GRATITUDE. I DID HELP YOU, DIDN'T I?
SHUFFLE
SHUFFLE
SHUFFLE
I DIDN'T ASK FOR YOUR HELP.
EH?
SO ARE YOU SAYING YOU WOULD PREFER TO HAVE BEEN ROBBED BY THOSE THUGS?
WE HADN'T BEEN ROBBED.
TALKING TO YOU IS MOST TIRESOME.

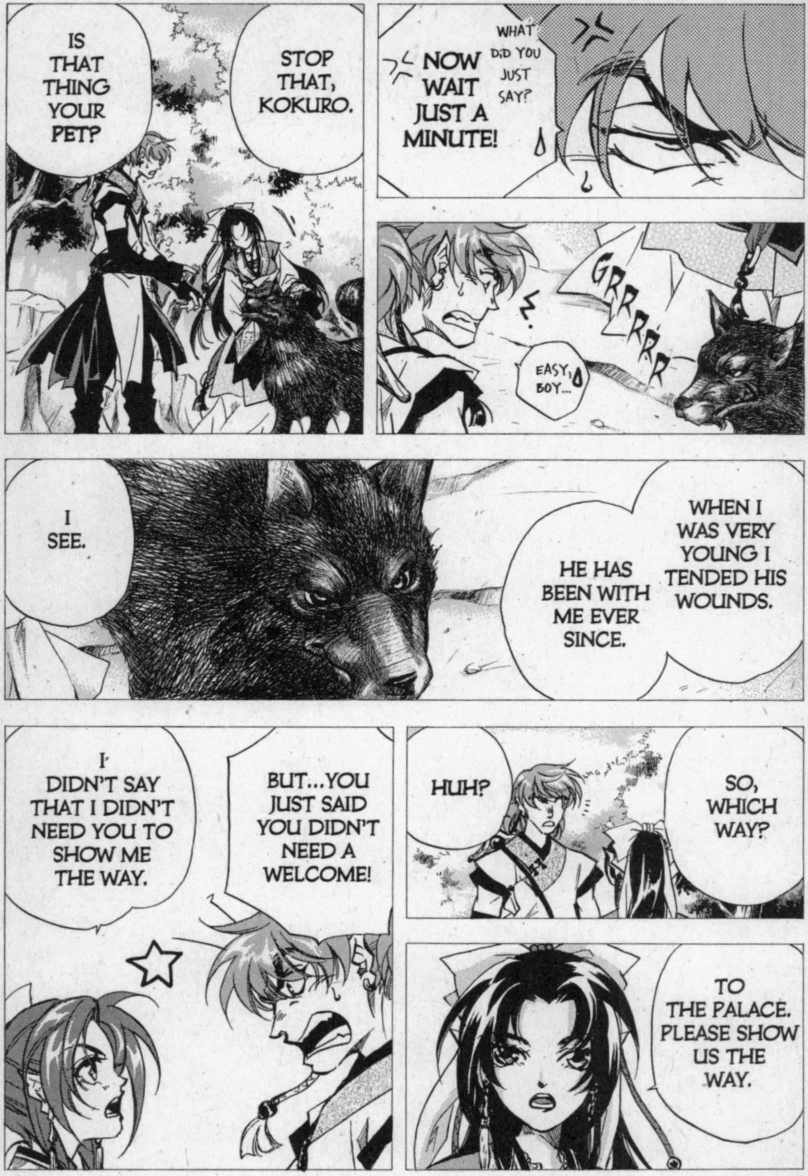
WHAT DID YOU JUST SAY?
NOW WAIT JUST A MINUTE!
GRRRRR
EASY, BOY...
STOP THAT, KOKURO.
IS THAT THING YOUR PET?
WHEN I WAS VERY YOUNG I TENDED HIS WOUNDS.
HE HAS BEEN WITH ME EVER SINCE.
I SEE.
SO, WHICH WAY?
HUH?
TO THE PALACE. PLEASE SHOW US THE WAY.
BUT...YOU JUST SAID YOU DIDN'T NEED A WELCOME!
I DIDN'T SAY THAT I DIDN'T NEED YOU TO SHOW ME THE WAY.

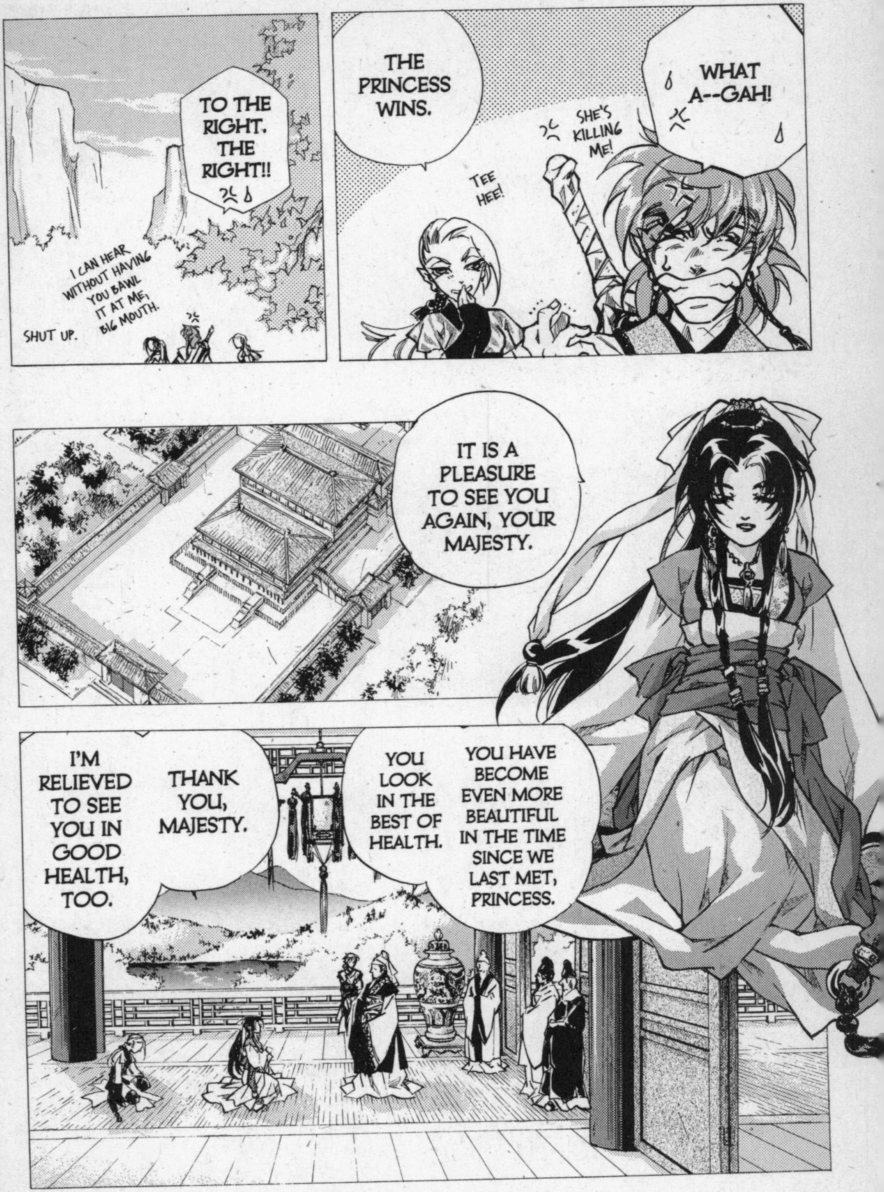
WHAT A--GAH!
THE PRINCESS WINS.
SHE'S KILLING ME!
TEE HEE!
TO THE RIGHT. THE RIGHT!!
I CAN HEAR WITHOUT HAVING YOU BAWL IT AT ME, BIG MOUTH.
SHUT UP.
IT IS A PLEASURE TO SEE YOU AGAIN, YOUR MAJESTY.
YOU HAVE BECOME EVEN MORE BEAUTIFUL IN THE TIME SINCE WE LAST MET, PRINCESS.
YOU LOOK IN THE BEST OF HEALTH.
THANK YOU, MAJESTY.
I'M RELIEVED TO SEE YOU IN GOOD HEALTH, TOO.

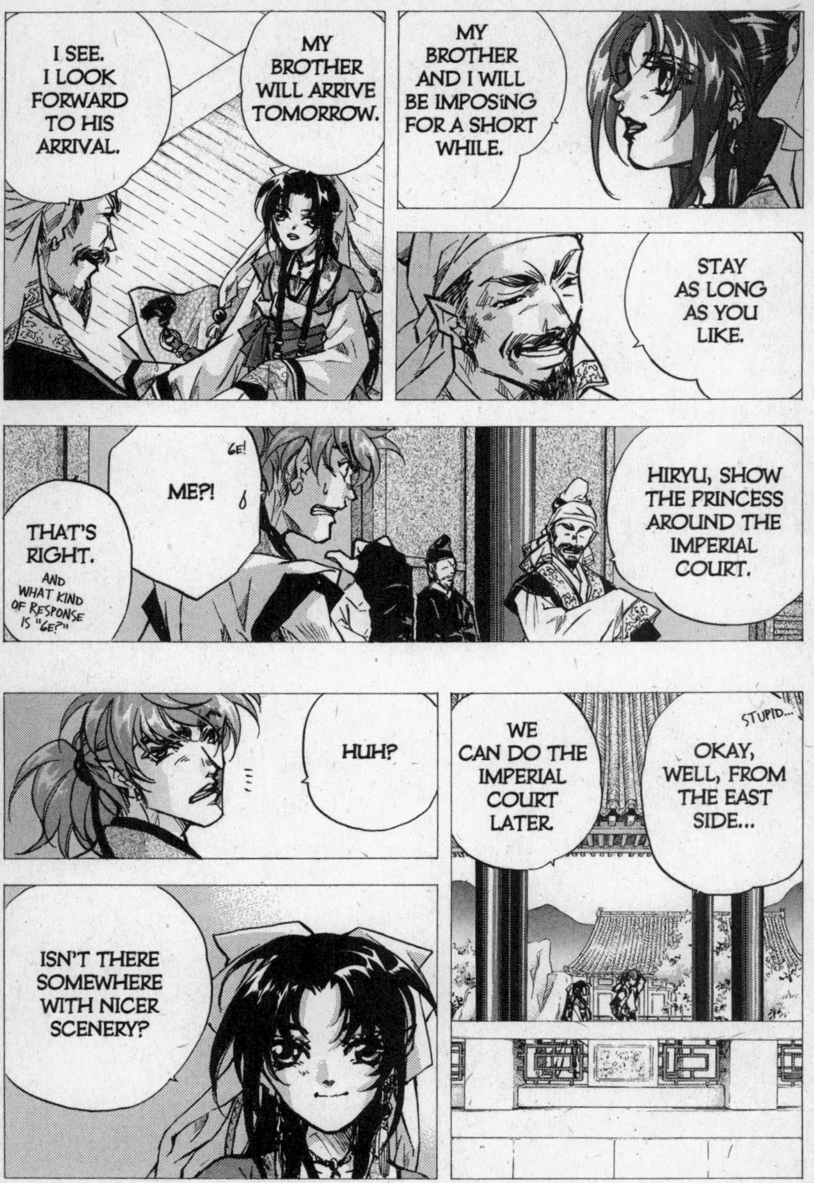
MY BROTHER AND I WILL BE IMPOSING FOR A SHORT WHILE.
STAY AS LONG AS YOU LIKE.
MY BROTHER WILL ARRIVE TOMORROW.
I SEE. I LOOK FORWARD TO HIS ARRIVAL.
HIRYU, SHOW THE PRINCESS AROUND THE IMPERIAL COURT.
GE!
ME?!
THAT'S RIGHT.
AND WHAT KIND OF RESPONSE IS "GE?"
STUPID...
OKAY, WELL, FROM THE EAST SIDE...
WE CAN DO THE IMPERIAL COURT LATER.
HUH?
ISN'T THERE SOMEWHERE WITH NICER SCENERY?

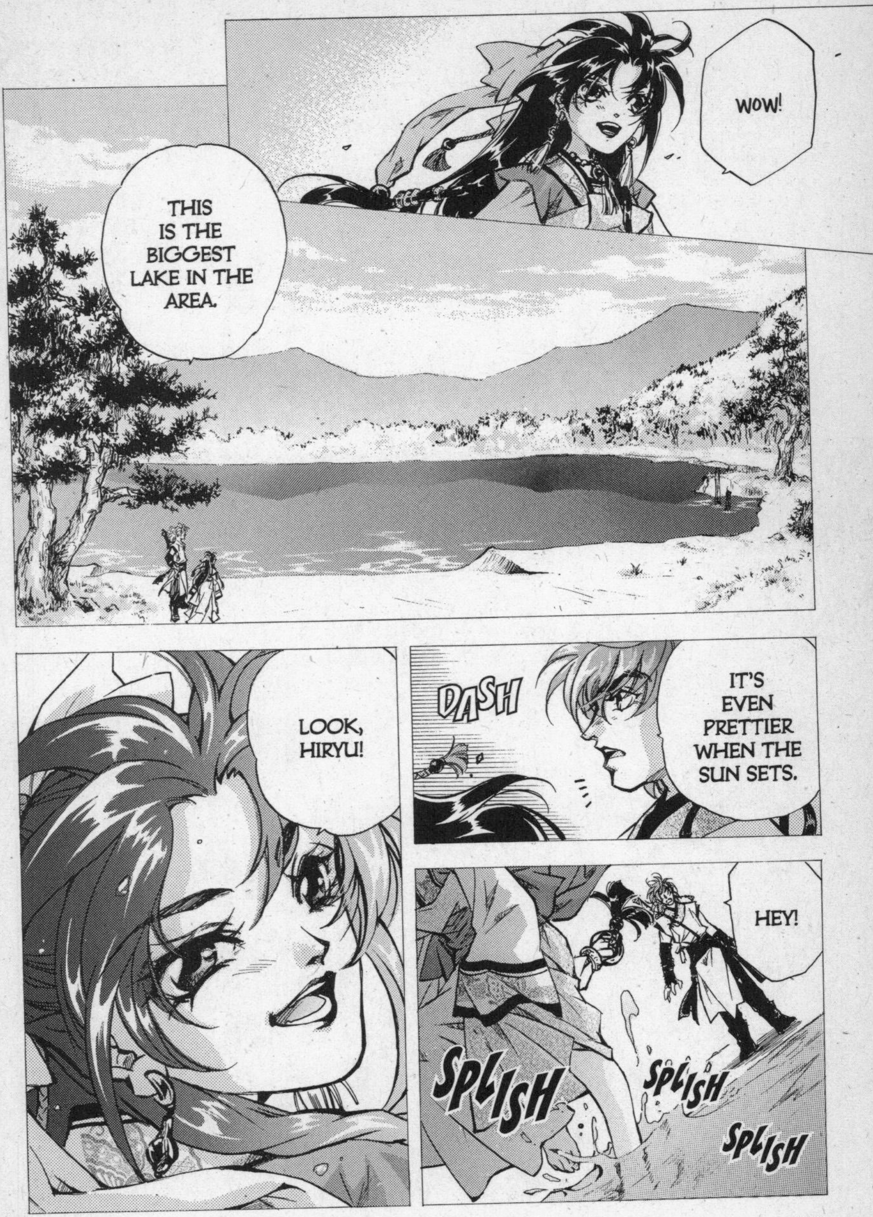
WOW!
THIS IS THE BIGGEST LAKE IN THE AREA.
DASH
IT'S EVEN PRETTIER WHEN THE SUN SETS.
HEY!
SPLISH
SPLISH
SPLISH
LOOK, HIRYU!

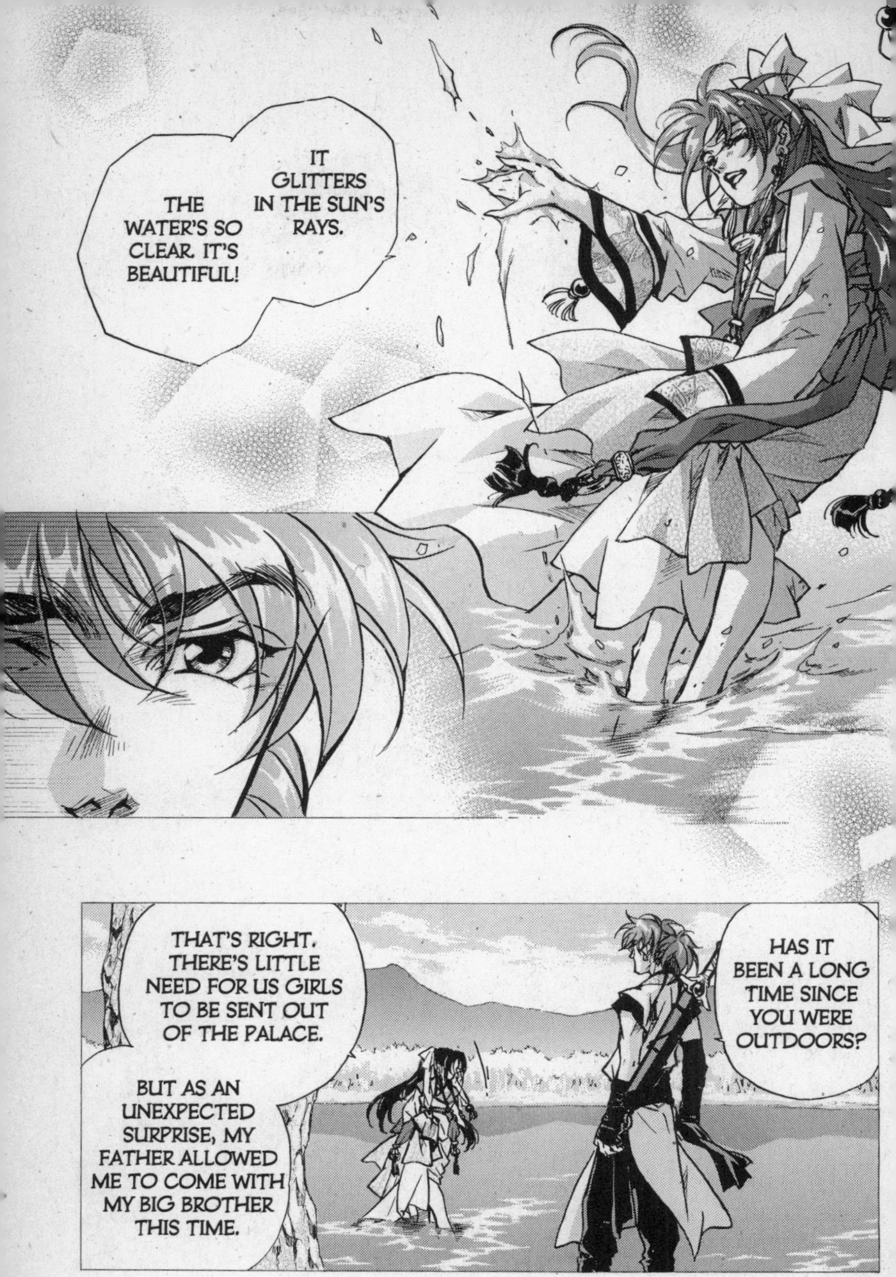
IT GLITTERS IN THE SUN'S RAYS.
THE WATER'S SO CLEAR. IT'S BEAUTIFUL!
HAS IT BEEN A LONG TIME SINCE YOU WERE OUTDOORS?
THAT'S RIGHT. THERE'S LITTLE NEED FOR US GIRLS TO BE SENT OUT OF THE PALACE.
BUT AS AN UNEXPECTED SURPRISE, MY FATHER ALLOWED ME TO COME WITH MY BIG BROTHER THIS TIME.

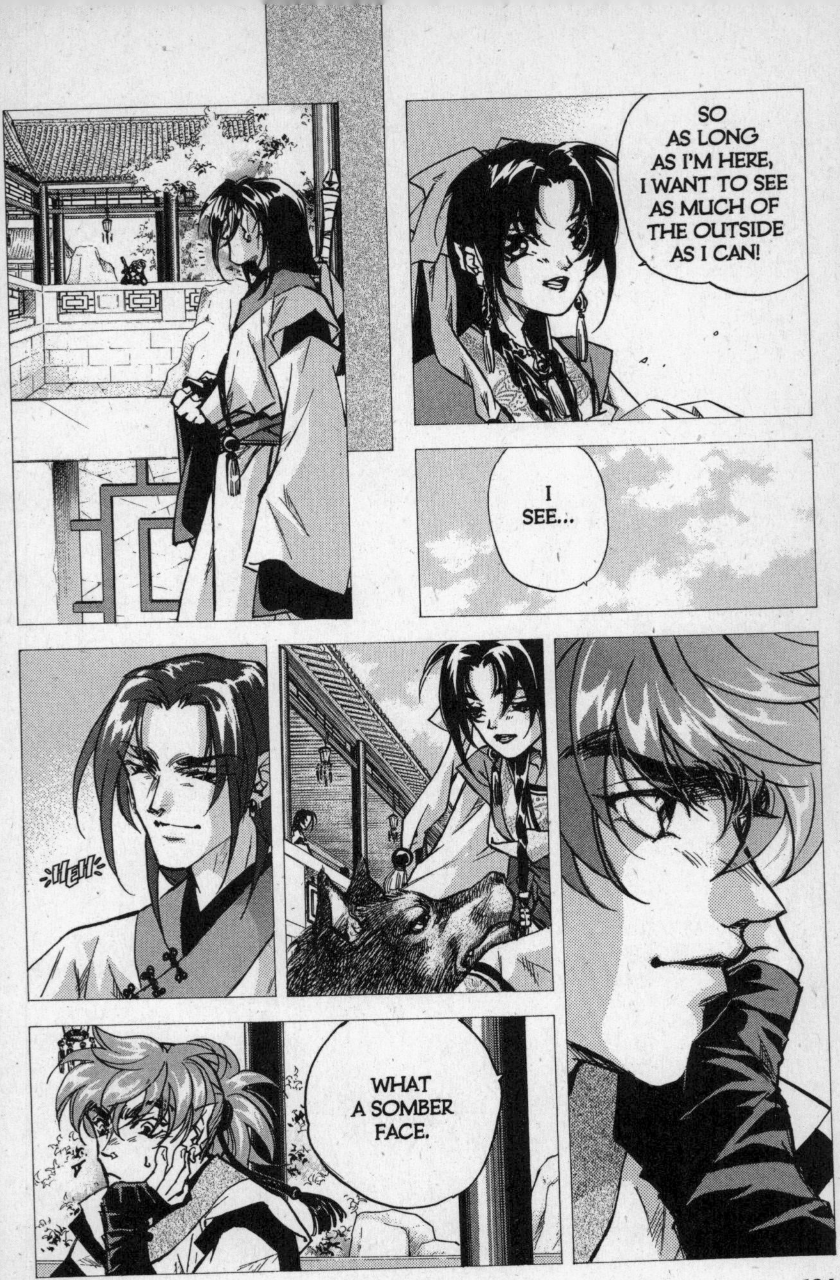
SO AS LONG AS I'M HERE, I WANT TO SEE AS MUCH OF THE OUTSIDE AS I CAN!
I SEE...
HEH
WHAT A SOMBER FACE.

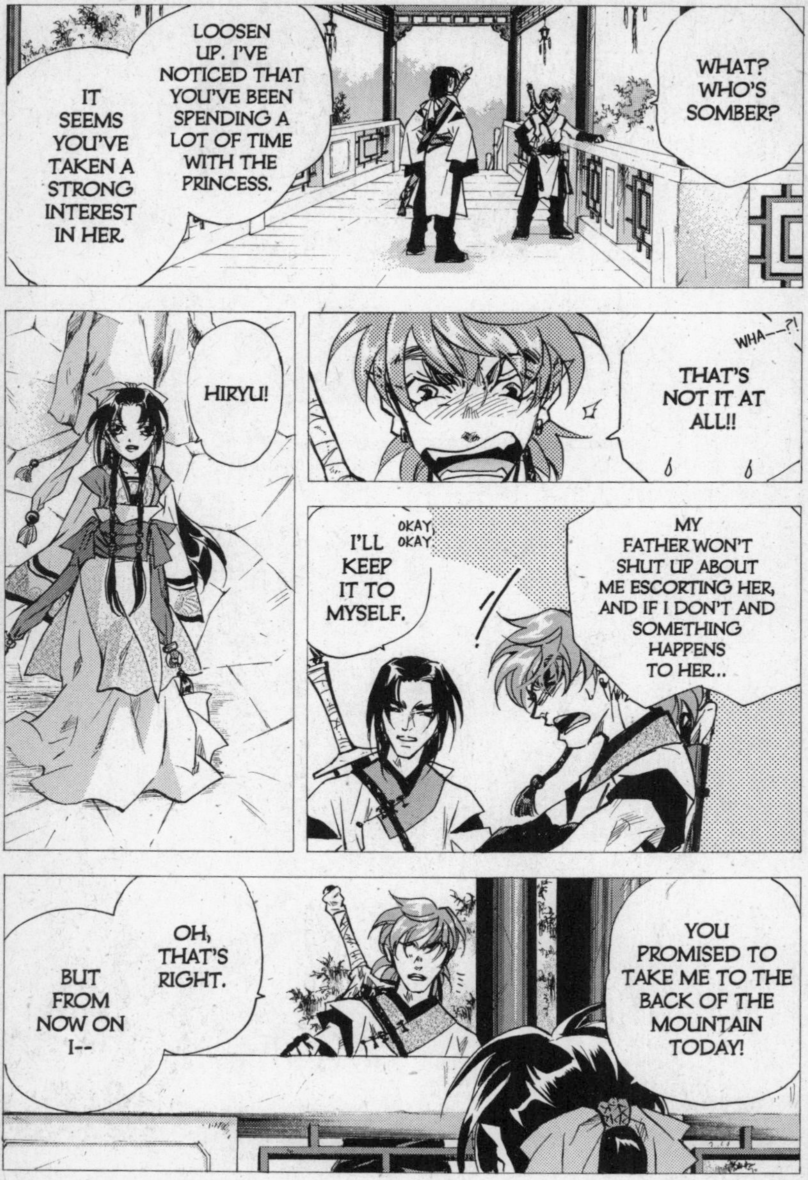
WHAT? WHO'S SOMBER?
LOOSEN UP. I'VE NOTICED THAT YOU'VE BEEN SPENDING A LOT OF TIME WITH THE PRINCESS.
IT SEEMS YOU'VE TAKEN A STRONG INTEREST IN HER.
WHA--?!
THAT'S NOT IT AT ALL!!
MY FATHER WON'T SHUT UP ABOUT ME ESCORTING HER, AND IF I DON'T AND SOMETHING HAPPENS TO HER...
OKAY, OKAY.
I'LL KEEP IT TO MYSELF.
HIRYU!
YOU PROMISED TO TAKE ME TO THE BACK OF THE MOUNTAIN TODAY!
OH, THAT'S RIGHT.
BUT FROM NOW ON I--

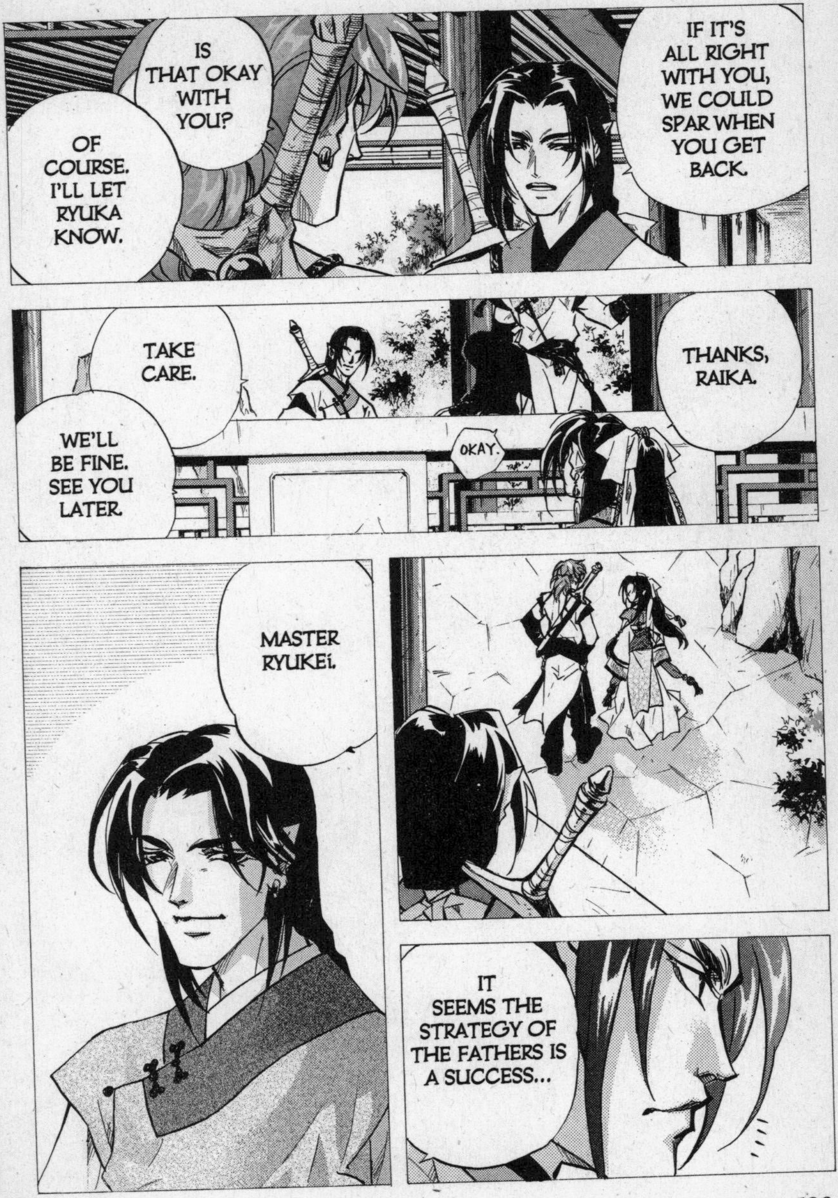
IF IT'S ALL RIGHT WITH YOU, WE COULD SPAR WHEN YOU GET BACK.
IS THAT OKAY WITH YOU?
OF COURSE. I'LL LET RYUKA KNOW.
THANKS, RAIKA.
OKAY.
TAKE CARE.
WE'LL BE FINE. SEE YOU LATER.
IT SEEMS THE STRATEGY OF THE FATHERS IS A SUCCESS...
MASTER RYUKEi.

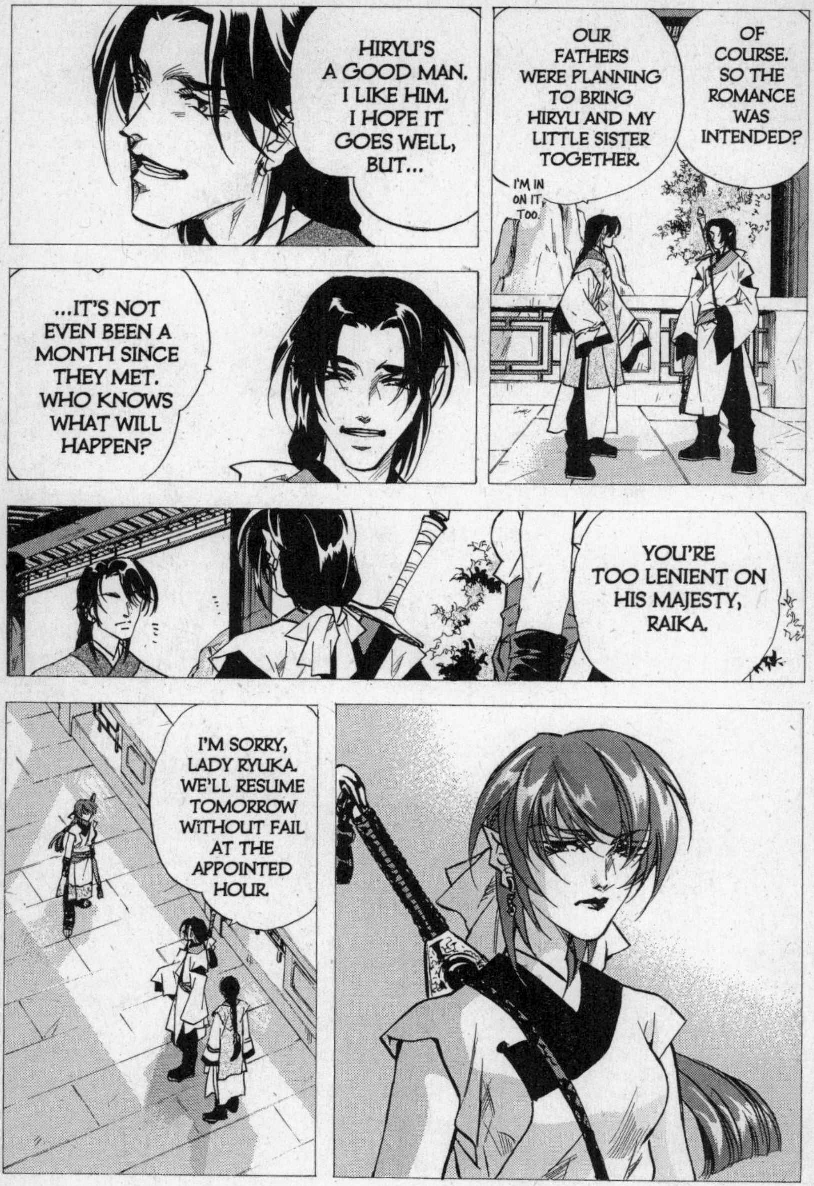
OF COURSE. SO THE ROMANCE WAS INTENDED?
OUR FATHERS WERE PLANNING TO BRING HIRYU AND MY LITTLE SISTER TOGETHER.
I'M IN ON IT, TOO.
HIRYU'S A GOOD MAN. I LIKE HIM. I HOPE IT GOES WELL, BUT...
...IT'S NOT EVEN BEEN A MONTH SINCE THEY MET. WHO KNOWS WHAT WILL HAPPEN?
YOU'RE TOO LENIENT ON HIS MAJESTY, RAIKA.
I'M SORRY, LADY RYUKA. WE'LL RESUME TOMORROW WITHOUT FAIL AT THE APPOINTED HOUR.

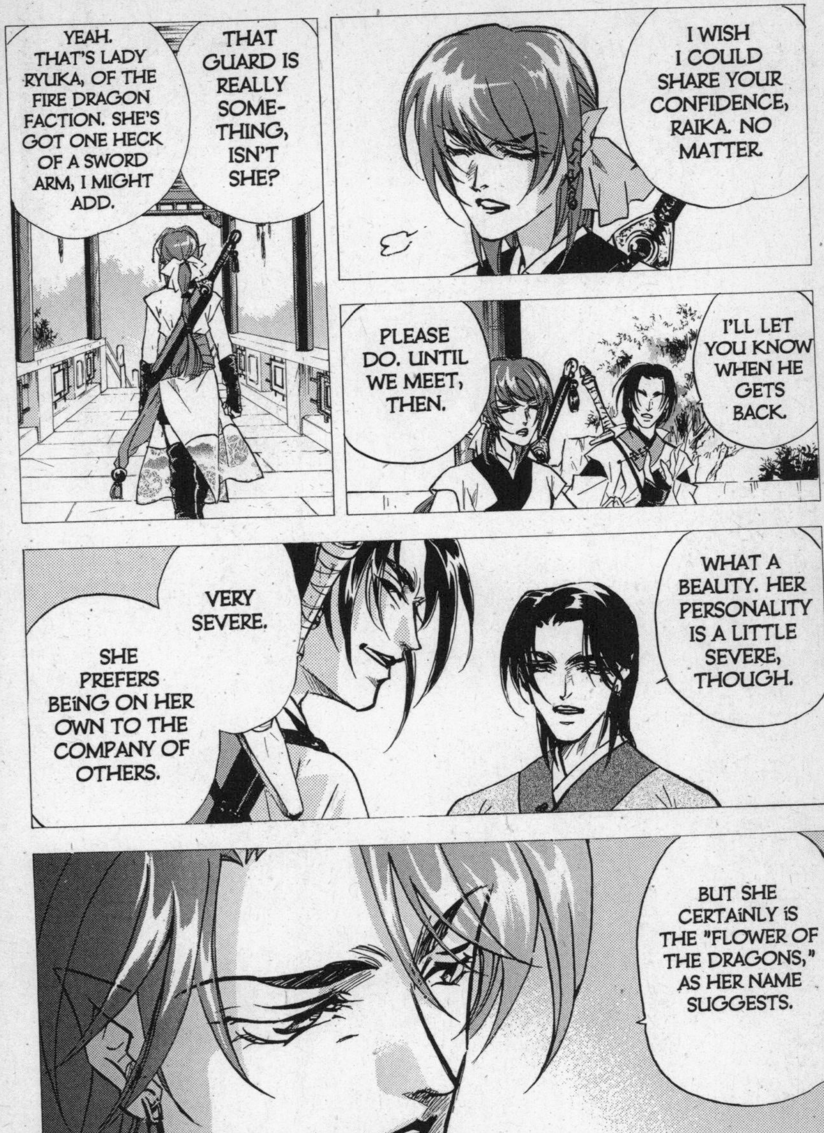
I WISH I COULD SHARE YOUR CONFIDENCE, RAIKA. NO MATTER.
I'LL LET YOU KNOW WHEN HE GETS BACK.
PLEASE DO. UNTIL WE MEET, THEN.
THAT GUARD IS REALLY SOME-THING, ISN'T SHE?
YEAH. THAT'S LADY RYUKA, OF THE FIRE DRAGON FACTION. SHE'S GOT ONE HECK OF A SWORD ARM, I MIGHT ADD.
WHAT A BEAUTY. HER PERSONALITY IS A LITTLE SEVERE, THOUGH.
VERY SEVERE.
SHE PREFERS BEING ON HER OWN TO THE COMPANY OF OTHERS.
BUT SHE CERTAINLY IS THE "FLOWER OF THE DRAGONS," AS HER NAME SUGGESTS.

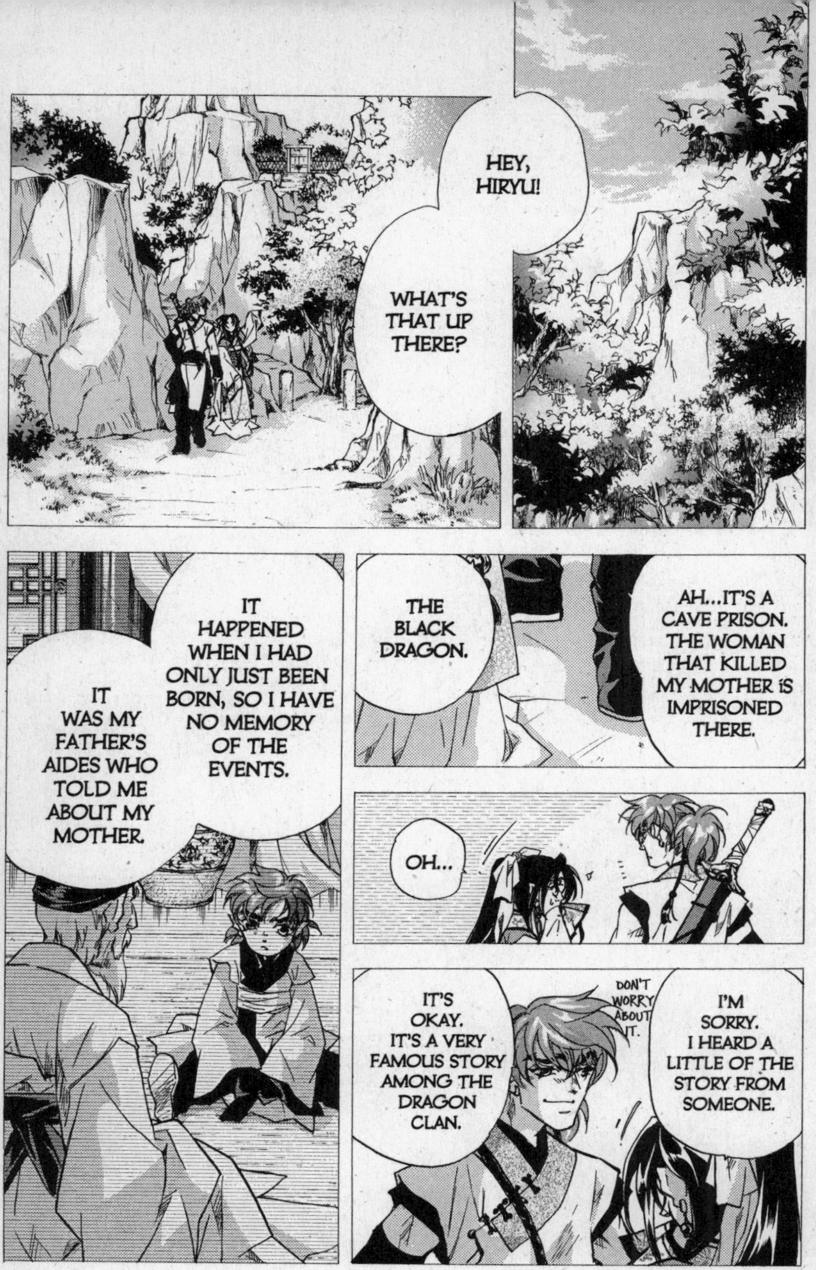
HEY, HIRYU!
WHAT'S THAT UP THERE?
AH...IT'S A CAVE PRISON. THE WOMAN THAT KILLED MY MOTHER iS IMPRISONED THERE.
THE BLACK DRAGON.
OH...
I'M SORRY. I HEARD A LITTLE OF THE STORY FROM SOMEONE.
DON'T WORRY ABOUT IT.
IT'S OKAY. IT'S A VERY FAMOUS STORY AMONG THE DRAGON CLAN.
IT HAPPENED WHEN I HAD ONLY JUST BEEN BORN, SO I HAVE NO MEMORY OF THE EVENTS.
IT WAS MY FATHER'S AIDES WHO TOLD ME ABOUT MY MOTHER.

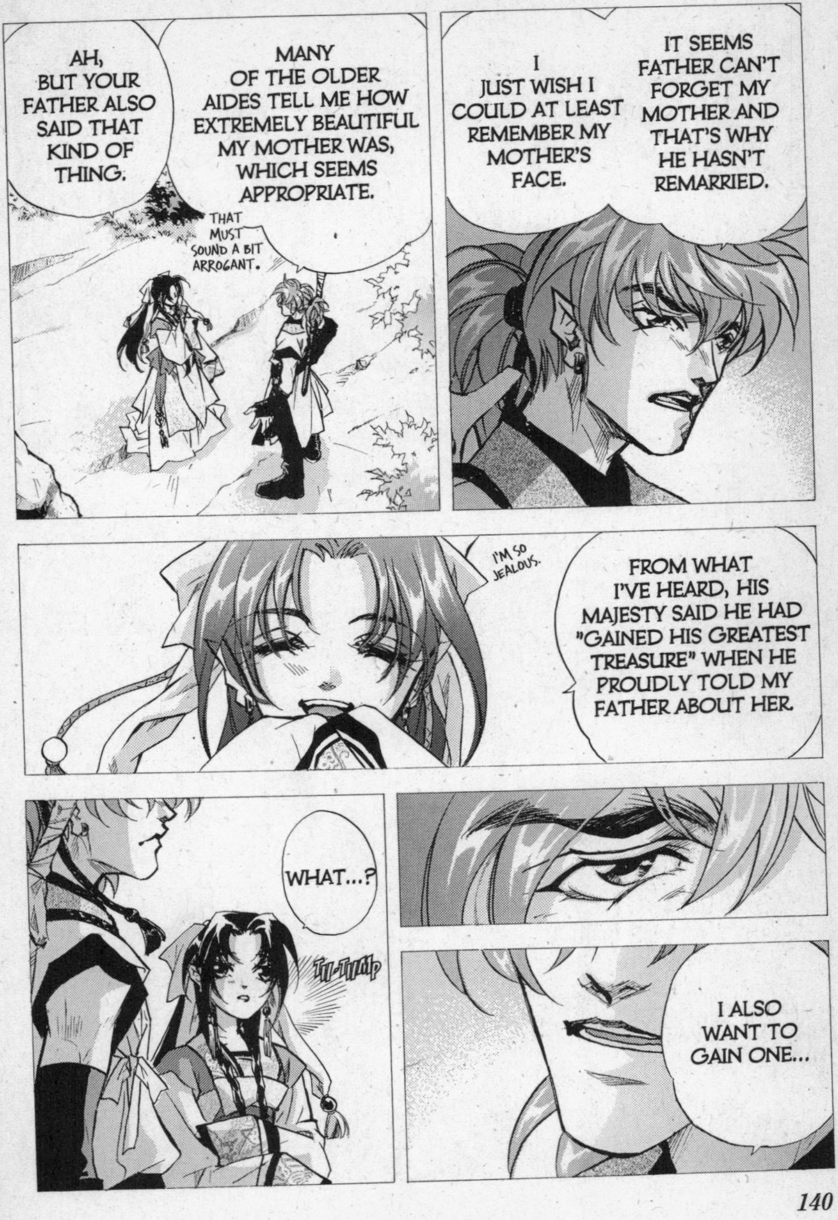

IT SEEMS FATHER CAN'T FORGET MY MOTHER AND THAT'S WHY HE HASN'T REMARRIED.
I JUST WISH I COULD AT LEAST REMEMBER MY MOTHER'S FACE.
MANY OF THE OLDER AIDES TELL ME HOW EXTREMELY BEAUTIFUL MY MOTHER WAS, WHICH SEEMS APPROPRIATE.
THAT MUST SOUND A BIT ARROGANT.
AH, BUT YOUR FATHER ALSO SAID THAT KIND OF THING.
FROM WHAT I'VE HEARD, HIS MAJESTY SAID HE HAD "GAINED HIS GREATEST TREASURE" WHEN HE PROUDLY TOLD MY FATHER ABOUT HER.
I'M SO JEALOUS.
I ALSO WANT TO GAIN ONE...
WHAT...?

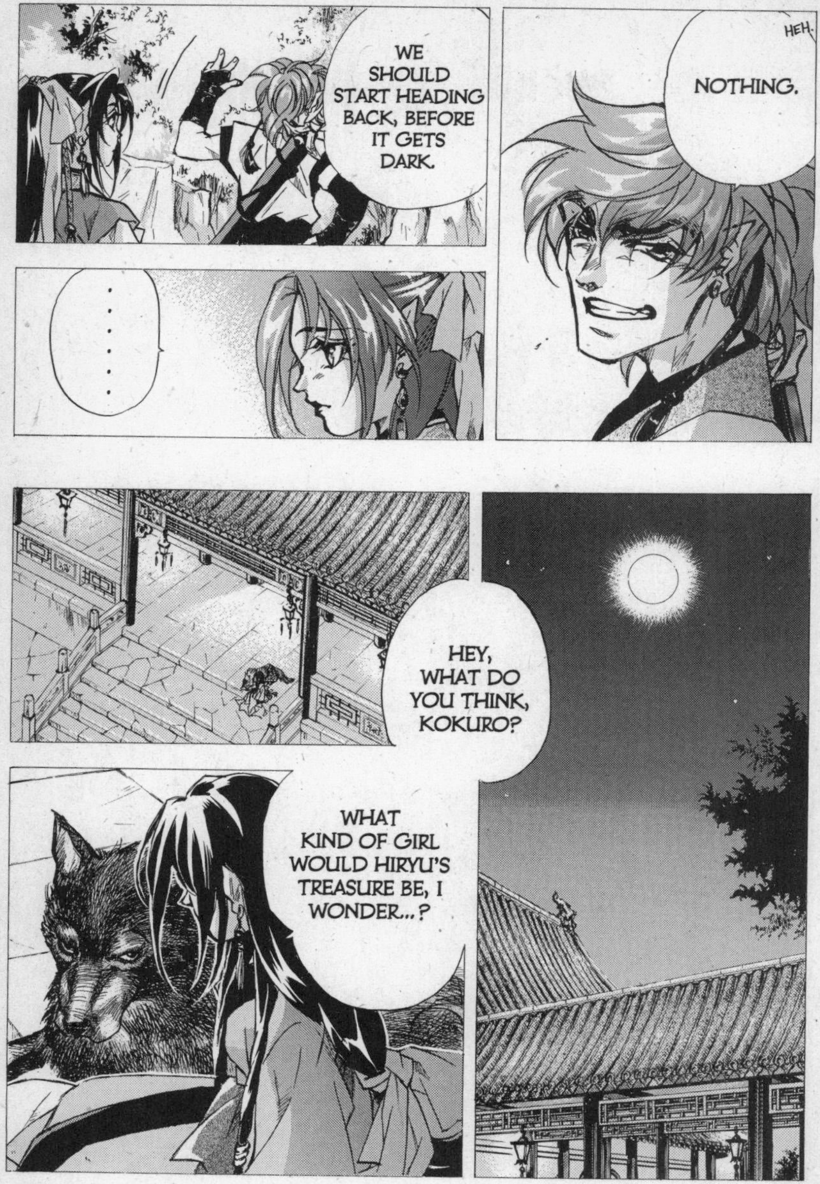
WE SHOULD START HEADING BACK, BEFORE IT GETS DARK.
. . . . . .
HEH.
NOTHING.
HEY, WHAT DO YOU THINK, KOKURO?
WHAT KIND OF GIRL WOULD HIRYU'S TREASURE BE, I WONDER...?

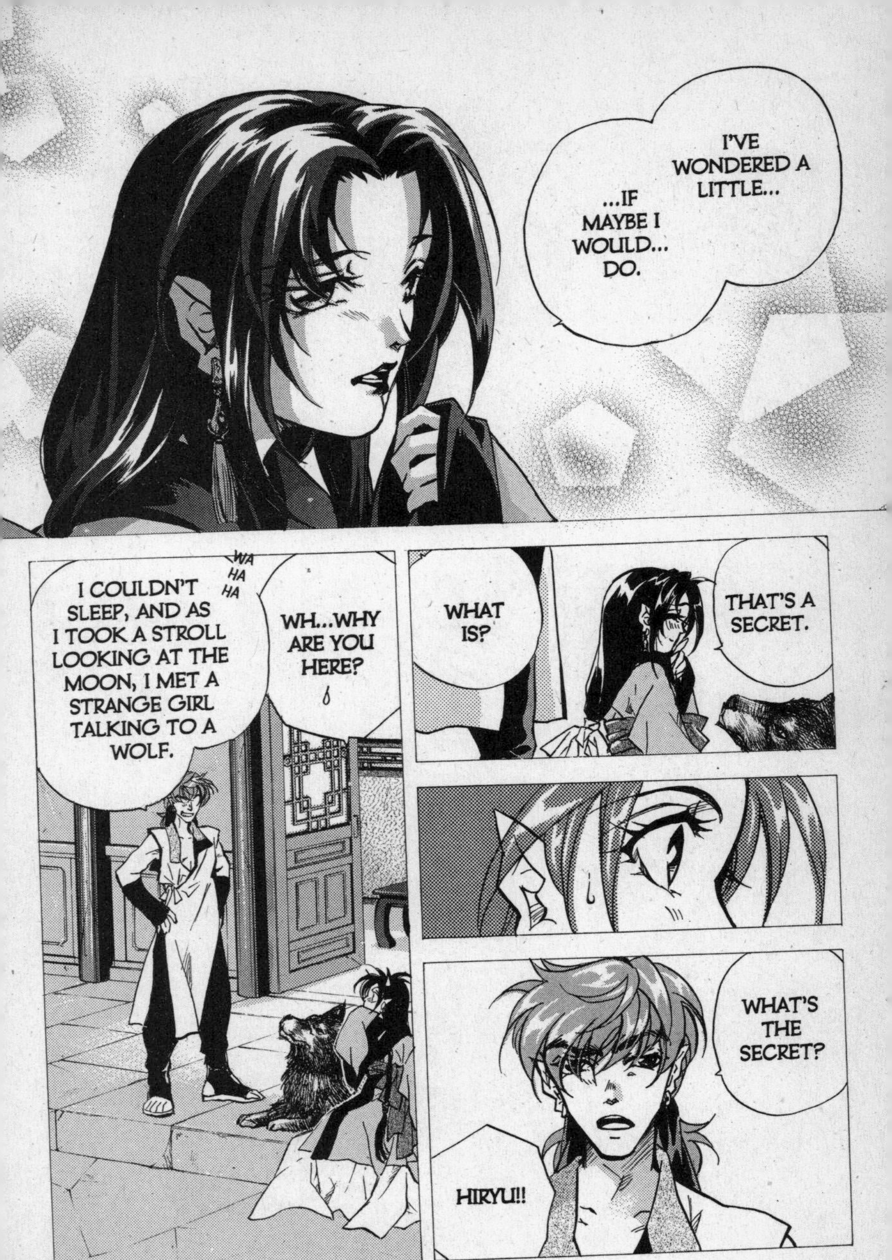
I'VE WONDERED A LITTLE...
...IF MAYBE I WOULD... DO.
THAT'S A SECRET.
WHAT IS?
WHAT'S THE SECRET?
HIRYU!!
WH...WHY ARE YOU HERE?
WA HA HA
I COULDN'T SLEEP, AND AS I TOOK A STROLL LOOKING AT THE MOON, I MET A STRANGE GIRL TALKING TO A WOLF.

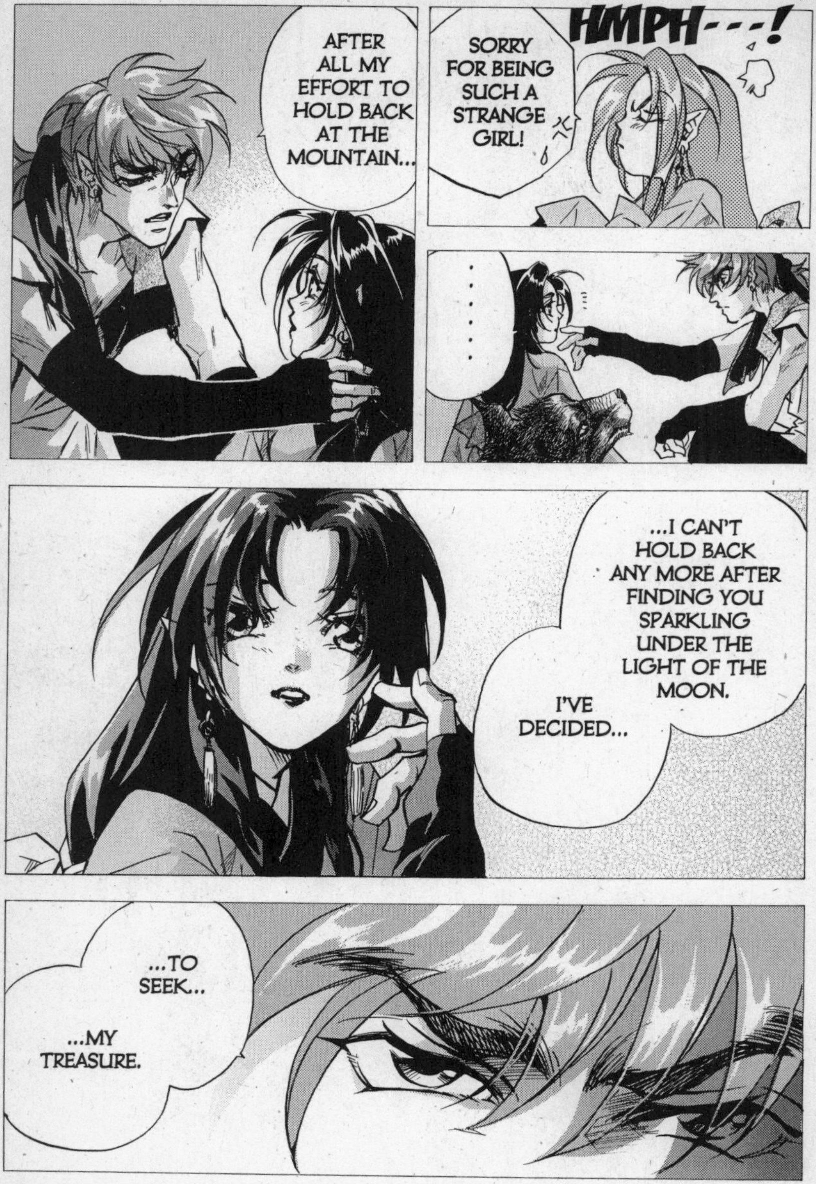
HMPH---!
SORRY FOR BEING SUCH A STRANGE GIRL!
......
AFTER ALL MY EFFORT TO HOLD BACK AT THE MOUNTAIN...
...I CAN'T HOLD BACK ANY MORE AFTER FINDING YOU SPARKLING UNDER THE LIGHT OF THE MOON.
I'VE DECIDED...
...TO SEEK...
...MY TREASURE.

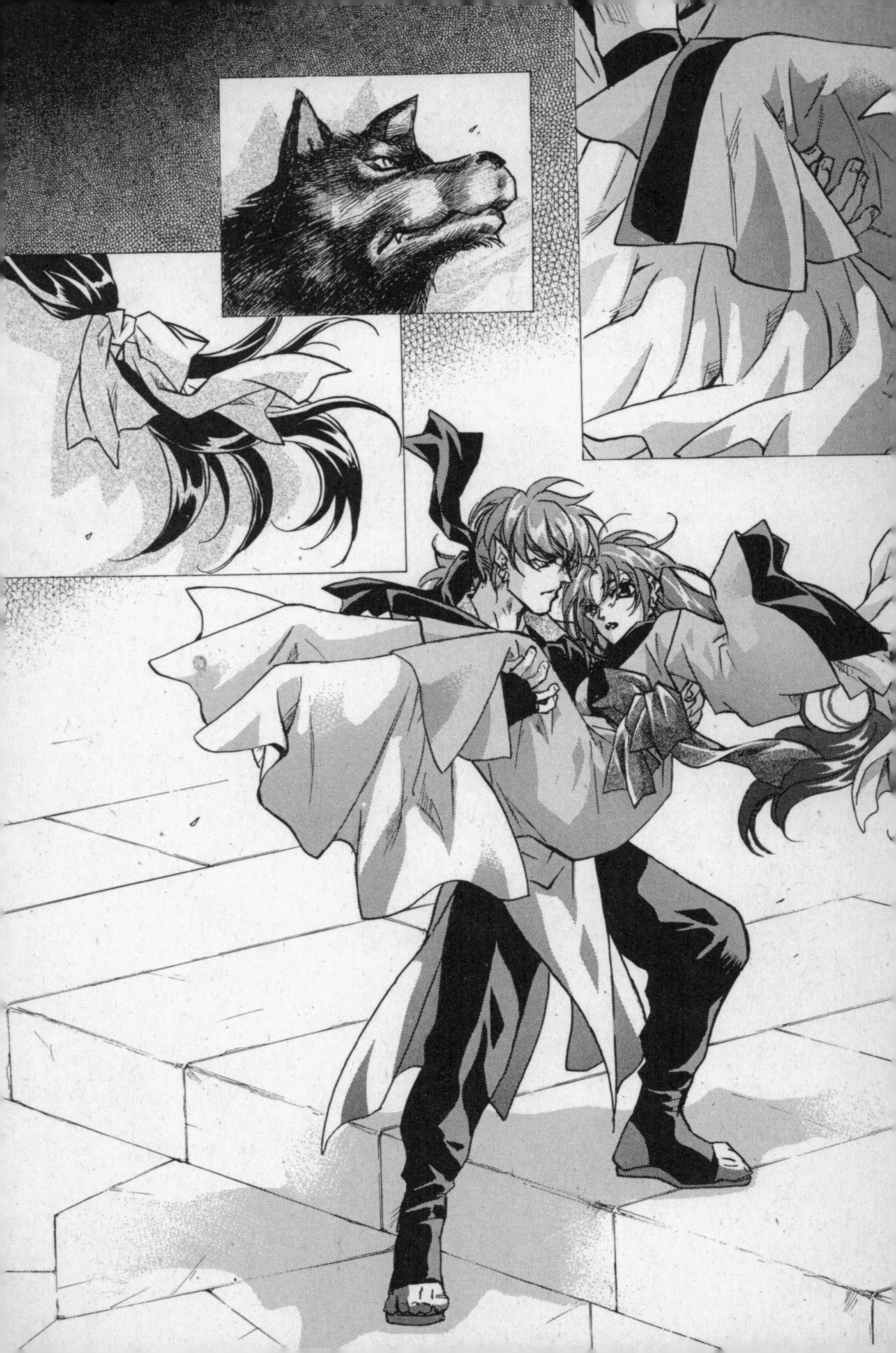

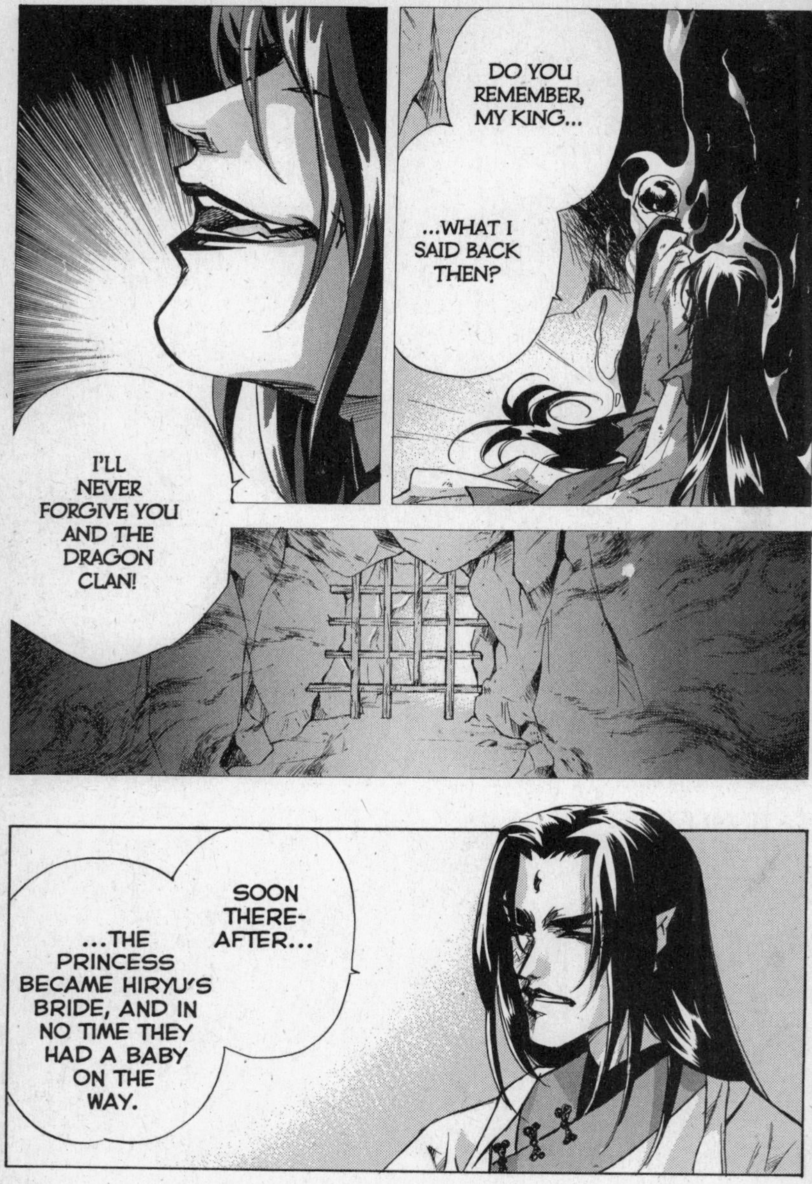
DO YOU REMEMBER, MY KING...
...WHAT I SAID BACK THEN?
I'LL NEVER FORGIVE YOU AND THE DRAGON CLAN!
SOON THERE-AFTER...
...THE PRINCESS BECAME HIRYU'S BRIDE, AND IN NO TIME THEY HAD A BABY ON THE WAY.

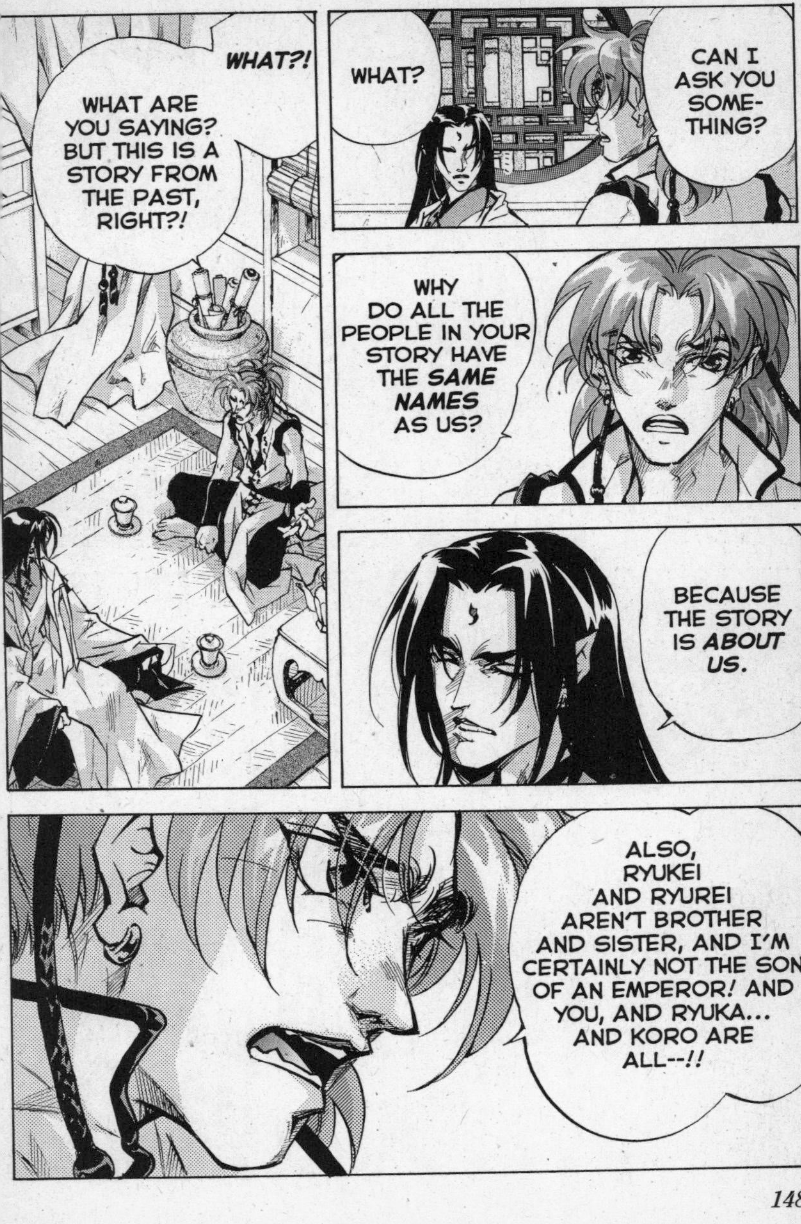
CAN I ASK YOU SOME-THING?
WHAT?
WHY DO ALL THE PEOPLE IN YOUR STORY HAVE THE *SAME NAMES* AS US?
BECAUSE THE STORY IS *ABOUT US.*
WHAT?!
WHAT ARE YOU SAYING? BUT THIS IS A STORY FROM THE PAST, RIGHT?!
ALSO, RYUKEI AND RYUREI AREN'T BROTHER AND SISTER, AND I'M CERTAINLY NOT THE SON OF AN EMPEROR! AND YOU, AND RYUKA... AND KORO ARE ALL--!!

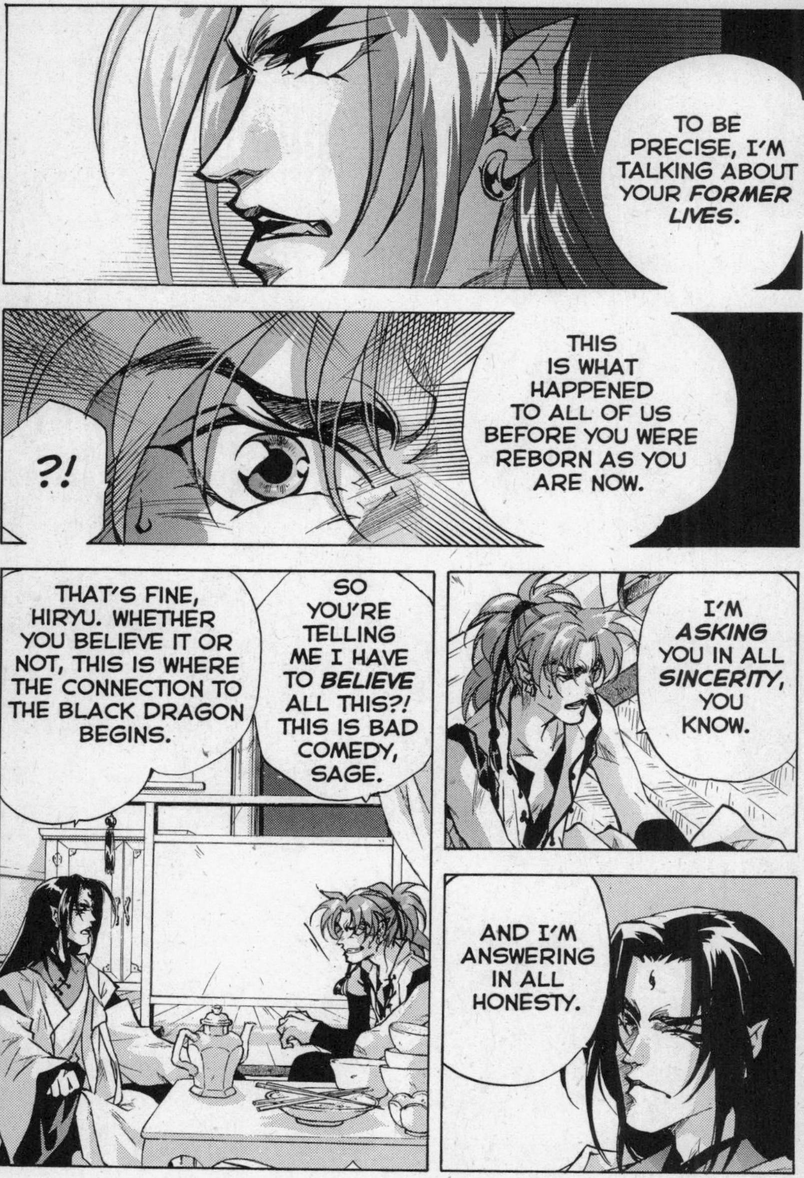
TO BE PRECISE, I'M TALKING ABOUT YOUR *FORMER LIVES*.
THIS IS WHAT HAPPENED TO ALL OF US BEFORE YOU WERE REBORN AS YOU ARE NOW.
?!
I'M *ASKING* YOU IN ALL *SINCERITY*, YOU KNOW.
AND I'M ANSWERING IN ALL HONESTY.
SO YOU'RE TELLING ME I HAVE TO *BELIEVE* ALL THIS?! THIS IS BAD COMEDY, SAGE.
THAT'S FINE, HIRYU. WHETHER YOU BELIEVE IT OR NOT, THIS IS WHERE THE CONNECTION TO THE BLACK DRAGON BEGINS.

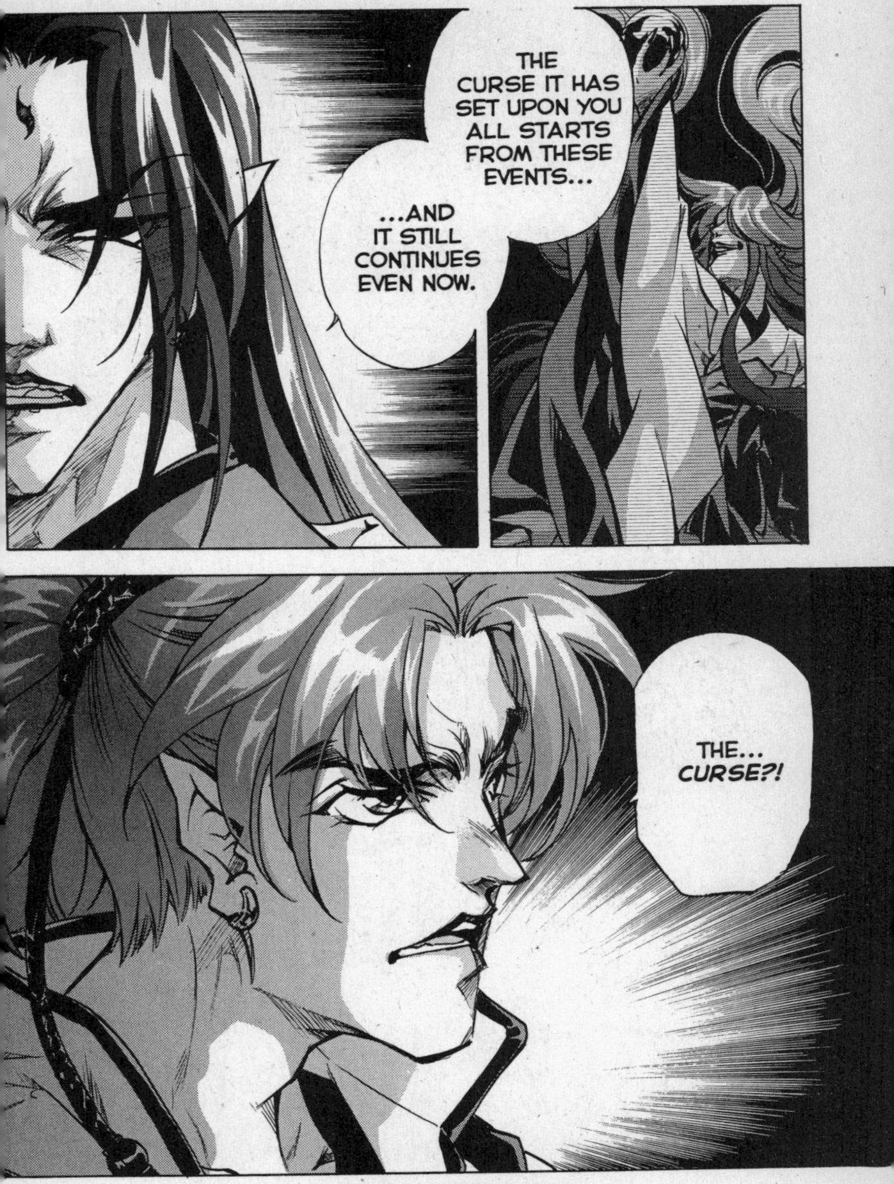
THE CURSE IT HAS SET UPON YOU ALL STARTS FROM THESE EVENTS...
...AND IT STILL CONTINUES EVEN NOW.
THE... *CURSE?!*

END OF CHAPTER 16

CHAPTER 17

(SUPPLEMENTARY STORY • NOW IS THE PAST PART 2)

天龍

TEN-RYU

TENRYU

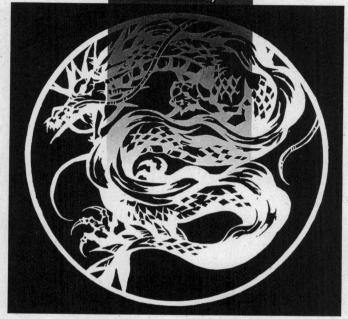

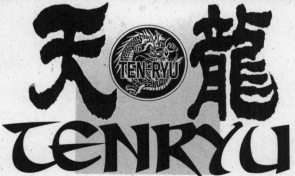

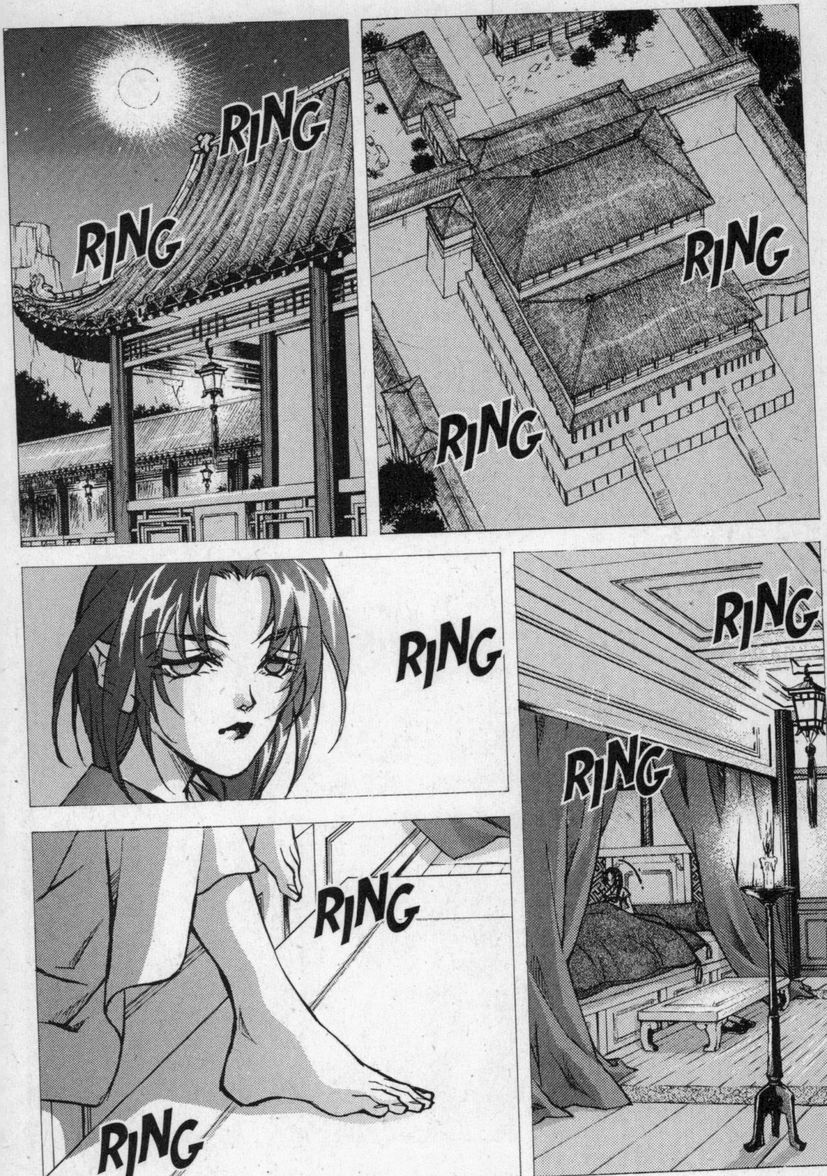
RING
RING
RING
RING
RING
RING
RING
RING
RING
RING

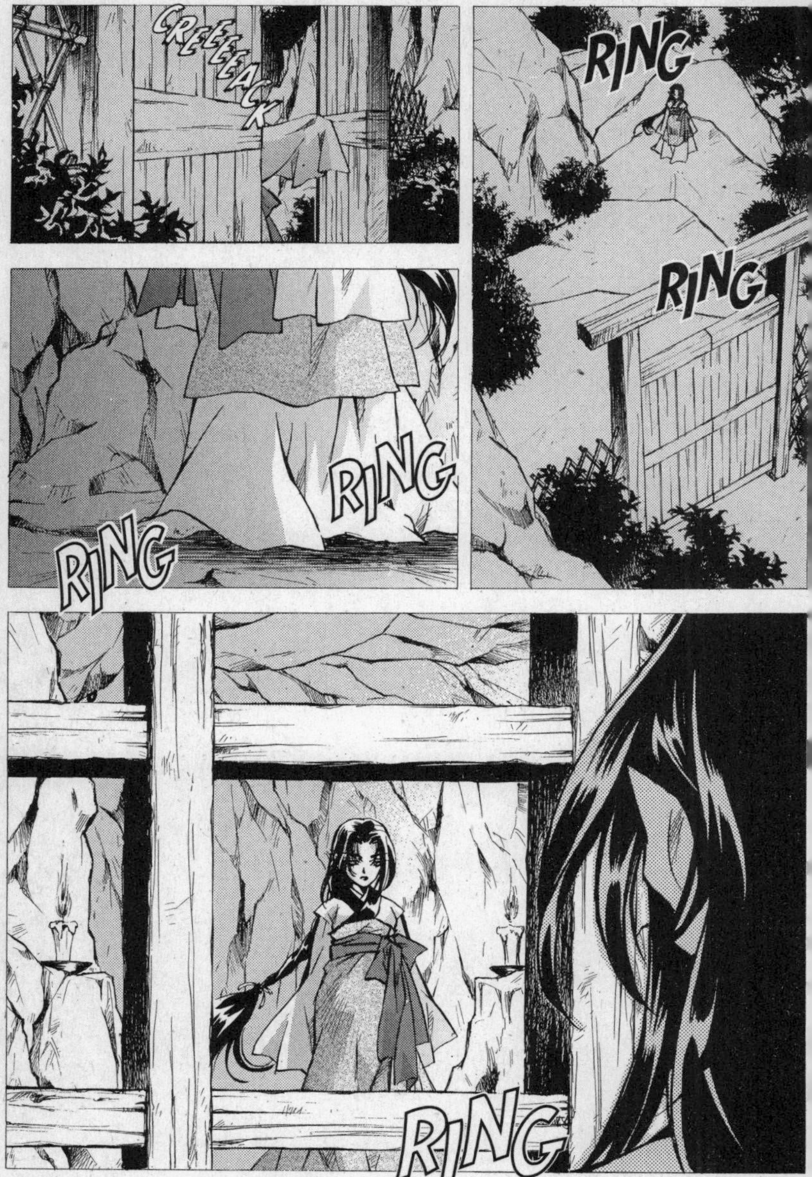
RING
RING
CREEEEACK
RING
RING
RING

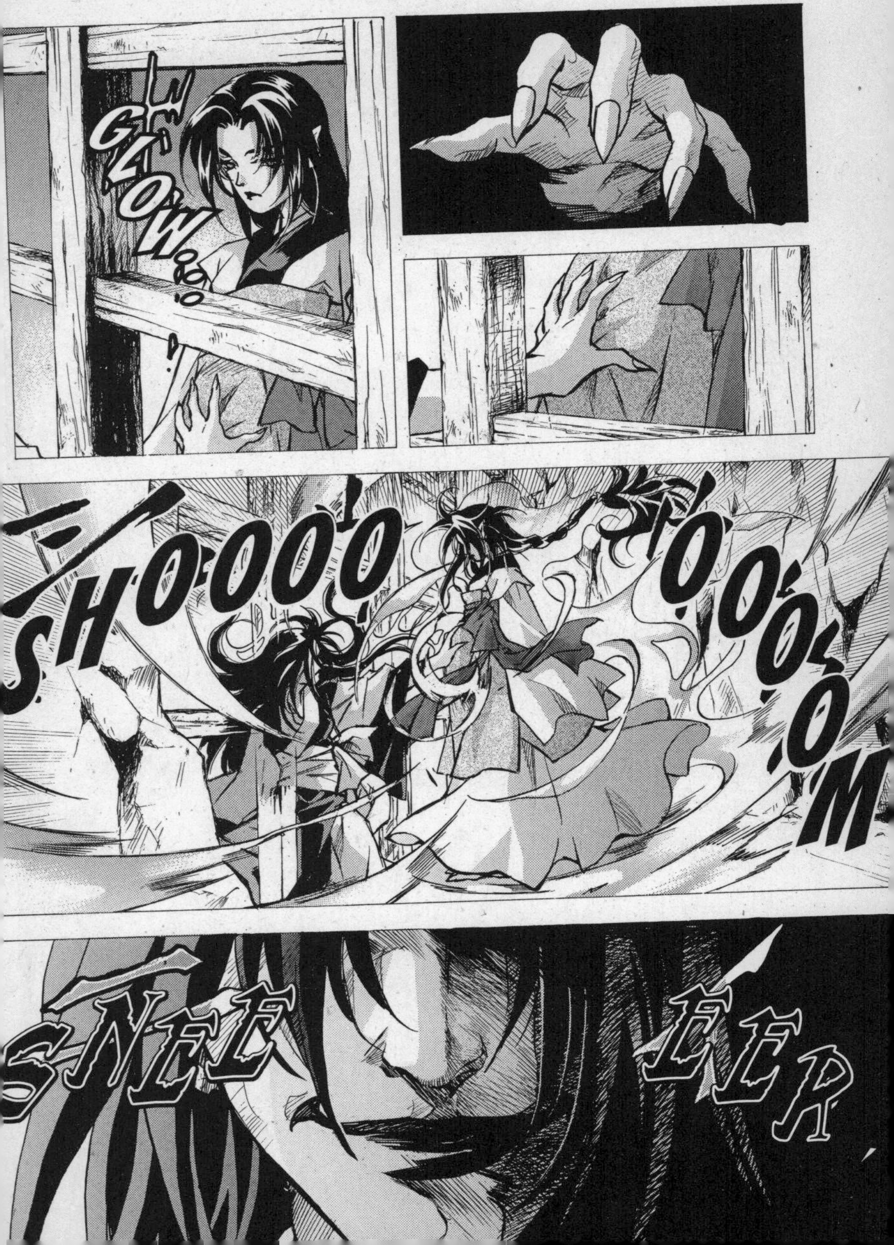
GLOWooo
SHOOOOO
OOOOM
SNEE
EER

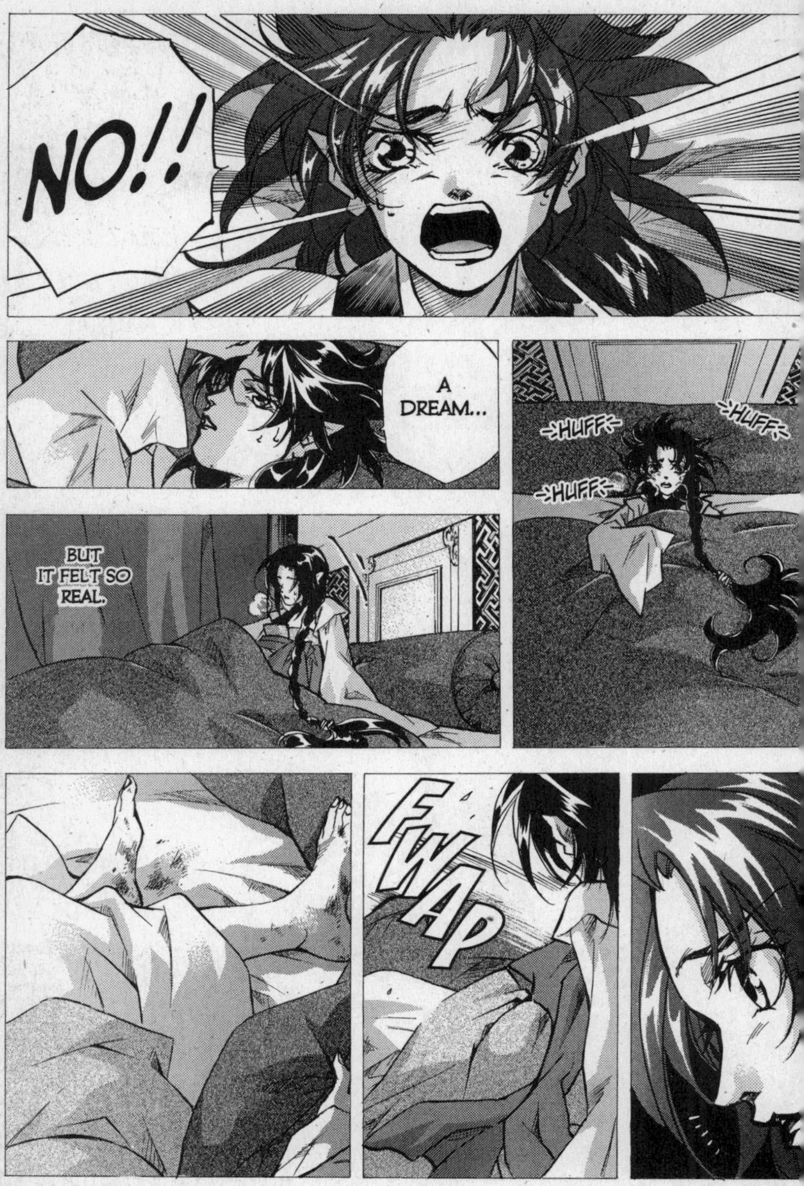
NO!!
HUFF
HUFF
HUFF
A DREAM...
BUT IT FELT SO REAL.
FWAP

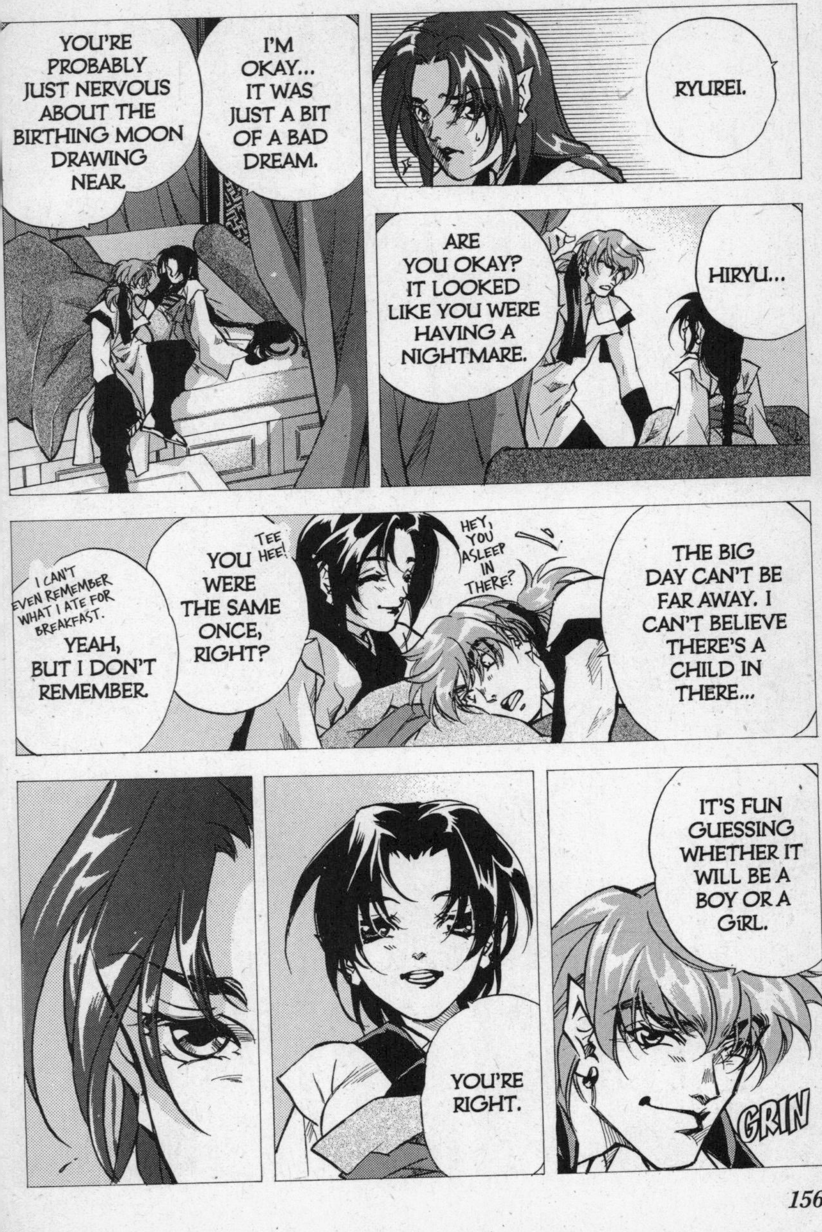
RYUREI.
HIRYU...
ARE YOU OKAY? IT LOOKED LIKE YOU WERE HAVING A NIGHTMARE.
I'M OKAY... IT WAS JUST A BIT OF A BAD DREAM.
YOU'RE PROBABLY JUST NERVOUS ABOUT THE BIRTHING MOON DRAWING NEAR.
THE BIG DAY CAN'T BE FAR AWAY. I CAN'T BELIEVE THERE'S A CHILD IN THERE...
HEY, YOU ASLEEP IN THERE?
TEE HEE!
YOU WERE THE SAME ONCE, RIGHT?
YEAH, BUT I DON'T REMEMBER.
I CAN'T EVEN REMEMBER WHAT I ATE FOR BREAKFAST.
IT'S FUN GUESSING WHETHER IT WILL BE A BOY OR A GIRL.
GRIN
YOU'RE RIGHT.

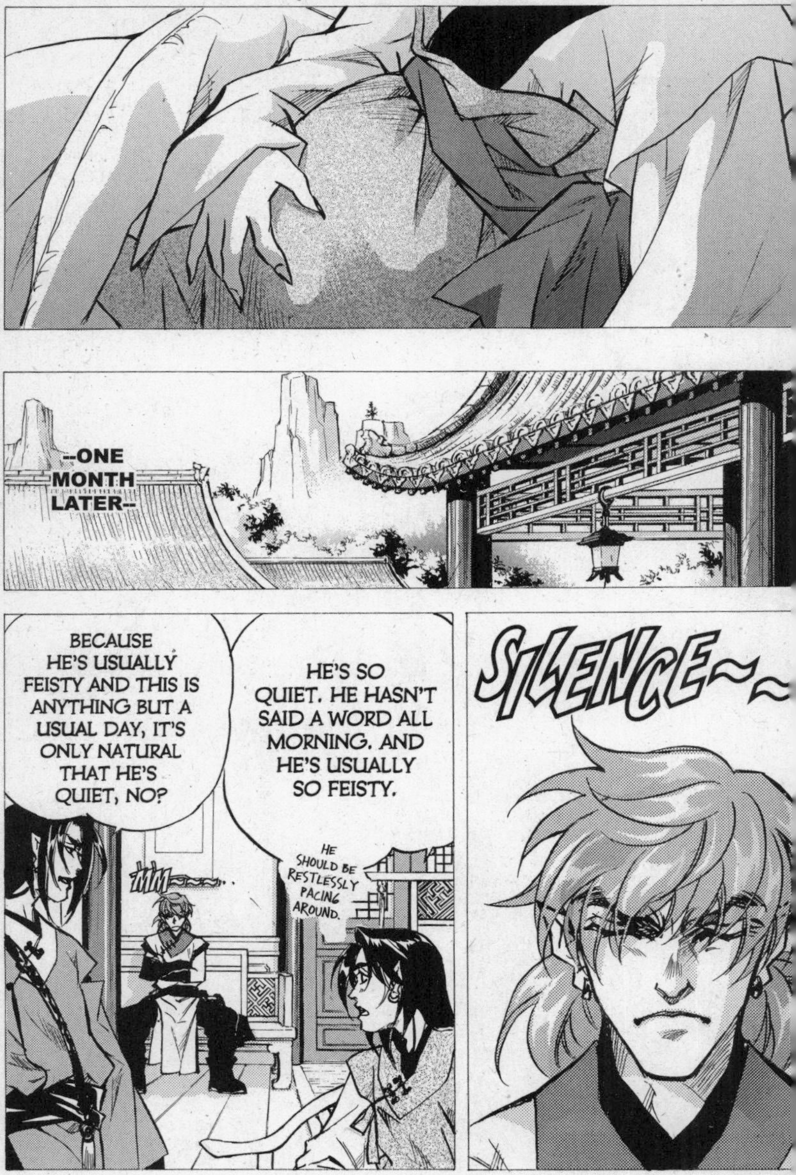
--ONE MONTH LATER--
SILENCE~~
HE'S SO QUIET. HE HASN'T SAID A WORD ALL MORNING. AND HE'S USUALLY SO FEISTY.
BECAUSE HE'S USUALLY FEISTY AND THIS IS ANYTHING BUT A USUAL DAY, IT'S ONLY NATURAL THAT HE'S QUIET, NO?
HE SHOULD BE RESTLESSLY PACING AROUND.
MM~~...

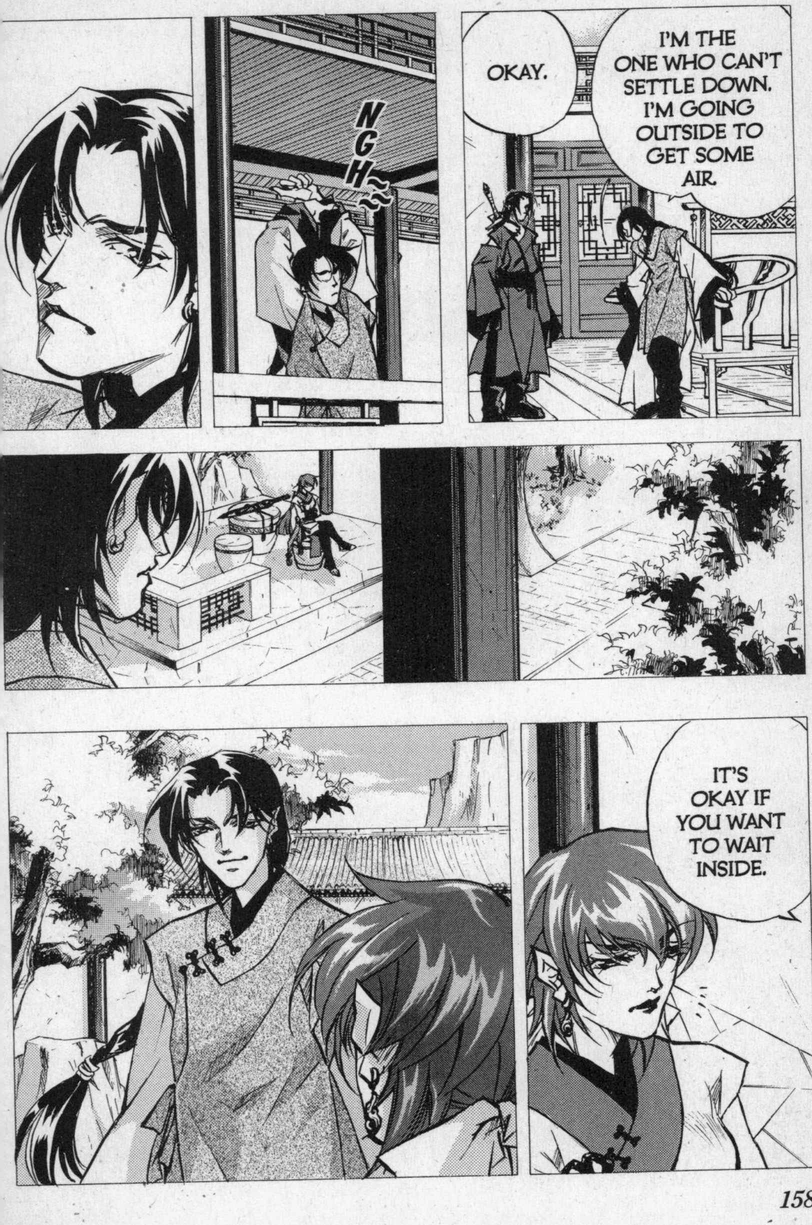
I'M THE ONE WHO CAN'T SETTLE DOWN. I'M GOING OUTSIDE TO GET SOME AIR.
OKAY.
NGH~
IT'S OKAY IF YOU WANT TO WAIT INSIDE.

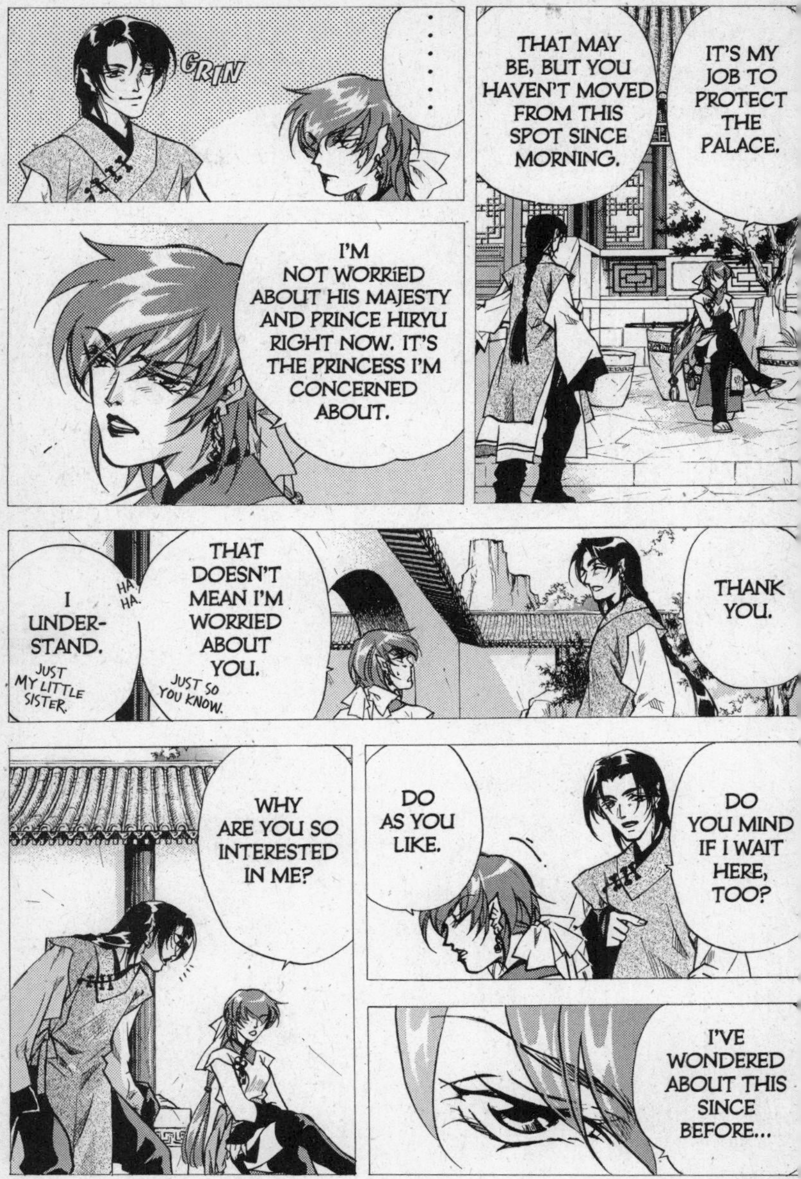
IT'S MY JOB TO PROTECT THE PALACE.
THAT MAY BE, BUT YOU HAVEN'T MOVED FROM THIS SPOT SINCE MORNING.
GRIN
. . . . .
I'M NOT WORRiED ABOUT HIS MAJESTY AND PRINCE HIRYU RIGHT NOW. IT'S THE PRINCESS I'M CONCERNED ABOUT.
THANK YOU.
THAT DOESN'T MEAN I'M WORRIED ABOUT YOU.
JUST SO YOU KNOW.
HA HA.
I UNDER-STAND.
JUST MY LITTLE SISTER.
DO YOU MIND IF I WAIT HERE, TOO?
DO AS YOU LIKE.
I'VE WONDERED ABOUT THIS SINCE BEFORE...
WHY ARE YOU SO INTERESTED IN ME?

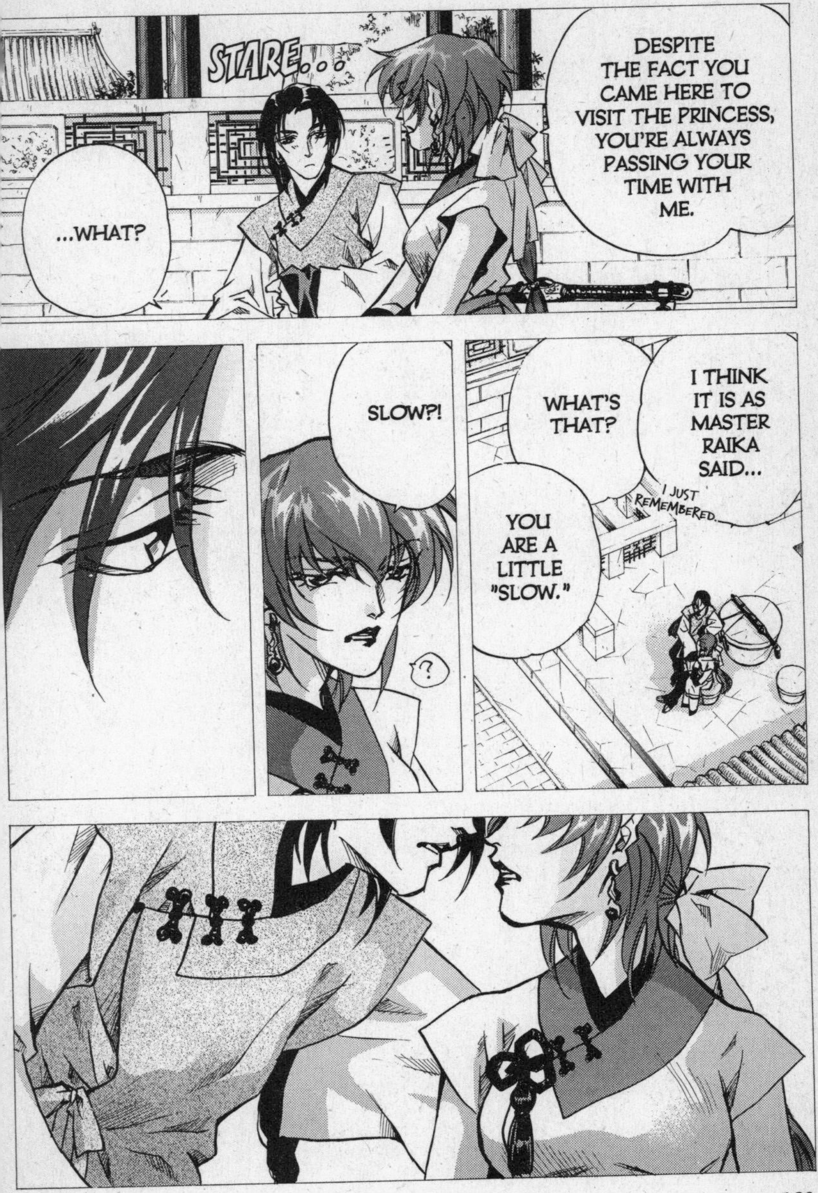
DESPITE THE FACT YOU CAME HERE TO VISIT THE PRINCESS, YOU'RE ALWAYS PASSING YOUR TIME WITH ME.
STARE...
...WHAT?
I THINK IT IS AS MASTER RAIKA SAID...
WHAT'S THAT?
I JUST REMEMBERED...
YOU ARE A LITTLE "SLOW."
SLOW?!
?

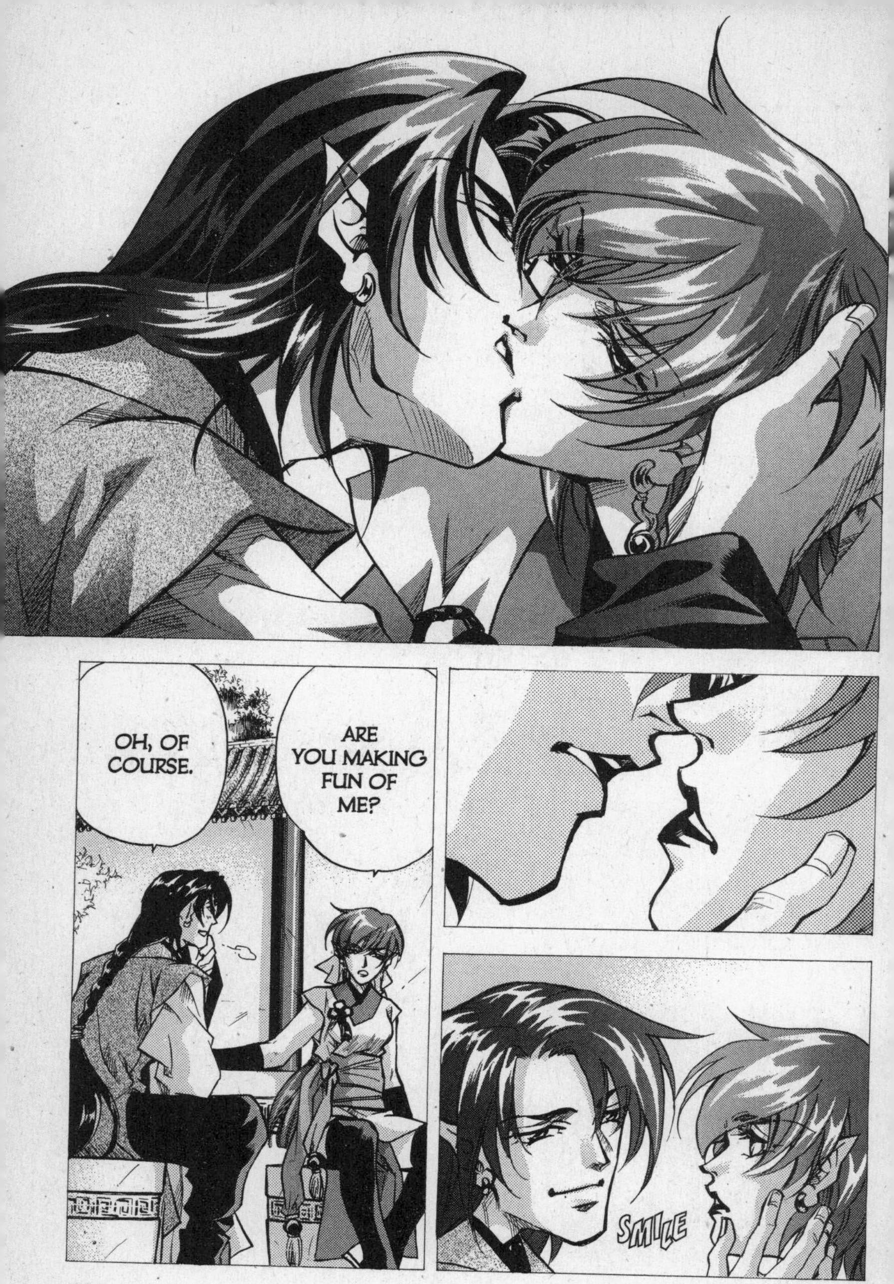
ARE YOU MAKING FUN OF ME?
OH, OF COURSE.
SMILE

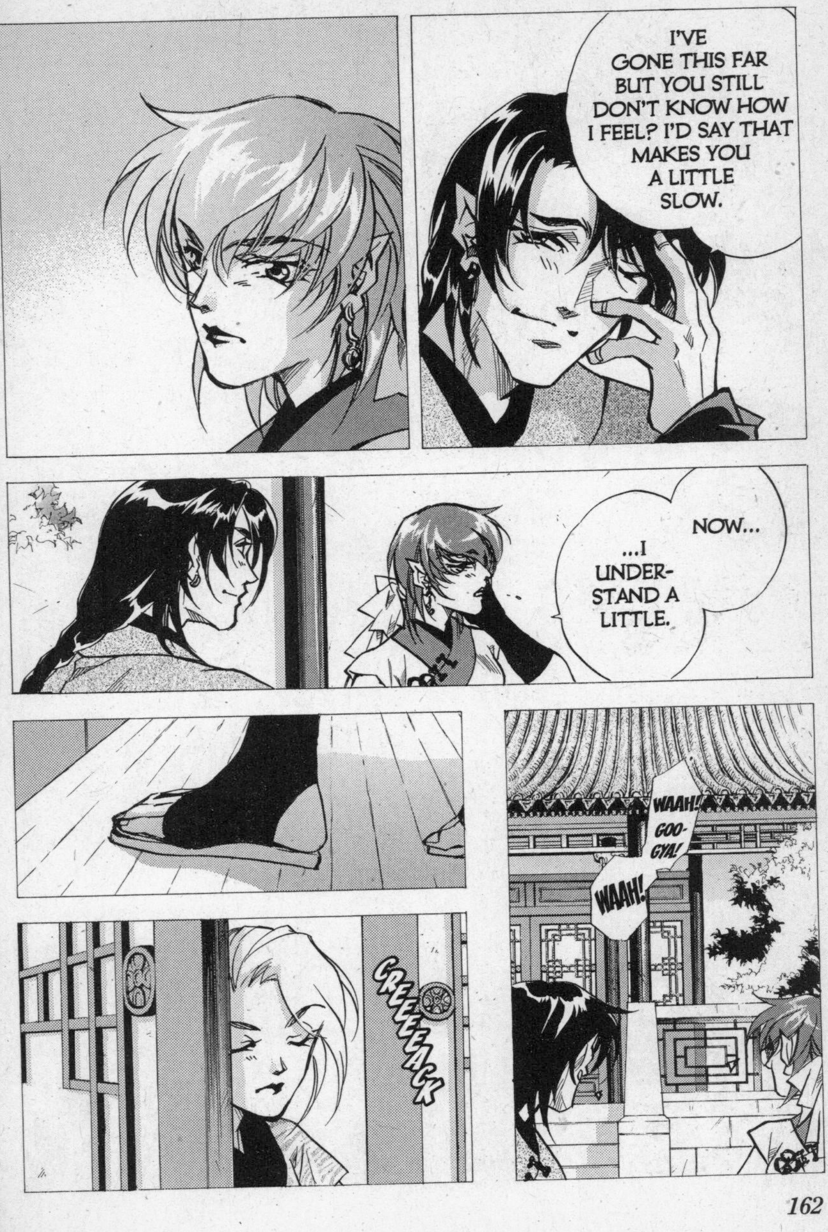
I'VE GONE THIS FAR BUT YOU STILL DON'T KNOW HOW I FEEL? I'D SAY THAT MAKES YOU A LITTLE SLOW.
NOW...
...I UNDER-STAND A LITTLE.
WAAH! GOO-GYA!
WAAH!
CREEEACK

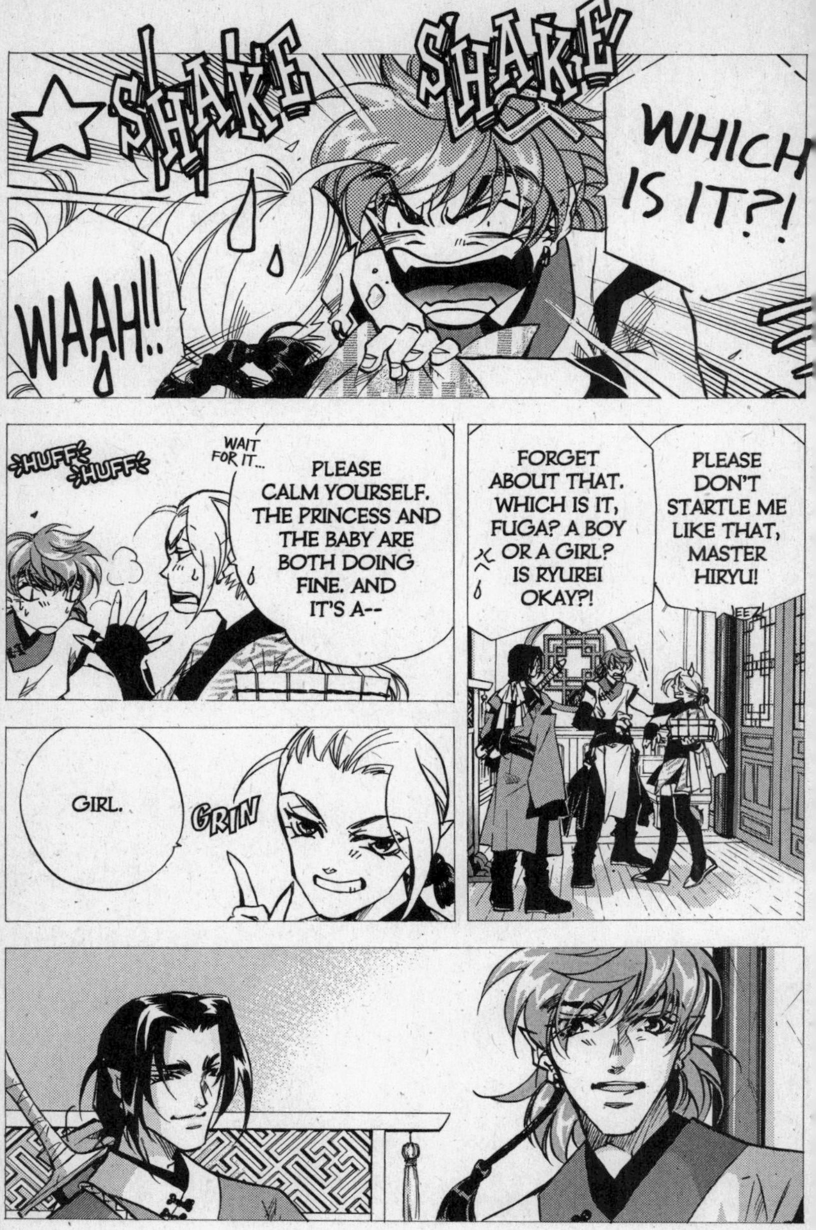
WHICH IS IT?!
SHAKE
SHAKE
WAAH!!
PLEASE DON'T STARTLE ME LIKE THAT, MASTER HIRYU!
FORGET ABOUT THAT. WHICH IS IT, FUGA? A BOY OR A GIRL? IS RYUREI OKAY?!
PLEASE CALM YOURSELF. THE PRINCESS AND THE BABY ARE BOTH DOING FINE. AND IT'S A--
WAIT FOR IT...
HUFF HUFF
GRIN
GIRL.

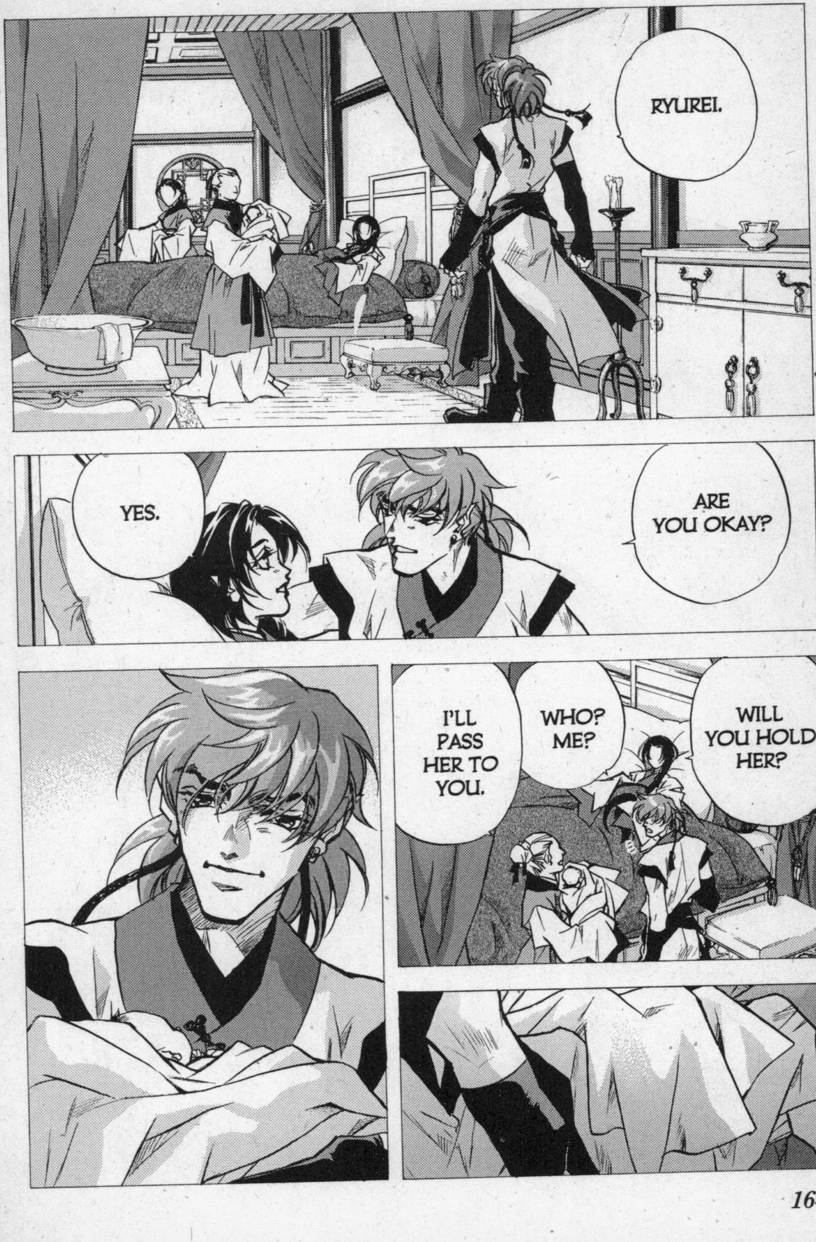
RYUREI.
ARE YOU OKAY?
YES.
WILL YOU HOLD HER?
WHO? ME?
I'LL PASS HER TO YOU.

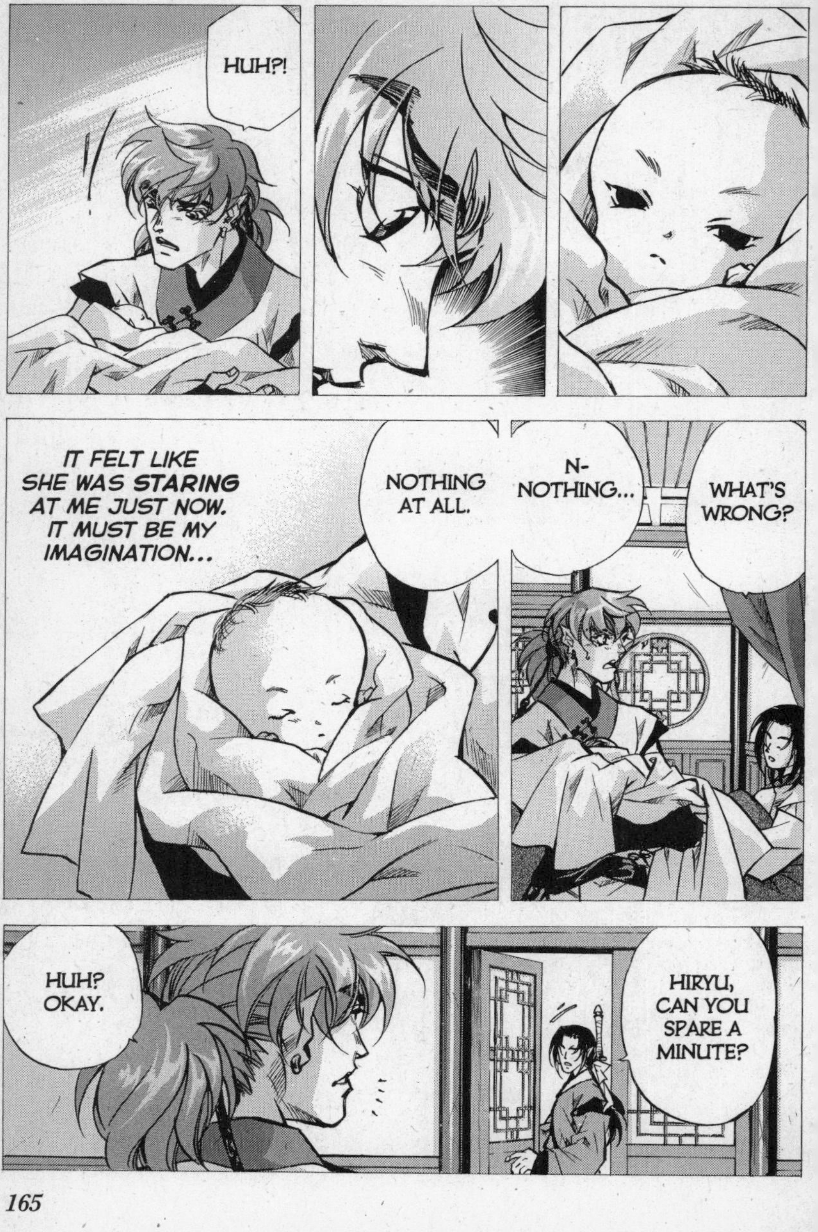
HUH?!
WHAT'S WRONG?
N- NOTHING...
NOTHING AT ALL.
IT FELT LIKE SHE WAS *STARING* AT ME JUST NOW. IT MUST BE MY IMAGINATION...
HIRYU, CAN YOU SPARE A MINUTE?
HUH? OKAY.

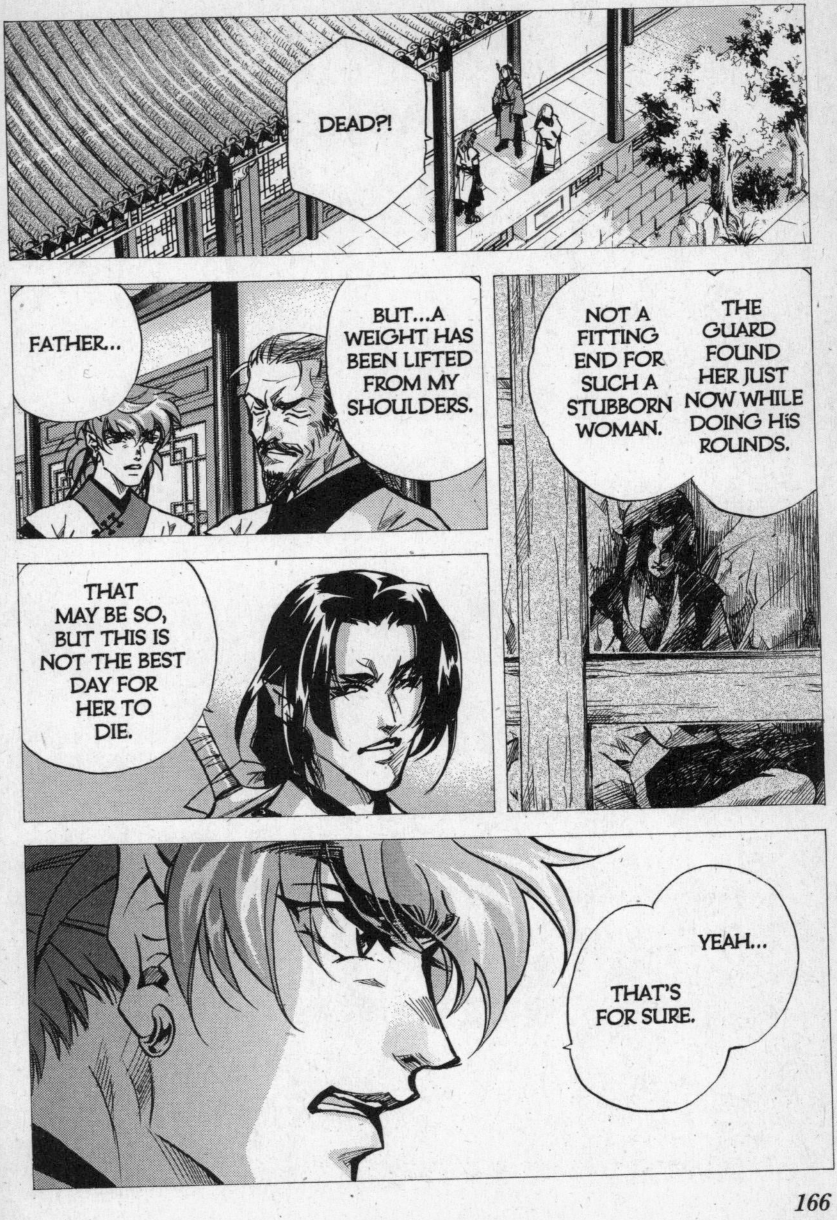
DEAD?!
THE GUARD FOUND HER JUST NOW WHILE DOING HIS ROUNDS.
NOT A FITTING END FOR SUCH A STUBBORN WOMAN.
BUT...A WEIGHT HAS BEEN LIFTED FROM MY SHOULDERS.
FATHER...
THAT MAY BE SO, BUT THIS IS NOT THE BEST DAY FOR HER TO DIE.
YEAH...
THAT'S FOR SURE.

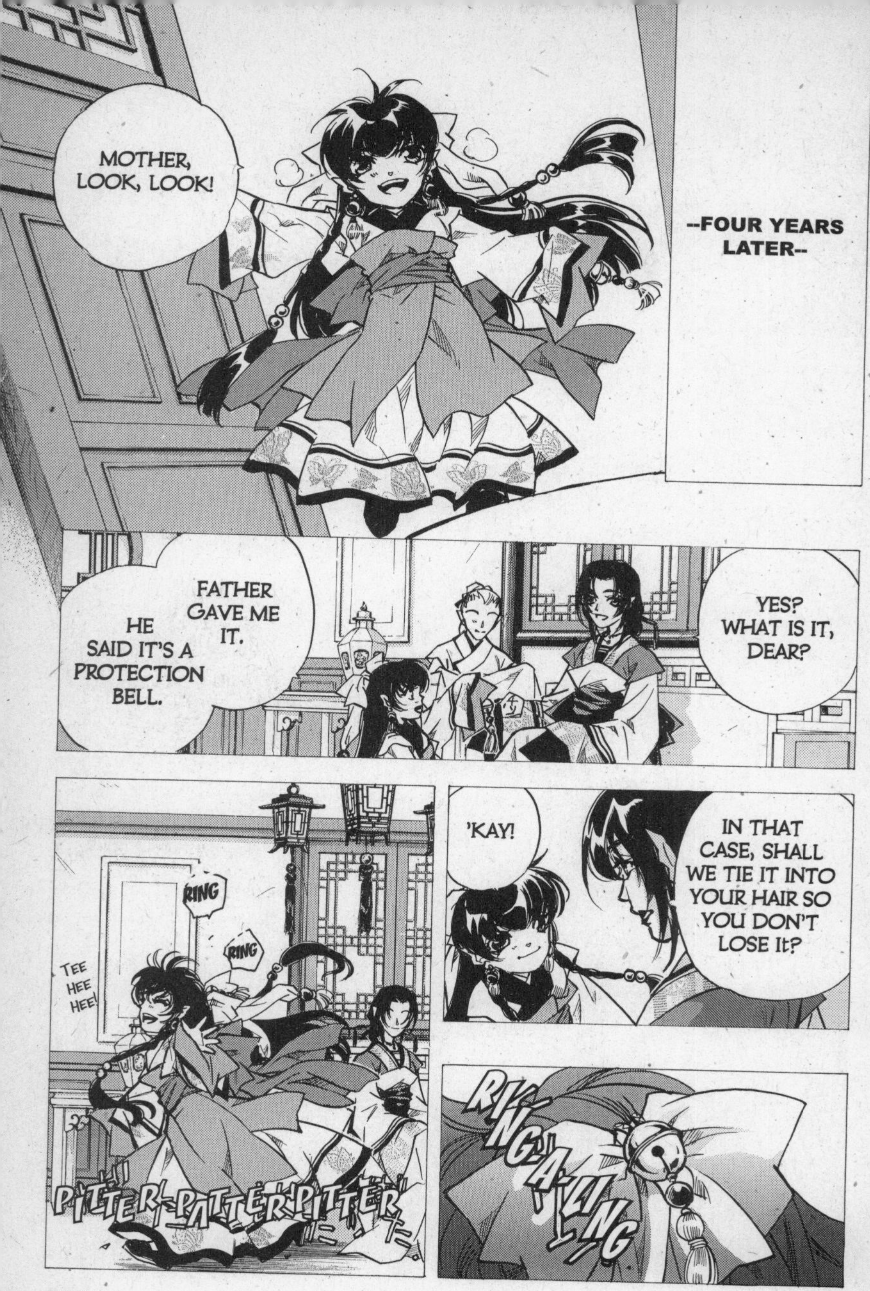
--FOUR YEARS LATER--
MOTHER, LOOK, LOOK!
YES? WHAT IS IT, DEAR?
FATHER GAVE ME IT.
HE SAID IT'S A PROTECTION BELL.
IN THAT CASE, SHALL WE TIE IT INTO YOUR HAIR SO YOU DON'T LOSE It?
'KAY!
RING-A-LING
RING
RING
TEE HEE HEE!
PITTER-PATTER-PITTER

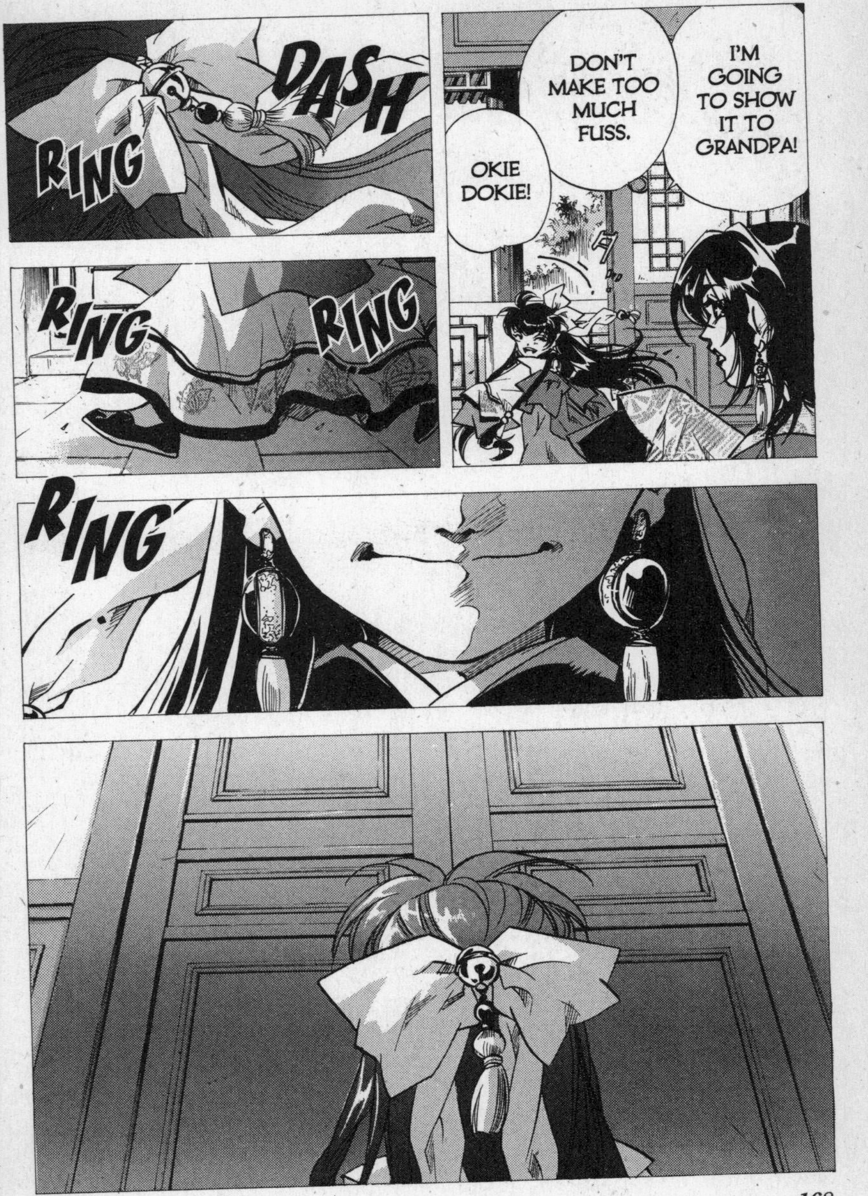
I'M GOING TO SHOW IT TO GRANDPA!
DON'T MAKE TOO MUCH FUSS.
OKIE DOKIE!
DASH
RING
RING
RING
RING

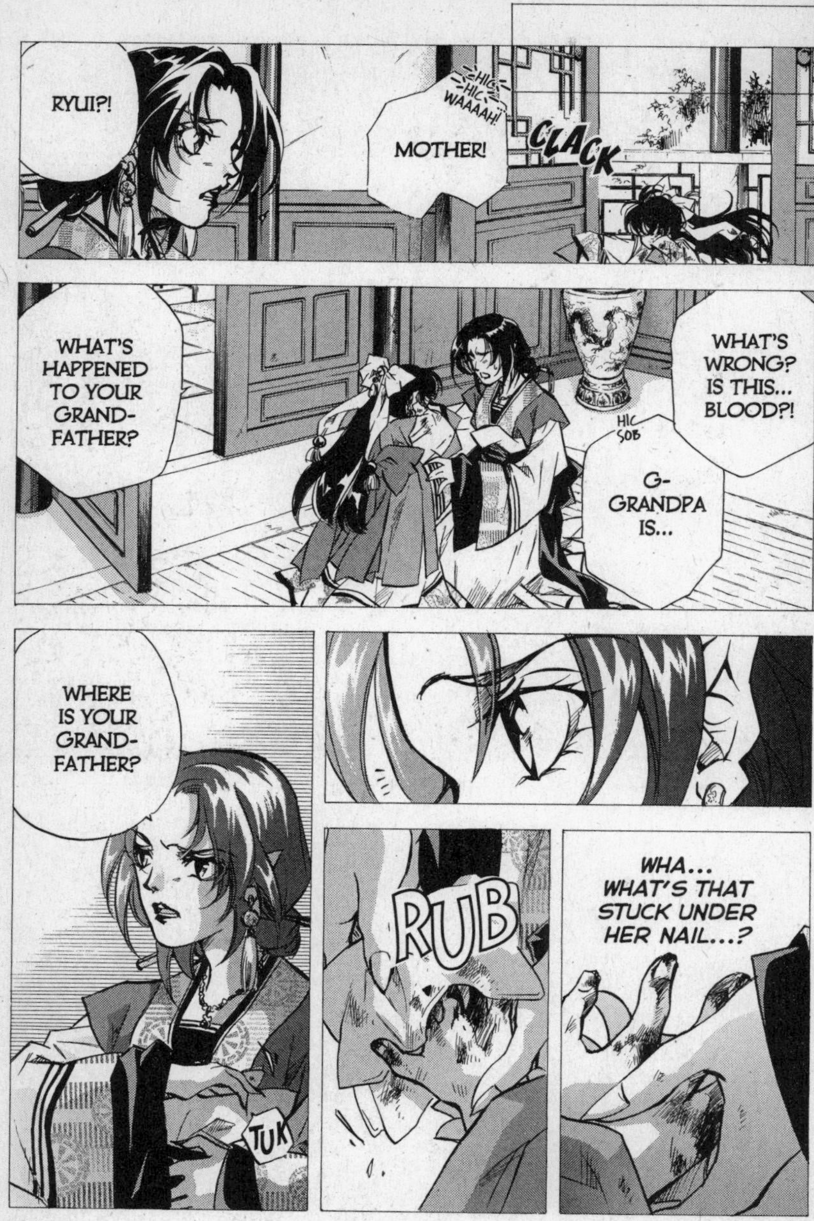
HIC HIC WAAAAH!
MOTHER!
CLACK
RYUI?!
WHAT'S WRONG? IS THIS... BLOOD?!
HIC SOB
G-GRANDPA IS...
WHAT'S HAPPENED TO YOUR GRAND-FATHER?
WHA... WHAT'S THAT STUCK UNDER HER NAIL...?
RUB
WHERE IS YOUR GRAND-FATHER?
TUK

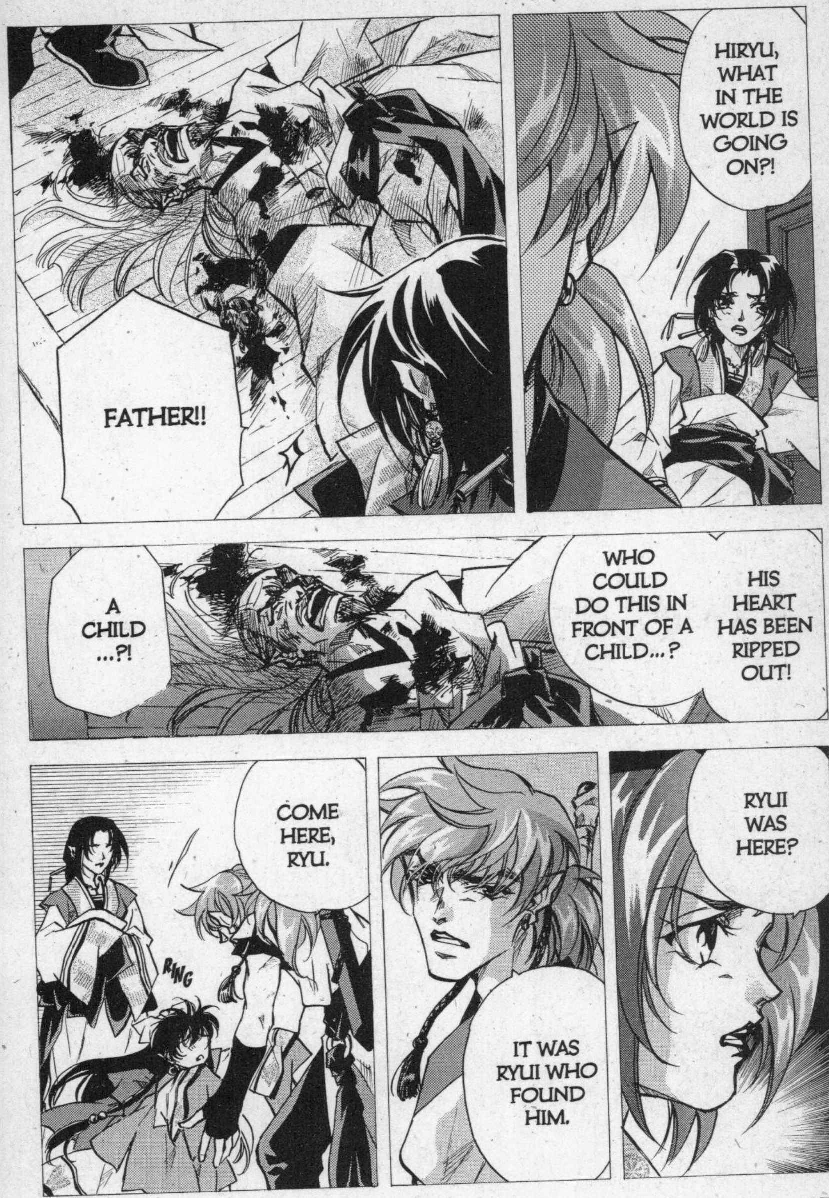
HIRYU, WHAT IN THE WORLD IS GOING ON?!
FATHER!!
HIS HEART HAS BEEN RIPPED OUT!
WHO COULD DO THIS IN FRONT OF A CHILD...?
A CHILD ...?!
RYUI WAS HERE?
IT WAS RYUI WHO FOUND HIM.
COME HERE, RYU.
RING

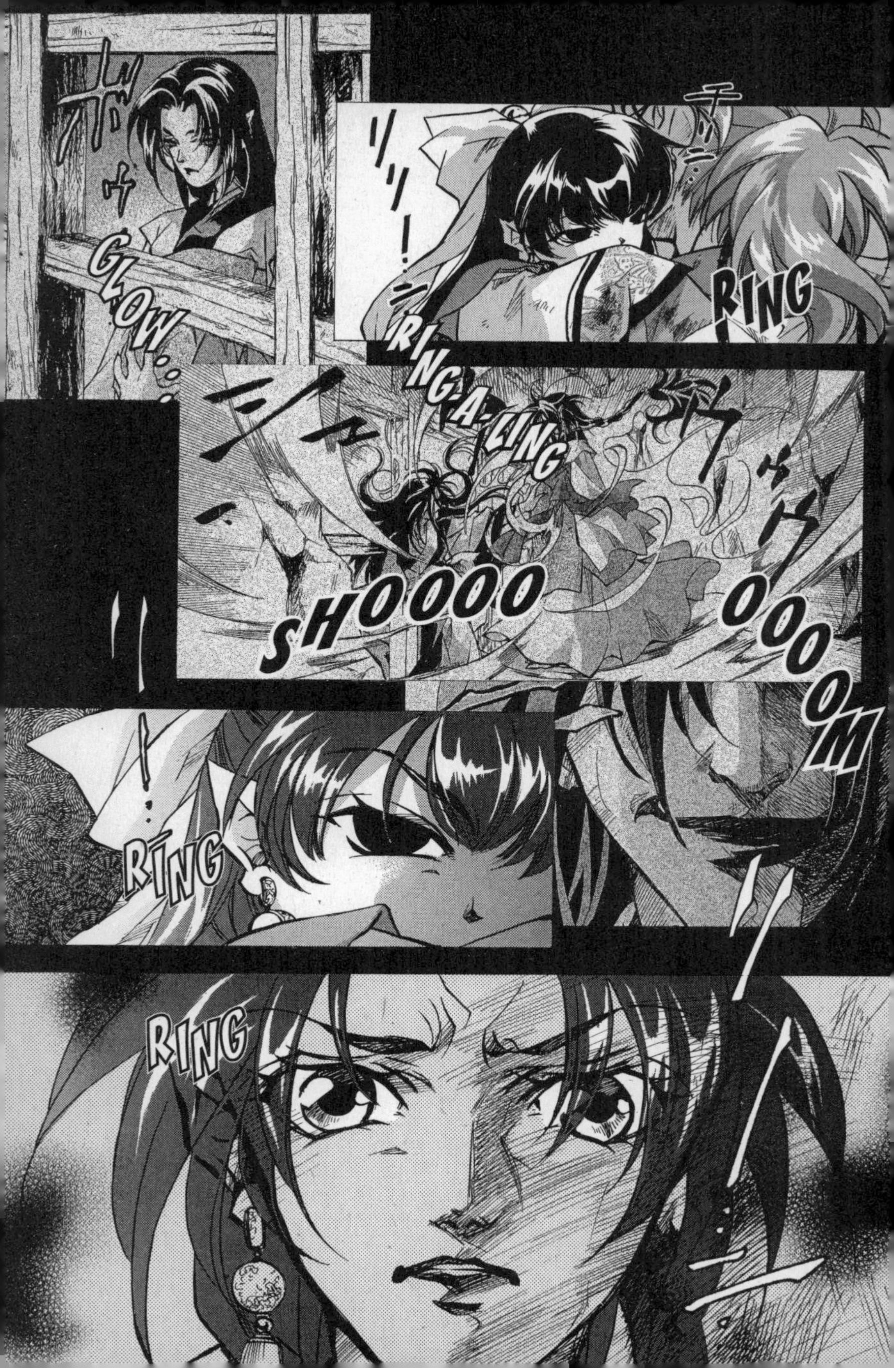
RING
RINGA-LING
GLOW...
SHOOOOO
OOOOOM
RING
RING

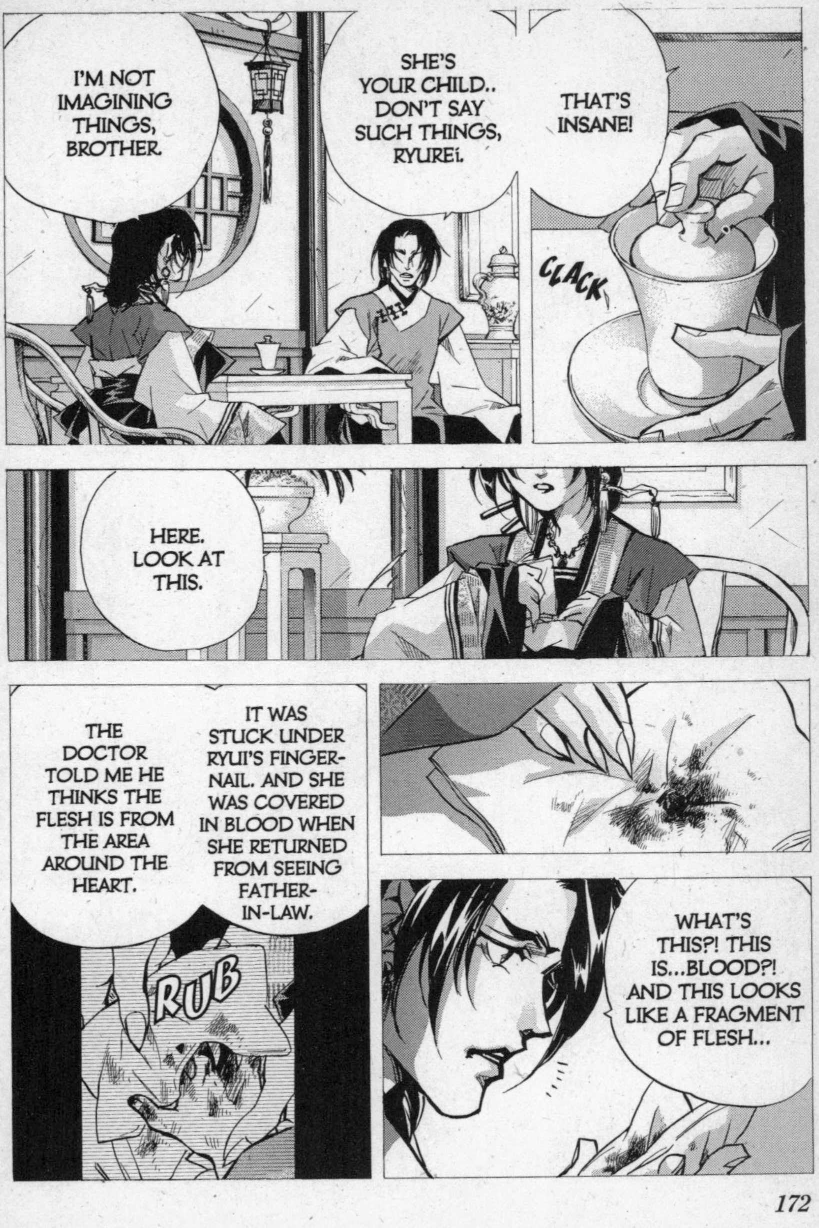
THAT'S INSANE!
CLACK
SHE'S YOUR CHILD.. DON'T SAY SUCH THINGS, RYUREi.
I'M NOT IMAGINING THINGS, BROTHER.
HERE. LOOK AT THIS.
WHAT'S THIS?! THIS IS...BLOOD?! AND THIS LOOKS LIKE A FRAGMENT OF FLESH...
IT WAS STUCK UNDER RYUI'S FINGER-NAIL. AND SHE WAS COVERED IN BLOOD WHEN SHE RETURNED FROM SEEING FATHER-IN-LAW.
THE DOCTOR TOLD ME HE THINKS THE FLESH IS FROM THE AREA AROUND THE HEART.
RUB

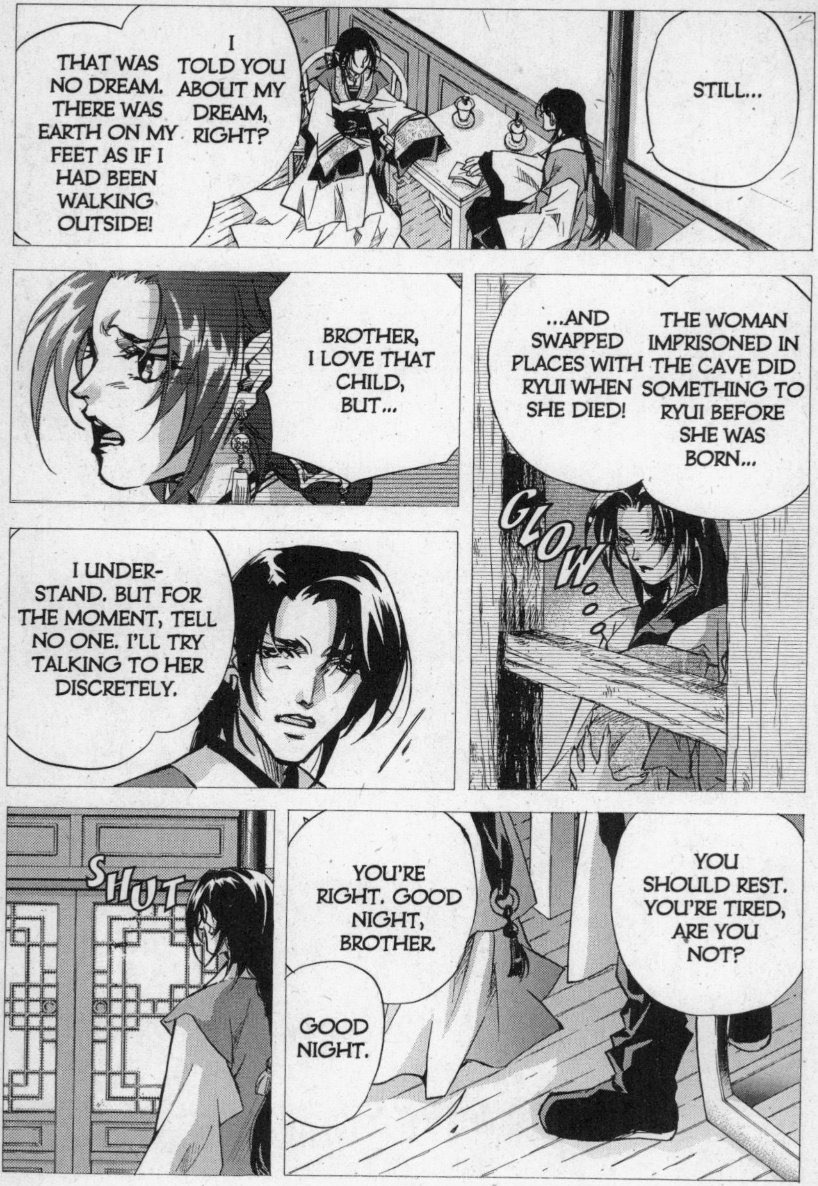
STILL...
I TOLD YOU ABOUT MY DREAM, RIGHT?
THAT WAS NO DREAM. THERE WAS EARTH ON MY FEET AS IF I HAD BEEN WALKING OUTSIDE!
THE WOMAN IMPRISONED IN THE CAVE DID SOMETHING TO RYUI BEFORE SHE WAS BORN...
...AND SWAPPED PLACES WITH RYUI WHEN SHE DIED!
GLOW
BROTHER, I LOVE THAT CHILD, BUT...
I UNDER-STAND. BUT FOR THE MOMENT, TELL NO ONE. I'LL TRY TALKING TO HER DISCRETELY.
YOU SHOULD REST. YOU'RE TIRED, ARE YOU NOT?
YOU'RE RIGHT. GOOD NIGHT, BROTHER.
GOOD NIGHT.
SHUT

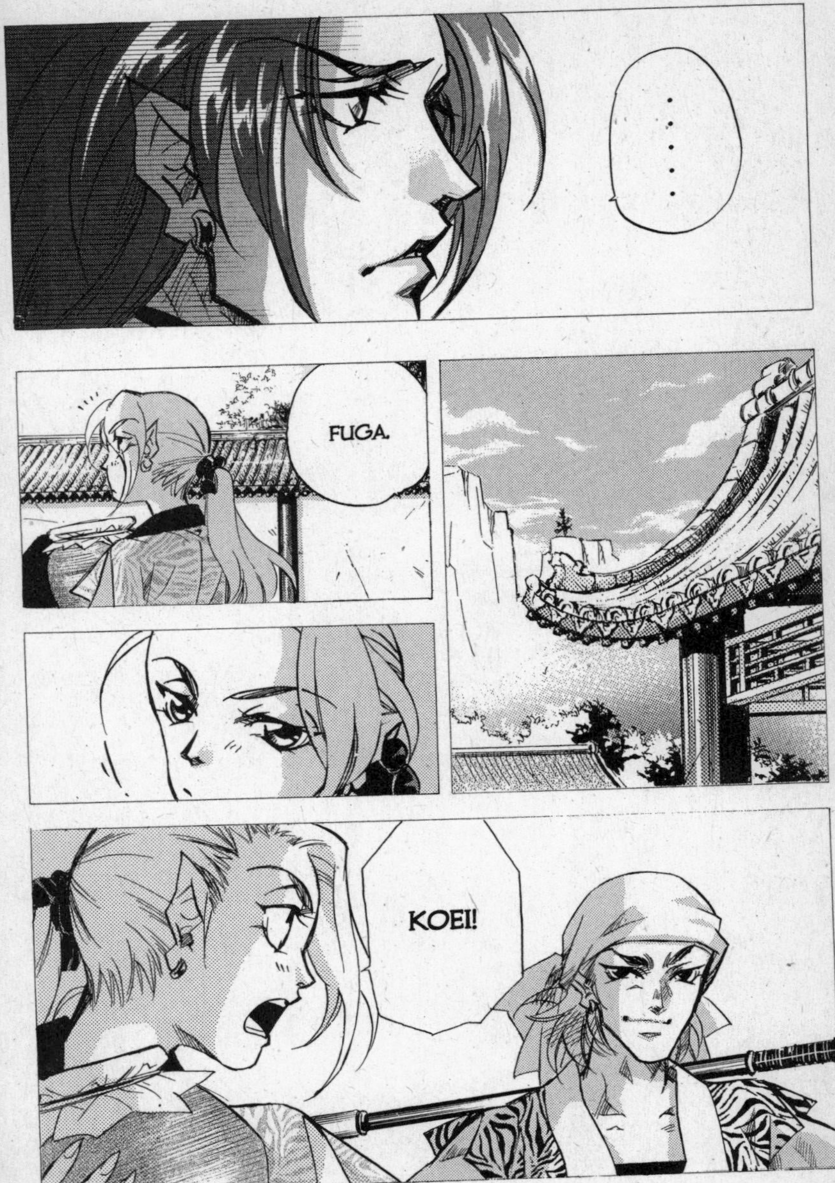
.....
FUGA.
KOEI!

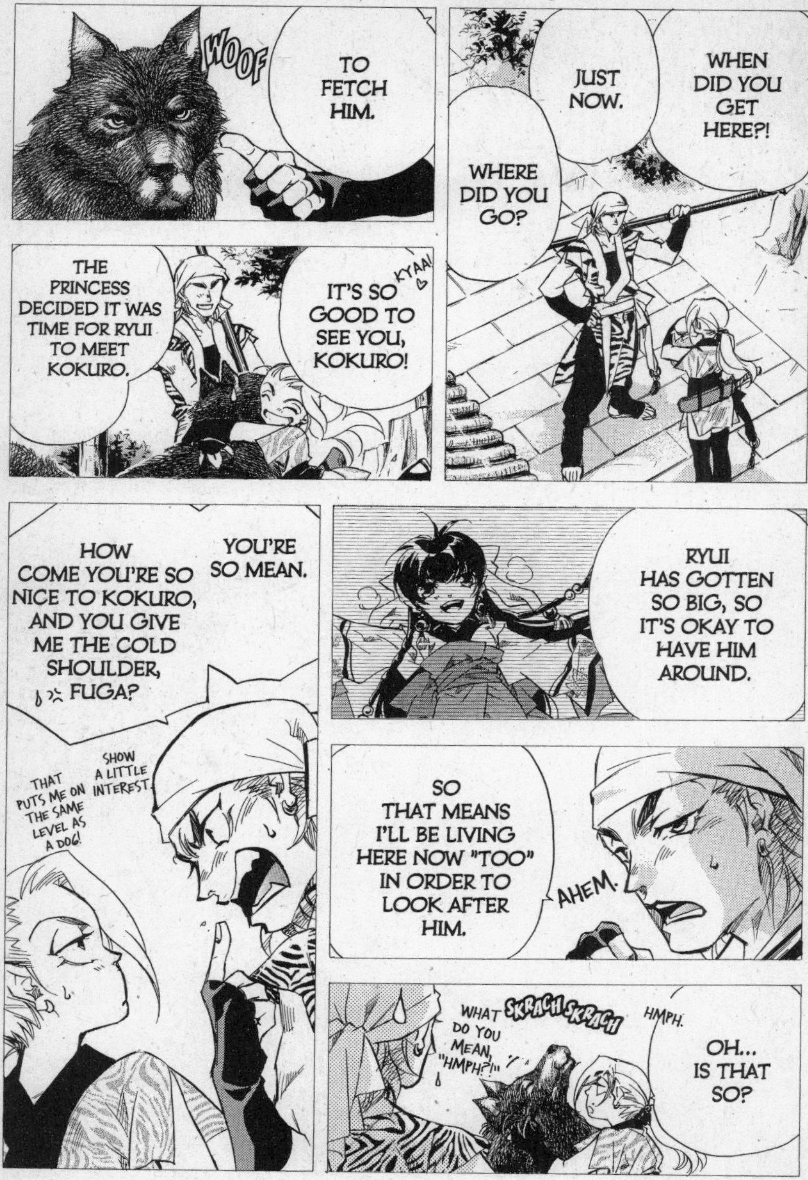
WHEN DID YOU GET HERE?!
JUST NOW.
WHERE DID YOU GO?
TO FETCH HIM.
WOOF
IT'S SO GOOD TO SEE YOU, KOKURO!
KYAA!
THE PRINCESS DECIDED IT WAS TIME FOR RYUI TO MEET KOKURO.
RYUI HAS GOTTEN SO BIG, SO IT'S OKAY TO HAVE HIM AROUND.
SO THAT MEANS I'LL BE LIVING HERE NOW "TOO" IN ORDER TO LOOK AFTER HIM.
AHEM.
HMPH.
OH... IS THAT SO?
SKRACH SKRACH
WHAT DO YOU MEAN, "HMPH?!"
YOU'RE SO MEAN.
HOW COME YOU'RE SO NICE TO KOKURO, AND YOU GIVE ME THE COLD SHOULDER, FUGA?
SHOW A LITTLE INTEREST.
THAT PUTS ME ON THE SAME LEVEL AS A DOG!

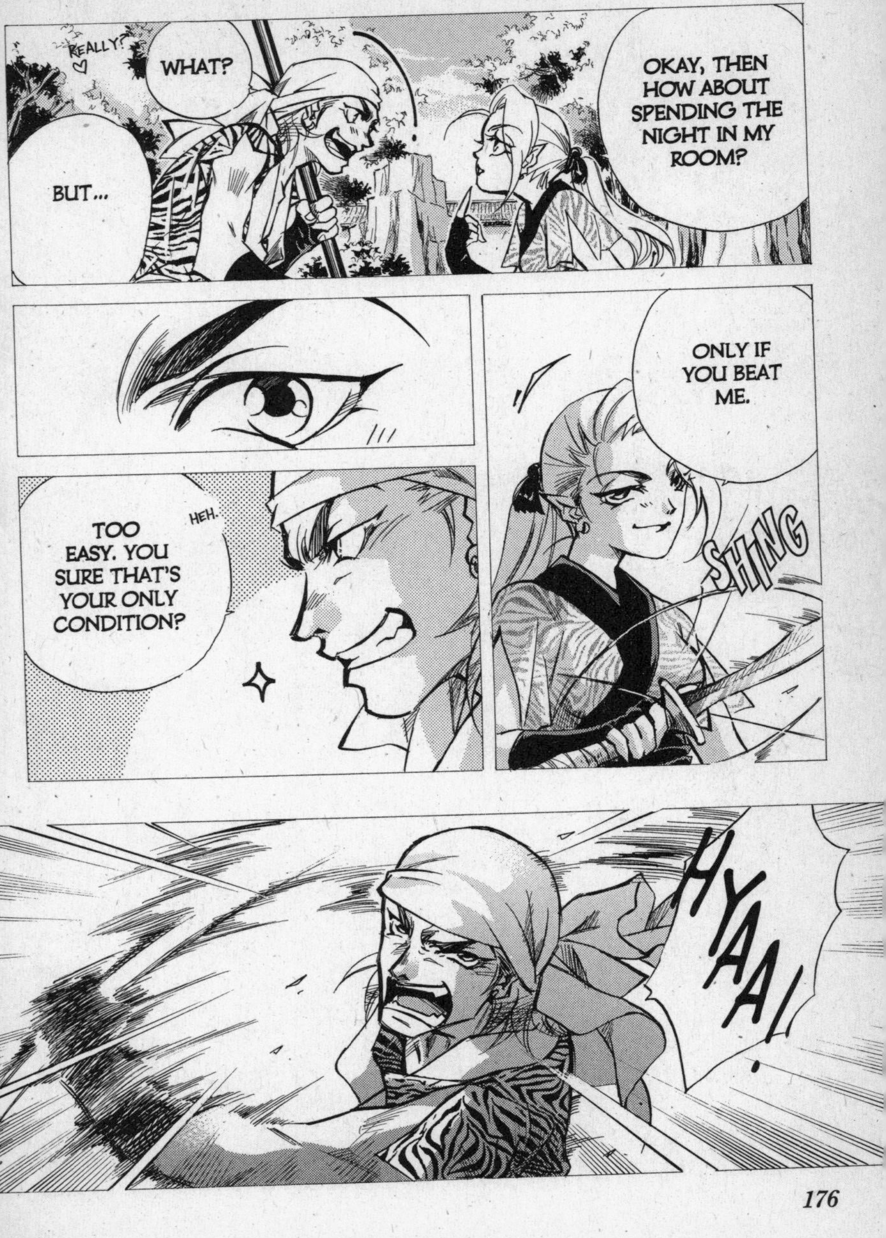
OKAY, THEN HOW ABOUT SPENDING THE NIGHT IN MY ROOM?
WHAT?
REALLY? ♡
BUT...
ONLY IF YOU BEAT ME.
SHING
HEH.
TOO EASY. YOU SURE THAT'S YOUR ONLY CONDITION?
HYAA!

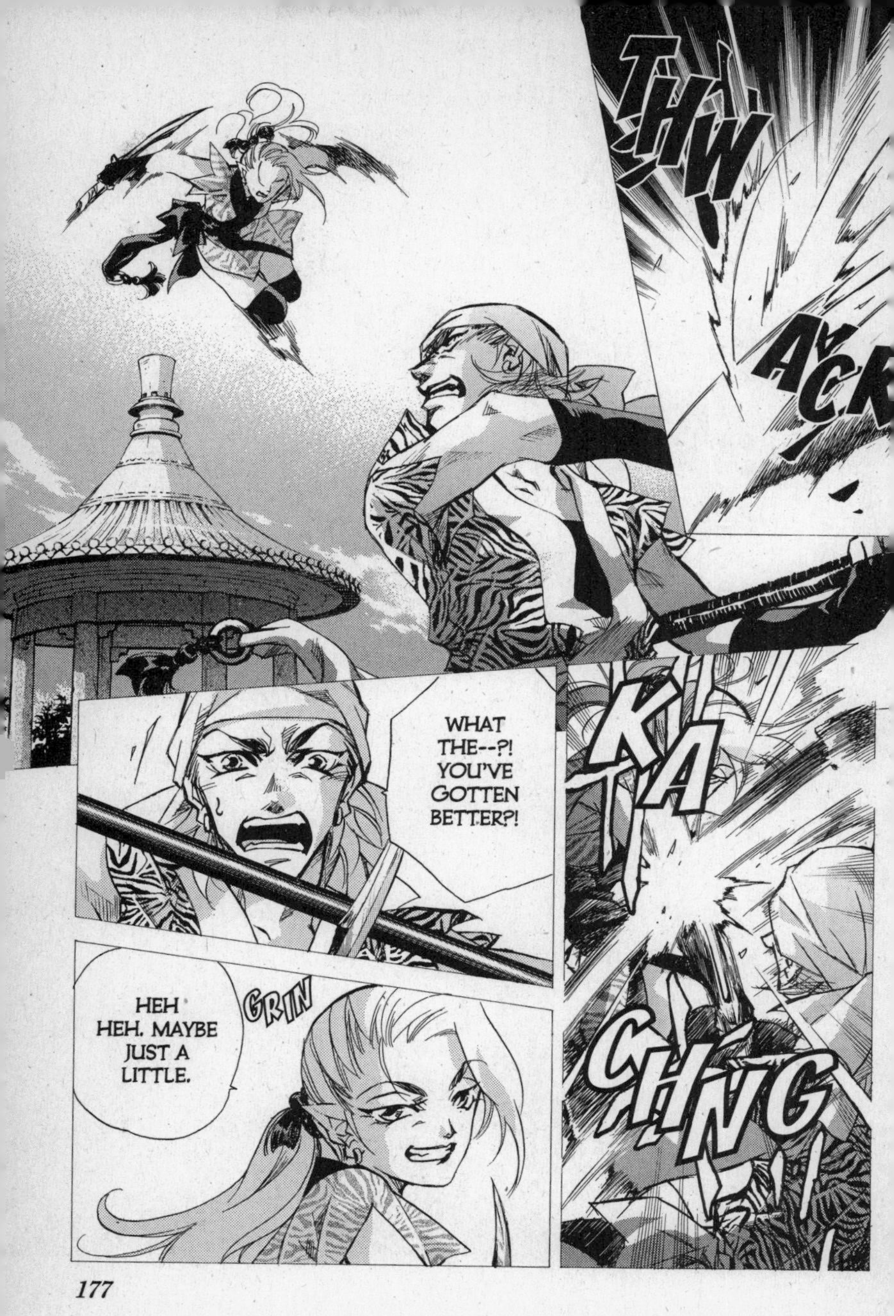
THW
ACK
KA
CHNG
WHAT THE--?! YOU'VE GOTTEN BETTER?!
GRIN
HEH HEH. MAYBE JUST A LITTLE.

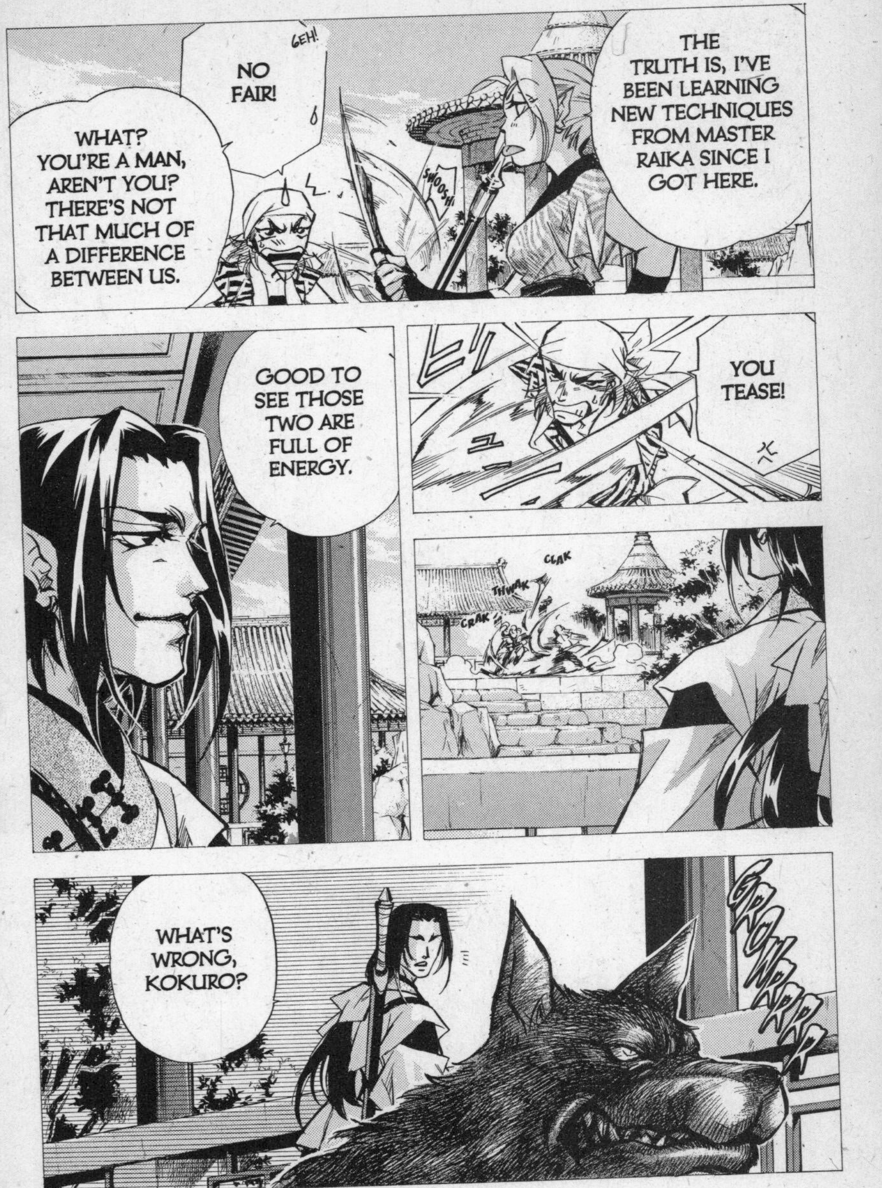
THE TRUTH IS, I'VE BEEN LEARNING NEW TECHNIQUES FROM MASTER RAIKA SINCE I GOT HERE.
SWOOSH!
GEH!
NO FAIR!
WHAT? YOU'RE A MAN, AREN'T YOU? THERE'S NOT THAT MUCH OF A DIFFERENCE BETWEEN US.
YOU TEASE!
CLAK
THWAK
CRAK
GOOD TO SEE THOSE TWO ARE FULL OF ENERGY.
WHAT'S WRONG, KOKURO?

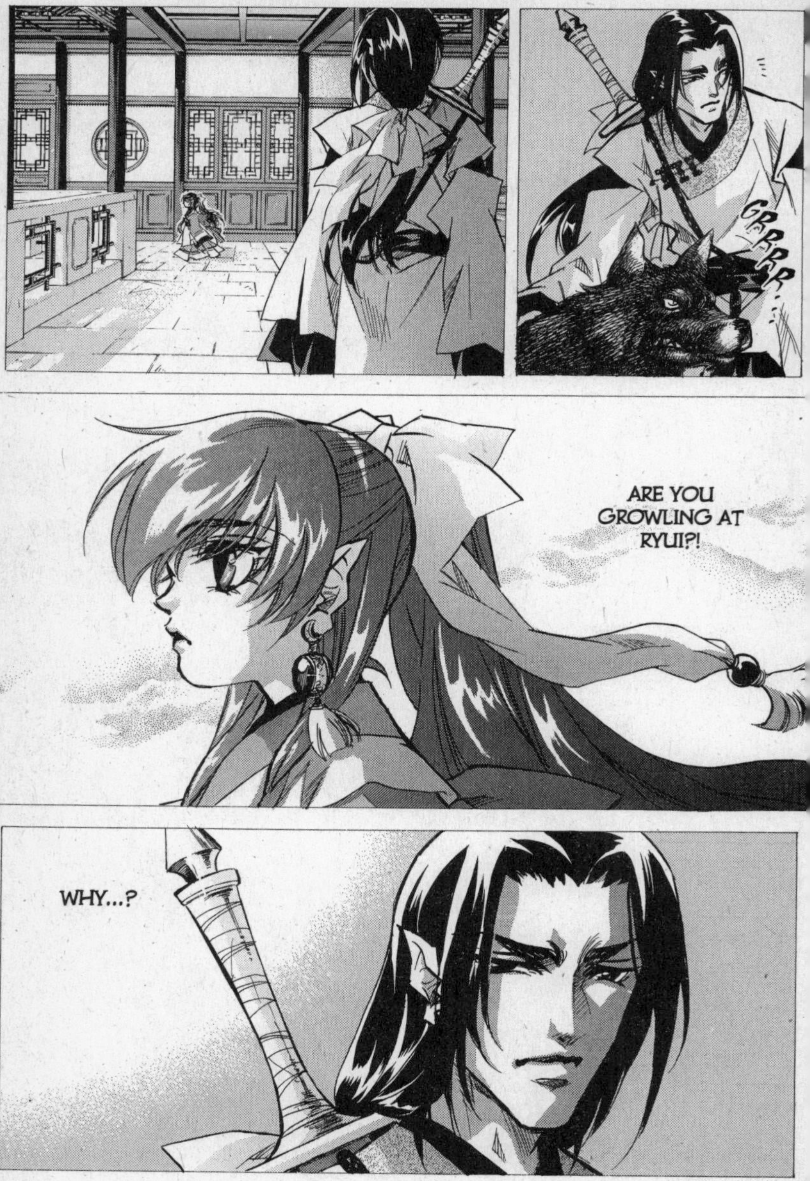
GRRRR...
ARE YOU GROWLING AT RYUI?!
WHY...?

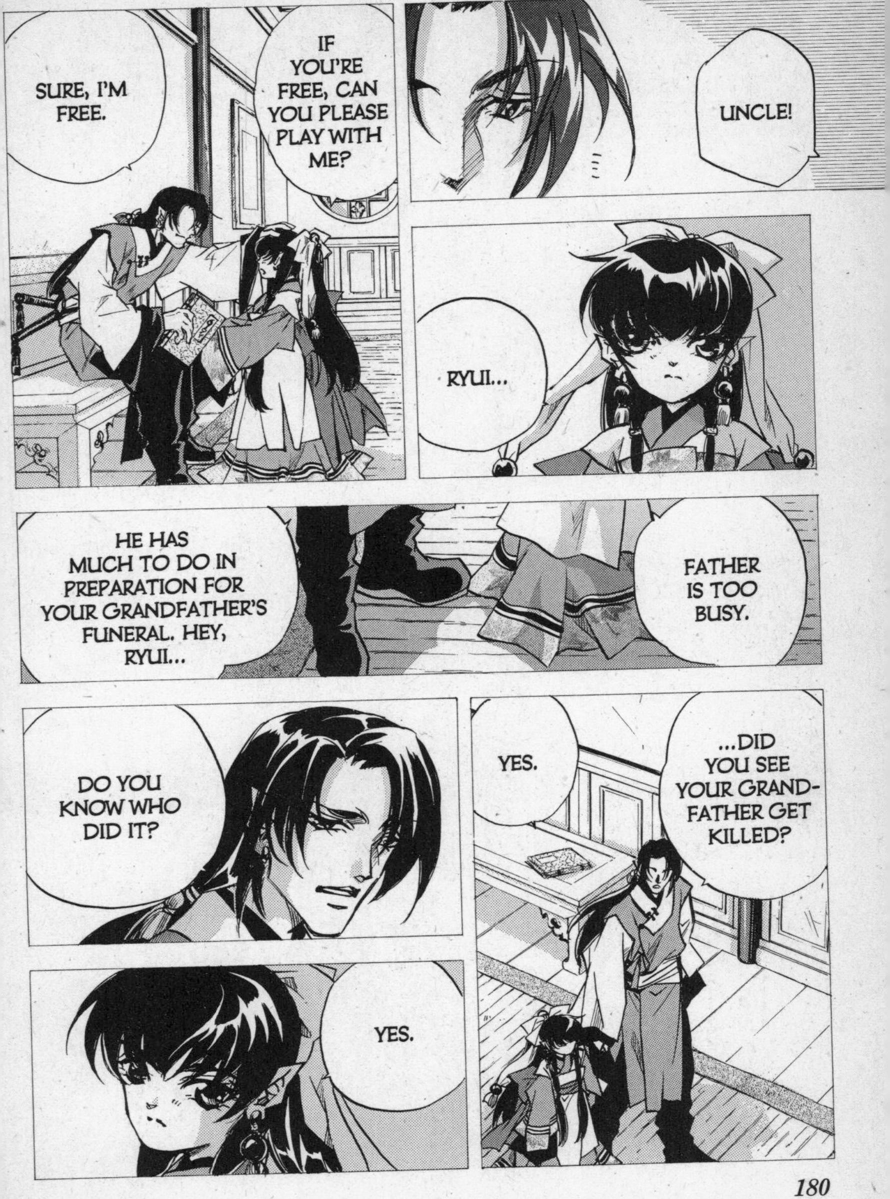
UNCLE!
RYUI...
IF YOU'RE FREE, CAN YOU PLEASE PLAY WITH ME?
SURE, I'M FREE.
FATHER IS TOO BUSY.
HE HAS MUCH TO DO IN PREPARATION FOR YOUR GRANDFATHER'S FUNERAL. HEY, RYUI...
...DID YOU SEE YOUR GRAND-FATHER GET KILLED?
YES.
DO YOU KNOW WHO DID IT?
YES.

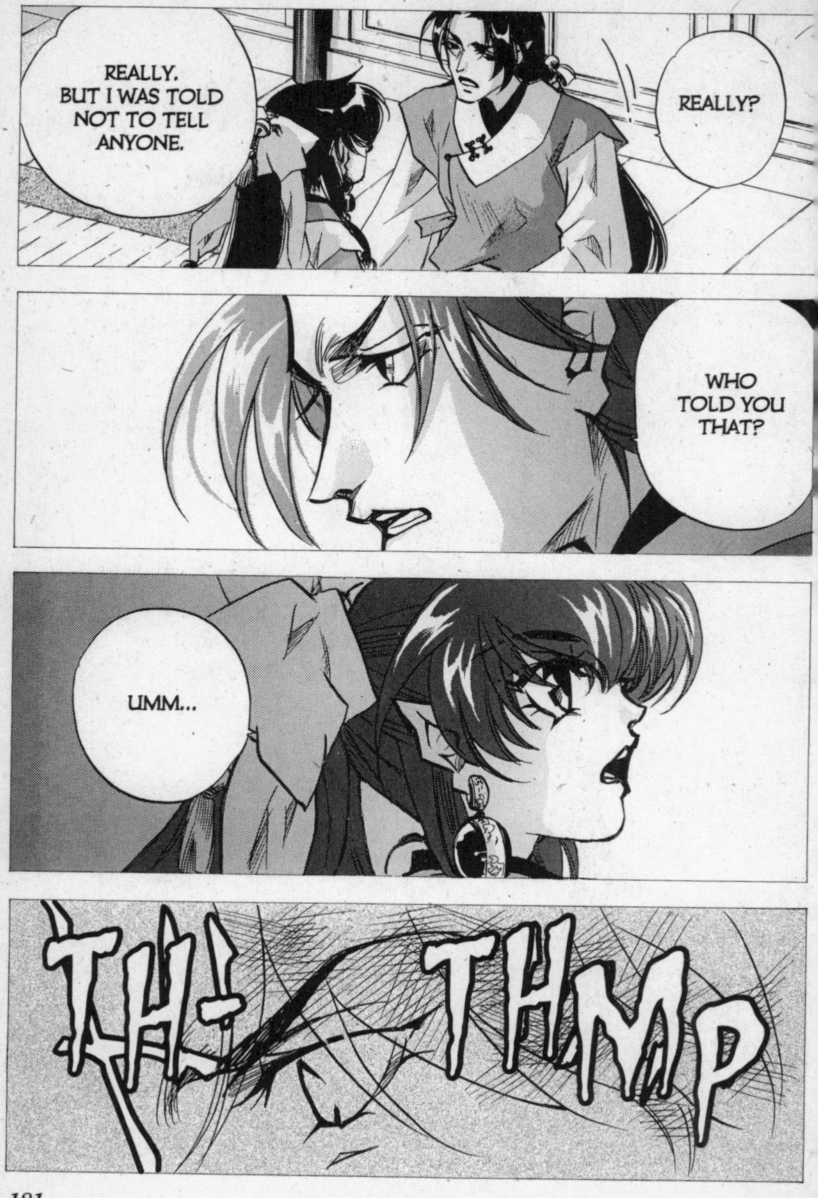
REALLY?
REALLY. BUT I WAS TOLD NOT TO TELL ANYONE.
WHO TOLD YOU THAT?
UMM...
THI- THMP

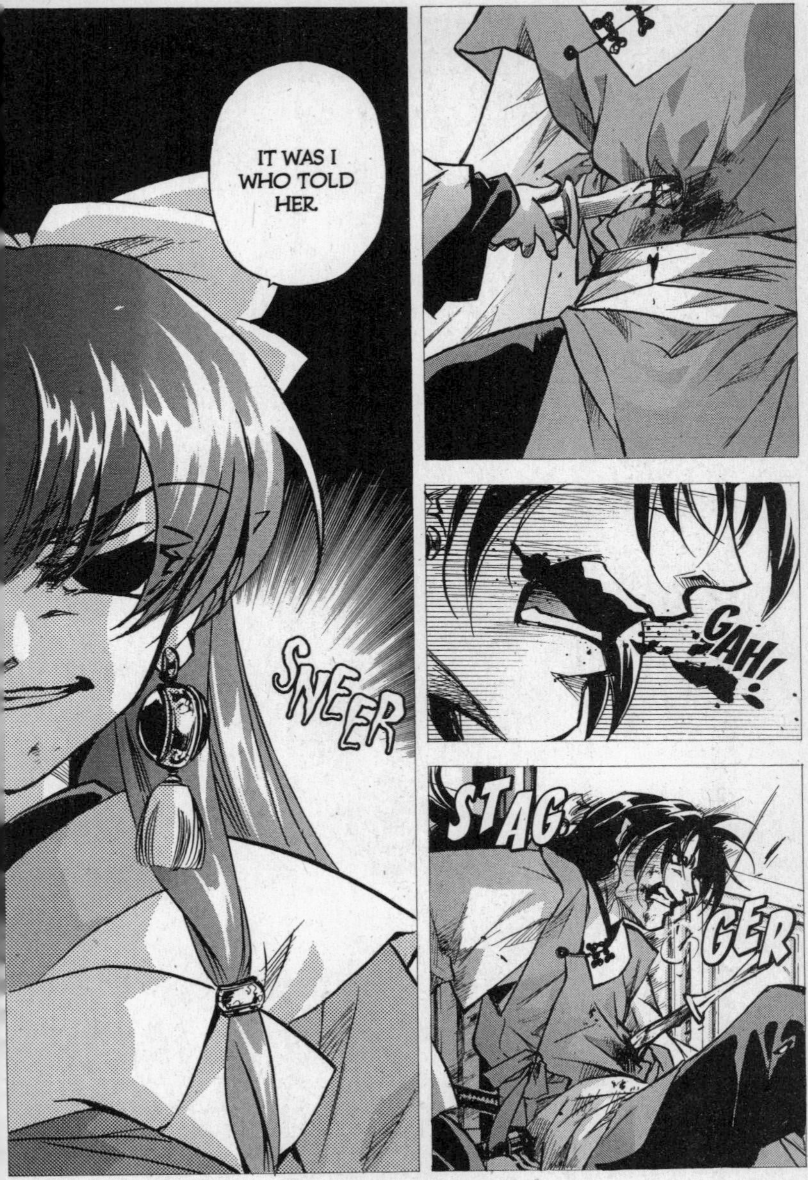
GAH!
STAG
GER
IT WAS I WHO TOLD HER.
SNEER

END OF CHAPTER 17

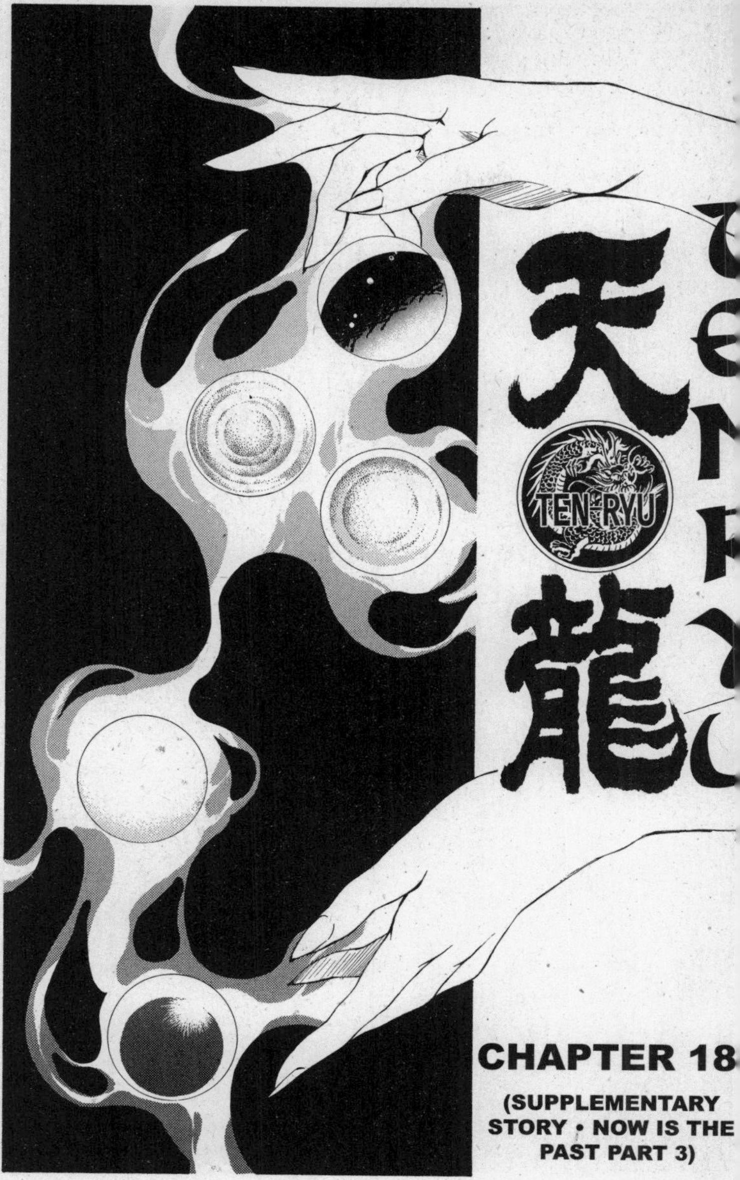
天龍
TEN-RYU

CHAPTER 18

(SUPPLEMENTARY STORY • NOW IS THE PAST PART 3)

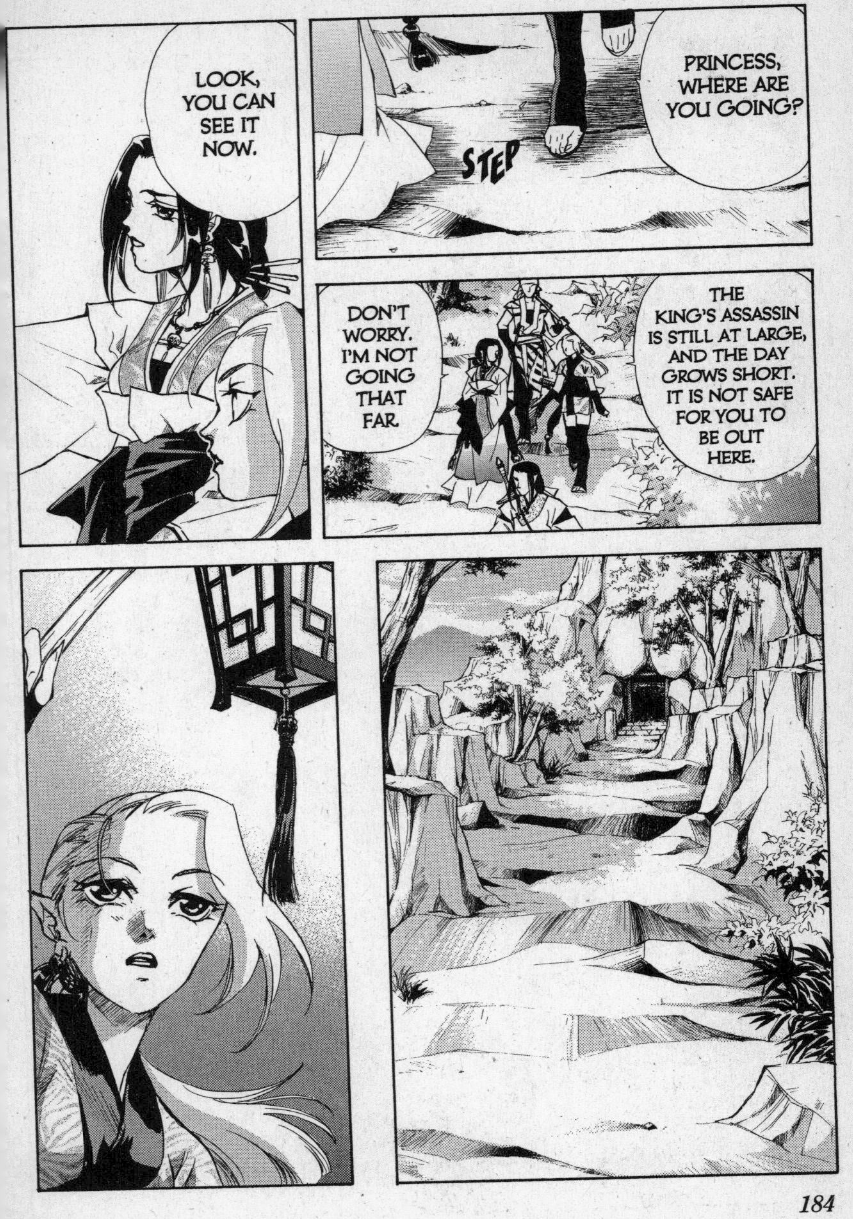
PRINCESS, WHERE ARE YOU GOING?
STEP
THE KING'S ASSASSIN IS STILL AT LARGE, AND THE DAY GROWS SHORT. IT IS NOT SAFE FOR YOU TO BE OUT HERE.
DON'T WORRY. I'M NOT GOING THAT FAR.
LOOK, YOU CAN SEE IT NOW.

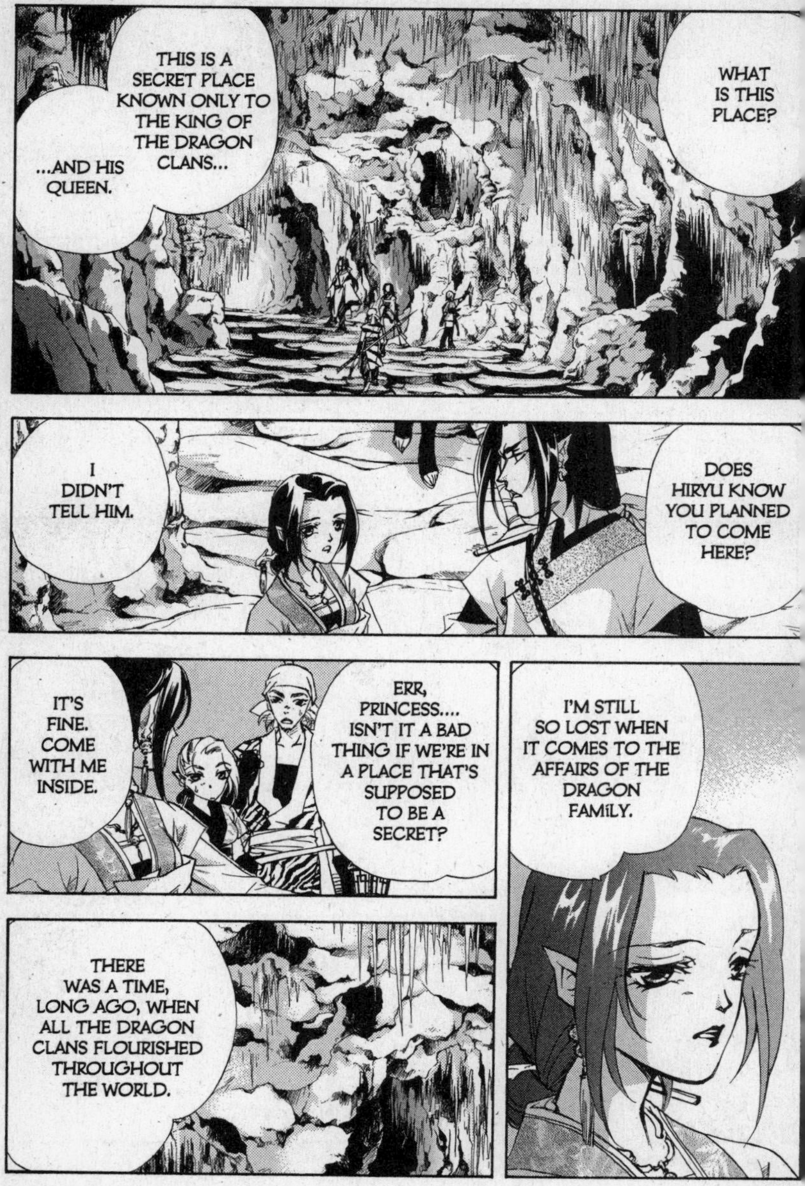
WHAT IS THIS PLACE?
THIS IS A SECRET PLACE KNOWN ONLY TO THE KING OF THE DRAGON CLANS...
...AND HIS QUEEN.
DOES HIRYU KNOW YOU PLANNED TO COME HERE?
I DIDN'T TELL HIM.
I'M STILL SO LOST WHEN IT COMES TO THE AFFAIRS OF THE DRAGON FAMILY.
ERR, PRINCESS.... ISN'T IT A BAD THING IF WE'RE IN A PLACE THAT'S SUPPOSED TO BE A SECRET?
IT'S FINE. COME WITH ME INSIDE.
THERE WAS A TIME, LONG AGO, WHEN ALL THE DRAGON CLANS FLOURISHED THROUGHOUT THE WORLD.

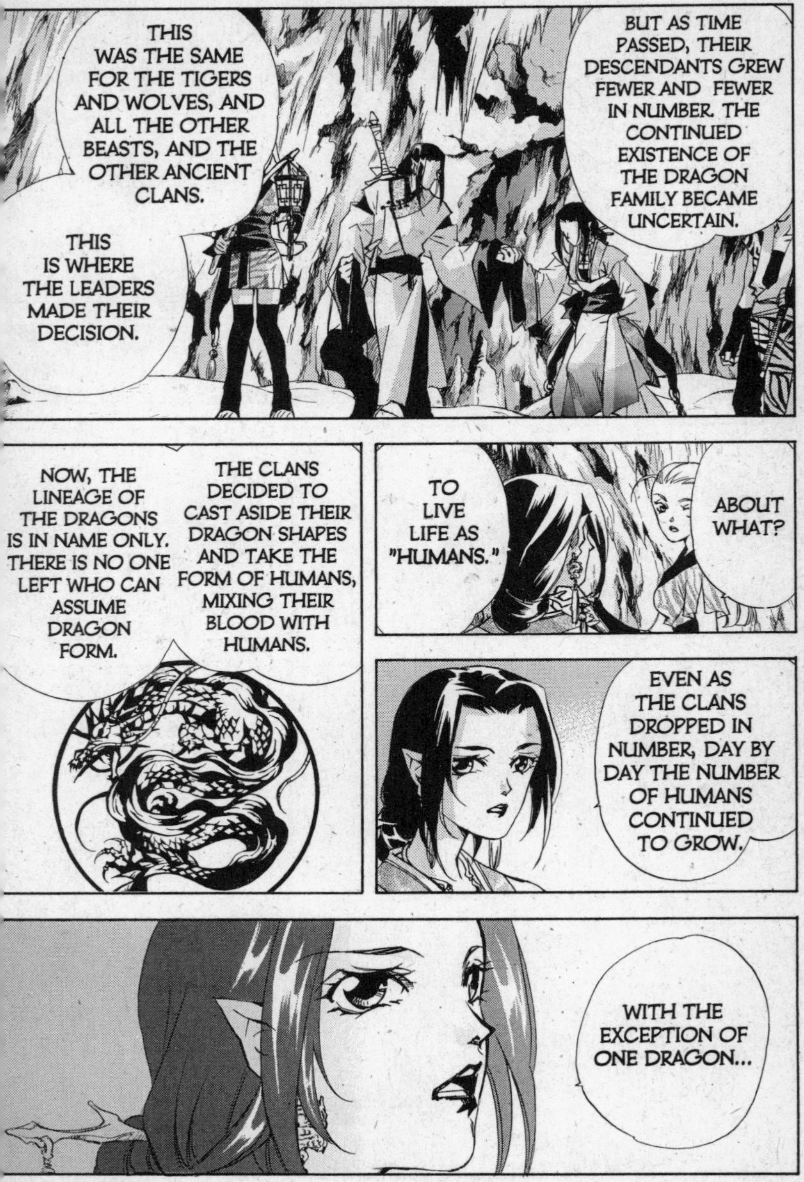

BUT AS TIME PASSED, THEIR DESCENDANTS GREW FEWER AND FEWER IN NUMBER. THE CONTINUED EXISTENCE OF THE DRAGON FAMILY BECAME UNCERTAIN.
THIS WAS THE SAME FOR THE TIGERS AND WOLVES, AND ALL THE OTHER BEASTS, AND THE OTHER ANCIENT CLANS.
THIS IS WHERE THE LEADERS MADE THEIR DECISION.
ABOUT WHAT?
TO LIVE LIFE AS "HUMANS."
EVEN AS THE CLANS DROPPED IN NUMBER, DAY BY DAY THE NUMBER OF HUMANS CONTINUED TO GROW.
THE CLANS DECIDED TO CAST ASIDE THEIR DRAGON SHAPES AND TAKE THE FORM OF HUMANS, MIXING THEIR BLOOD WITH HUMANS.
NOW, THE LINEAGE OF THE DRAGONS IS IN NAME ONLY. THERE IS NO ONE LEFT WHO CAN ASSUME DRAGON FORM.
WITH THE EXCEPTION OF ONE DRAGON...

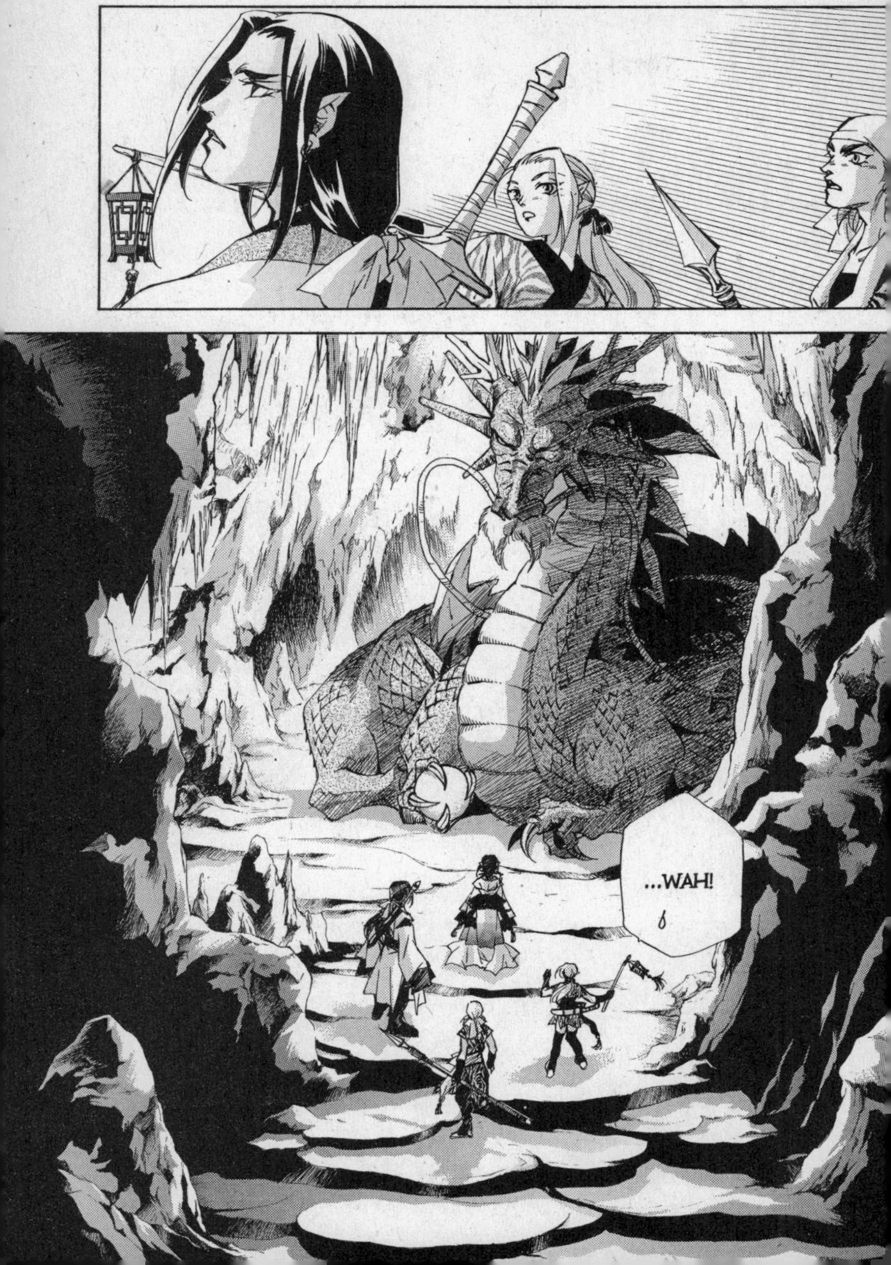
...WAH!

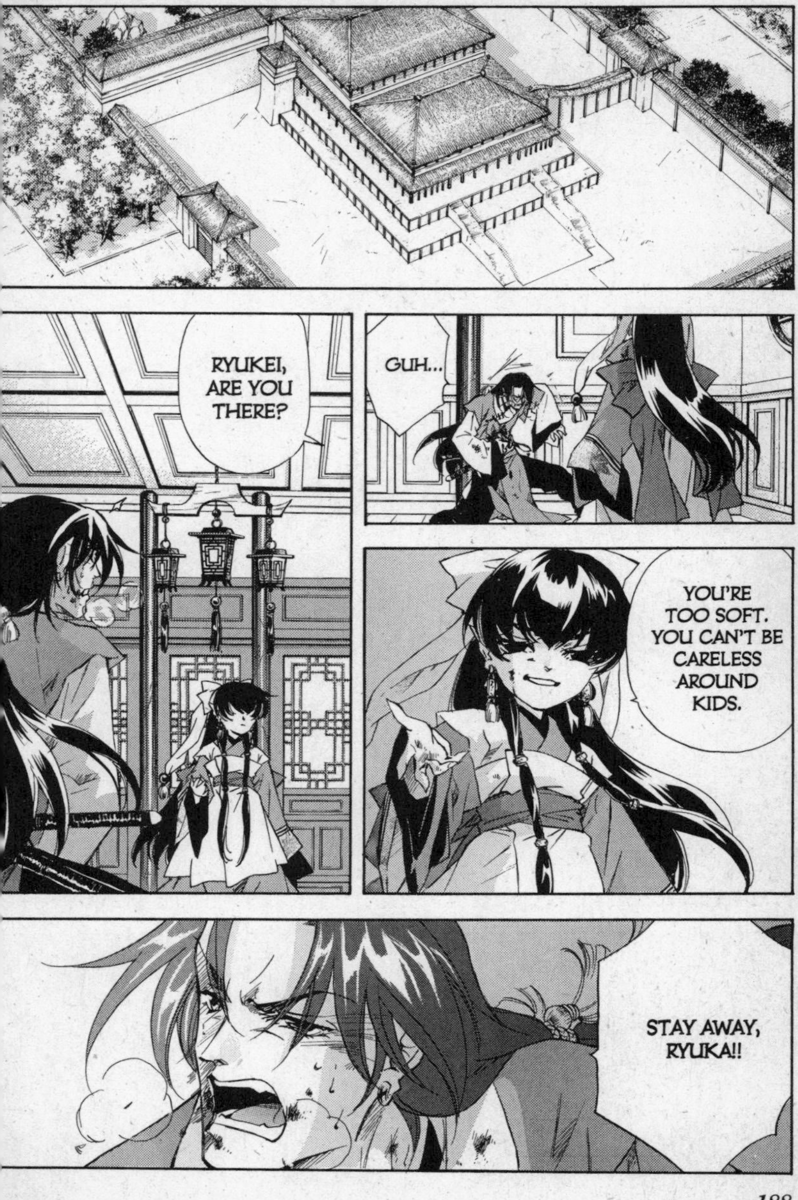
GUH...
YOU'RE TOO SOFT. YOU CAN'T BE CARELESS AROUND KIDS.
RYUKEI, ARE YOU THERE?
STAY AWAY, RYUKA!!

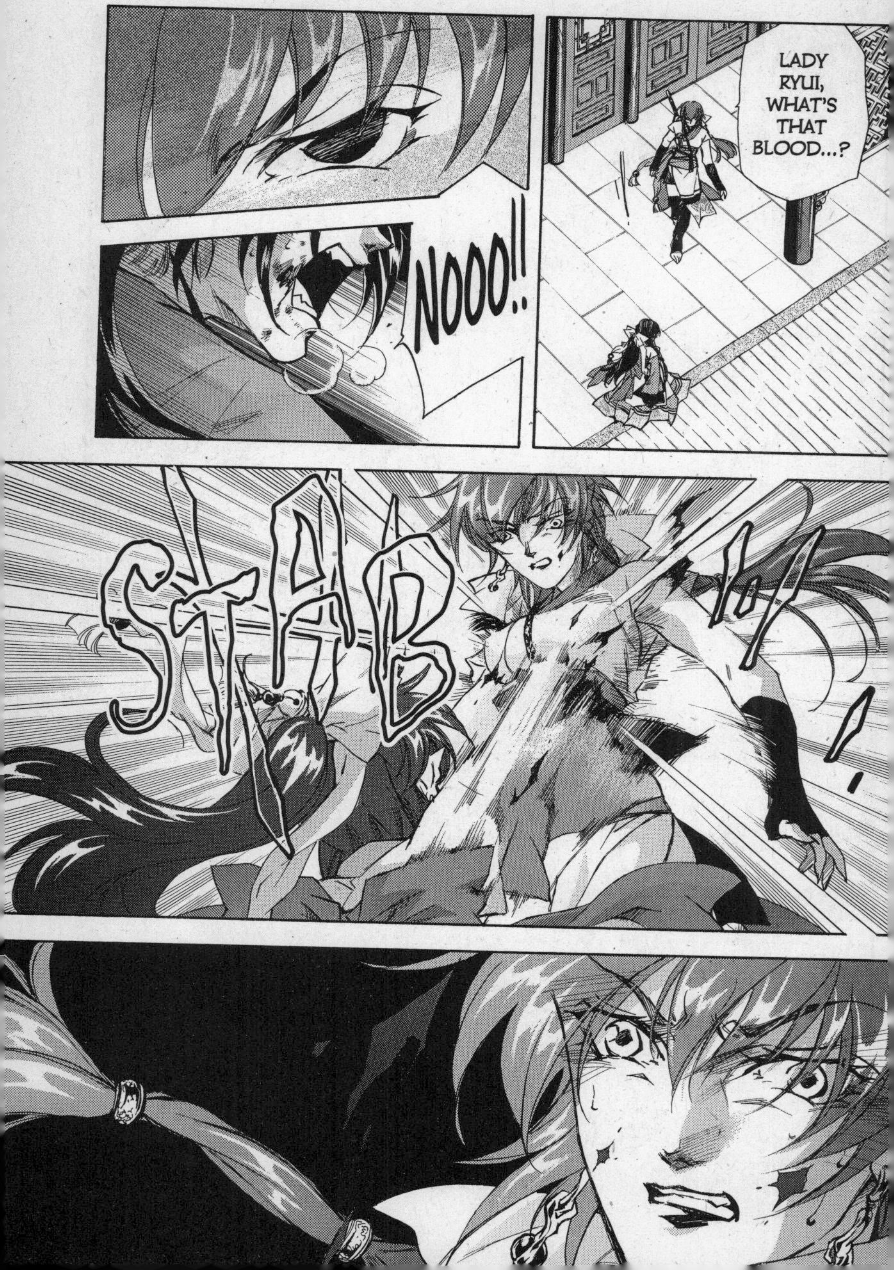
LADY RYUI, WHAT'S THAT BLOOD...?
NOOO!!
STAB
!!

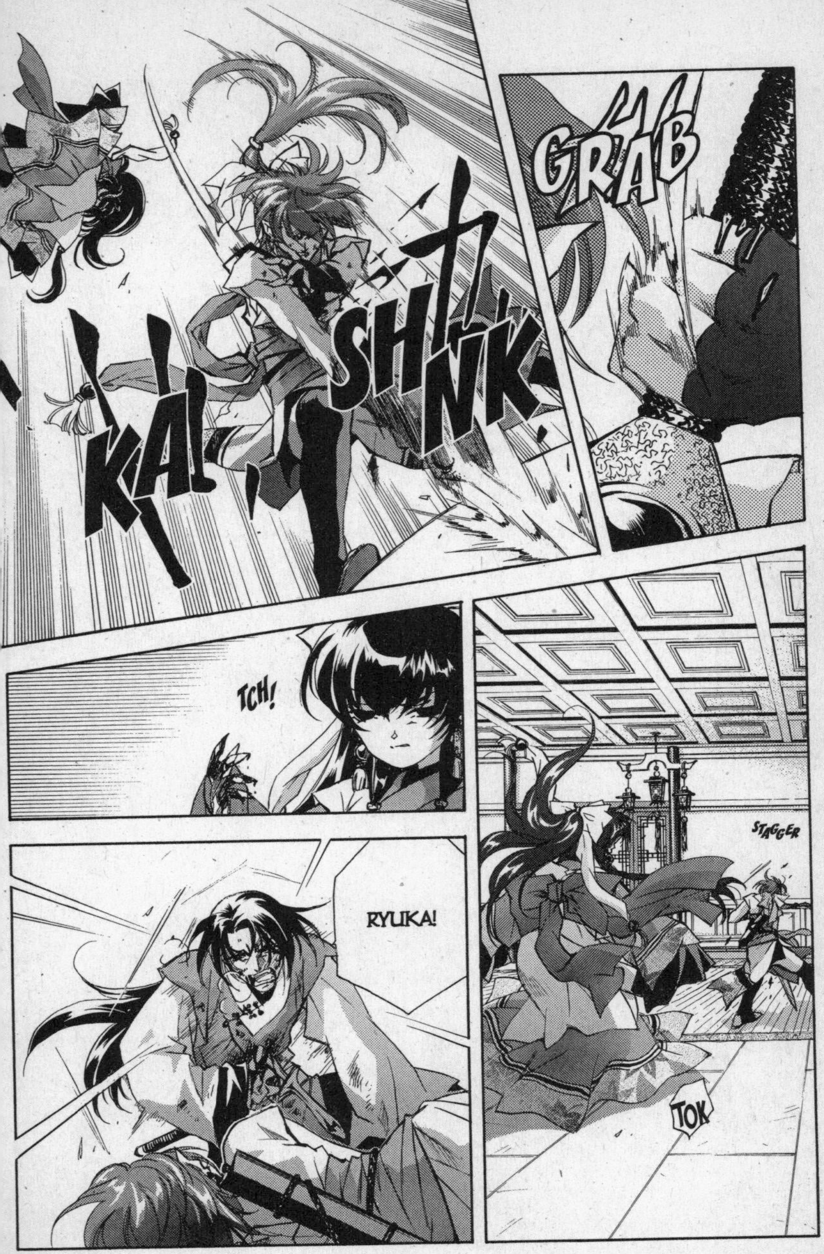
GRAB
SHINK
KA!
STAGGER
TOK
TCH!
RYUKA!

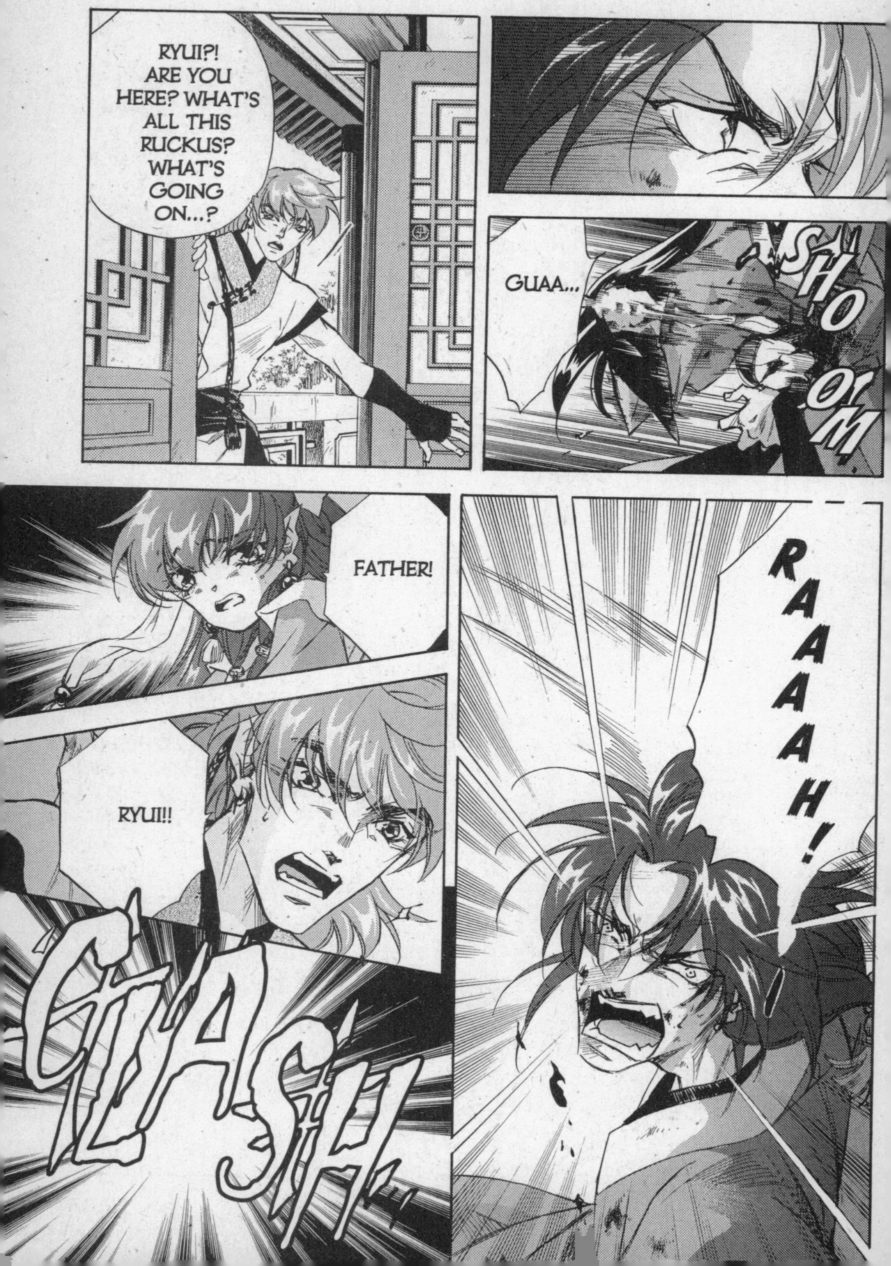
GUAA...
SHOOOM
RYUI?! ARE YOU HERE? WHAT'S ALL THIS RUCKUS? WHAT'S GOING ON...?
RAAAAH!
FATHER!
RYUI!!
CLASH...

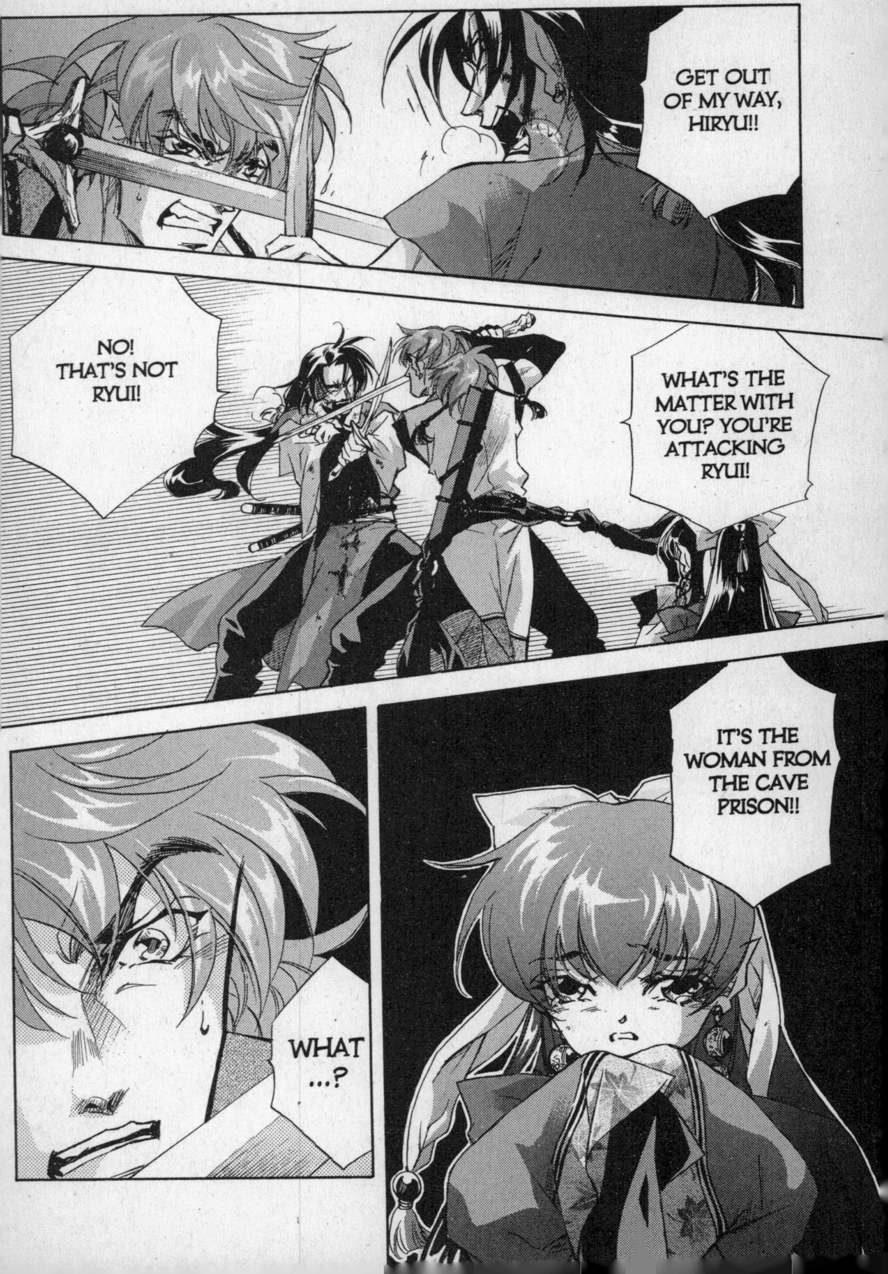
GET OUT OF MY WAY, HIRYU!!
WHAT'S THE MATTER WITH YOU? YOU'RE ATTACKING RYUI!
NO! THAT'S NOT RYUI!
IT'S THE WOMAN FROM THE CAVE PRISON!!
WHAT ...?

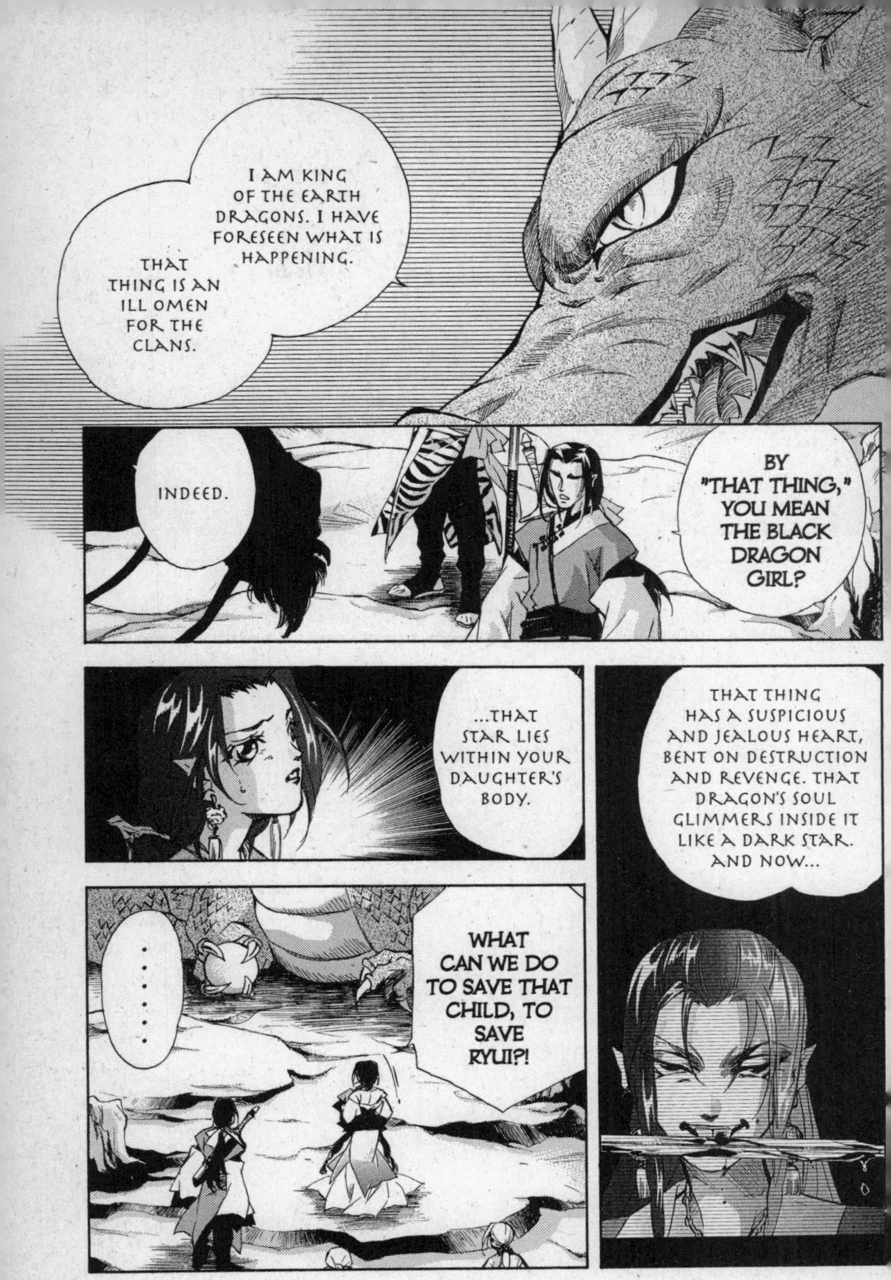
I AM KING OF THE EARTH DRAGONS. I HAVE FORESEEN WHAT IS HAPPENING.
THAT THING IS AN ILL OMEN FOR THE CLANS.
BY "THAT THING," YOU MEAN THE BLACK DRAGON GIRL?
INDEED.
THAT THING HAS A SUSPICIOUS AND JEALOUS HEART, BENT ON DESTRUCTION AND REVENGE. THAT DRAGON'S SOUL GLIMMERS INSIDE IT LIKE A DARK STAR. AND NOW...
...THAT STAR LIES WITHIN YOUR DAUGHTER'S BODY.
WHAT CAN WE DO TO SAVE THAT CHILD, TO SAVE RYUI?!
....

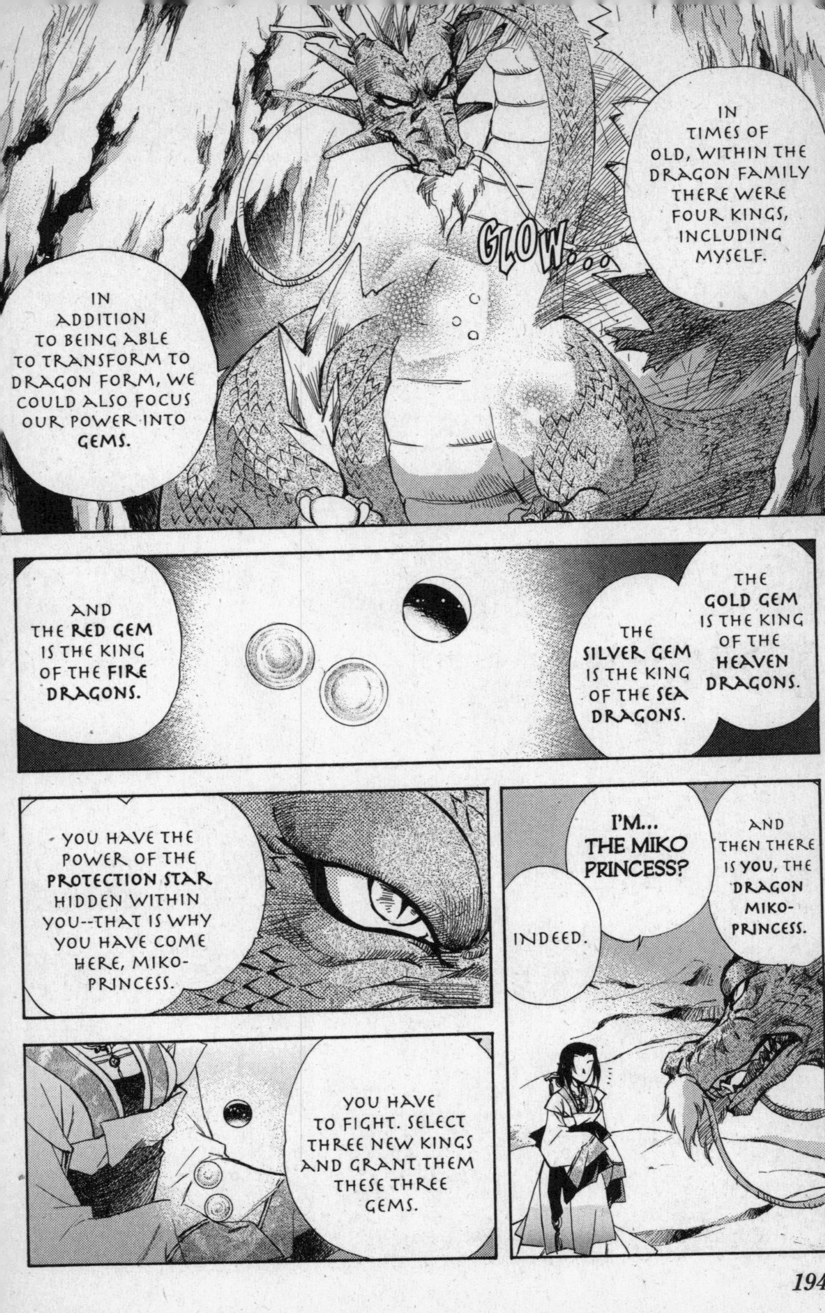
IN TIMES OF OLD, WITHIN THE DRAGON FAMILY THERE WERE FOUR KINGS, INCLUDING MYSELF.
GLOW...
IN ADDITION TO BEING ABLE TO TRANSFORM TO DRAGON FORM, WE COULD ALSO FOCUS OUR POWER INTO GEMS.
THE GOLD GEM IS THE KING OF THE HEAVEN DRAGONS.
THE SILVER GEM IS THE KING OF THE SEA DRAGONS.
AND THE RED GEM IS THE KING OF THE FIRE DRAGONS.
AND THEN THERE IS YOU, THE DRAGON MIKO-PRINCESS.
I'M... THE MIKO PRINCESS?
INDEED.
YOU HAVE THE POWER OF THE PROTECTION STAR HIDDEN WITHIN YOU--THAT IS WHY YOU HAVE COME HERE, MIKO-PRINCESS.
YOU HAVE TO FIGHT. SELECT THREE NEW KINGS AND GRANT THEM THESE THREE GEMS.

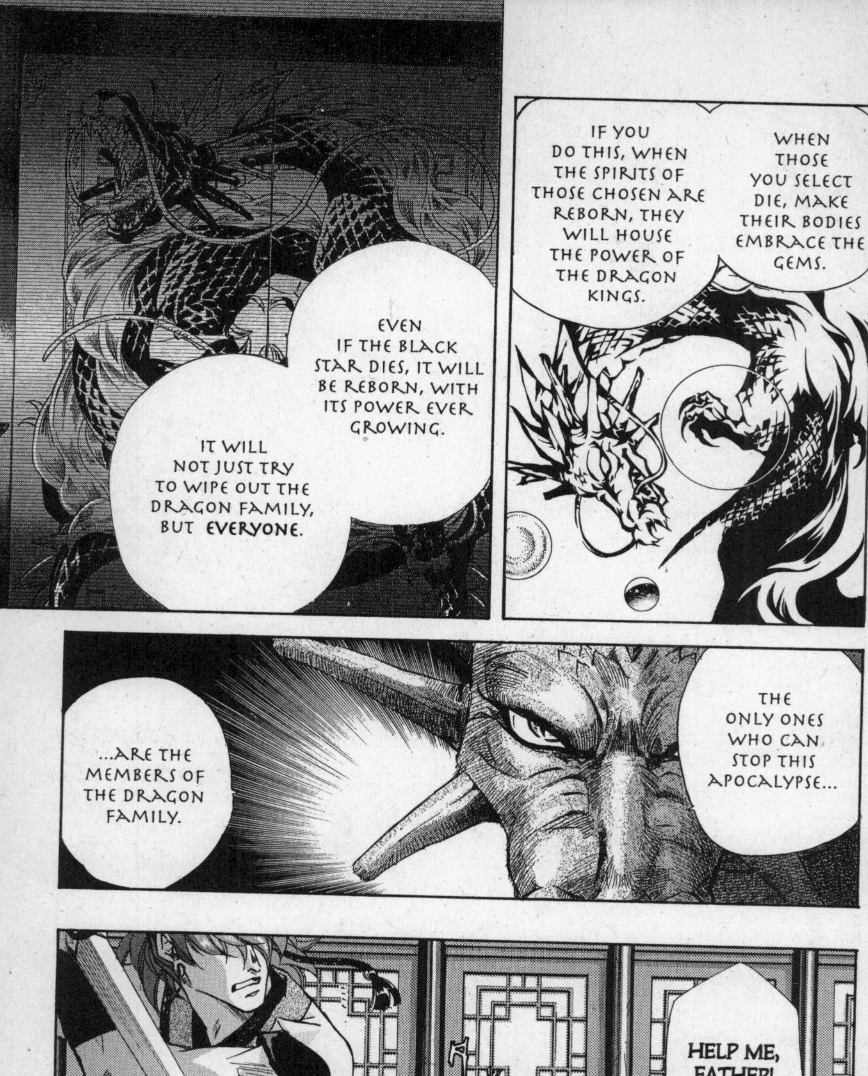
WHEN THOSE YOU SELECT DIE, MAKE THEIR BODIES EMBRACE THE GEMS.
IF YOU DO THIS, WHEN THE SPIRITS OF THOSE CHOSEN ARE REBORN, THEY WILL HOUSE THE POWER OF THE DRAGON KINGS.
EVEN IF THE BLACK STAR DIES, IT WILL BE REBORN, WITH ITS POWER EVER GROWING.
IT WILL NOT JUST TRY TO WIPE OUT THE DRAGON FAMILY, BUT EVERYONE.
THE ONLY ONES WHO CAN STOP THIS APOCALYPSE...
...ARE THE MEMBERS OF THE DRAGON FAMILY.
HELP ME, FATHER!

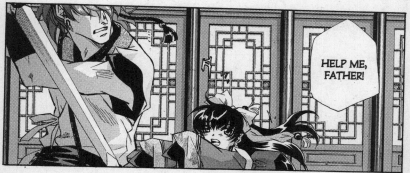

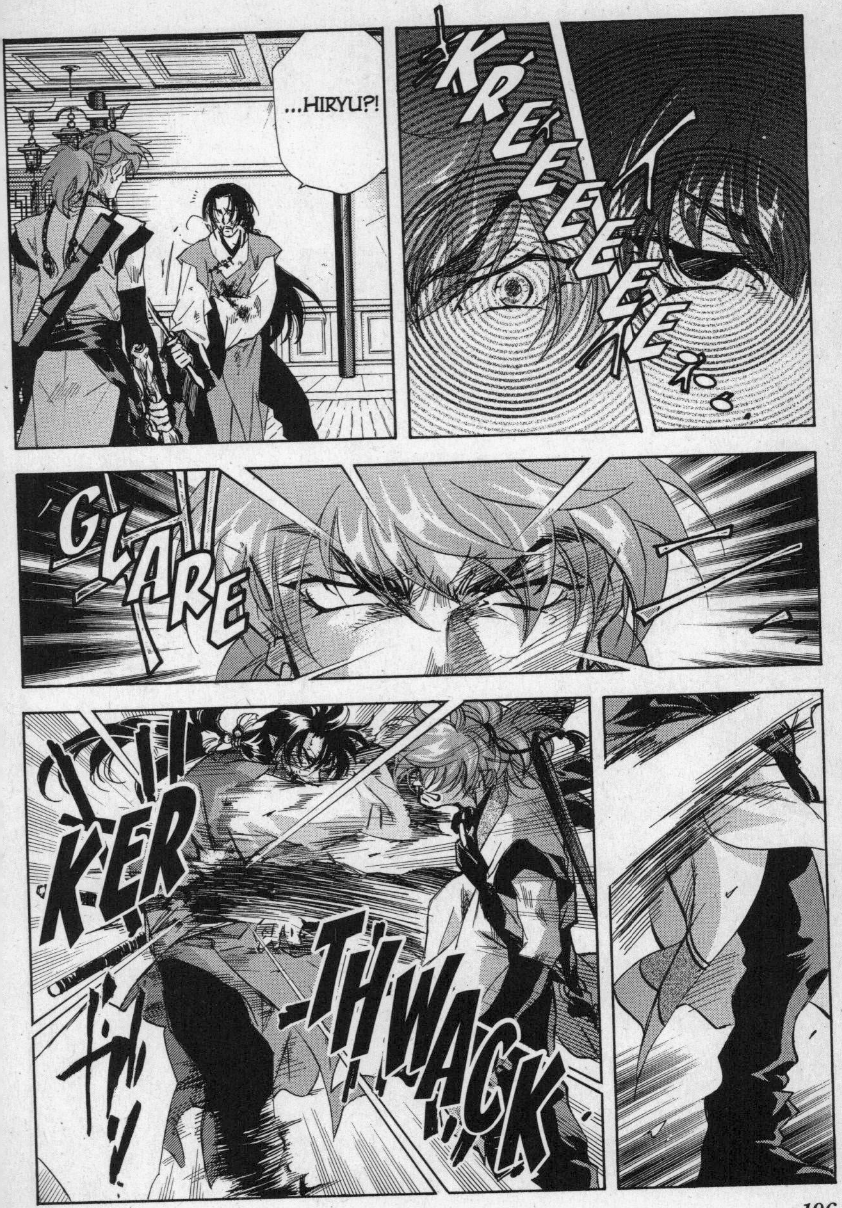
KREEEEEEE
...HIRYU?!
GLARE
KER-THWACK

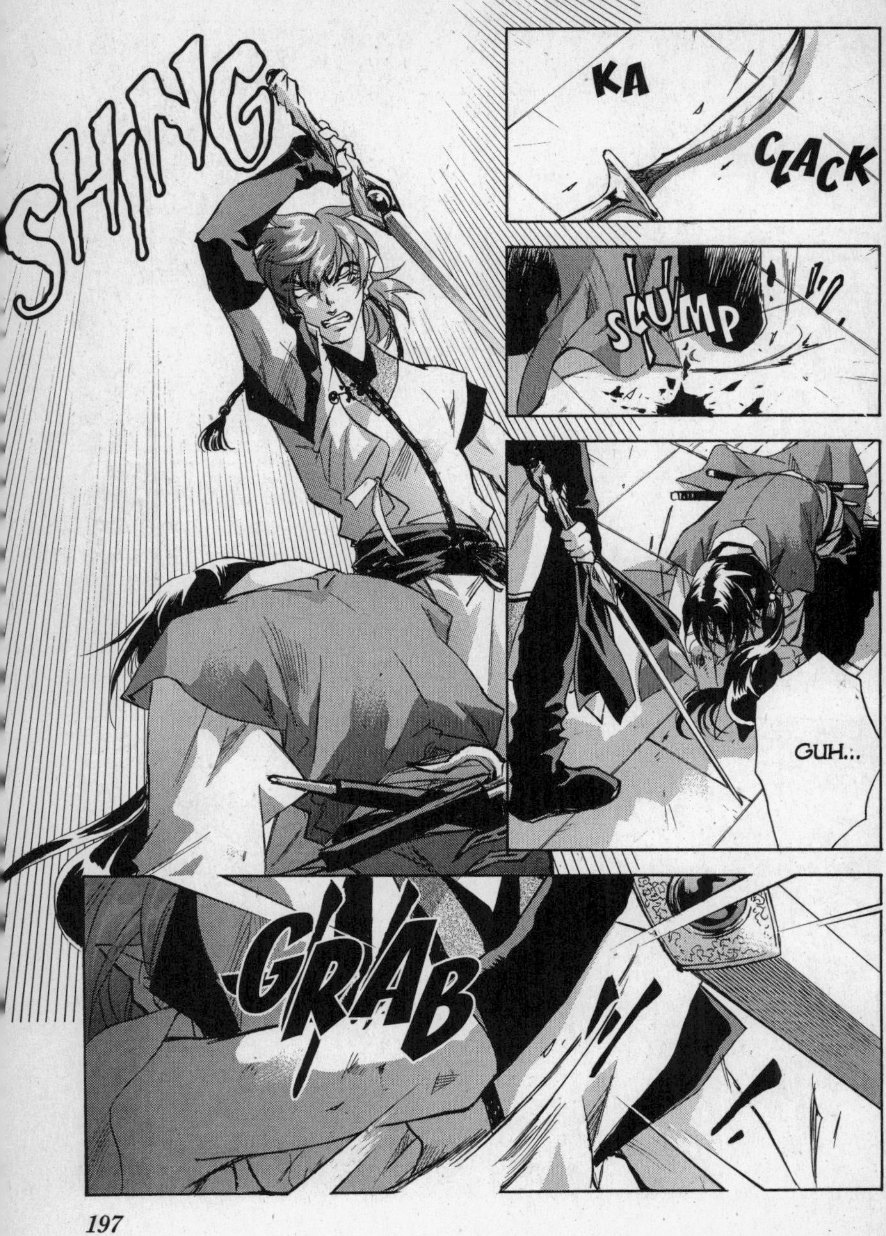
KA
CLACK
SLUMP
GUH...
SHING
GRAB

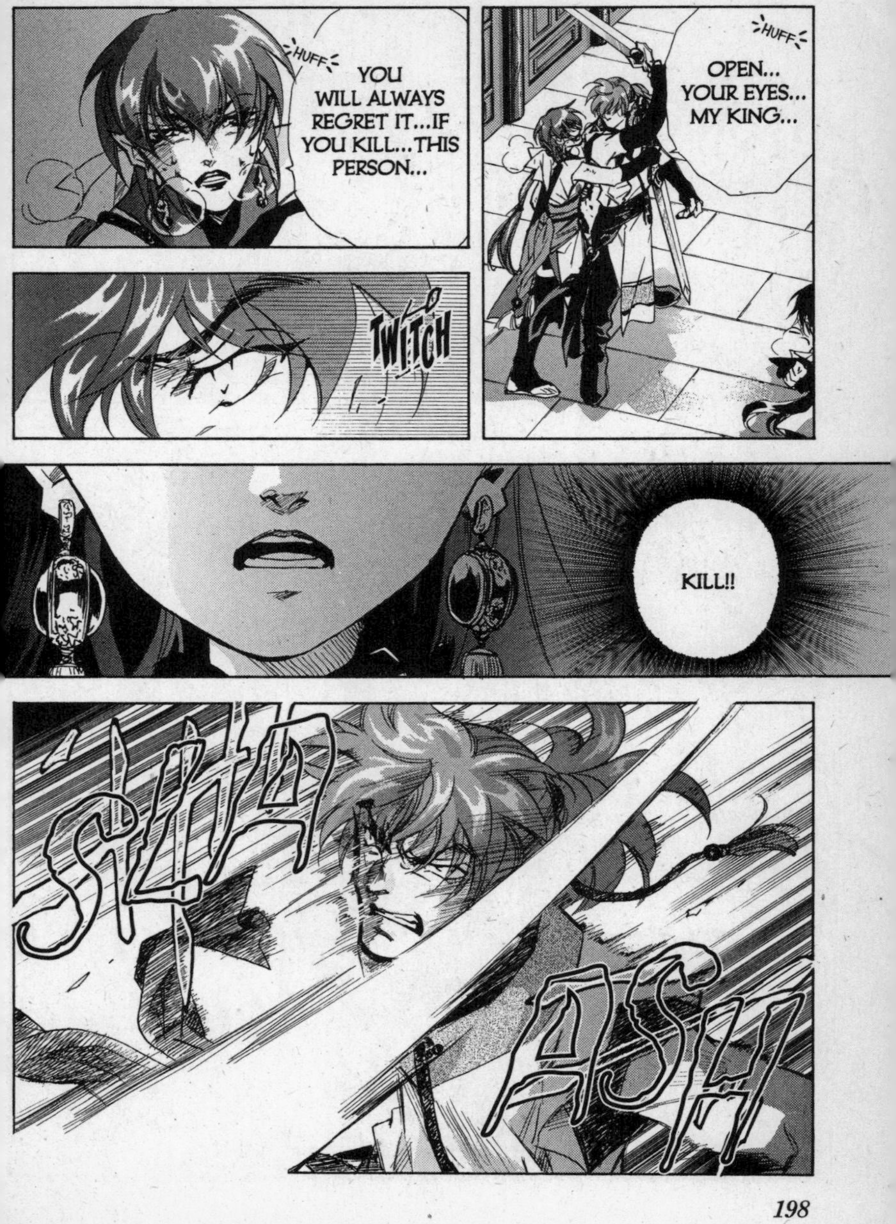
HUFF
OPEN... YOUR EYES... MY KING...
HUFF
YOU WILL ALWAYS REGRET IT...IF YOU KILL...THIS PERSON...
TWITCH
KILL!!
SLASH

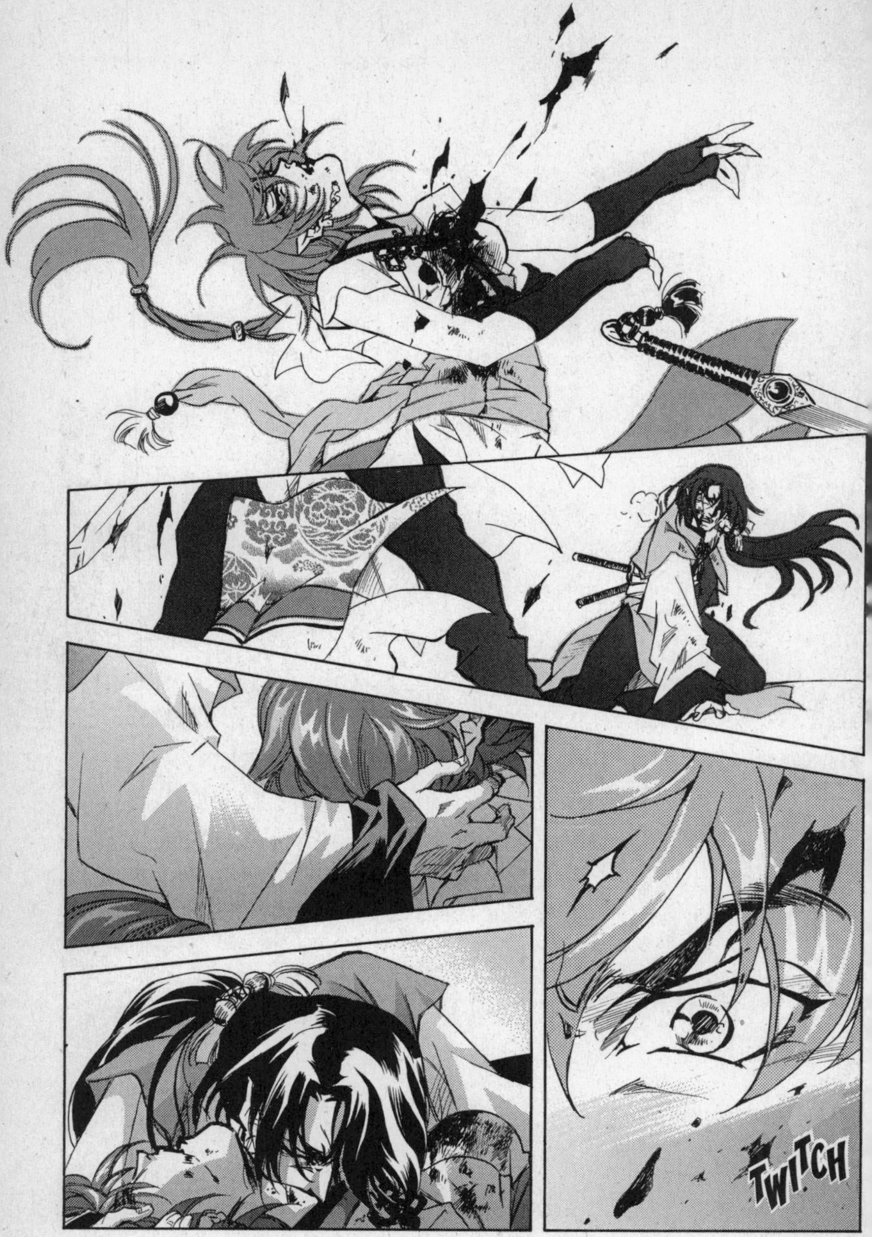
TWITCH

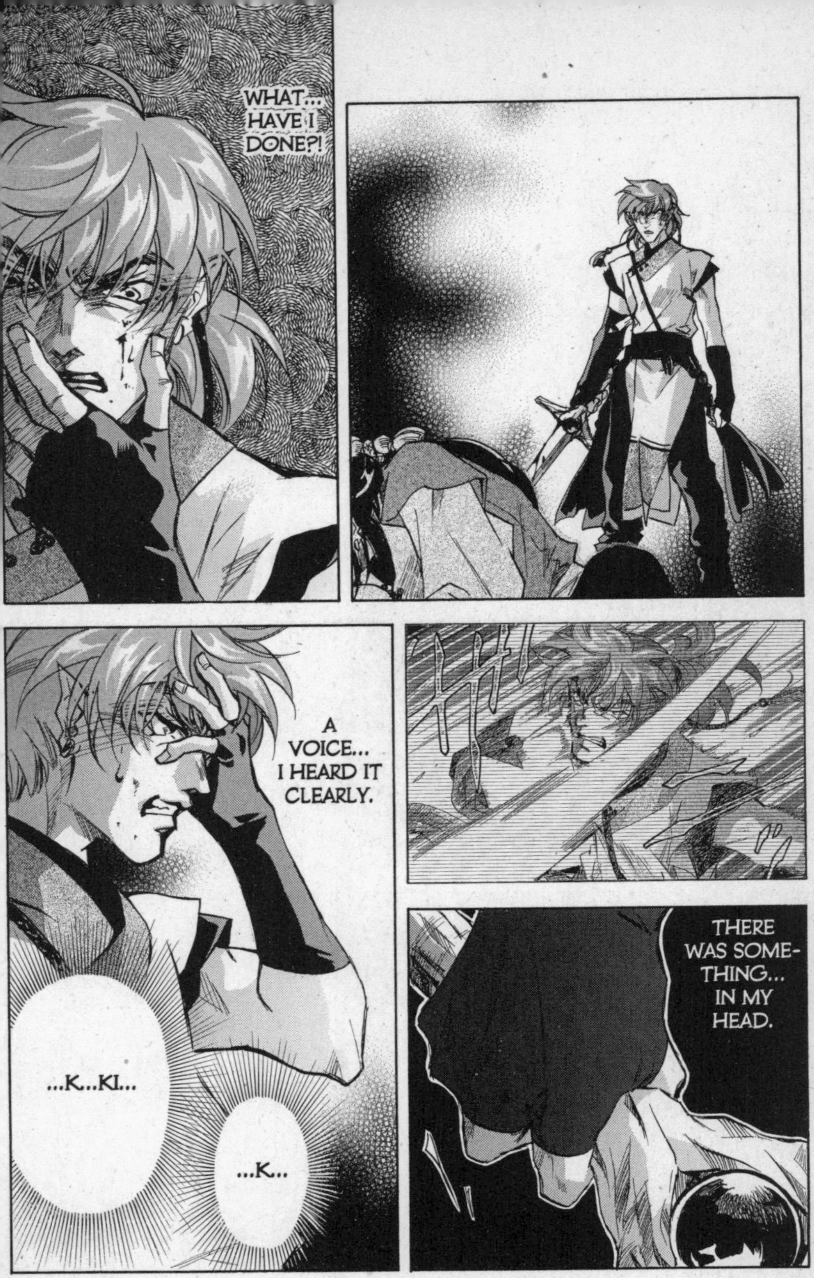
WHAT... HAVE I DONE?!
THERE WAS SOME-THING... IN MY HEAD.
A VOICE... I HEARD IT CLEARLY.
...K..KI...
...K...

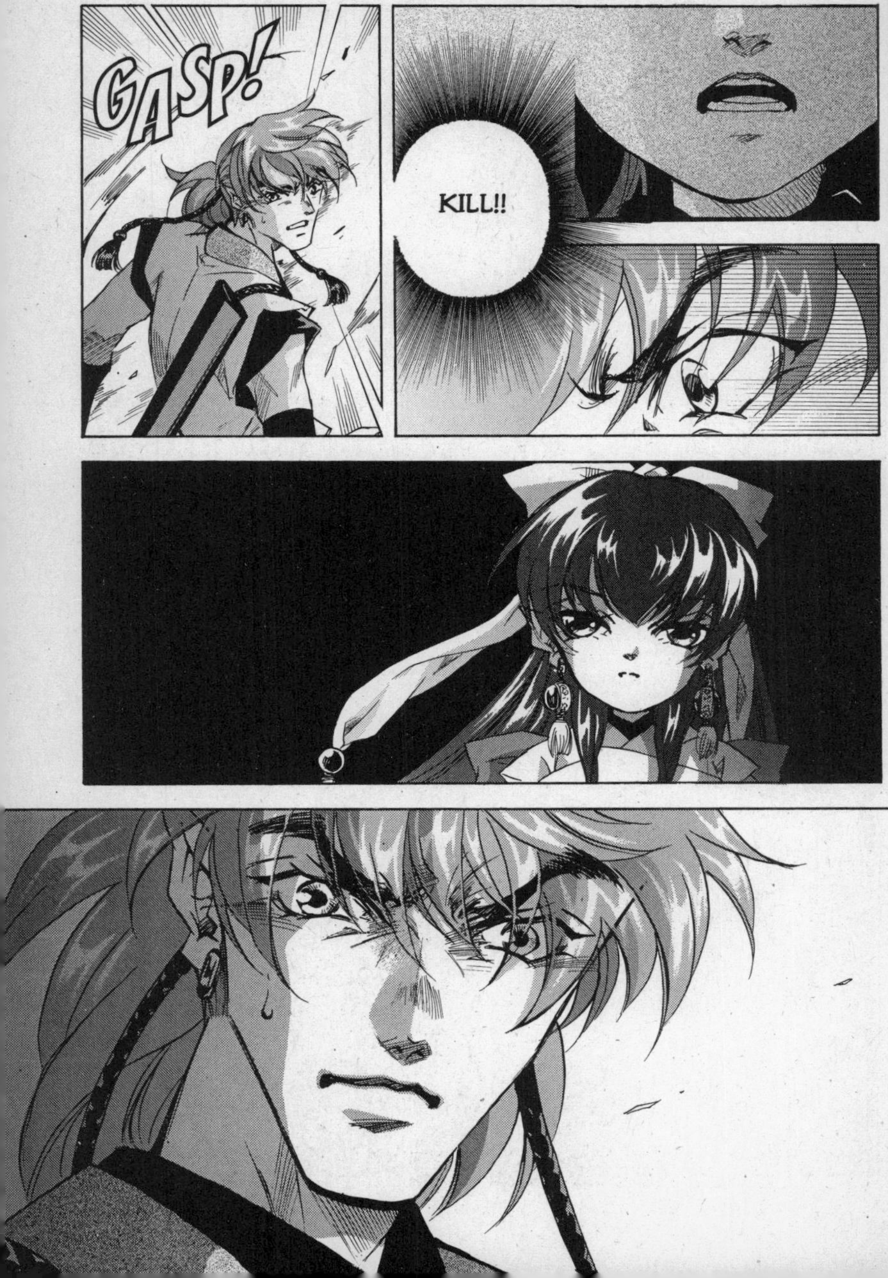
KILL!!
GASP!

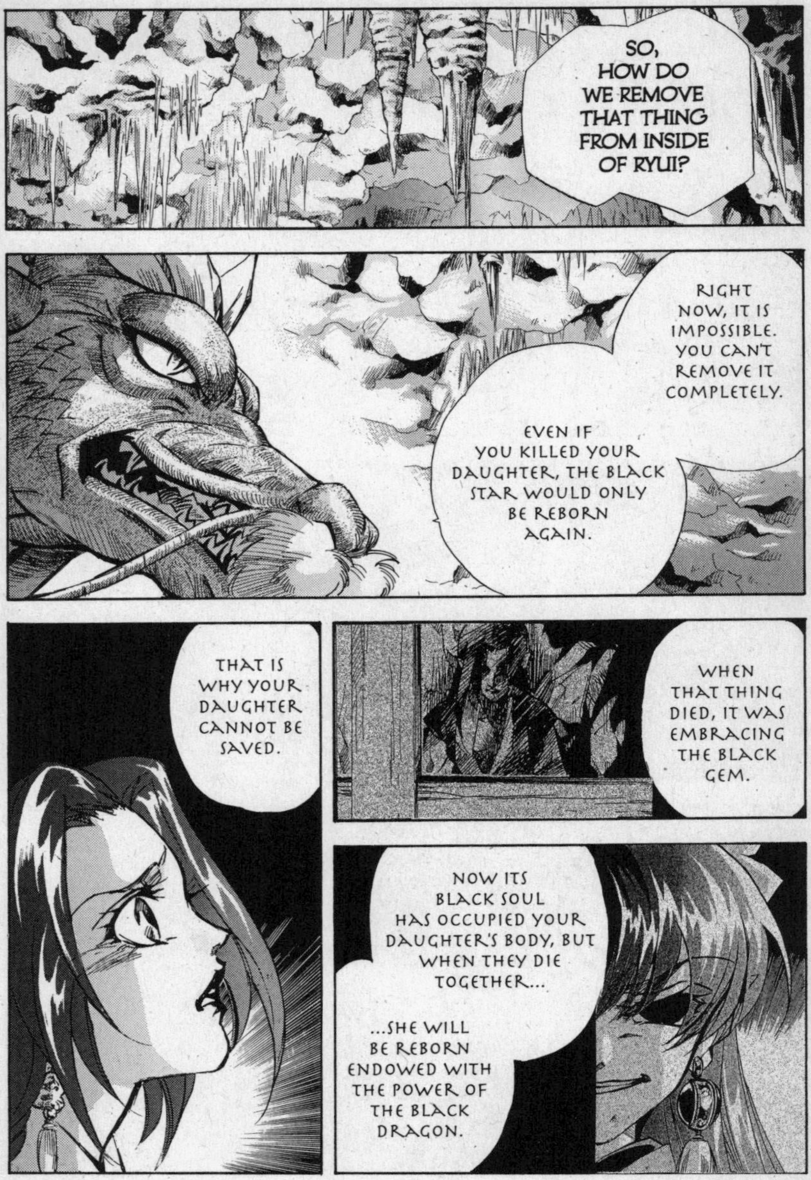
SO, HOW DO WE REMOVE THAT THING FROM INSIDE OF RYUI?
RIGHT NOW, IT IS IMPOSSIBLE. YOU CAN'T REMOVE IT COMPLETELY.
EVEN IF YOU KILLED YOUR DAUGHTER, THE BLACK STAR WOULD ONLY BE REBORN AGAIN.
WHEN THAT THING DIED, IT WAS EMBRACING THE BLACK GEM.
NOW ITS BLACK SOUL HAS OCCUPIED YOUR DAUGHTER'S BODY, BUT WHEN THEY DIE TOGETHER...
...SHE WILL BE REBORN ENDOWED WITH THE POWER OF THE BLACK DRAGON.
THAT IS WHY YOUR DAUGHTER CANNOT BE SAVED.

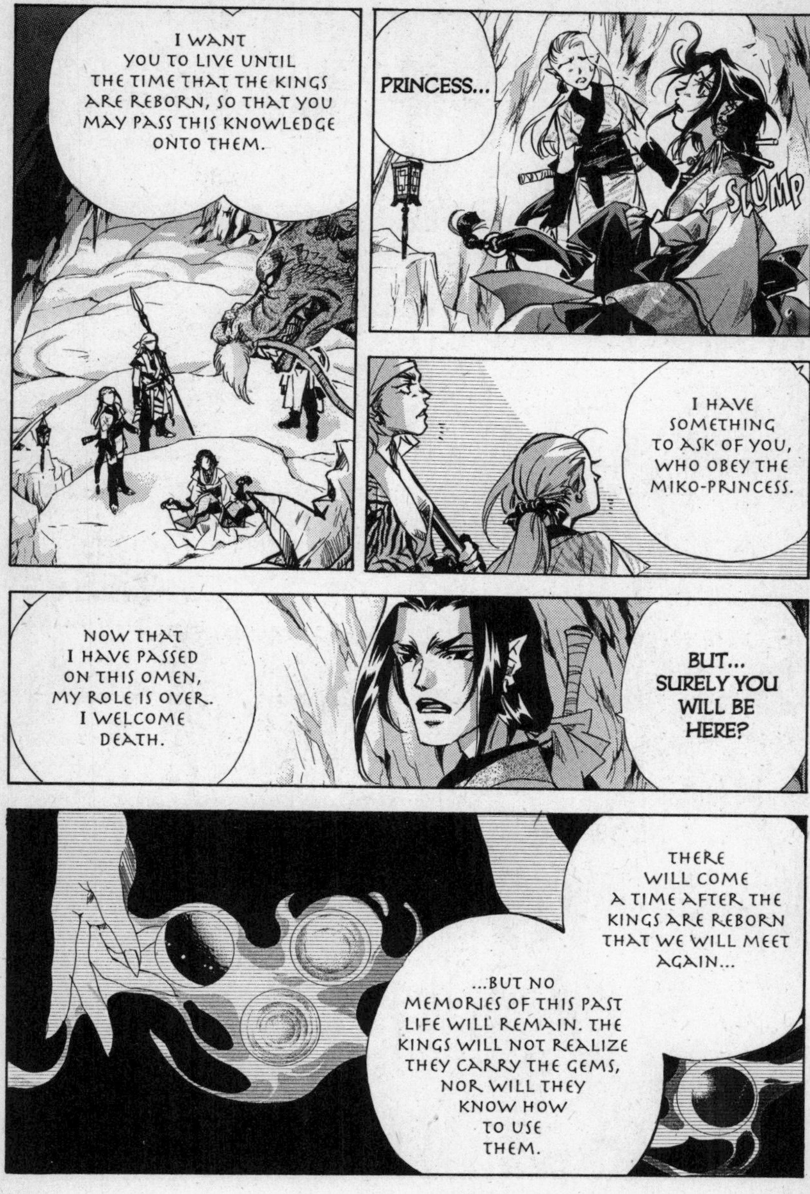
PRINCESS...
SLUMP
I HAVE SOMETHING TO ASK OF YOU, WHO OBEY THE MIKO-PRINCESS.
I WANT YOU TO LIVE UNTIL THE TIME THAT THE KINGS ARE REBORN, SO THAT YOU MAY PASS THIS KNOWLEDGE ONTO THEM.
BUT... SURELY YOU WILL BE HERE?
NOW THAT I HAVE PASSED ON THIS OMEN, MY ROLE IS OVER. I WELCOME DEATH.
THERE WILL COME A TIME AFTER THE KINGS ARE REBORN THAT WE WILL MEET AGAIN...
...BUT NO MEMORIES OF THIS PAST LIFE WILL REMAIN. THE KINGS WILL NOT REALIZE THEY CARRY THE GEMS, NOR WILL THEY KNOW HOW TO USE THEM.

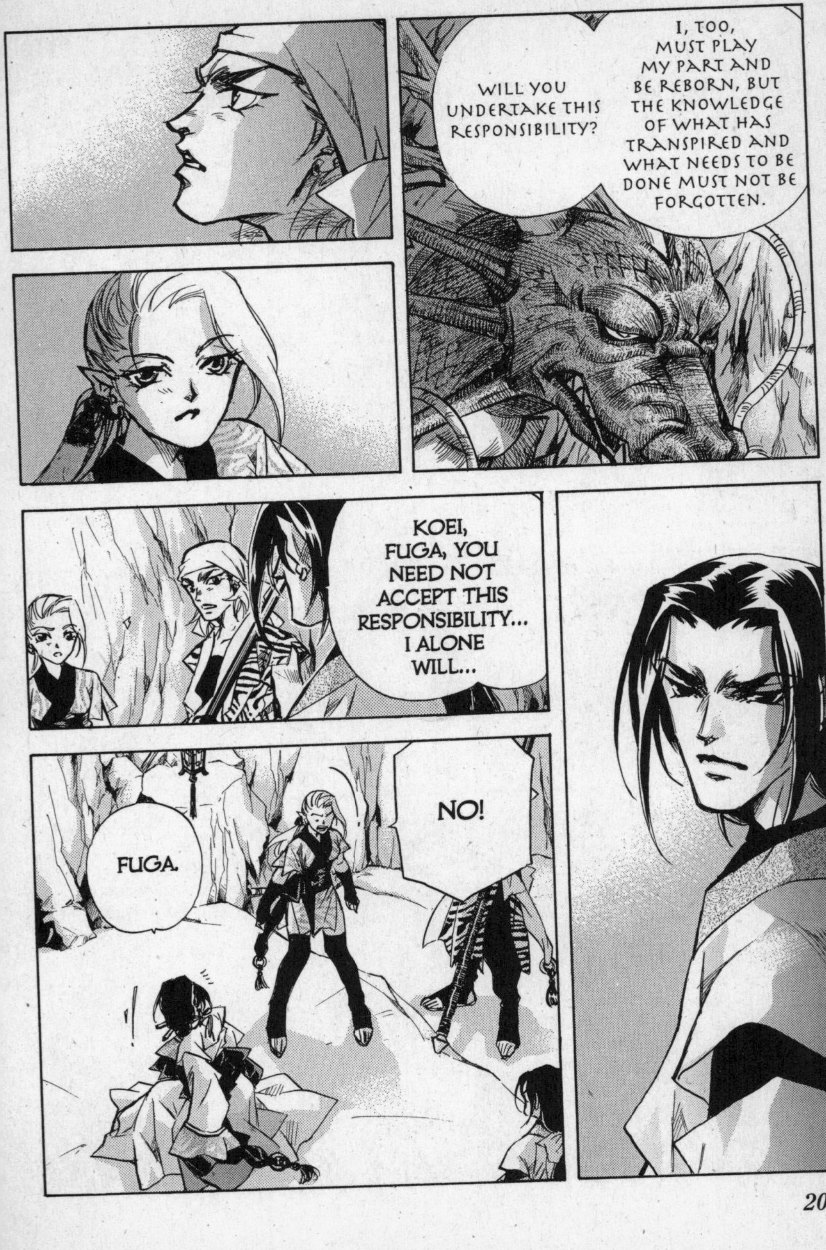

I, TOO, MUST PLAY MY PART AND BE REBORN, BUT THE KNOWLEDGE OF WHAT HAS TRANSPIRED AND WHAT NEEDS TO BE DONE MUST NOT BE FORGOTTEN.
WILL YOU UNDERTAKE THIS RESPONSIBILITY?
KOEI, FUGA, YOU NEED NOT ACCEPT THIS RESPONSIBILITY... I ALONE WILL...
NO!
FUGA.

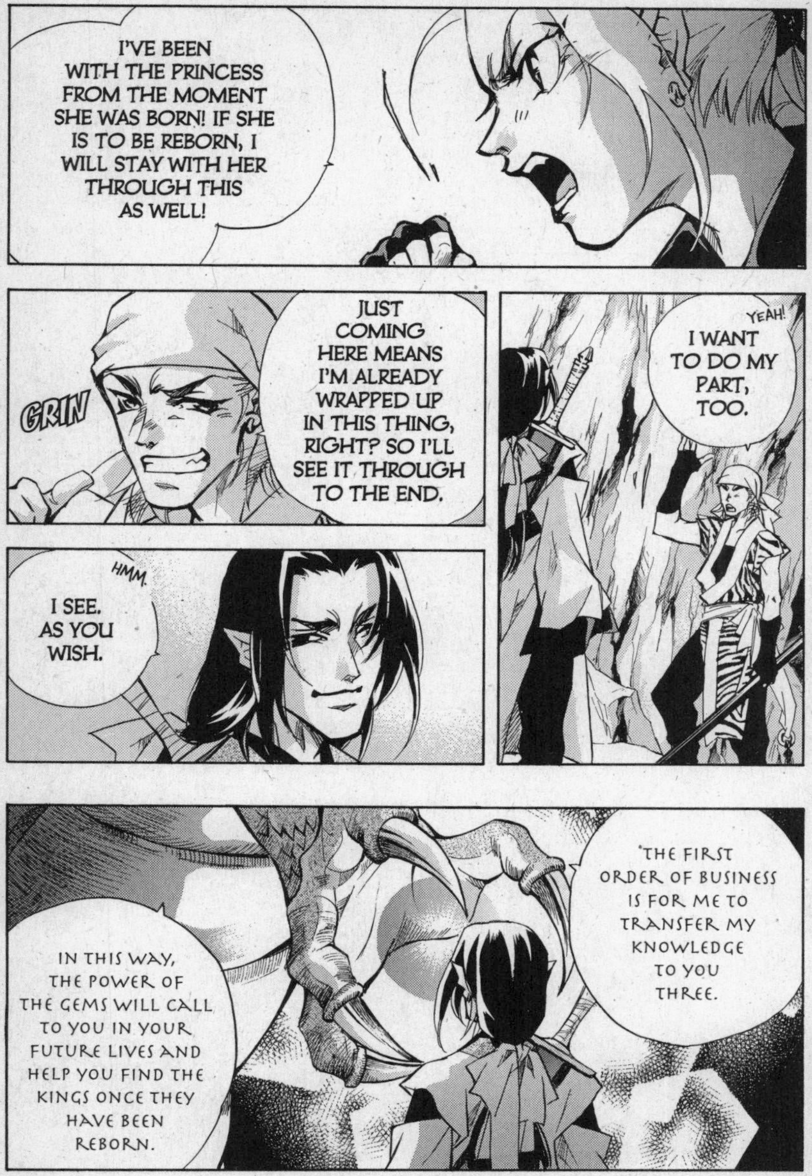
I'VE BEEN WITH THE PRINCESS FROM THE MOMENT SHE WAS BORN! IF SHE IS TO BE REBORN, I WILL STAY WITH HER THROUGH THIS AS WELL!
YEAH!
I WANT TO DO MY PART, TOO.
JUST COMING HERE MEANS I'M ALREADY WRAPPED UP IN THIS THING, RIGHT? SO I'LL SEE IT THROUGH TO THE END.
GRIN
HMM.
I SEE. AS YOU WISH.
THE FIRST ORDER OF BUSINESS IS FOR ME TO TRANSFER MY KNOWLEDGE TO YOU THREE.
IN THIS WAY, THE POWER OF THE GEMS WILL CALL TO YOU IN YOUR FUTURE LIVES AND HELP YOU FIND THE KINGS ONCE THEY HAVE BEEN REBORN.

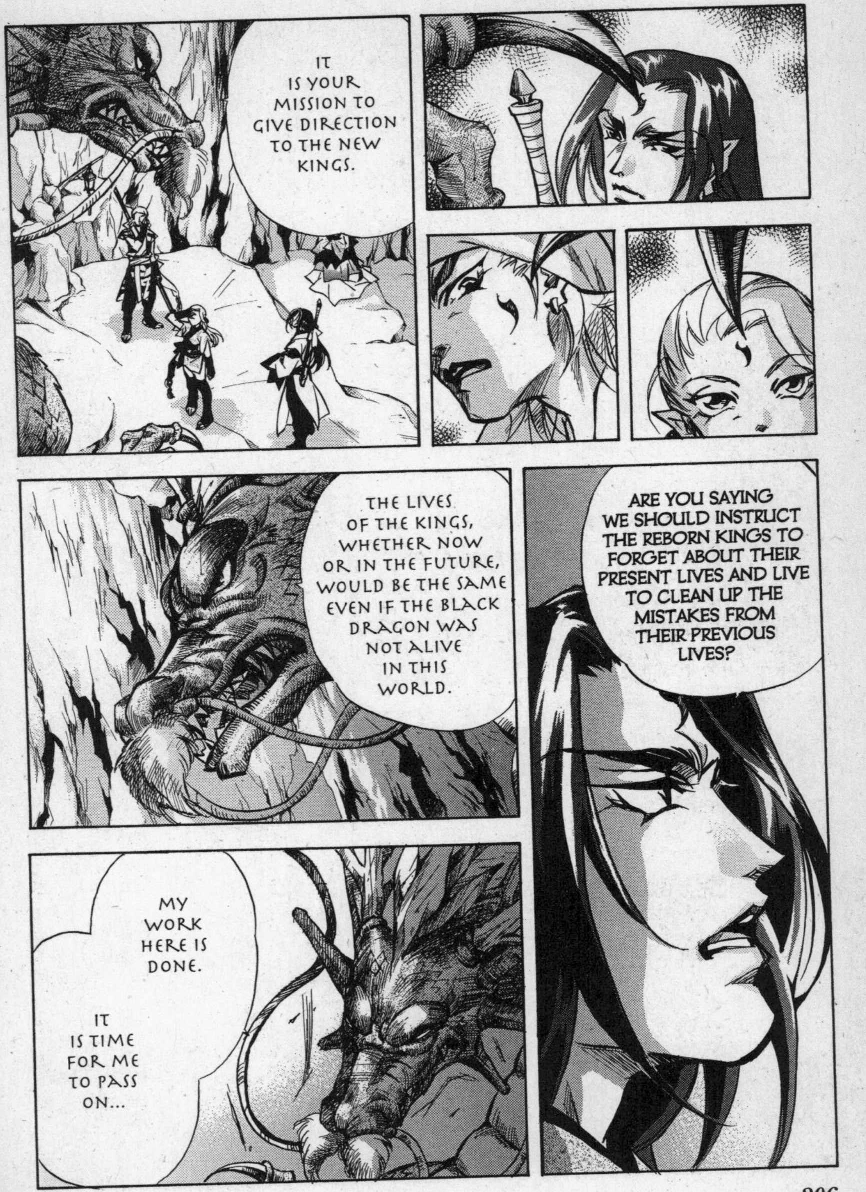
IT IS YOUR MISSION TO GIVE DIRECTION TO THE NEW KINGS.
ARE YOU SAYING WE SHOULD INSTRUCT THE REBORN KINGS TO FORGET ABOUT THEIR PRESENT LIVES AND LIVE TO CLEAN UP THE MISTAKES FROM THEIR PREVIOUS LIVES?
THE LIVES OF THE KINGS, WHETHER NOW OR IN THE FUTURE, WOULD BE THE SAME EVEN IF THE BLACK DRAGON WAS NOT ALIVE IN THIS WORLD.
MY WORK HERE IS DONE.
IT IS TIME FOR ME TO PASS ON...

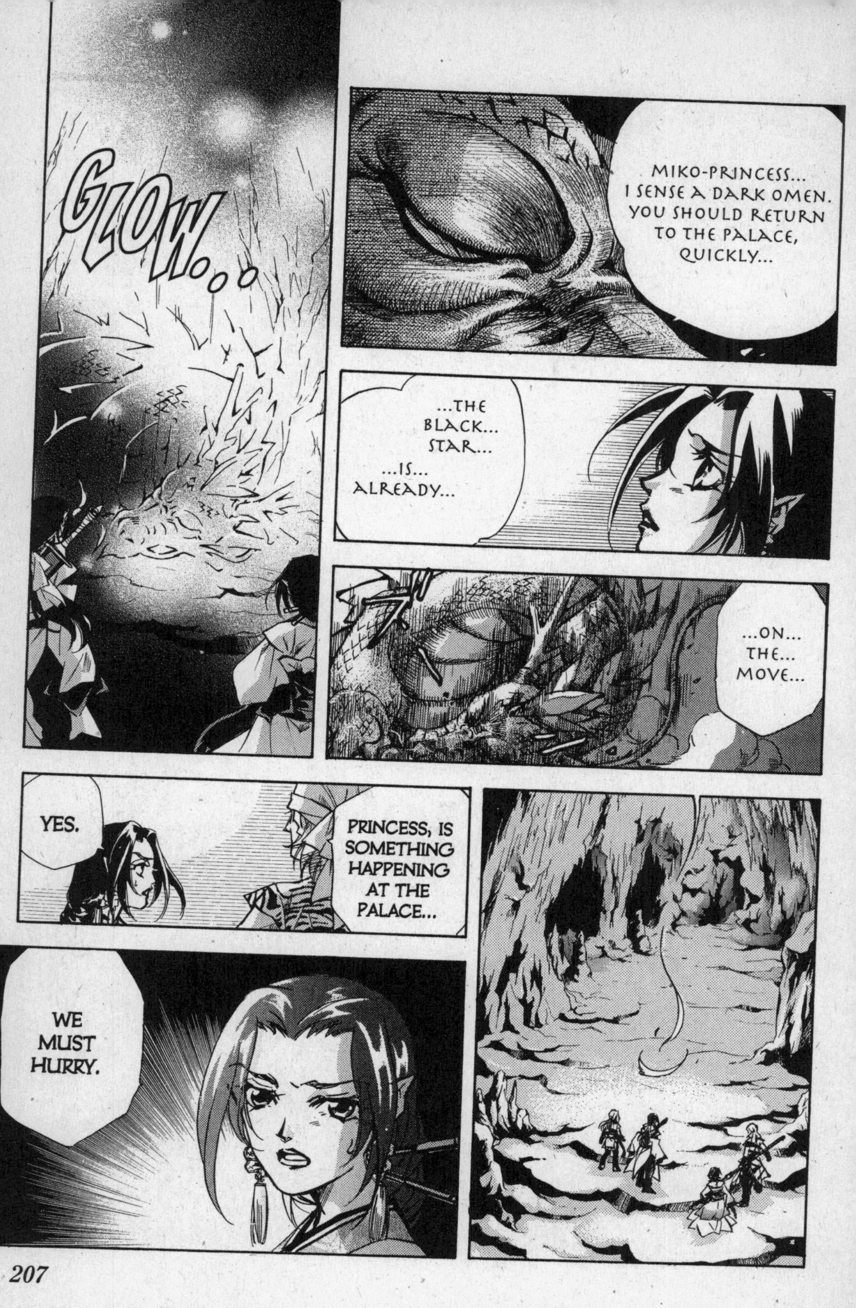
MIKO-PRINCESS... I SENSE A DARK OMEN. YOU SHOULD RETURN TO THE PALACE, QUICKLY...
...THE BLACK... STAR...
...IS... ALREADY...
...ON... THE... MOVE...
GLOW...
PRINCESS, IS SOMETHING HAPPENING AT THE PALACE...
YES.
WE MUST HURRY.

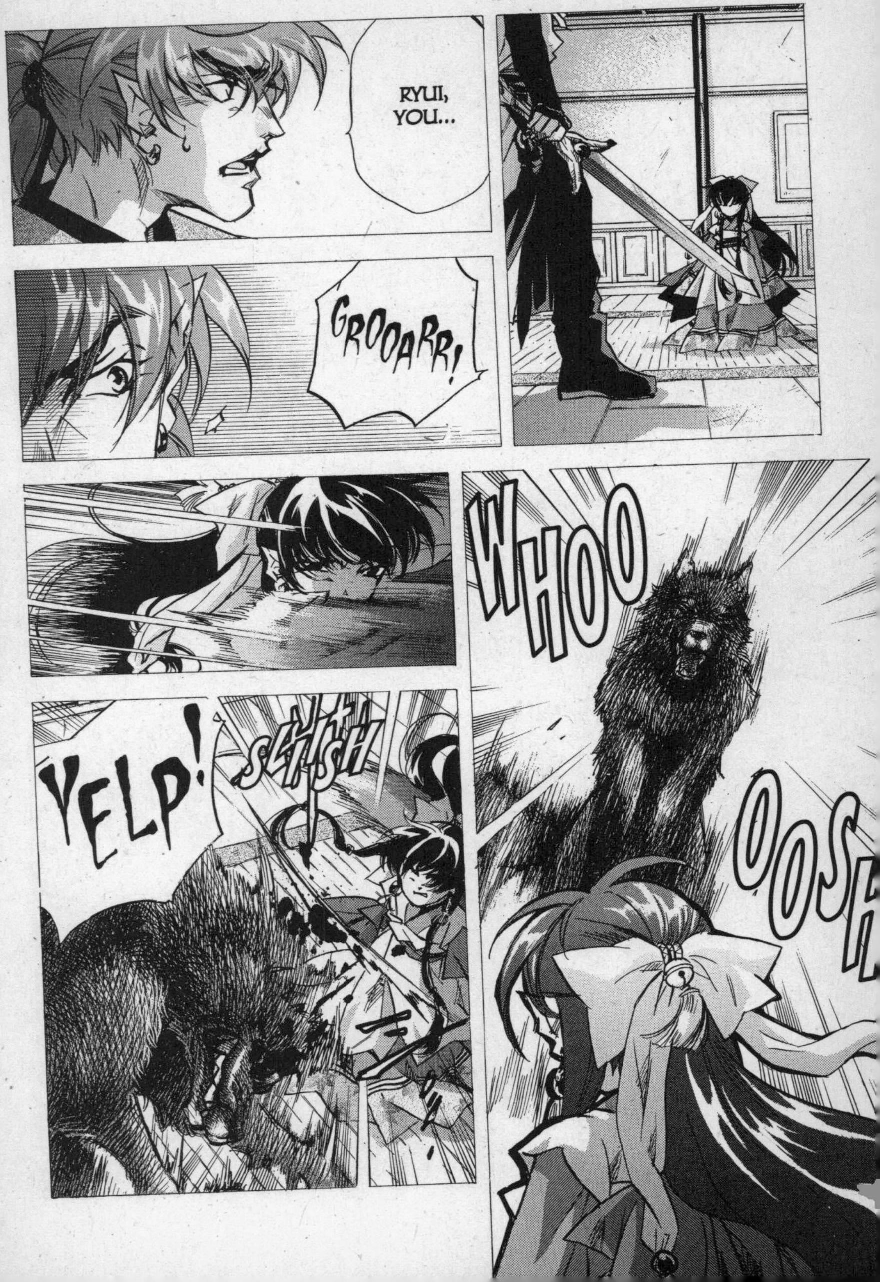
RYUI, YOU...
GROOARR!
WHOO
OOSH
YELP!
SLISH

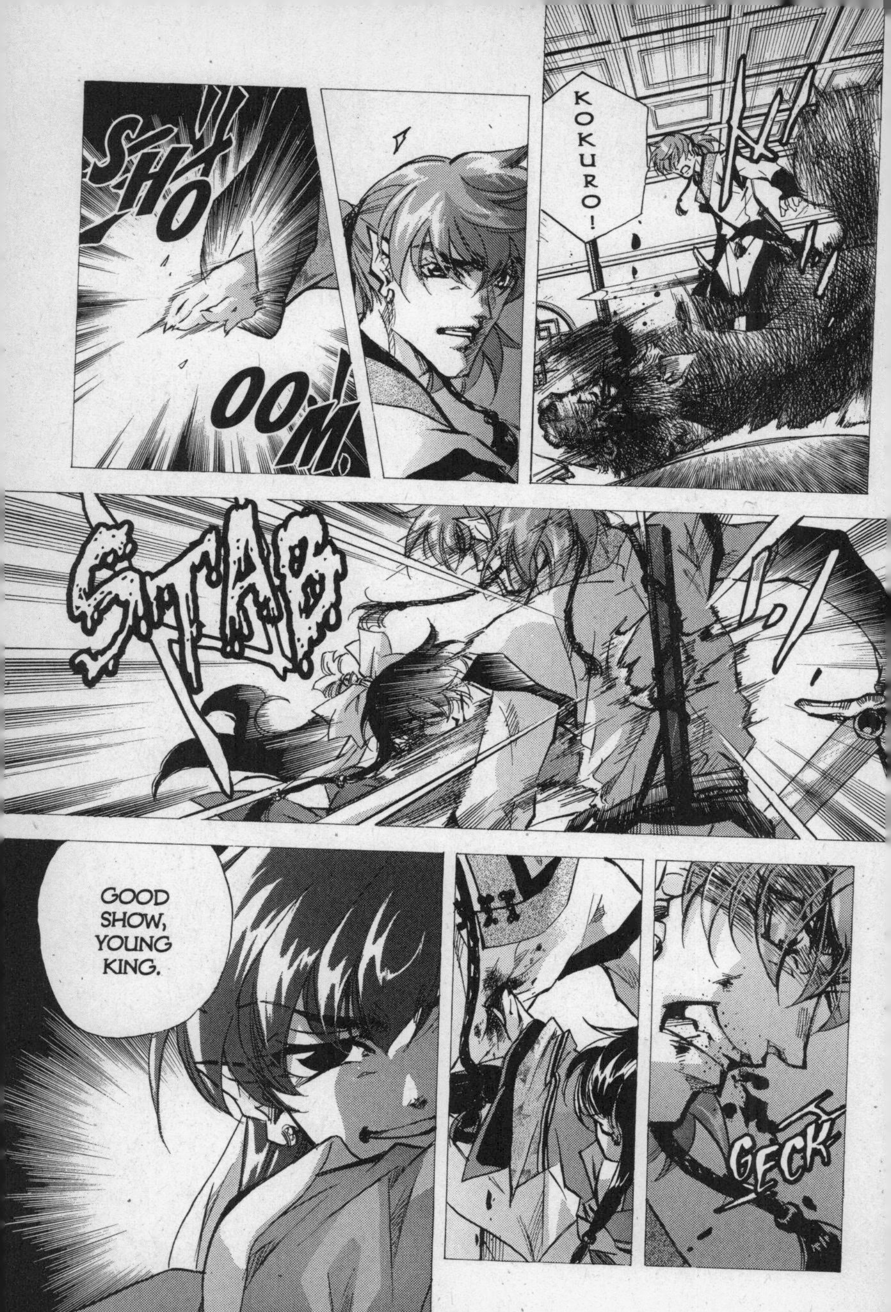
KOKURO!
SHOOOM!
STAB
GECK
GOOD SHOW, YOUNG KING.

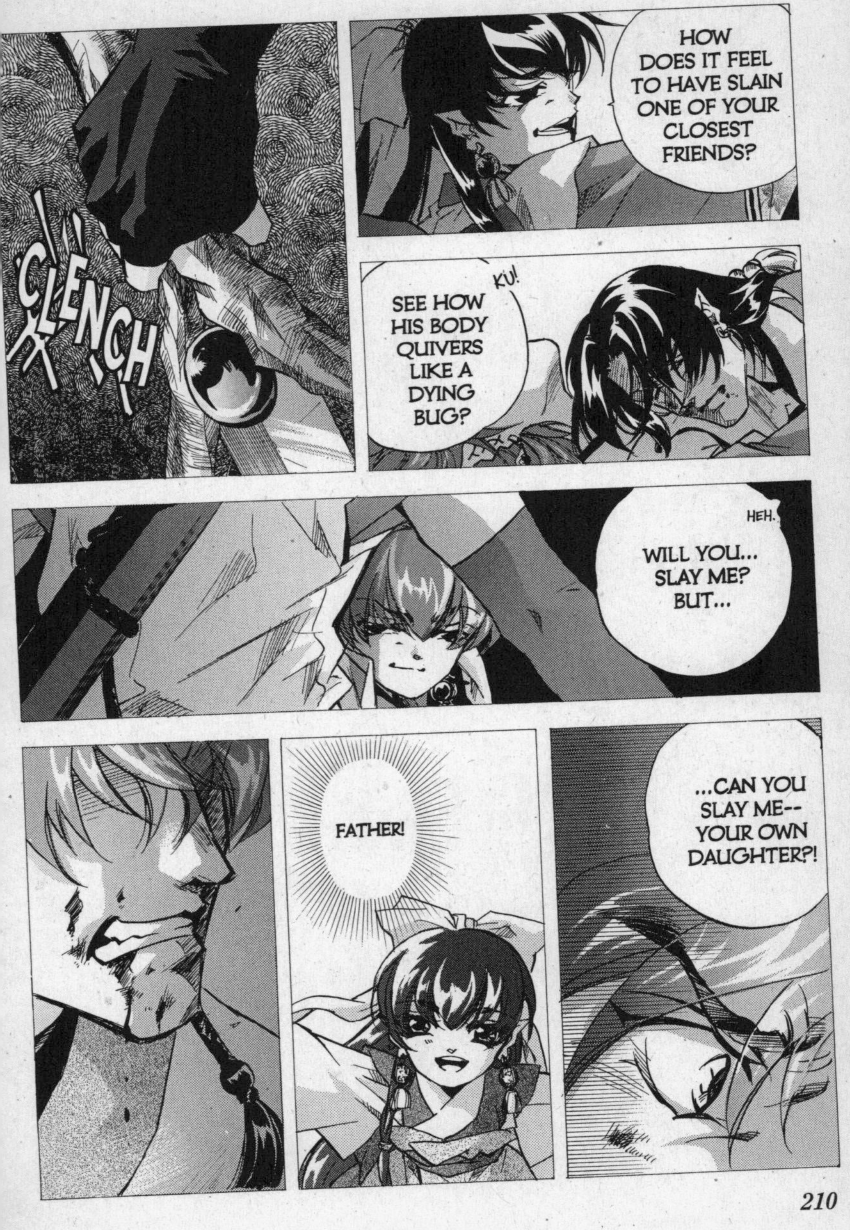
HOW DOES IT FEEL TO HAVE SLAIN ONE OF YOUR CLOSEST FRIENDS?
KU!
SEE HOW HIS BODY QUIVERS LIKE A DYING BUG?
CLENCH
HEH.
WILL YOU... SLAY ME? BUT...
...CAN YOU SLAY ME-- YOUR OWN DAUGHTER?!
FATHER!

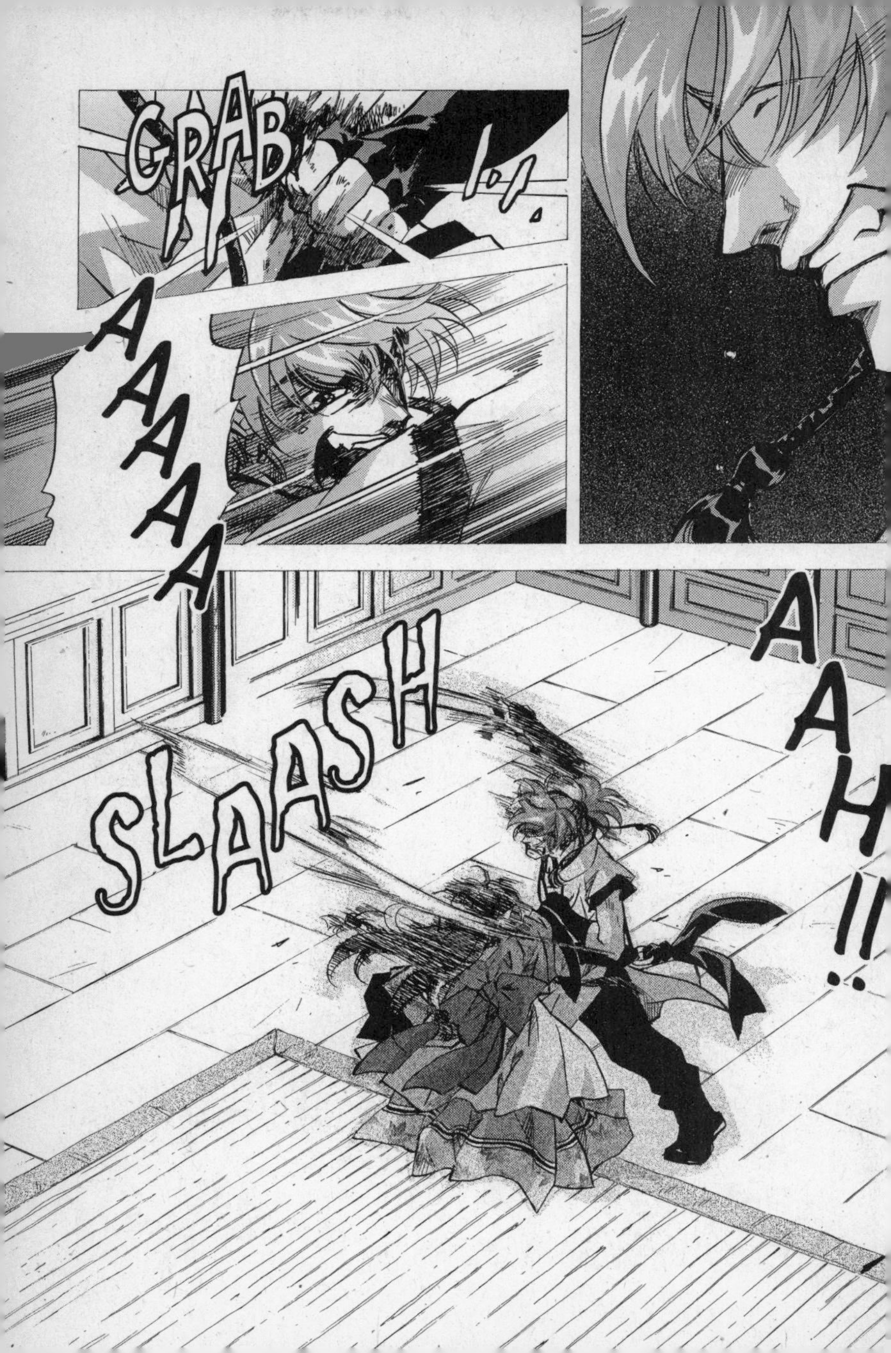
GRAB
AAAAAA
AAH!!
SLAASH

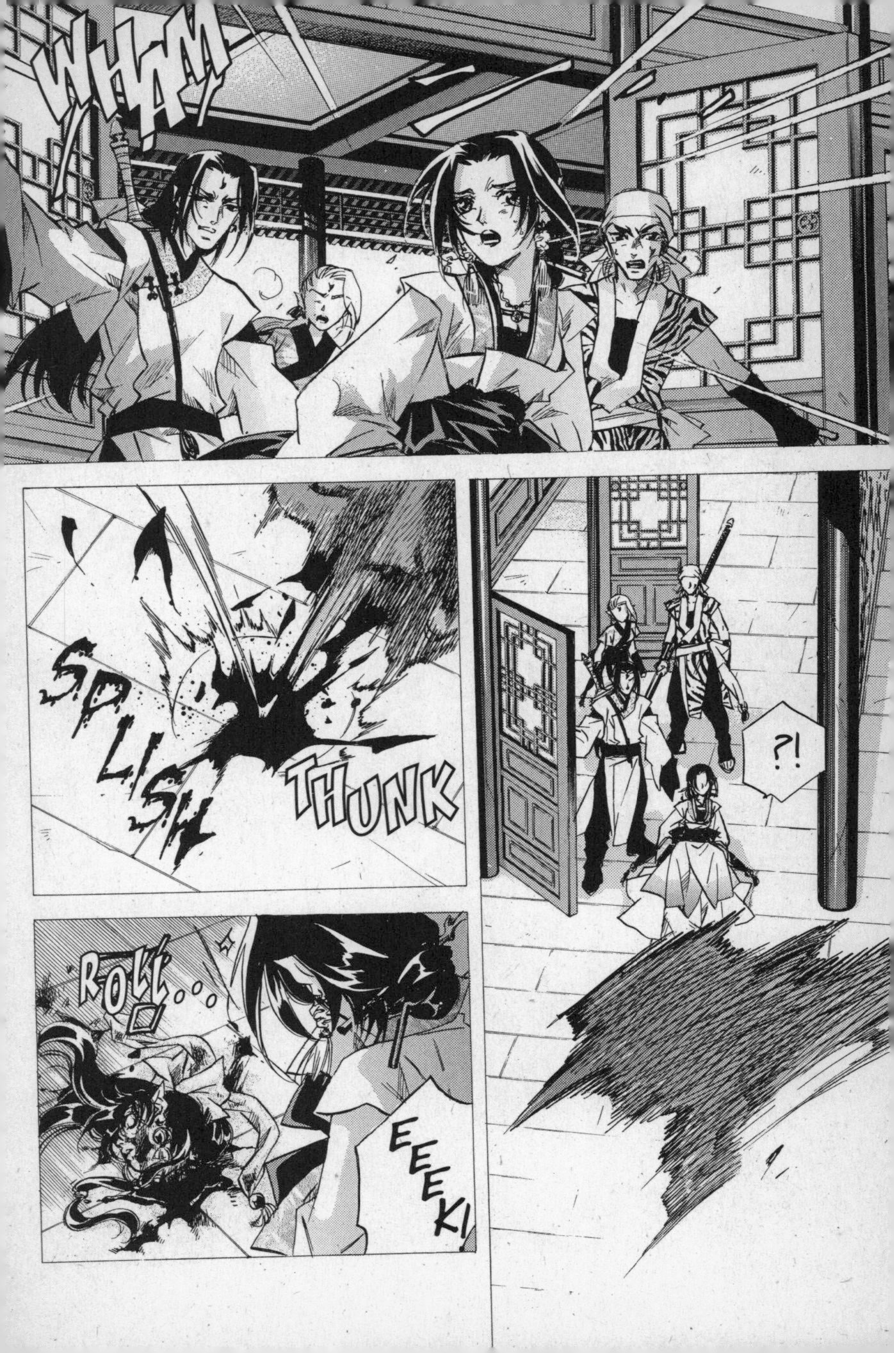
WHAM
?!
SPLISH
THUNK
ROLL...
EEEK!

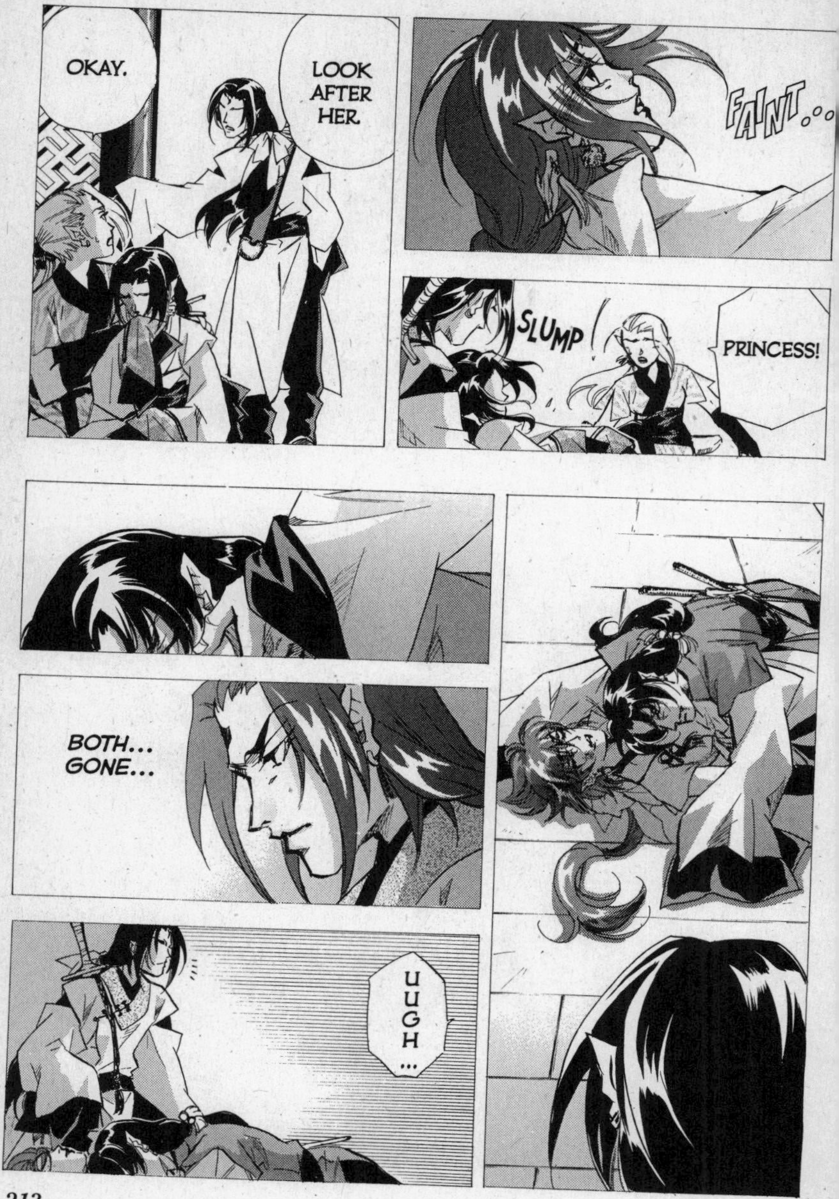
FAINT...
PRINCESS!
SLUMP!
LOOK AFTER HER.
OKAY.
BOTH... GONE...
UUGH...

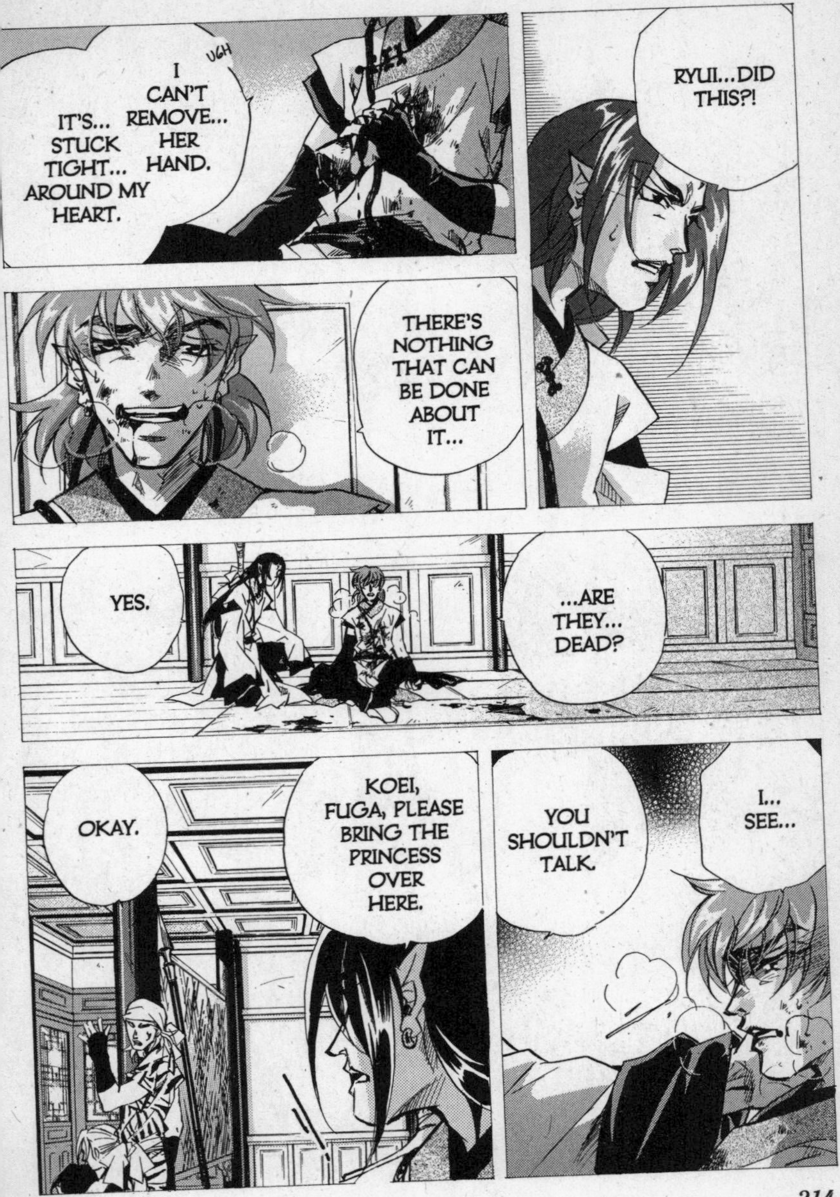
RYUI...DID THIS?!
UGH
I CAN'T REMOVE... HER HAND.
IT'S... STUCK TIGHT... AROUND MY HEART.
THERE'S NOTHING THAT CAN BE DONE ABOUT IT...
...ARE THEY... DEAD?
YES.
I... SEE...
YOU SHOULDN'T TALK.
KOEI, FUGA, PLEASE BRING THE PRINCESS OVER HERE.
OKAY.

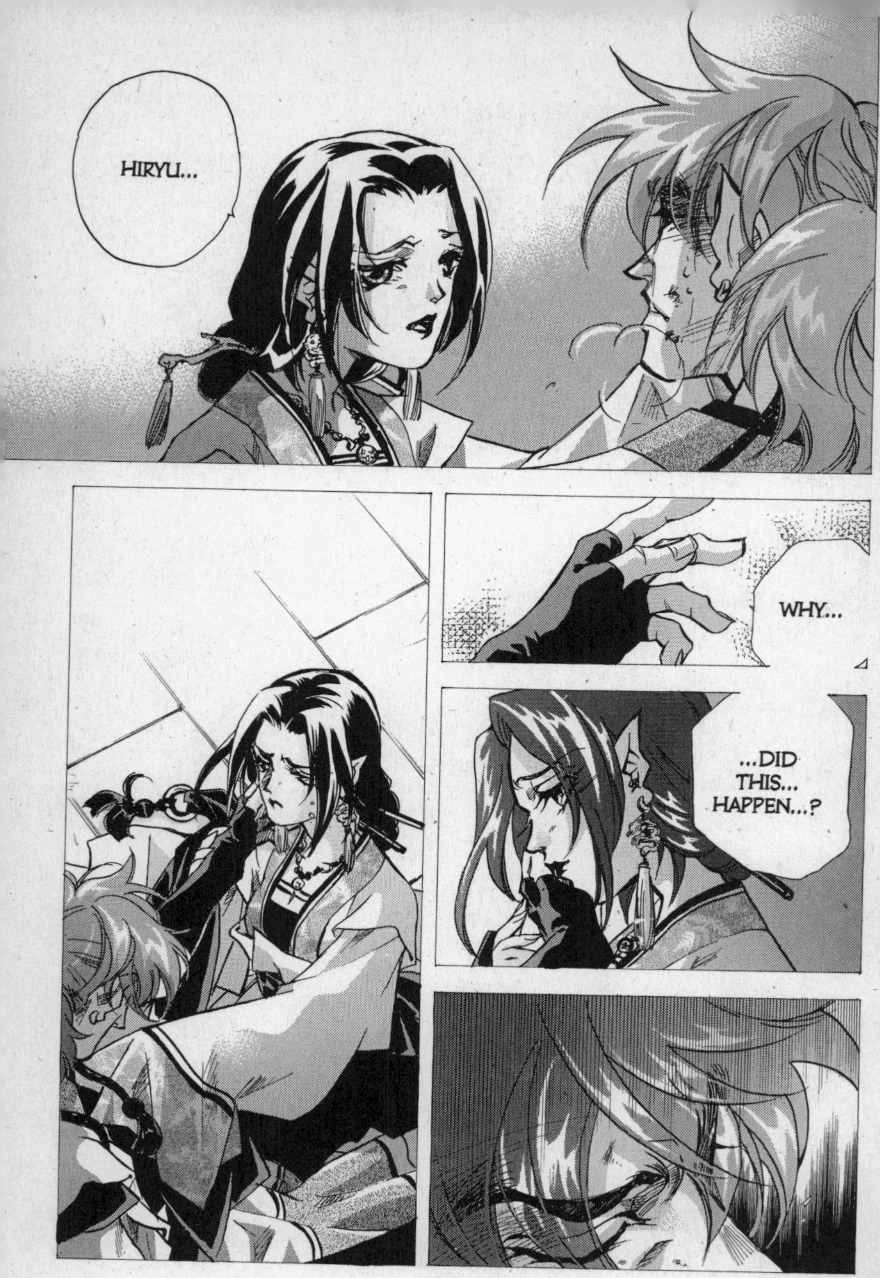
HIRYU...
WHY...
...DID THIS... HAPPEN...?

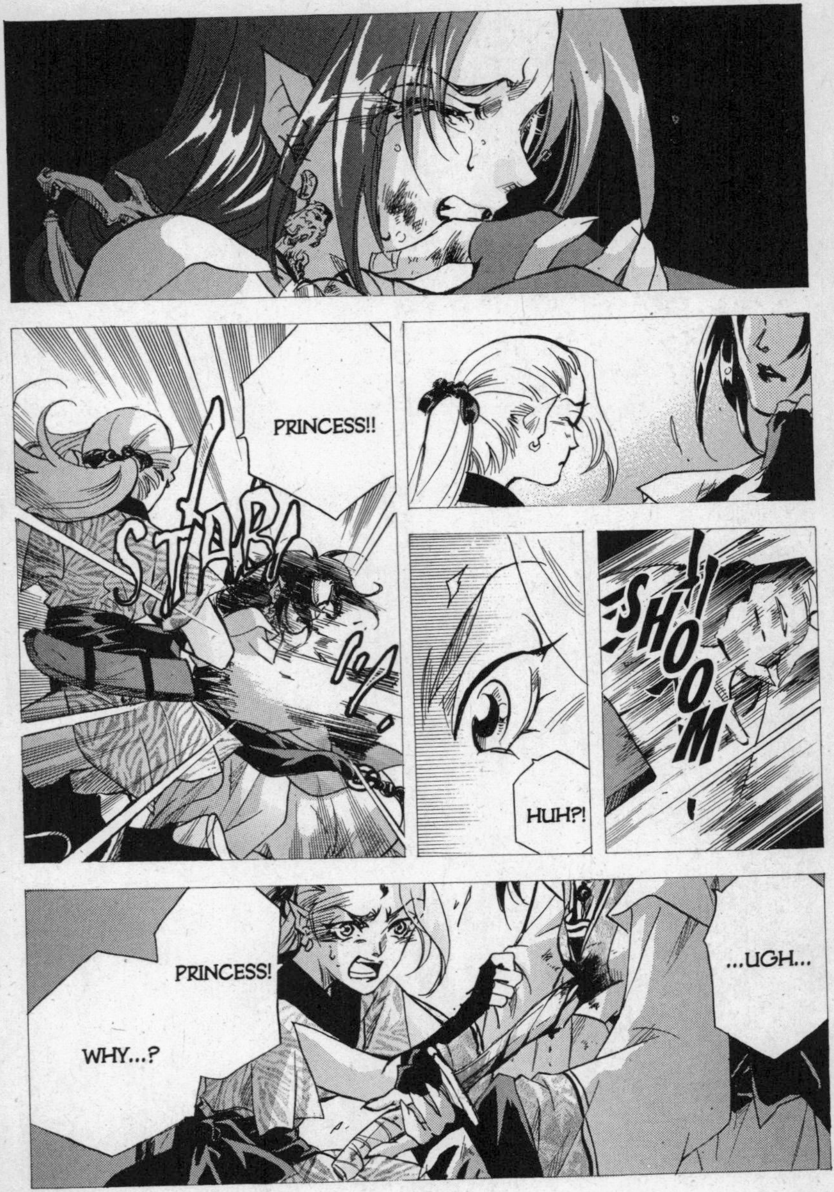
SHOOM
HUH?!
PRINCESS!!
STAB
...UGH...
PRINCESS!
WHY...?

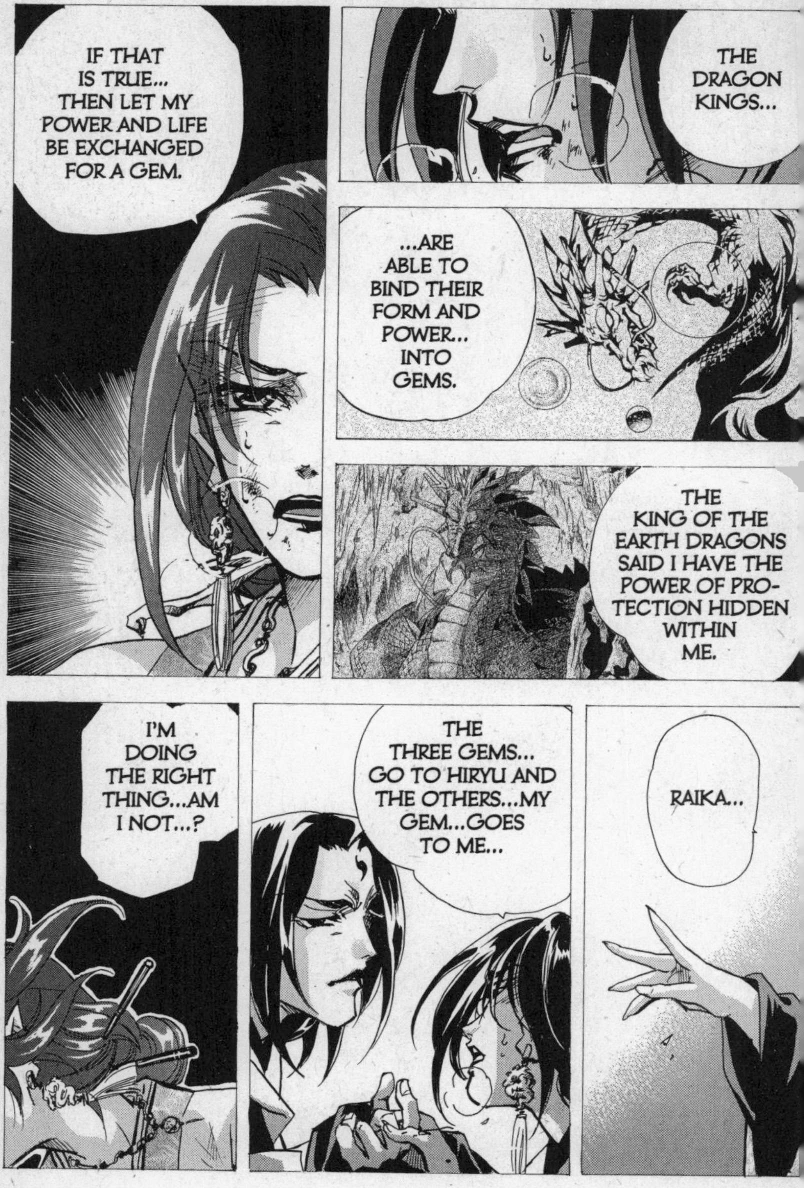
THE DRAGON KINGS...
...ARE ABLE TO BIND THEIR FORM AND POWER... INTO GEMS.
THE KING OF THE EARTH DRAGONS SAID I HAVE THE POWER OF PRO-TECTION HIDDEN WITHIN ME.
IF THAT IS TRUE... THEN LET MY POWER AND LIFE BE EXCHANGED FOR A GEM.
RAIKA...
THE THREE GEMS... GO TO HIRYU AND THE OTHERS...MY GEM...GOES TO ME...
I'M DOING THE RIGHT THING...AM I NOT...?

PRINCESS!

A VERMILION GEM...

GLOW...

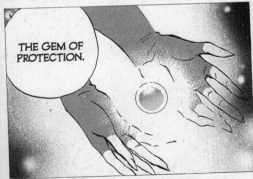

THE GEM OF PROTECTION.

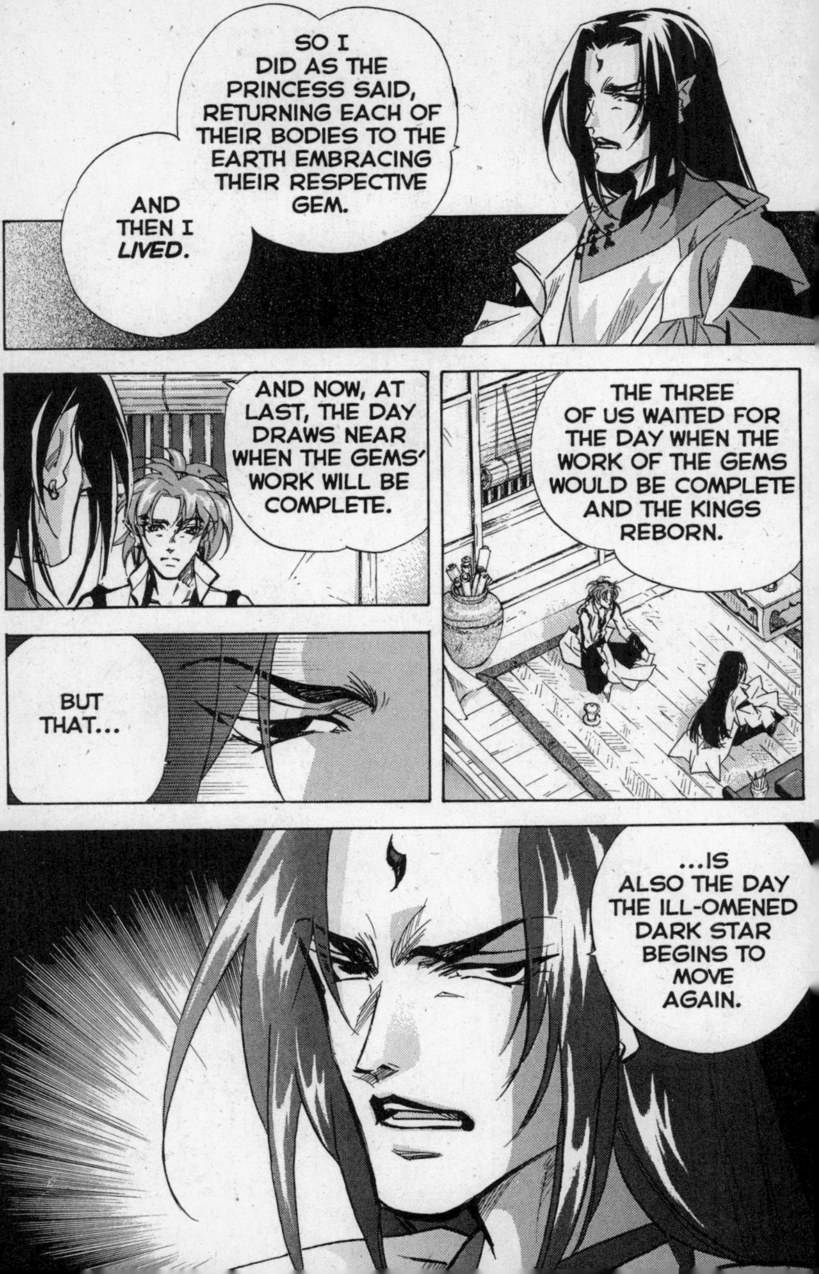
SO I DID AS THE PRINCESS SAID, RETURNING EACH OF THEIR BODIES TO THE EARTH EMBRACING THEIR RESPECTIVE GEM.
AND THEN I *LIVED*.
THE THREE OF US WAITED FOR THE DAY WHEN THE WORK OF THE GEMS WOULD BE COMPLETE AND THE KINGS REBORN.
AND NOW, AT LAST, THE DAY DRAWS NEAR WHEN THE GEMS' WORK WILL BE COMPLETE.
BUT THAT...
...IS ALSO THE DAY THE ILL-OMENED DARK STAR BEGINS TO MOVE AGAIN.

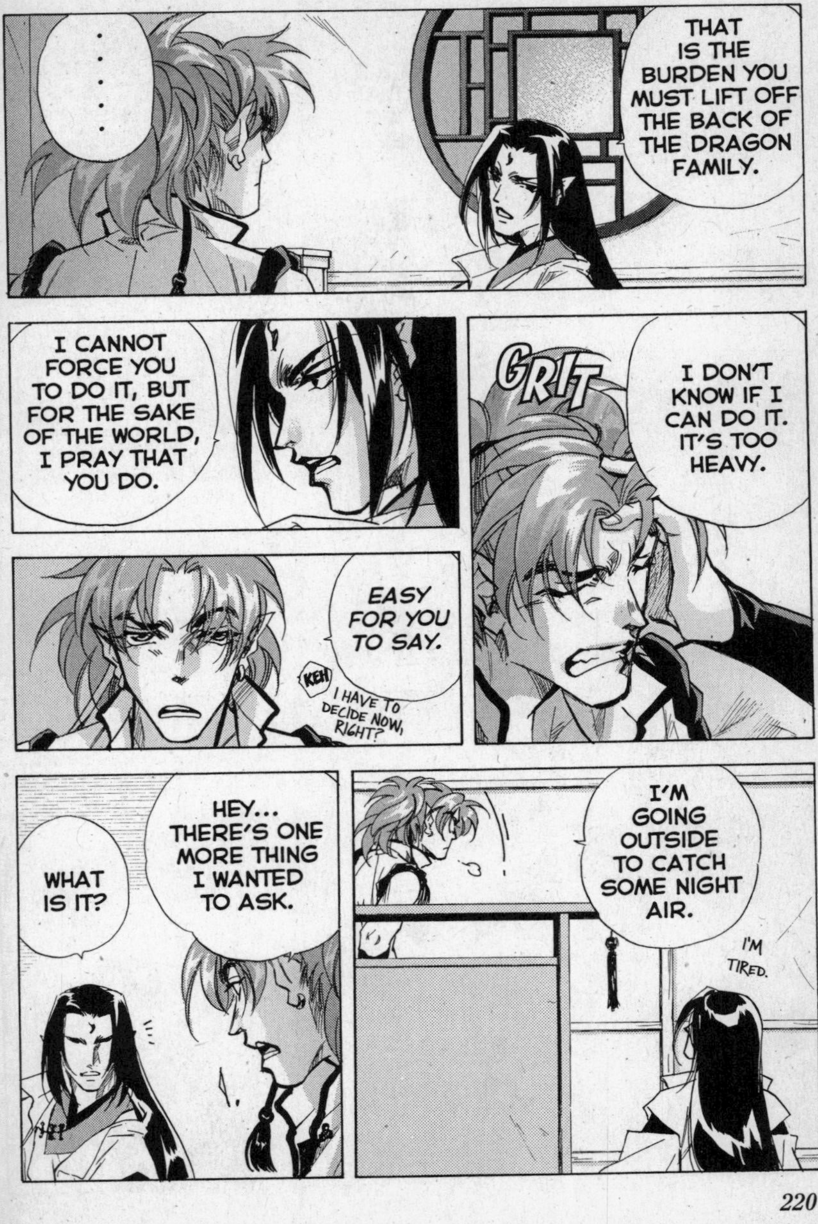
THAT IS THE BURDEN YOU MUST LIFT OFF THE BACK OF THE DRAGON FAMILY.
. . . . .
GRIT
I DON'T KNOW IF I CAN DO IT. IT'S TOO HEAVY.
I CANNOT FORCE YOU TO DO IT, BUT FOR THE SAKE OF THE WORLD, I PRAY THAT YOU DO.
EASY FOR YOU TO SAY.
KEH
I HAVE TO DECIDE NOW, RIGHT?
I'M GOING OUTSIDE TO CATCH SOME NIGHT AIR.
I'M TIRED.
HEY... THERE'S ONE MORE THING I WANTED TO ASK.
WHAT IS IT?

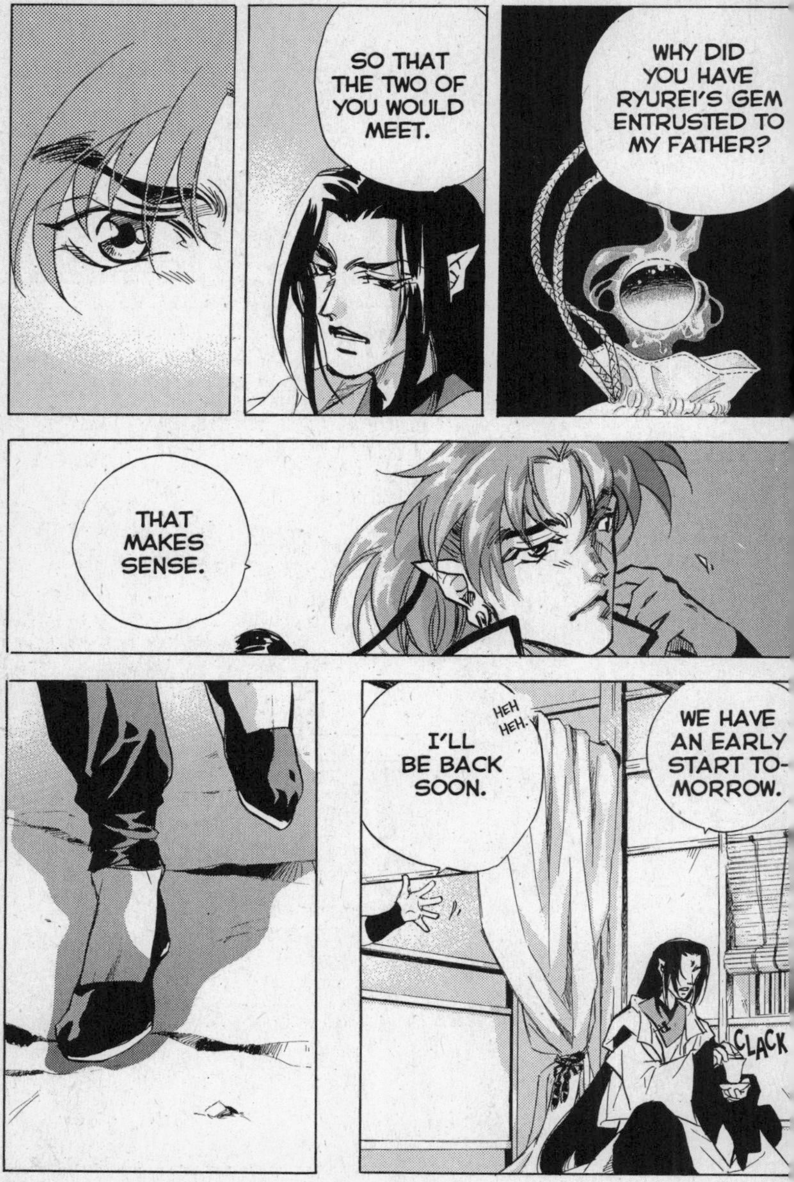
WHY DID YOU HAVE RYUREI'S GEM ENTRUSTED TO MY FATHER?
SO THAT THE TWO OF YOU WOULD MEET.
THAT MAKES SENSE.
WE HAVE AN EARLY START TO-MORROW.
HEH HEH.
I'LL BE BACK SOON.
CLACK

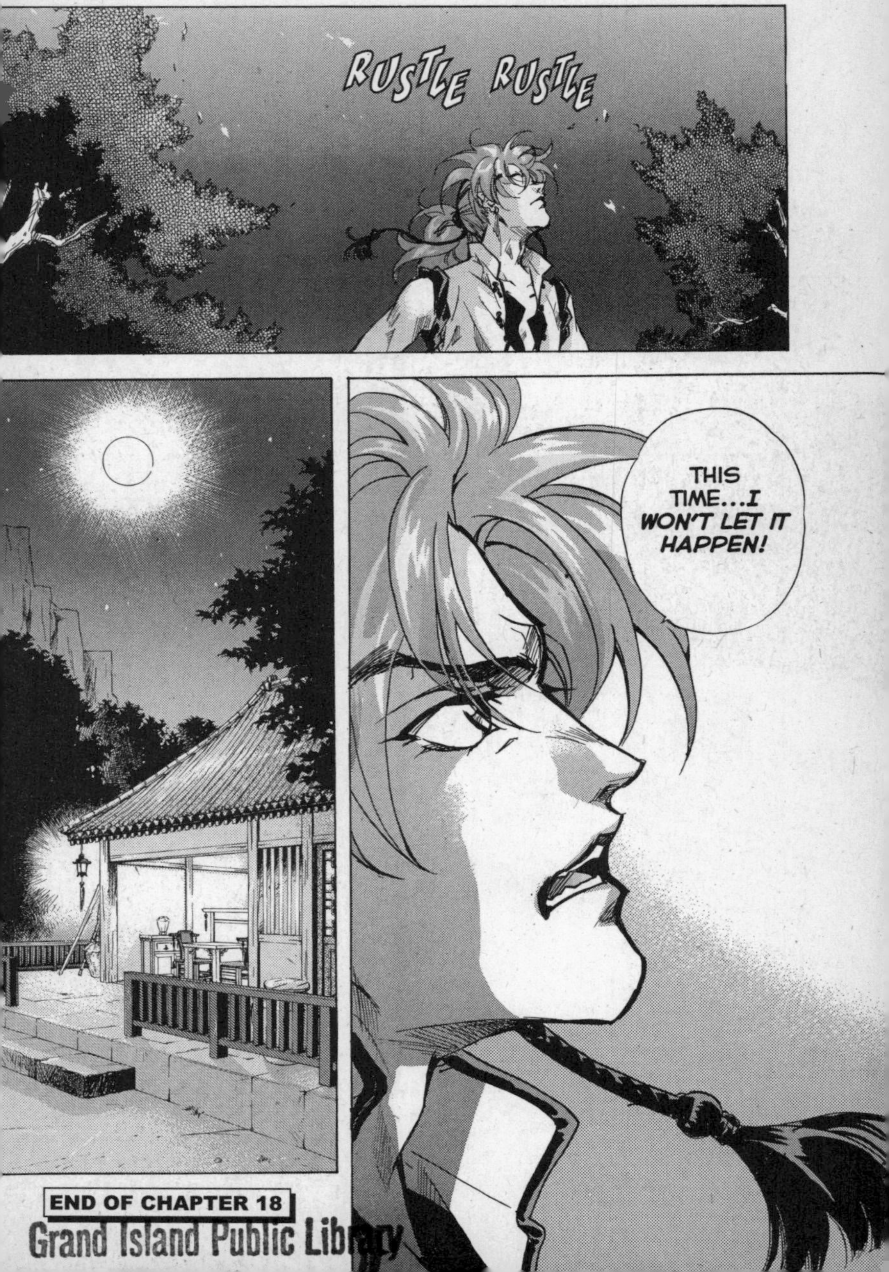
RUSTLE RUSTLE
THIS TIME...I WON'T LET IT HAPPEN!
END OF CHAPTER 18

CMX

Jim Lee
Editorial Director

John Nee
VP—Business Development

Hank Kanalz
VP—General Manager, WildStorm

Paul Levitz
President & Publisher

Georg Brewer
VP—Design & DC Direct Creative

Richard Bruning
Senior VP—Creative Director

Patrick Caldon
Senior VP—Finance & Operations

Chris Caramalis
VP—Finance

Terri Cunningham
VP—Managing Editor

Stephanie Fierman
Senior VP—Sales & Marketing

Alison Gill
VP—Manufacturing

Rich Johnson
VP—Book Trade Sales

Lillian Laserson
Senior VP & General Counsel

Paula Lowitt
Senior VP—Business & Legal Affairs

David McKillips
VP—Advertising & Custom Publishing

Gregory Noveck
Senior VP—Creative Affairs

Cheryl Rubin
Senior VP—Brand Management

Jeff Trojan
VP—Business Development, DC Direct

Bob Wayne
VP—Sales

TENRYU Volume 4, published by WildStorm
Productions, an imprint of DC Comics, 888 Prospect
St. #240, La Jolla, CA 92037. English Translation ©
2006. All Rights Reserved. English translation rights in
U.S.A. and Canada arranged by AKITA PUBLISHING
CO., LTD., Tokyo,through Tuttle-Mori Agency, Inc.,
Tokyo. The stories, characters, and incidents mentioned in this magazine are entirely fictional. Printed
on recyclable paper. WildStorm does not read or
accept unsolicited submissions of ideas, stories or artwork. Printed in Canada.

 DC Comics, a Warner Bros.
Entertainment Company.

Neil Rae —Translation
Jake Forbes — Adaptation
Wilson Ramos — Lettering
Larry Berry — Design
Thierry Frissen — Additional Design
Jim Chadwick — Editor

ISBN: 1-4012-0672-7
ISBN-13: 978-1-4012-0672-7

FLIP IT!!

All the pages in this book were created—and are printed here—in Japanese RIGHT-to-LEFT format. No artwork has been reversed, so you can read the stories the way the creators meant for them to be read.

RIGHT TO LEFT?!

Traditional Japanese manga starts at the upper right-hand corner, and moves right-to-left as it goes down the page. Follow this guide for an easy understanding.

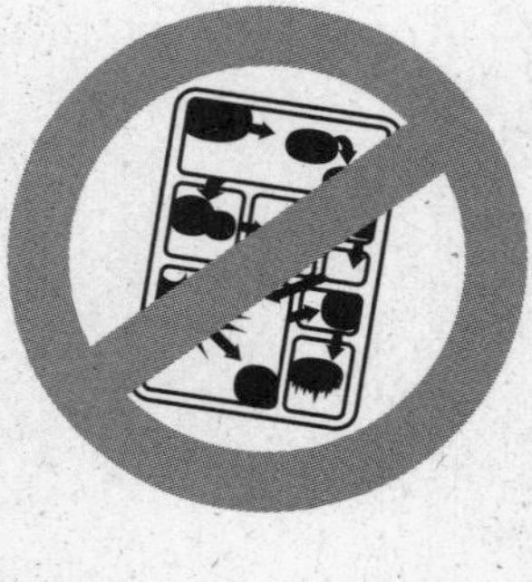

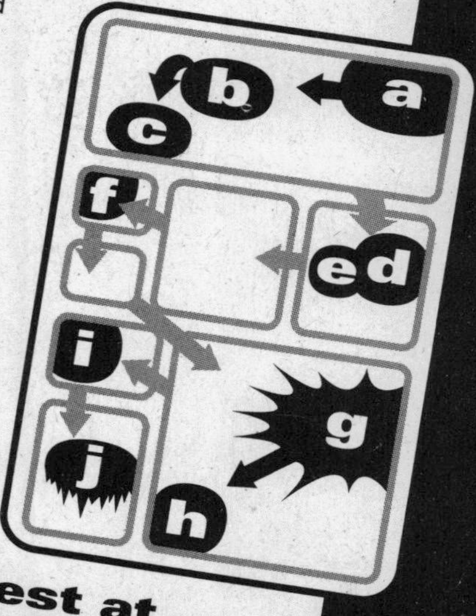
a
b
c
ed
f
g
h
i
j

Catch the latest at cmxmanga.com!